ENGINEERING METALLURGY

Part II
METALLURGICAL PROCESS TECHNOLOGY

ENGINEERING METALLURGY

Part II
METALLURGICAL PROCESS TECHNOLOGY

RAYMOND A. HIGGINS
B.Sc. (Birm.), F.I.M.

Senior Lecturer in Materials Science, The College of Commerce and Technology, West Bromwich; Examiner in Metallurgy to the Institution of Production Engineers, the Union of Lancashire and Cheshire Institutes, the Union of Educational Institutes, and the City and Guilds of London Institute; formerly Chief Metallurgist, Messrs. Aston Chain and Hook Co., Ltd., Birmingham

HODDER AND STOUGHTON
LONDON SYDNEY AUCKLAND TORONTO

To the Memory of my

MOTHER

whose self-sacrifice and devotion to me
during my student years enabled me to
become a metallurgist

ISBN 0 340 18506 6 (paperback edition)

First edition 1960
Reprinted 1964, 1967, 1968
Second edition (completely revised) 1970
Reprinted (with amendments) 1974
Reprinted 1975, 1976, 1978, 1980

Printed in Great Britain for
Hodder and Stoughton Educational,
a division of Hodder and Stoughton Ltd,
Mill Road, Dunton Green, Sevenoaks, Kent
by Richard Clay (The Chaucer Press) Ltd
Bungay, Suffolk

PREFACE TO THE FIRST EDITION

In Part I of 'Engineering Metallurgy' the basic principles of applied physical metallurgy were covered. The present volume is primarily intended for those engineers who have acquired such a knowledge, either by studying metallurgy as a subject in an engineering Higher National Certificate course or by careful reading of Part I of this work. For the benefit of any engineer who may find himself concerned with metallurgical processes in advance of adequate preliminary studies, it may be noted that in both Parts of this book sections are numbered on the decimal system. In Part II frequent references to appropriate sections of Part I make it easy for the reader to look up the metallurgical principles governing any particular process under consideration.

This volume deals with many processes of which an engineer might well have to take charge. In industries where the output of metallurgical products is high such control will properly be the job of a qualified metallurgical specialist. In some organisations, however, circumstances may not justify such an appointment. This book throughout approaches its subject matter on the assumption that the responsibilities to technical control are falling upon an engineer.

It is hoped therefore that, as well as being complementary to the study of applied physical metallurgy in Part I, this volume will provide a useful introduction to some of the more important industrial metallurgical processes. Clearly, a book of this type cannot do more than give a very brief outline of such processes. For this reason a short selection of material for further reading is included at the end of each chapter.

In addition it is hoped that this volume will prove to be a useful textbook for those students taking Associateship examinations of the various Engineering Institutions. Moreover, much of the subject-matter contained in the syllabus for Mechanical and Thermal Treatment (for the examinations of the Institution of Metallurgists) will be found here.

The author wishes once more to record his thanks to his friend and one-time colleague, A. N. Wyres, Esq., A.I.M., of the College of Technology, Oxford, for reading through the original MS. and making many constructive suggestions for its improvement. He also remembers with gratitude the help given to him in the early stages of the preparation of the book by the late J. H. Parry, Esq., F.I.M. The author wishes to record his deep appreciation of the encouragement and help given to him at all times by W. E. Fisher, Esq., O.B.E., D.Sc., A.M.I.Mech.E., the General Editor of the Higher Technical Series. Finally, he wishes to thank A. N. Skeldon, Esq., of the West Bromwich Technical College, for help given in the production of a number of the photographs; and all those connected with the various industrial organisations who have contributed photographs and other material used in the preparation of this book.

R. A. HIGGINS

Department of Science,
The Technical College,
West Bromwich, Staffs.

PREFACE TO THE SECOND EDITION

Since this book was first published considerable progress has been made in many of the processes used for forming and treating metals. In a 'technological age' this was to be expected. An attempt has been made, therefore, to bring this book up to date.

In common with Part I, SI units have been introduced in this edition and the reader will find useful notes describing this system of 'metrication' in the introductory pages of Part I.

During recent years the introduction of high energy rate metal-forming operations has constituted possibly the most interesting new field of development. The reader will find a number of references to it in this volume, where 'HERF' is discussed in simple terms.

Progress in the welding industries has been such that chapters dealing with welding processes have, of necessity, been almost completely rewritten. However, whilst a number of new and exciting processes have been introduced, the continued importance of arc- and oxy-acetylene welding should not be overlooked.

When a new book is published it is inevitably reviewed in the appropriate trade journals. Any author would do well to read carefully such reviews as he will often find they contain many useful observations. Thus, when this volume was first published one critic considered that it could be improved by the inclusion of relevant British Standards references in the 'Bibliography' at the end of each chapter. In the present edition this suggestion has been complied with as it was felt that BSI specifications contain a mine of information in a readily-available form.

Another critic complained that the 'Bibliography' contained references to too many American publications. However, the more optimistic authors do write for a world market. Since both volumes of this work have been published in Mexico and more recently in the U.S.A., the international character of the extended 'Bibliography' has been preserved in this edition. Moreover, few would disagree with the suggestion that, with a large market to exploit, American publishers are able to produce many excellent works which it would be economically difficult to publish here.

Finally the author would like to thank those industrial organisations who have helped in the provision of new illustrations for this volume. He would also like to thank E. Bancalari, Esq., M.A., and his staff of the West Bromwich Technical Library for help in compiling not only the BSI extracts mentioned above but also the contents of the 'Bibliography' generally, and for help in providing many trade journals both current and past.

R. A. HIGGINS

The College of Commerce and Technology,
West Bromwich, Staffs.

CONTENTS

ix

Chapter one
THE INDUSTRIAL MELTING OF METALS AND ALLOYS

1.10

In the early days of iron and steel manufacture, fusion of the metal was not an integral part of the process. The ore was chemically reduced by charcoal and the resultant spongy mass of iron forged to a compact shape. Techniques for the production of high temperatures were not sufficiently advanced at that time to render the melting of iron possible on an industrial scale, and even today some metals, for example tungsten, which have very high melting points are more conveniently produced by powder-metallurgy methods (Chapter Six, Part II). Nevertheless, in the bulk of metallurgical production melting and casting constitute the primary stages in the manufacturing process, whether the alloy be cast into its finished shape or as an ingot which will undergo further mechanical processes.

The introduction of metals such as titanium into the sphere of metallurgical operations brings with it new difficulties which must be overcome. Not only does molten titanium react with most gases but it also attacks all orthodox furnace refractories. The somewhat novel method of melting titanium by means of an electric arc in a water-cooled copper crucible is therefore used. A layer of titanium solidifies on to the copper crucible, thus protecting it from attack, and the net result is that titanium is virtually being melted in a titanium crucible. The complete operation is conducted in a vacuum chamber in order to protect the titanium from attack by atmospheric gases.

1.11

The main requirements of a molten metal just prior to casting are:

(*a*) that its chemical composition and purity shall have been maintained during melting;

(*b*) that it should be at the correct casting temperature.

Attainment of the correct casting temperature is most important. If a metal or alloy is cast at too low a temperature it may not flow adequately to fill all the recesses of the mould and, at best, a casting riddled with shrinkage cavities (4.17—Part I) may result. The use of a needlessly high casting temperature, on the other hand, may lead to a 'gassy' melt and the formation of blow holes in the resultant casting. Moreover, the grain may be coarse so that the mechanical properties suffer as a result.

Changes in the composition of the charge may take place during melting. This is liable to happen when one of the ingredients is volatile at the casting temperature of the alloy. Likewise, high affinity for oxygen of one of the components may cause it to oxidise rapidly during the melting process and be lost in the slag. Both of these difficulties can be largely overcome as a result of experience and the adoption of a standardised melting technique, together with the development of suitable chemical conditions during the melting process.

It is essential to maintain a high standard of purity with some metals and alloys. The most common source of impurities during a melting process is the fuel or its products of combustion, so that when high purity is of paramount importance the charge may need to be totally enclosed in a crucible or, alternatively, a chemically clean fuel such as electricity used. The adoption of either method will increase the cost of melting.

A CLASSIFICATION OF FURNACES USED FOR MELTING
1.20
Furnaces used for the melting of metals and alloys vary widely in capacity and design. They range from small crucible furnaces holding but a few kilograms of metal to open-hearth furnaces of up to 200 tonnes capacity. The type of furnace used for a melting process will be largely dictated by the following factors:

(a) the necessity of melting the alloy as rapidly as possible and raising it to the required casting temperature;

(b) the need for maintaining both the purity of the charge and the accuracy of its composition;

(c) the output required from the furnace;

(d) the cost of running the furnace.

Generally metals with high melting points are more expensive to melt than those with low melting points, for it is not only more difficult and expensive to attain a high temperature but also insulation must be more effective to reduce heat losses. Moreover, the wear on the refractory lining of the furnace will be greater at high temperatures, so that a special refractory must often be used.

As mentioned above, the purity of the charge can be maintained either by the use of electricity as a fuel or by using a furnace, such as a crucible furnace, where the charge can be isolated from the fuel and its products of combustion. The use of a crucible furnace is expensive because it involves a relatively inefficient method of heating, whilst the basic cost of electricity is high, even though this is to some extent offset by the possibility of using it efficiently.

Furnaces for the melting of metals can conveniently be classified into four main groups according to the degree of contact which takes place between the charge and the fuel or its products of combustion.

1.21 Furnaces in which the Charge Is in Intimate Contact with the Fuel and the Products of Combustion
The most important furnace in this group is, of course, the foundry cupola, in which the iron being melted is charged to the furnace along with the coke.

The thermal efficiency of such a furnace will obviously be high since, in addition to the direct heat transfer from burning fuel to charge, heat losses will be small because of the continuous nature of the process. Furnaces which work intermittently by melting small batches of metal dissipate considerable quantities of heat from their refractory linings during the interval between pouring one melt and charging the next.

The main disadvantage of the cupola is that the charge, being in direct contact with both the fuel and the products of combustion, can pick up considerable amounts of impurity—particularly sulphur. On this score alone the utility of the cupola is strictly limited. Moreover, the chemical conditions in the cupola cannot be controlled, since the presence of carbon in the form of coke will ensure an atmosphere which is very strongly reducing, and consequently suitable for the melting of only a very limited number of alloys.

In recent years the relative scarcity of good metallurgical coke has made the cupola somewhat less competitive in terms of melting costs. For this and other reasons increased use of electric melting with coreless induction furnaces has to some extent displaced the cupola and this trend will undoubtedly continue.

1.22 Furnaces in which the Charge Is Isolated from the Fuel but Is in Contact with the Products of Combustion

A furnace of this type with which the reader may already be familiar is the open-hearth furnace for the manufacture of steel (2.90—Part I). Many other furnaces of similar design exist in which the same method of firing is employed; the fuel being either lump coal, pulverised coal, coke, oil or gas. Some of these furnaces are quite small, and few, other than the steel furnaces, use a regenerative system of heat transfer. They can be classified generally as 'reverberatory' furnaces, in which the hot products of combustion are deflected by the furnace roof on to the charge being heated.

The fuel efficiency will obviously be lower than that in the previous group, since there is a bigger heat loss in the outgoing products of combustion (in a cupola the products of combustion actually pass amongst the incoming charge and give up their heat to it, whereas in a reverberatory furnace they merely pass across its surface and give up a correspondingly smaller amount of their heat). Moreover, in a reverberatory furnace there is a bigger surface of refractory lining at which heat loss can occur, per unit mass of charge.

The pick-up of impurities from the fuel, however, will be limited to those of a gaseous nature. These may still cause trouble, and unless they can be eliminated by further treatment before the alloy is cast, such a furnace may prove unsuitable.

One important advantage that the reverberatory furnace has over the cupola is in the more effective control which can be exercised over the furnace atmosphere. By regulating the amount of secondary air admitted to the hearth of the reverberatory furnace the atmosphere can be made reducing, neutral or oxidising at will.

1.23 Furnaces in which the Charge Is Isolated from Both the Fuel and Products of Combustion

The principal example of this group is the furnace employing a crucible which may be heated by either coke, gas or oil. The charge may be almost completely isolated from the products of combustion if the crucible is fitted with a lid; a more convenient, and often more efficient, method is to cover the molten charge with a layer of flux. The pick-up of impurities during melting is thus reduced almost to zero.

The main disadvantages of the crucible furnace are that both fuel efficiency and output are low. Whilst the crucible furnace may be ideal for melting small amounts of an alloy, it is a slow method of melting where large scale output is concerned.

1.24 Electric Furnaces

Melting furnaces employing electricity as a source of energy are for the most part either of the arc or the induction type, though a few small-capacity furnaces dealing with low melting-point alloys employ resistance heating. The main disadvantage of the use of electricity is, of course, its high cost, though this cost may be reduced if the melting schedule can be so planned as to use 'off-peak' electricity. Further, the melting costs of an alloy depend upon factors additional to the simple cost of the fuel. For example, when an electric furnace is used it is often possible to deal with a greater proportion of cheap, low-grade scrap, thus reducing substantially the overall cost of the hot metal. Other advantages associated with the use of electric melting include:

(i) contamination of the charge is reduced to a minimum;

(ii) a high temperature is quickly obtained and easily controlled;

(iii) vacuum melting can be used to give complete freedom from oxidation and the solution of other gases.

TYPES OF FURNACE USED IN MELTING

1.30

Some of the more important melting furnaces relative to the above groups will now be considered.

1.31 Shaft-type Furnaces

Shaft-type furnaces are those in which the charge passes progressively downwards under gravity and so meets a flow of hot gases passing upwards. A high thermal efficiency results from the close contact between charge and burning fuel and the fact that such a furnace is continuous in operation.

1.311 THE FOUNDRY CUPOLA. The cupola is still the standard melting unit in most iron foundries. In principle it is rather like a small blast furnace, but whereas the function of the latter is *smelting*, the cupola is used only for melting, and little change in composition takes place in the charge during the process.

The cupola (Fig. 1.1) consists of a vertical steel shell lined with fire-bricks or rammed refractory material and mounted on a base-plate which is supported by four steel columns. Modern cupolas are usually of the 'drop-bottom' type, that is, they are fitted with hinged doors in the base-plate which can be lowered to allow residue from the furnace to be removed at the end of the melt.

The air blast is admitted to the cupola through tuyères situated at a height of about 1 metre above the drop bottom and connected to the air blower by means of a wind-belt or blast-box which encircles the furnace. The number

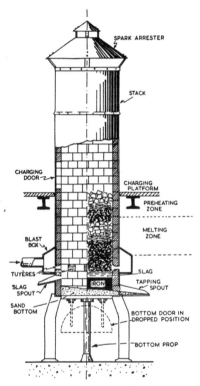

FIG. 1.1—The Foundry Cupola.

of tuyères will depend upon the size of the furnace, and generally one tuyère is allowed for every 0·15 m of the internal diameter at the tuyères.

Before the cupola is charged a bed of sand about 0·15 m thick is built up on the drop bottom and made to slope towards the metal tap-hole. In addition, a slag hole is provided about 0·15 m below the tuyères for the removal of slag at suitable intervals during the melt. A platform and charging hole are provided at a height of between 4 and 5 m above the tuyères, and here coke, pig iron, scrap and limestone are charged to the furnace.

Both cold- and hot-blast cupolas are in use. In the latter the in-going air is preheated in some form of recuperator which is heated by the hot gases from the cupola. The recuperator may be an external unit, or it may consist of vertical tubes built into the cupola itself. These tubes enter the furnace about 2 m above the tuyères and extend to within a foot of the charging door. The in-going air passes through these tubes and is thus heated before it reaches the tuyères.

1.312 'TOWER' MELTING FURNACES were introduced recently for melting aluminium alloys. These are furnaces fired by town gas and are generally composed of three main sections: charging elevator, melting unit and holding furnace.

In the melting unit itself (Fig. 1.2) burners fire beneath a grate which

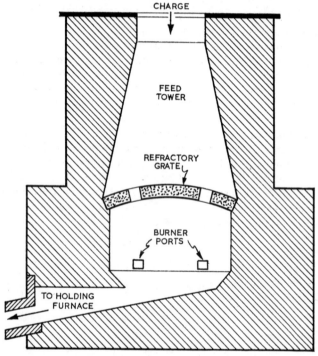

CHARGE

FEED
TOWER

REFRACTORY
GRATE

BURNER
PORTS

TO HOLDING
FURNACE

FIG. 1.2—A 'Tower' Furnace for Melting Aluminium.

supports the solid charge. Products of combustion pass up through the grate, heating the charge which melts and runs down through the grate. As the molten metal falls through the hot zone beneath the grate it is effectively super-heated.

The complete plant is automatically controlled, temperature measuring equipment serving both melting and holding furnaces and adjusting the heat input as necessary. Feed is also controlled automatically as described in connection with a similar furnace mentioned later (1.324).

The holding furnace is a cylindrical rotary unit (1.323) which in this instance is indirectly heated by a 0·15 m diameter recuperative radiant tube.

Indirect heating is used in order to maintain quality in the molten charge particularly in respect of limiting the ingress of gaseous impurities.

In recent years the availability of low-sulphur gas has encouraged the development of large shaft furnaces (similar in some respects to a cupola) which are used in the melting of copper-base alloys. These gas-fired furnaces are generally run in conjunction with channel-type induction furnaces (1.342) which are used for holding and superheating the charge. This system is very suitable when the unit is to supply molten metal for a continuous-casting plant (2.341). The fluctuating demands of the latter could not be met by using the shaft furnace alone but by incorporating the holding furnace into the system a sufficient reservoir of molten metal is held available.

1.32 Reverberatory Furnaces

Furnaces of this type range in size from small units used for melting non-ferrous metals, and holding 50 kg or so, to large furnaces capable of holding 25 tonnes. Although open-hearth furnaces are usually associated with the manufacture of steel (2.90—Part I) they fall into this group, since small ones of about 10 tonnes capacity are sometimes used for melting iron for the production of blackheart malleable castings.

1.321 AIR FURNACES. The term air furnace is generally employed to describe the type of reverberatory used for melting cast iron when the maintenance of composition and purity of the product is particularly important. Consequently the melting of iron for the manufacture of rolling-mill rolls and blackheart malleable castings is carried out in such furnaces, which usually hold about 15 tonnes of metal. Since the charge is out of contact with the fuel, it absorbs less sulphur, whilst the longer melting time allows for a greater degree of

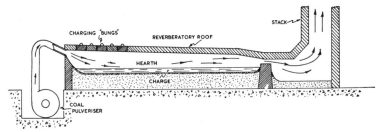

FIG. 1.3—An Air Furnace Using Pulverised Fuel.

control in the composition of the product. Control of composition is also easier in a batch-type furnace such as this than in the continuous-running cupola. Moreover, large pieces of scrap can be dealt with effectively by the air furnace.

Lump coal, pulverised fuel or oil are used to fire air furnaces. Pulverised fuel and oil are blown into the furnace through a burner situated at one end (Fig. 1.3), but if solid coal is used this is burned in a grate and the draught created by means of an efficient stack and systems of dampers situated at the end of the hearth opposite to the grate.

The outer shell of the furnace is constructed with steel plates and lined with good-quality firebricks. The hearth is also lined with firebrick, but in addition a layer of silica sand is fritted on to the surface to reduce the wear on the bricks beneath. The hearth usually slopes towards a tapping hole situated at the side of the furnace. Charging is effected either through sliding doors in the sides of the furnace or, in some cases, through the furnace roof, a section of which is movable, allowing the charge to be lowered into the furnace by a crane. Furnaces of this type are usually between 7 and 10 m long.

1.322 SMALL REVERBERATORY FURNACES are used for the melting and refining of non-ferrous metals. Their capacities range from 50 to 5 000 kg, and they are usually fired by oil or gas. The smaller units are sometimes made to tilt to facilitate pouring of the charge, but in the large stationary furnaces the hearth is sloped for this purpose as with the large air furnaces used to melt iron.

Although brasses and bronzes are the non-ferrous alloys most commonly melted in reverberatories, similar furnaces have been developed for melting aluminium alloys. An interesting modification of the reverberatory furnace

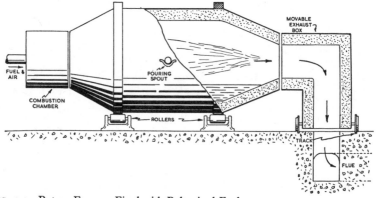

FIG. 1.4—Rotary Furnace Fired with Pulverised Fuel.
The furnace is charged at the exhaust end, the exhaust box being moved aside for the purpose.

was developed at the end of the Second World War in order to deal with scrap air frames. This furnace was gas fired and consisted of a hearth which sloped steeply to a reservoir and tap hole situated at the firing end. The compressed scrap was fed through a charging door at the top of the sloping hearth, where the aluminium alloy melted and ran down into the reservoir, leaving behind any ferrous material used in the original frame.

1.323 ROTARY FURNACES are somewhat similar in principle to orthodox reverberatories, so will be mentioned here. The furnace consists essentially of a cylindrical steel shell (Fig. 1.4) tapered at each end and lined with a refractory material. A burner is situated at one end and a flue system at the other. The fuel may be gas, oil or pulverised fuel, and this is carried in an air blast supplied by a rotary blower.

These furnaces can be rocked or completely rotated during melting, the shell being mounted on rollers for this purpose. In this way rapid heat transfer from the heated refractories to the charge is effected both during melting and the subsequent super-heating stage. In addition to rapid melting, complete mixing of the molten charge is assured by the rotary motion. During rotation the tap hole is stopped with ganister.

The furnace is generally charged through one end, and to facilitate this a removable exhaust box which connects the furnace to the flue system is fitted. This can be moved aside on rails and a charge carrier brought into position on the same set of rails, to tip the charge into the furnace chamber.

Large rotary furnaces with capacities of up to 10 tonnes are used for melting iron and steel and are generally fired by pulverised fuel. In order to preheat the air blast a regenerative system is often used. Small furnaces with capacities up to 2 tonnes are used for melting brass and bronze and for refining low-grade brass scrap prior to casting it in ingot form. Such small furnaces are usually fired by oil or town gas, and regenerative systems are not used. Since charging and tapping take place through a single opening which is not completely closed during melting, these furnaces are usually of the rocking type.

1.324 THE 'HI-MELT' TOWER FURNACE. One type of tower-melting furnace has already been mentioned in 1.312. Here we shall describe a modified type of tower furnace in which a combination of reverberatory and shaft heating is employed. The Wild–Barfield 'Hi-Melt' tower furnace (Fig. 1.5) comprises three main parts—the charging conveyor, the melting unit and the holding furnace. In operation, the conveyor is controlled by the level of ingots in the preheater shaft section of the melting furnace and the melting rate is, in turn, controlled by the metal level in the holding furnace. Thus, with a full load of molten metal in the holding furnace and the required amount of ingots in the preheater shaft, the unit is temporarily inactive except for the radiant tube which maintains temperature in the holding furnace.

As soon as metal is drawn from the holding furnace, weight-loaded cells in the support legs sense the reduction in load and automatically bring the burners of the melting section on to full heat. As a result, molten metal runs into the holding furnace until increased pressure on the weight-loaded cells causes them to reduce the gas flow to the burners.

In the preheater shaft of the melting furnace there are two light-sensitive cell units, one above the other. When the level of ingots falls below the height of the lower cell, the conveyor is brought into action to feed more aluminium ingots into the preheater shaft. This continues until the ingot level reaches the upper of the two cells, when charging ceases.

In the melting furnace proper conventional reverberatory firing is used. Aluminium ingots fed into the top of the preheater shaft reach a semi-plastic state by the time they have descended to the inclined hearth. They are then moved into the hot reverberatory zone by hydraulic pushers.

In addition to the advantages associated with automatic operation, this type of furnace is characterised by a high thermal efficiency coupled with a low metal loss.

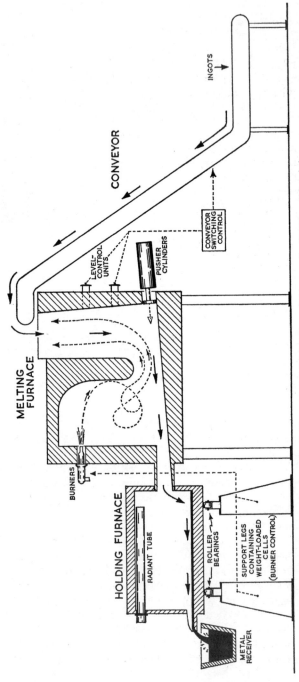

FIG. 1.5—The Wild–Barfield 'Hi-Melt' Tower Furnace for Melting Aluminium.

1.33 Crucible Furnaces

Crucible furnaces vary considerably in design and capacity, and range from laboratory furnaces melting but a few kilograms of metal to industrial units holding as much as 1 tonne. The smaller crucibles are usually heated in stationary 'pit' furnaces, from which they are withdrawn for pouring, whilst large crucibles are generally built into a tilting furnace chamber and the complete unit tilted for pouring the charge.

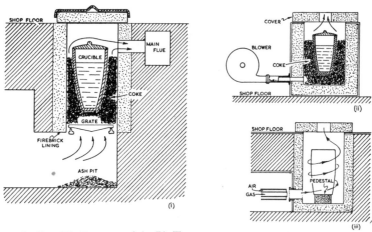

FIG. 1.6—Crucible Furnaces of the Pit Type.
(i) Coke-fired with natural draught; (ii) coke-fired with forced draught; (iii) gas-fired.

1.331 PIT FURNACES (Fig. 1.6) are those which are sunk below the working level of the shop floor in order that the crucible can be removed from the furnace either manually or by lifting tackle.

These furnaces may be fired by coke, gas or oil. Coke-fired furnaces are generally of square cross-section with a grate at the bottom. A bed of coke is laid on the grate to act as a foundation for the crucible, around which more coke is packed. Since sufficient coke must be added at one charge to melt the metal and raise it to the required casting temperature, it is normal practice to provide the crucible with a lid so that it can be covered with coke if desired. In the older installations natural draught was used exclusively, and is still popular, but with many modern coke-fired furnaces a forced draught is employed. Gas- or oil-fired furnaces are not fitted with a grate and are usually of circular cross-section. Forced draught is, of course, used, the flame from the burner entering the furnace chamber tangentially so that it encircles the crucible to follow a spiral path. Pit furnaces of this type are used to melt steel, brass and bronze, and the crucible capacity is generally between 50 and 100 kg.

Stationary gas- or oil-fired furnaces (Fig. 1.7), in which the crucible is built into the melting chamber, are commonly used for melting aluminium

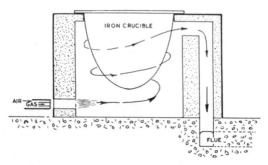

FIG. 1.7—Stationary Gas-fired Bale-out Crucible Furnace.

alloys. Such furnaces are only partially sunk into the ground, so that small amounts of metal can be baled out as required for making small sand- or die-castings. A particular advantage of this type of furnace for melting aluminium alloys is that the surface of the metal is exposed to the atmosphere rather than to the furnace gases, from which it could dissolve hydrogen, thus causing unsoundness in the resultant castings.

Courtesy of Messrs Morgan Crucible Company Ltd, London, S.W.11.

PLATE 1.1—Oil-fired Lift-out Crucible Furnace for Melting Ferrous and Non-ferrous Alloys.
Capacities range between 25 and 150 kg of copper.

1.332 TILTING FURNACES may also be heated by coke, but gas or oil is now more often used. The tilting chamber consists of a cylindrical steel shell (Fig. 1.8), which in the larger units is lined with shaped refractory bricks and in the smaller ones with rammed refractory material. The crucible is built into the refractory-lined combustion chamber, and the pouring spout projects through the side of the furnace.

PLATE 1.2—Electrically Heated Bale-out Furnace for Aluminium Alloys.
This furnace is being used as a holding furnace in the production of gravity die castings.

These furnaces are usually made to tilt about an axis which passes through the pouring spout. In this way a steady stream of metal can be poured into a relatively small aperture.

In order to obtain high temperatures with furnaces of this type a forced draught must always be used whether the fuel be coke, gas or oil. The products of combustion are allowed to escape from the top of the furnace through apertures spaced around the crucible. Oil-fired tilting furnaces of about 250 kg capacity are very popular for melting copper alloys, though furnaces holding up to 1 tonne are sometimes used.

1.34 Electric Furnaces

Electric melting furnaces are generally either of the arc or the induction type. The former are used almost entirely for melting and producing high-grade carbon and alloy steels. Initially, induction furnaces were used principally for melting relatively small amounts of expensive alloy steels and non-ferrous metals, but improvements in design in the early 1950s have led to their adoption for large-scale melting, particularly in the iron foundry.

1.341 ARC FURNACES are generally of the direct-arc type, in which an arc is

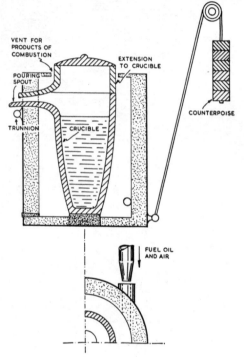

FIG. 1.8—Oil-fired Tilting Crucible Furnace.

struck from the carbon electrodes on to the charge itself (Fig. 1.9). The electrodes are three or four in number and are connected in series so that the current flows through the charge from one electrode to its neighbour. The furnace chamber is bowl shaped and is fitted with a domed roof which carries the electrodes. The roof is mounted on rails so that it can be moved aside whilst the furnace is being charged. Alternatively, a charging door is fitted in that side of the furnace opposite to the spout.

The associated electrical equipment consists essentially of a step-down transformer which reduces the mains supply voltage to that required. The

Plates 1.2 and 1.3 by courtesy of Messrs Morgan Crucible Company Ltd, London, S.W.11.

PLATE 1.3—Oil-fired Tilting Crucible Furnace Used for the Bulk Melting of Aluminium and Copper Alloys.
The molten metal is being transferred to a ladle.

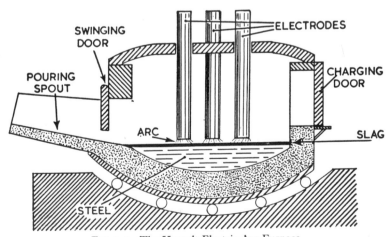

FIG. 1.9—The Heroult Electric Arc Furnace.

voltage applied to the electrode system can be varied, and is usually over 100 volts at the beginning of the melt, reduced to about 40 volts when melting is compete.

The indirect-arc furnace (Fig. 1.10) is sometimes used for melting alloy steels, brasses and bronzes, its capacity varying between 50 and 500 kg. The furnace consists of a cylindrical shell lined with a suitable refractory and has two electrodes mounted horizontally. The arc is struck between these electrodes so that the current does not pass through the charge, heat transfer being by radiation from the arc. The furnace is designed to rock during melting, and this movement not only helps to mix the charge but also assists the transfer of heat.

1.342 INDUCTION FURNACES may differ from each other in design but all work on principles which are similar to those of the electric transformer. An alternating current, carried by a primary coil placed in suitable proximity to

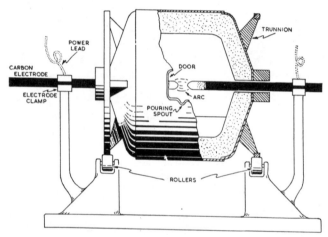

FIG. 1.10—Rocking Indirect-Arc Furnace.

the metal charge, induces secondary currents in the latter. These secondary currents lead to the production of heat in accordance with the 'I^2R' law, and hence to melting. There are two different types of induction furnace, known respectively as the 'coreless' furnace and the cored-type or 'channel' furnace.

The principles of the coreless induction furnace are shown in Fig. 1.11 (i). Here a primary coil of wire is wound around a refractory crucible which carries the charge. Secondary currents are induced in the latter when an alternating current is passed through the coil. Originally, the alternating currents employed in these furnaces were always of high frequency— 1 000 or more Hz (cycles per second)—which led to their being known generally as 'high-frequency' furnaces. The very high capital and maintenance costs of frequency-converting equipment tended to restrict the use of these furnaces to melting high-grade steels and valuable non-ferrous metals. Fortunately, developments in the early 1950s brought about a significant reduction in the capital cost of these furnaces. The first of these developments concerned the introduction, simultaneously in the U.S.A. and in Europe, of the 'mains-frequency' (or 'line-frequency') coreless furnace. This, as its name implies, needs no frequency-converting equipment and though its use

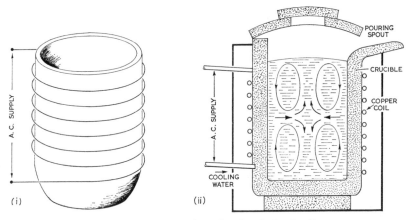

FIG. 1.11—The Principle of the Coreless Induction Furnace.

may be limited as compared with a high-frequency coreless furnace, it can nevertheless be used economically for large scale melting, particularly in the iron foundry.

At about the same time progress was being made in Canada and the U.S.A. in the production of a static 'frequency-multiplier' so that much cheaper equipment became available for melting, using moderately high frequencies in the range 500 to 10000 Hz.

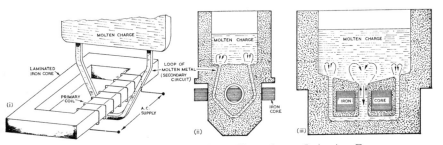

FIG. 1.12—The Principle of the Cored- or Channel-type Induction Furnace.

In both coreless and channel-type furnaces, an effect known as electro-magnetic stirring occurs. If two conductors, carrying currents in opposite directions, are placed side by side, they will repel each other. In induction furnaces this state of affairs occurs in the molten charge, in which, therefore, a stirring motion is produced (Figs. 1.11 and 1.12). In the coreless furnace the extent of this stirring motion is governed largely by the power employed and by the frequency used in the primary coil, such that:

$$\text{Turbulence} \propto \sqrt{\frac{1}{\text{Frequency}}} \text{ (approximately).}$$

Since the power employed is dictated by the necessary melting rate, it follows that the degree of stirring can only be controlled by varying the frequency. In some small furnaces, undue turbulence would be undesirable,

Plates 1.4 and 1.5 by courtesy of Messrs I.C.I. Metals Division.

PLATE 1.4—Ajax-Wyatt Induction Furnace for Melting Copper Alloys.

since, amongst other effects, it would increase erosion of the furnace refractories. Consequently, high-frequency primary currents are often used in furnaces of this type. With large furnaces melting, for example, iron and steel swarf, the stirring effect is extremely useful and line-frequency furnaces are employed for this work in order that increased turbulence will be produced.

A further factor which influences furnace selection involves the relationship between frequency and the ease of starting. It is generally necessary for line-frequency furnaces to be operated with a residual 'heel' of molten metal left in from the previous charge. This limits any change in composition which can be effected between charges, but in cases where long runs of a constant composition are programmed this obviously introduces no problems and certainly does not place such a furnace at a disadvantage with respect to the cupola which is its main competitor in the iron foundry. Coreless furnaces operating at higher frequencies can be started with little or no 'heel' so that for many specialised applications in which small furnaces are used, higher frequencies can be employed.

PLATE 1.5—I.C.I. Titanium Melting Plant, Birmingham. Ingots of titanium are produced by electric arc melting of consumable electrodes in a vacuum chamber. Once the electrode is in position the furnace cubicle is sealed and all operations carried out by remote control.

The elements of design of a coreless induction furnace are shown in Fig. 1.11 (ii) and there is little or no variation in basic design between very small units and large ones with a capacity of many tonnes.

The cored-type or channel-furnace, based on the original Ajax–Wyatt design, generally uses alternating current at mains frequency. Its principles of operation are indicated in Fig. 1.12 (i) and here the similarity to an electric transformer is more obvious than in the case of the coreless furnace. Many readers will be familiar with the operation of an electrical transformer. Briefly it consists of two coils of wire wound round a soft iron core. If an alternating current is passed through one coil, called the primary, an electro-magnetic field is induced in the iron core, and this in turn induces a current in the other coil, called the secondary. If the number of turns of wire in the secondary is greater than in the primary, then the potential difference across the terminals of the secondary will be greater than that applied to the primary. The current flowing in each coil, however, will be in inverse proportion to the potential differences across its terminals. The primary of the Ajax–Wyatt furnace consists of a copper coil, whilst the secondary is a single loop of the molten charge. Since the transformer is a high-ratio one, of the step-down variety, its secondary will carry a high current at low voltage. This heavy current will naturally have a pronounced heating effect in accordance with the 'I^2R law'.

The main disadvantage of this furnace is that sufficient molten metal must be left in the crucible in order to provide a circuit for the next charge. Naturally it must be 'primed' with molten metal when starting up. Consequently, only alloy of a single composition can be melted during any one run of this furnace.

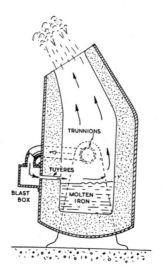

FIG. 1.13—The Tropenas Side-blown Converter.

The Ajax–Wyatt 'Vee'-shaped channel furnace (Fig. 1.12 (ii)) has been popular for some fifty years and is still used for metals which do not 'clog' the channels. Cleaning of these channels is difficult and this was made easier by designing channels with parallel sides and in which a greater degree of metal circulation is achieved as in the 'Uni-Directional-Flow' induction furnace (Fig. 1.12 (iii)). In most channel furnaces with capacities of up to a few tonnes the metal reservoir is a refractory-lined vertical cylinder with the inductor unit attached at the bottom as shown in Fig. 1.12, and the charge is poured by tilting the furnace about an axis approximately in line with the top of the furnace case. Larger furnaces are of the 'drum' type in which the metal reservoir is a horizontal cylinder with the inductor units attached to the circumference on the underside of the cylinder.

1.35 Converters

The converter is not primarily a melting furnace, although used in the production of steel for the manufacture of castings. In a plant designed for the production of steel ingots by one of the L-D processes, the molten pig iron is invariably transferred from the blast furnace to a 'mixer'—a large furnace for the storage of molten pig iron—and from there to an L-D converter. A foundry, however, generally functions as a self-contained unit, the pig iron being melted in a cupola and then converted into steel by using a converter of the Tropenas type (Fig. 1.13).

The Tropenas converter is of relatively small capacity, 1 or 2 tonnes, and is side-blown, that is, the tuyères are situated in the side of the converter so that the blast impinges on the surface of the molten iron instead of passing through it as in the old Bessemer converter, which is now generally obsolete.

MELTING CAST IRON

1.40

For melting cast iron the cupola is still used more extensively than any other kind of furnace. It is a convenient and efficient unit capable of providing molten iron in continuous supply, though its virtual monopoly in the matter of iron melting has in recent years been challenged by the coreless induction furnace. Cupola size is generally expressed in terms of internal diameter at the tuyère level. This dimension governs the cross-sectional area of the melting zone and the melting rate in tonnes per hour, though a certain amount of latitude exists in speed of melting due to the influence of other variables. It is satisfactory in practice, however, to allow a melting rate of 7 tonnes of iron per hour for every square metre of cross-sectional area at the melting zone. Thus a cupola of 0·75 m internal diameter at tuyère level has a cross-sectional area of 0·442 m² and consequently a melting rate of 3·1 tonnes per hour.

1.41

The metal charge to the cupola consists of pig iron, foundry scrap, purchased cast-iron scrap and often some steel scrap. Pig iron from the blast furnace is now generally cast into metal moulds in pig-casting machines. The rate of solidification of the iron is much greater than it was when cast into sand channels. It is therefore almost impossible to classify an iron by the appearance of its fracture (2.51—Part I), and the modern tendency is to purchase pig iron according to chemical analysis. Purchased cast-iron scrap can be used with safety in the production of general-purpose grey iron castings, but where high-duty iron is concerned only foundry returns from the same grade of casting should be used. Steel scrap is used mainly in the production of high-duty iron castings.

1.42

Coke used as fuel in the cupola should be of the hard, dense 'metallurgical' variety with an ash content of not more than 10% and a sulphur content below 1·0%. The increasing scarcity of such coke is one of the factors which makes it necessary for the foundryman to consider other ways of melting iron. In starting up the cupola a coke bed is first built up in the hearth of the furnace. It is essential that this bed is deep enough, since a shallow coke bed will mean that some of the air which is blown in at the tuyères will not have reacted with coke to produce either carbon monoxide or carbon dioxide, and will therefore be free to oxidise some of the iron. Conditions such as these not only favour the oxidation of much of the silicon and manganese in the iron but also allow a considerable pick-up of sulphur to take place. Both of these factors will tend to make the iron more 'white', and whilst this is a normal tendency in cupola melting, it is one which must be adequately controlled.

1.43

Having established a bed of coke to a depth of about 1 m above the tuyère level in the hearth of the cupola, alternate layers of the metal charge and coke are then added. The amounts of each must obviously be accurately controlled

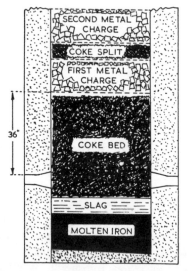

FIG. 1.14—Charging the Foundry Cupola.

if the cupola is to run efficiently. The optimum weight of metal charge corresponding to the size of the cupola is usually about one-tenth of the hourly melting rate. Thus for the 0·75 m cupola we have been considering a single metal charge would consist of about 300 kg of pig iron and scrap. Due to variations in the bulk of scrap, it is difficult consistently to estimate the charge by visual means or measurement by volume, and accurate weighing is a much better method of ensuring that the charges shall be equal.

As the first charge of metal is melted, the height of the coke bed will fall by about 0·15 m. This coke burned from the bed must be replaced by a coke charge, or 'split' as it is called, which follows the metal charge. An easy way of estimating the coke split is to find out how much coke is contained in a circle of firebricks 0·15 m high and of the same internal diameter as the cupola. Having derived the amount of a single split in this way, a measure of the correct capacity can be made for subsequent use. Alternatively, of course, the coke can be weighed for each split. For our 0·75 m cupola a metal-to-coke ratio of 10 to 1 is usual, but for smaller cupolas, and also in large cupolas where steel scrap is being used, the ratio may be as low as 8 to 1.

Thus alternate layers of metal and coke are added to the cupola so that production is continuous, with obvious advantage in respect of output and fuel economy.

As the coke burns some ash will be formed. This will be joined by other foreign matter, such as sand from foundry scrap and possibly rust and scale from other types of scrap. Some type of flux must therefore be added which will combine with these materials to form a fluid slag which can be run from the cupola at convenient intervals. Limestone is universally employed as a flux for this purpose, and assuming that the coke has an ash content of 10% the amount of limestone required will be about 3% of the weight of the metal charge. The fluxing action of the limestone is similar to that which prevails in the blast furnace (2·44—Part I).

Sometimes small quantities of fluorspar are added along with the limestone. This is a chemically neutral mineral which melts at a low temperature and thus helps to produce a more fluid cupola slag. Soda ash is also often added in order to reduce sulphur pick-up by the iron:

$$FeS + Na_2O + C = Fe + CO + Na_2S \text{ (joins slag)}.$$

Recently research has been carried out to remove sulphur from the iron by intermittently blowing powered calcium carbide into the cupola via the tuyères.

As the metal melts it runs down and collects in the hearth of the cupola. A layer of molten slag floats on top of the molten iron and the metal is tapped as required into a ladle. When the melting run has been completed the supporting bar is pulled away so that the bottom of the furnace is 'dropped'. The doors fall open, and any remaining slag, unburned coke or metal droplets fall from the furnace, which is then allowed to cool so that necessary patching of the lining can be carried out.

1.44

The development of the coreless induction furnace to operate on mains frequency has led to its adoption for the melting of cast iron in recent years. If one considers only the relative fuel costs of induction furnace and cupola, the cupola still has the simple advantage despite the increasing scarcity of metallurgical coke. The induction furnace, however, can accept a wide range of cheap raw materials such as borings, punchings, swarf and other scrap of low economic value. These are not easily dealt with in a cupola but are melted with a very high rate of recovery in the coreless furnace and there is little or no change in the composition of the charge, particularly in terms of contamination. Further, the advent of off-peak tariffs for electric power, coupled with the development of very large storage furnaces, has helped to make electric melting economically attractive.

The advent of the line-frequency coreless furnace has led to its adoption for primary melting for reasons given above and because of the high degree of turbulence in the charge which makes the use of borings and other low-density scrap possible. The current tendency is to employ such a furnace for melting during off-peak periods and then to transfer the molten iron to a large storage furnace of the channel-drum type (1.342) for subsequent use during the day shift.

More recently still the shortage of metallurgical coke has resulted in the adaption of the cupola to work either partially or completely on natural gas. Gas-assisted melting involves the use of gas to supplement coke, thus reducing the amount of coke required, but cupolas are also now in use where gas is the sole fuel.

MELTING ALUMINIUM ALLOYS

1.50

Molten aluminium has a very high affinity for oxygen, but the oxide skin which forms on the surface of the melt effectively protects it from further oxidation. The tendency therefore is to use melting furnaces in which the minimum of turbulence is produced at the surface of the molten metal so that the oxide skin remains unbroken. Consequently crucible furnaces were widely used for melting aluminium alloys but in recent years the tendency has been to use such furnaces for holding molten metal rather than for melting it, bearing in mind the low thermal efficiency of the crucible. These holding furnaces may be bale-out or tilter furnaces fired by gas or oil. Reverberatory furnaces are now more widely used for melting purposes and these are generally designed so that instead of the flame impinging on the surface of the charge it is directed at the roof of the furnace, thus reducing turbulence of the molten metal. A modern unit used for melting aluminium alloys and working either on the shaft or shaft/reverberatory principle is the 'tower' furnace (1.312 and 1.324).

The recovery of swarf, baled foil, decorated foil scrap and tube off-cuts is often carried out in the coreless induction furnace where the stirring action assists in absorbing thin scrap before it is oxidised. The channel-type induction furnace, however, is generally more attractive from a cost point of view when melting ordinary scrap and ingots. The principal disadvantage in its use is that the channel tends to become clogged with small particles of aluminium oxide. Since these particles are not affected by the magnetic field they tend to be 'squeezed' to the outside of the metal stream and on to the refractory walls of the channel itself. Hence the Tama-type channel furnace is generally used for melting aluminium. It has rectangular channels which can be cleaned periodically using suitable broaches.

In recent years the bulk melting of aluminium and its alloys has become popular. Thus, in the Birmingham area, delivery of the molten metal from melter to user sometimes involves a road journey of up to 16 km.

1.51
Hydrogen, which may arise from various sources, dissolves readily in molten aluminium alloys, but is almost insoluble in solid alloys. As solidification takes place therefore, the gas is liberated in the partly solid casting, producing blow-holes. Reverberatory melting increases the danger of hydrogen absorption, since the gas may exist in considerable quantities in the furnace atmosphere. Hence the reverberatory furnace is used mainly for melting alloys for die-casting, where, due to the rapid solidification which takes place gas porosity is less able to manifest itself.

1.52
Both oxidation and gas solution increase with temperature, and it is therefore important that accurate pyrometric control is available to avoid overheating the melt. It is particularly important that those alloys containing zinc or magnesium should not be overheated. Much of the former would be lost by volatilisation, whilst the latter oxidises readily at high temperatures. The necessity for super-heating molten aluminium alloys should be avoided where possible by preheating stirrers, plungers and ladles so that their chilling effect on the molten metal is reduced.

1.53
Whilst overheating will accelerate the formation of dross, it is by no means the only cause. As already mentioned, unnecessary turbulence or stirring of the melt will repeatedly expose fresh metal surfaces which immediately oxidise and form additional scum. Likewise the use of small scrap, with its relatively large area of oxide skin, and corroded scrap will increase the amount of dross produced.

Undoubtedly the most frequent cause for the rejection of aluminium alloy castings is porosity due to the liberation, during solidification, of hydrogen which has been dissolved by the metal at some stage in the melting process. This hydrogen does not arise from the negligible amount of the free gas present in the atmosphere, but is generally produced as a result of a chemical reaction between the molten aluminium and water vapour from some other source:

$$2Al + 3H_2O = Al_2O_3 + 6H.$$

Whilst this hydrogen is still in its atomic state it is readily absorbed by the molten aluminium.

It is interesting to note that 1 m³ of air may contain as much as 10 g of water vapour. If this water vapour reacts with molten aluminium according to the above equation more than 1 g of hydrogen will be liberated, and this would be sufficient to cause such unsoundness in about 1 tonne of castings as to make necessary their rejection.

As shown in Fig. 1.15 the solubility of hydrogen in solid aluminium is very, low, but as the metal melts the solubility increases very rapidly. Conversely as the molten aluminium solidifies the solubility of hydrogen falls again so that it is rejected from solution. Since dendrites of metal have already begun

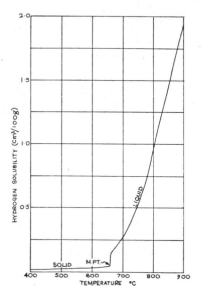

FIG. 1.15

to form, the tiny bubbles of gas are trapped between the growing arms, forming blow holes in the resultant casting. In practice, molten aluminium with a gas content of less than 100 mm^3/kg will produce castings virtually free from porosity.

Common sources of moisture which give rise to the production of hydrogen include:

(a) products of combustion in the furnace atmosphere;

(b) water vapour in the atmosphere of the foundry itself;

(c) corrosion products on the surface of the scrap;

(d) condensed moisture on the surface of the scrap;

(e) badly dried melting pots and foundry tools;

(f) sand adhering to scrap, such as runners and risers.

The oxide skin which forms on the surface of the melt prevents to some extent contact between the metal and either the foundry atmosphere or the products of combustion. The skin must therefore be disturbed as little as possible when further additions of the charge are being made. When aluminium alloys are melted in pit furnaces the crucible should be covered with a lid or, better still, the molten charge should be protected by a layer of flux. The use of flux is essential with alloys containing more than 2% magnesium, since these alloys are very prone to the solution of hydrogen.

In order to expel moisture from corrosion products present on the surface of ingots or scrap, the material should be preheated on the side of the melting furnace before being charged to the crucible. Because of their greater heat capacity, ingots require heating for a longer period than thin scrap. This prolonged preheating is necessary to evaporate moisture, which condenses initially on the ingot surfaces from the products of combustion emitted from the furnace. Preheating of ingots should be common practice with all metals, since the presence of moisture on the ingot surface will cause molten metal to be thrown out of the furnace with explosive violence when such ingots are charged to the crucible.

Hydrogen may also be produced as a result of reactions between the molten charge and various lubricants adhering to process scrap, whilst ingot metal which was originally melted under unfavourable conditions may contain blow-holes filled with hydrogen. This hydrogen may be dissolved again by the metal as it melts.

1.54 De-gassing Aluminium Alloys

If an aluminium alloy has been melted under conditions which have allowed the absorption of hydrogen to take place, then a de-gassing treatment must be applied to the molten metal just before casting it. The bulk of the dissolved hydrogen can be removed in one of the following ways:

(a) by bubbling another gas through the molten alloy;
(b) by treatment of the molten alloy with a suitable liquid flux in the presence of a hydrogen-free atmosphere;
(c) by pre-solidification.

If the hydrogen in solution in the molten alloy is in equilibrium with an atmosphere containing a certain amount of hydrogen, then, obviously, removal of all the hydrogen from the atmosphere in contact with the melt will lead to the evolution by the metal of its hydrogen content. As this evolved hydrogen is continually swept away, more will diffuse from the metal into the atmosphere until equilibrium is reached at zero hydrogen content of both metal and atmosphere.

The removal of hydrogen from the melt by diffusion into a hydrogen-free atmosphere is not quite so simple as it sounds, because not only must the atmosphere be free from hydrogen and hydrogen-containing gases, such as water vapour, but the metal surface must also be clean and free from oxide-film barriers, to enable the gas to diffuse into the atmosphere. Thus methods (a) and (b) mentioned above are similar in principle. In each case intimate contact is effected between a dry hydrogen-free gas and the molten metal; on the one hand, by passing bubbles of the gas through the melt and, on the other, by fluxing the oxide skin at the surface of the melt and exposing the metal itself to dry air.

1.541 THE GAS METHOD is the most frequently used, and involves passing either nitrogen or chlorine through the melt. The function of this process as indicated above is to 'flush' hydrogen from the molten alloy.

The gas, whether nitrogen or chlorine, is supplied in cylinders, and it goes without saying that it must be as free as possible from moisture, since the latter would tend to introduce hydrogen into the melt. A graphite or refractory tube is used to bubble the gas through the molten alloy, and it is connected to the gas cylinder by rubber tubing which carries an asbestos-wool filter. The refractory tube, which should reach to the bottom of the melt, is best closed at the lower end and drilled with a number of 3 mm diameter holes rather in the manner of a domestic gas poker.

Before de-gassing is carried out the fuel supply should be turned off. Treatment is usually carried out with the melt at a temperature of 730° C if chlorine is used, but de-gassing with nitrogen is not very effective below 740° C. The flow of gas should not be such that excessive turbulence is caused at the surface of the melt; a steady stream of bubbles is all that is required. It is advisable to remove most of the dross from the surface by means of a suitable liquid flux before de-gassing is attempted. Fluxes commonly employed for this purpose contain mixtures of the fluorides and chlorides of magnesium and potassium for use with magnesium-bearing alloys, and mixtures of sodium chloride and sodium silicofluoride for use with magnesium-free alloys. When the dross has been removed along with the layer of flux the surface of the melt is protected by the addition of a further layer of flux.

Effective de-gassing takes from 10 to 20 minutes, depending largely upon the size of the melt, which is then allowed to stand for a further 10 minutes before removing the flux layer with a perforated ladle. The melt is then cast.

The main advantage in the use of nitrogen for de-gassing is that unlike chlorine it is not poisonous. In other respects, however, nitrogen is less satisfactory than chlorine. Not only does cylinder nitrogen contain some moisture and oxygen but, being lighter than chlorine, it also disperses more quickly into the atmosphere. Chlorine, being a heavy gas, forms a protective layer on the surface of the melt, and this further assists in the removal of hydrogen. Moreover, some aluminium chloride forms as a heavy vapour along with the chlorine and makes its own contribution towards de-gasification and protection.

Despite its toxicity therefore, chlorine is much more widely used than nitrogen as a de-gassing agent. Provided that efficient fume extraction is employed, chlorine is quite safe to use, and has the further advantage that it has a cleansing action on the melt. The use of chlorine tends to produce coarse grain in some alloys, but this can be overcome by adding a grain refiner after de-gassing is complete.

All the advantages attendant on the use of chlorine as a de-gasser can be obtained by treating the melt with the compound hexachlorethane, $C_2 Cl_6$. This is a solid which when plunged below the surface of the melt decomposes with the liberation of chlorine. Obviously this provides a convenient method of de-gassing, since gas cylinders and ancilliary apparatus are not required.

Suppliers of foundry equipment sell hexachlorethane—generally under a trade name—as either powder or tablets in weighed units for the treatment of a specific amount of molten alloy.

When de-gassing with hexachlorethane the furnace is first shut off before the melt has reached its casting temperature. The temperature which the melt should have reached when the fuel supply is cut off will be determined largely by experience, and will be related to the size of the charge and the heat capacity of the furnace. The surface of the melt should be treated with flux to remove most of the dross and covered with another thin layer of flux. The temperature of the melt should be between 700° and 750° C. The required amount of hexachlorethane is plunged below the surface with a special bell-shaped plunger (Fig. 1.16) and held near to the bottom of the crucible until the evolution of chlorine has ceased. This should take about 3 minutes.

$$C_2Cl_6 \longrightarrow 2\,C + 3\,Cl_2$$

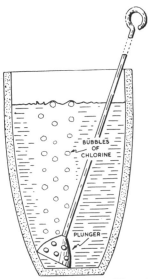

Fig. 1.16—De-gassing an Aluminium Alloy with Hexachlorethane.

The plunger is then removed and the melt allowed to stand for about 10 minutes during which time it should attain its pouring temperature (the fuel supply is, of course, still turned off). Finally, the flux is stirred into the surface of the melt in order that it shall dissolve dross and other suspended matter. The flux is then skimmed off with a perforated ladle and the melt is ready for casting.

1.542 TREATMENT WITH A LIQUID FLUX. It was mentioned earlier that the oxide scum which forms on the surface of molten aluminium is a fairly effective protection against the absorption of hydrogen and that, conversely, it will also prevent any dissolved gas from escaping again, as would happen if the surface of the molten alloy were exposed to dry air after the melting process was complete.

Reasonably effective de-gassing is therefore obtained by covering the surface of the melt with about 1% by weight of a dry mixture consisting of two parts sodium chloride to one part sodium fluoride. As soon as it melts this flux is rabbled into the surface of the melt for about 5 minutes. It is then thickened by the addition of some higher-melting-point flux so that it can be removed with a perforated ladle.

This treatment is most effective if the crucible is removed from the furnace before the flux is added, since water vapour from products of combustion may still be present in the furnace atmosphere after the fuel has been cut off. However, removal from the furnace may only be possible in the case of large crucibles with a big heat capacity, and small crucibles which cool quickly may have to remain in the furnace whilst treatment is carried out.

One disadvantage of treatment with flux of this nature is that the liquid flux attacks refractory crucibles. This can be overcome to a large extent by confining the flux in an iron ring which fits into the top of the crucible

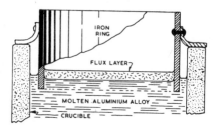

FIG. 1.17—Flux De-gasification of a Molten Aluminium Alloy.

(Fig. 1.17). Although the flux does not come into contact with the sides of the crucible, it cleans a sufficient area of the surface of the melt for its action to be effective.

1.543 PRE-SOLIDIFICATION is sometimes applied to reduce the gas content of very gassy melts. The molten metal is allowed to cool and solidify very slowly in the crucible, care being taken to prevent the surface from freezing over until the rest of the melt is solid. During cooling and subsequent solidification the solubility of the hydrogen falls almost to zero, and if the surface is prevented from freeezing over, most of the gas will be liberated. The charge can then be remelted under satisfactory conditions and should be relatively gas-free.

Treatment of this type is best carried out in iron or steel pots, since refractory crucibles would be liable to crack when attempts were made to remelt the solid charge.

THE MELTING OF COPPER-BASE ALLOYS
1.60

Although de-gassing is a process usually associated with the aluminium-base alloys, it is now applied to at least one group of copper-base alloys—namely the tin bronzes. Like aluminium alloys, these bronzes are very liable to dissolve hydrogen from various sources during the melting process. Bronze is often melted in pit-type crucible furnaces which are coke-fired. Any moisture present either in the coke or in the air drawn in at the bottom of the furnace will be reduced, resulting in the formation of hydrogen. Some of this hydrogen will dissolve in the melt, and treatment must be applied to remove it before the melt is cast. Although hydrogen is dissolved to a less extent by molten bronze than it is by molten aluminium alloys, its effect on the properties of the solid bronze may be just as serious, particularly if the bronze is cast as ingots for cold-rolling operations.

1.61

Due to coring phenomena, a 6% tin bronze (commonly used for cold-rolling) usually contains some of the hard brittle δ-phase (16.42—Part I). This solidifies last in the spaces between the dendrite arms which comprise the α-phase solid solution of which the alloy is largely composed. If any gas is present in the melt it will begin to bubble out of solution at about this stage, and in so doing will set up an internal pressure in the partly solid ingot. This pressure is sufficient to force the tin-rich liquid out on to the surface of the ingot, where it solidifies as a film of hard, brittle δ-phase. This is a bluish intermetallic compound, and a 'gassed' bronze ingot can be identified very easily by the bluish sheen on its surface. Such an ingot is useless for rolling since the brittle layer of the δ-phase cracks readily and produces a series of hair-like fissures on the surface of the ingot.

This defect was controlled originally by 'scalping' about 3 mm from the surface of the cast ingot, but during the Second World War a flux de-gassing treatment was developed. This consists in treating the molten bronze with an oxygen-bearing flux so that the oxidising conditions produced at the surface of the melt result in the elimination of hydrogen from the melt.

1.62

The standard melting practice for tin bronzes is as follows: the copper, along with any bronze scrap which constitutes part of the charge, is melted as quickly as possible. A flux of the type mentioned above, composed of equal, parts of copper mill-scale (copper oxide), fused borax and dry sand, is then added to the crucible in quantities amounting to about 3% by weight of the charge. When the charge reaches a temperature of 1 250° C the flux is drawn to one side and the tin added whilst the crucible is still in the furnace. The melt is stirred vigorously with a refractory rod and the crucible then withdrawn from the furnace. Dry sand is added to the flux to thicken it and the resulting slag skimmed off. Sufficient phosphor-copper* is then added to the melt in order completely to deoxidise it, that is, to remove all traces of copper oxide remaining from the flux treatment. The amount of phosphor-copper added is sufficient to ensure a residue of about 0·04% phosphorus, which

---

* Phosphor-copper is an alloy containing either 15 or 30% phosphorus, the remainder, copper. Its use for deoxidising is safer and more convenient than yellow phosphorus formerly used for this purpose.

dissolves in the bronze. More phosphor-copper will be used in the case of phosphor-bronzes in which the content of the residual phosphorus is much higher. When the reaction between the copper oxide and phosphor-copper is complete and the temperature of the melt has fallen to 1 200–1 250° C it is ready to cast.

Molten tin-bronzes may also be de-gassed by scavenging with nitrogen or air. In principle the process is similar to that already outlined for aluminium alloys (1.54).

1.63

Hydrogen is also highly soluble in molten aluminium bronze, and pinhole porosity can be experienced as it is with aluminium-base alloys if any considerable amount of hydrogen is absorbed during the melting of the alloy. Practical experience shows, however, that if the oxide film is allowed to form on the molten metal and is not broken or disturbed there is no occurrence of pinholes, unless the melt is grossly overheated or retained in a molten state in the furnace for too long. It therefore seems that the film is sufficiently impermeable to hydrogen to prevent it and other gases from gaining access to the melt except at a very slow rate.

If the oxide film is removed from the surface either mechanically or by the use of fluxes containing the fluorides of sodium and potassium whilst the crucible is still in the furnace, gas enters the molten metal and pinhole porosity is produced in the resultant casting. Occasionally dross is melted with a flux of this type in order to reclaim the valuable metal contained in such residues. Invariably the ingots cast contain large quantities of gas which makes them rise in the mould on solidification. In order to de-gas such ingots they are subjected to a flux treatment similar to that applied to aluminium-base alloys. That is, they are remelted under a flux and the melt withdrawn from the furnace, so that it may remain molten for a sufficient length of time in contact with dry air to permit the escape of dissolved hydrogen.

1.64

The solubility of hydrogen in molten brass is very low, and consequently there is no trouble from pinhole porosity in any of the commercial brasses. Zinc has a low boiling point and is volatilising freely at the casting temperature of brass. It is therefore suggested that this has a similar effect to the bubbling of an inert gas through the melt in that it 'flushes' away the hydrogen. The solubility of hydrogen in brass decreases as the partial pressure of zinc approaches atmospheric pressure, just as the solubility of air in water decreases with increasing vapour pressure of the water, becoming zero at the boiling point.

Unless precautions are taken to avoid it, oxidation, with consequent loss of zinc, can take place to a considerable extent during the melting of brass. In molten, and to a less extent in solid, brass the high zinc vapour pressure results in a steady loss of zinc, and if the unprotected surface is exposed to air the zinc vapour diffuses outwards and becomes oxidised, with the formation of a cloud of particles of zinc oxide. Because of the evolution of zinc vapour there is little or no penetration by oxygen into the melt itself, and oxidation of the zinc vapour occurs at a distance from the molten metal.

The most common method used to prevent undue loss of zinc is to cover the surface of the melt with a layer of charcoal, which acts very largely as a barrier to the outward diffusion of zinc and the inward diffusion of oxygen. Zinc and oxygen meet in the charcoal layer, forming zinc oxide, which clogs the interstices in the mechanical barrier and increases its effectiveness. Any disturbance of the charcoal layer results in an immediate evolution of zinc vapour from the surface of the melt, with the formation of a cloud of zinc oxide. Covering fluxes, composed mainly of borax and glass, are often used to increase the effectiveness of the charcoal barrier against zinc diffusion and also to facilitate the skimming operations prior to casting.

Zinc loss always tends to be greater when light or bulky scrap is melted. Such scrap is also awkward to charge, and for ease of handling it should be baled.

1.65

In the case of complex brasses containing elements such as lead, iron manganese, nickel, aluminium or silicon the melting technique may need to be modified. Lead is insoluble in molten or solid brass, and is added to improve the machinability of the alloy (20.24—Part I). Since it has a higher specific gravity than brass, lead tends to sink to the bottom of the crucible, so that its distribution in the resultant casting would be uneven. The channel-type induction furnace has proved very suitable for melting alloys of this type, since the constant movement and circulation of the charge produced electrically in this furnace causes very thorough mixing, without breaking or disturbing the surface from above as in stirring. This type of melting is also very suitable when easily oxidised elements, such as silicon or aluminium, are to be added.

1.66

In view of the changes which can occur both in composition and purity of charge it is not surprising that electric melting of copper alloys is gaining in popularity.

The channel-type induction furnace has long been used in the melting of high-quality cartridge brass and in recent years induction furnaces generally have been developed to deal with the melting of all types of copper-base alloy. The operating cost of an induction furnace is such that the economic advantage tends to increase as the value of the metal being melted increases. Generally speaking the channel furnace is used when long runs of a single alloy are envisaged. The reasons for this are the higher electrical efficiency, lower capital cost and lower rate of wear of refractories as compared with the coreless furnace.

The fact that some metal must always be left in a channel furnace in order to complete the electrical circuit, tends to rule it out when charges of different compositions are to be accommodated. In such cases the coreless induction furnace is used, and becomes particularly suitable when large quantities of swarf or low-density scrap are to be melted. Obviously some contamination between charges is still possible due to small quantities of metal remaining at the end of a melt. Thus, in highly-diversified foundries dealing with many different alloys, the 'lift-coil' furnace offers a means of overcoming possible contamination. The lift-coil furnace comprises a coil assembly in a suitably-insulated framework which can be raised or lowered from an overhead gantry on to a two-station bogie situated beneath the coil. The charge is contained in a separate crucible which is positioned on one station of the bogie. Whilst this charge is being melted another crucible, positioned on the second station, is being charged. On completion of melting in the first crucible the coil is raised from the first crucible and lowered over the second one. In this respect the operation is similar to that of the old coke-fired crucible furnace except that all the advantages of induction melting are available here.

1.67

Computer control has inevitably been incorporated into many metallurgical processes in recent years. In the brass trade, for example, it is now possible to use an on-line computer to guide production from the melting stage to the finishing process, balancing each operation against constantly changing conditions in addition to planning the original method of production.

During the melting process the computer schedules the sampling of the molten brass from the furnaces and arranges for its analysis by a spectro-meter. The analysis results are fed automatically into the computer, along with readings of temperature, pressure and weight data from the furnaces, other programmed factors and any relevant information from the caster. The computer then tells the operator what additions should be made to the melts in order to maintain correct compositions, and also what control adjustments are necessary on the melting equipment.

On a less sophisticated scale electric furnaces can be made to operate automatically so that they pour accurately controlled amounts of—for example —bronze at a specified temperature and at predetermined intervals. The pouring temperature is automatically controlled to within ± 1 °C and the operator merely supervises the charging of the melting furnace and transfer of the molten metal to the holding unit.

BIBLIOGRAPHY

1 'Principles of Metal Casting', F. W. Heine and P. C. Rosenthal (McGraw-Hill).
2 'The Metallurgy of Steel Castings', C. W. Briggs (McGraw-Hill).
3 'Melting Iron in the Cupola', J. E. Hurst (Penton Publishing Co.).
4 'Non-ferrous Foundry Metallurgy', A. J. Murphy (Pergamon Press).
5 'Casting of Brass and Bronze', D. R. Hull (The American Society for Metals).
6 'Chill-cast Tin Bronzes', D. Hanson and W. T. Pell-Walpole (Arnold).
7 'Aluminium Alloy Castings', E. Carrington (Griffin).

8 'Melting Practice for the Production of Aluminium Alloy Castings' (Alar Ltd.).

9 'Magnesium Casting Technology', A. W. Brace and F. A. Allen (Chapman and Hall).

10 'The Casting of Steel', W. C. Newell (Pergamon Press).

11 'The Making, Shaping and Treating of Steel', J. M. Camp and C. B. Francis (Carneigie-Illinois Steel Corp.).

12 'The Cupola and its Operation', American Foundrymens' Society.

13 'Aluminium', Vol III—Fabrication and Finishing, Ed. K. R. van Horn (The American Society for Metals).

14 'Principles of Magnesium Technology', E. F. Emley (Pergamon Press).

15 BS 2759: 1956—Glossary of terms used in industrial high-frequency induction and dielectric heating.

16 BS 3446: 1962—Glossary of terms relating to the manufacture and use of refractory materials.

Chapter two
INGOT CASTING

2.10

When a metal is to be produced in a wrought form it is first cast as an ingot of a shape and size suitable for processing in the plant available. Whilst steel is normally cast into ingots of approximately square section, non-ferrous alloys are frequently cast as flat slabs for rolling to strip or sheet; bars for the production of wire; and cylindrical billets for the extrusion of sections.

Metallurgical, as well as economic, considerations demand that molten metal shall solidify rapidly as soon as it is poured into the mould. Ingot moulds are therefore made from metal, and are either massive and of cast iron or of thin-walled copper which is water-cooled. In either case the molten metal will chill rapidly on making contact with the mould surface.

CASTING STEEL INGOTS
2.20

When the charge in the steel-making furnace is ready it is poured into a teeming ladle which has been conveyed to the teeming platform by means of a travelling electric crane. The ladle is a refractory-lined steel vessel equipped with a trunnion on each side, by means of which it is lifted. In order that the slag which floats on the top of the molten steel shall not enter the ingots the charge is poured from the bottom of the ladle (Fig. 2.1). Hence the steel outer shell has a hole in the bottom near to the rim, in which is fitted a refractory nozzle, together with a stopper of similar material which fits into the nozzle. The stopper is carried on the end of a steel rod, protected by refractory sleeving, which extends vertically through the molten bath. The stopper rod is connected to a lever mechanism by means of which an operator controls the raising and lowering of the stopper, and consequently the rate of pouring. The ladle is generally heated by gas before the charge is tapped into it.

When the molten steel has been poured into the ladle it may be de-oxidised with ferro-manganese, ferro-silicon or aluminium. It is then allowed to stand for some time, whilst slag and other non-metallic materials float to the surface, after which it is teemed into the ingot moulds.

2.201 The ingot moulds are made from cast iron. A typical composition for the purpose is as follows: carbon, 3·5%; silicon, 1·0%; manganese, 0·8%; phosphorous, 0·15%; sulphur, 0·07%. These moulds are of various shapes and sizes. In cross-section they may be square or rectangular with rounded

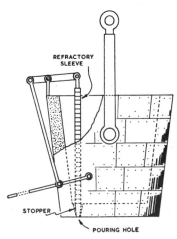

FIG. 2.1—The Principle of the Bottom-pouring Ladle.

edges, eight-sided, fluted, twelve-sided or circular with walls corrugated. The purpose of these corrugations is partly to accelerate solidification and thus produce a fine grain in the ingot and partly to minimise the formation of cracks in the ingot surface during the first rolling operation. Some typical ingot mould sections are shown in Fig. 2.2.

In order to facilitate 'stripping' the ingot from the mould it is necessary to taper the mould cavity to the extent of about 20 mm per metre on diameter. One end of the ingot is thus slightly larger than the other end, and moulds are commonly referred to as 'big-end-up' or 'big-end-down', according to whether they taper downwards or upwards. The big-end-down type of

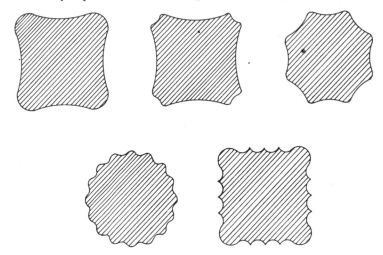

FIG. 2.2—Typical Steel Ingot Sections.

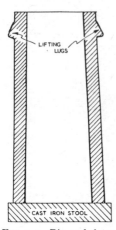

FIG. 2.3—Big-end-down
Ingot Mould.

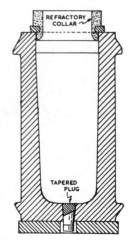

FIG. 2.4—Big-end-up Ingot
Mould, with 'Hot Top'.

mould (Fig. 2.3) is the older. It is open at both ends, and when ready for use stands on a thick cast-iron 'stool' which forms the bottom of the mould. Stripping of the ingot is thus relatively easy, since it is only necessary to lift the mould from off the solid ingot, which is left standing on the stool.

2.202 The newer big-end-up type of mould (Fig. 2.4) is usually closed at the bottom except for a round hole which is fitted with a tapered plug which facilitates the stripping of the solid ingot. This type of mould is generally fitted with a

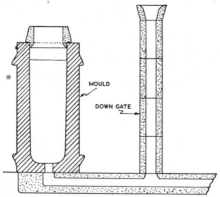

FIG. 2.5—Assembly for the Bottom Pouring
of Steel Ingots.

removable refractory collar or 'hot-top' which is placed on top of the mould. The function of this refractory collar is to slow down the rate of cooling at the top of the ingot and thus provide a reservoir of molten metal which can 'feed' into the main body of the ingot as its solidifies and hence contracts. The hot-top thus minimises piping (Fig. 2.6).

Courtesy of Messrs Newton Chambers & Co. Ltd, Thorncliffe, Sheffield.

PLATE 2.1—Teeming Steel from a Large Ladle into Ingot Moulds.

2.203 Some high-grade steel ingots are bottom-poured into big-end-up moulds, as shown in Fig. 2.5. The main reason for this procedure is to prevent splashing of the metal on to the sides of the mould, as is possible with the top-pouring method. These splashings freeze on to the mould walls and cause discontinuities in the surface of the solid ingot, with consequent imperfections on the surface of the rolled products. By using the more expensive bottom-pouring method, however, the mould is filled without agitation or splashing of the metal. In addition, the degree of oxidation of the metal during teeming is much less than it is with the top-pouring method.

2.204 The principles of continuous casting of aluminium alloys and other metals are mentioned later in this chapter (2.341). Similar processes have also

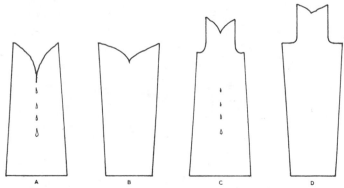

FIG. 2.6—The Influence of Mould Design on Pipe Formation.
A—Big-end-down; no hot top.   B—Big-end-up; no hot top.
C—Big-end-down; hot top.   D—Big-end-up; hot top.

been adapted to the casting of round, square and retangular sections in steel; and slabs of 0·1 m² or more in cross-section are currently in production.

Fig. 2.7 illustrates one development of this type of process for the manufacture of steel strip between 2·5 mm and 25 mm thick. After the metal has cooled sufficiently in the water-cooled mould to form a solid shell on the outside, it is passed through a pair of squeeze rolls, the distance between the axes of which exceeds the centre width of the interior of the mould exit. The degree of reduction in centre thickness is of the order of 2:1. A number of pairs of rolls in succession may be employed beneath the mould.

Courtesy of Messrs Newton Chambers & Co. Ltd, Thorncliffe, Sheffield.
PLATE 2.2—'Stripping' the Cast-iron Moulds from Steel Ingots.

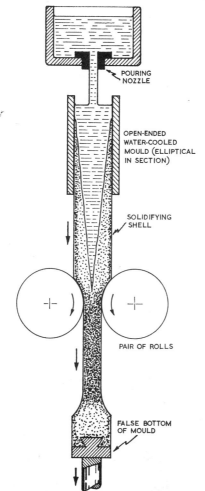

POURING
NOZZLE

OPEN-ENDED
WATER-COOLED
MOULD (ELLIPTICAL
IN SECTION)

SOLIDIFYING
SHELL

PAIR OF ROLLS

FALSE BOTTOM
OF MOULD

FIG. 2.7—A Method for the Continuous Casting of Steel.

2.21 Types of Steel Ingot

In Part I (4.30) it was shown that pipe formation is likely to be more extensive in an ingot cast in a big-end-down mould than in one cast in a big-end-up mould. In fact, in the former type of ingot the formation of a secondary pipe is a probability which will be further increased if any gas is liberated during solidification of the steel. In either type of mould the extent of the pipe can be limited by the use of a hot-top as indicated in Fig. 2.6.

It should not be assumed that all grades of steel are completely deoxidised before casting, for, whilst high-carbon steels are invariably completely killed, much semi-killed steel is produced, together with large quantities of low-carbon 'rimming' steel, which receives little or no deoxidation.

Most of the excess oxygen (present as the oxide FeO) in molten steel at the end of the refining process is removed by the carbon which is added, according to the following reaction:

$$FeO + C = Fe + CO \quad . \quad . \quad . \quad . \quad . \quad (1).$$

Some oxygen, however, can remain in the melt in equilibrium with carbon, and the relationship between the amounts of oxygen and carbon which can exist together in the melt in this way is shown in Fig. 2.8.

If the carbon content of the molten steel is known, therefore, the exact amount of deoxidant necessary completely to deoxidise the steel can be calculated, and if only partial deoxidation is required, then the amount of

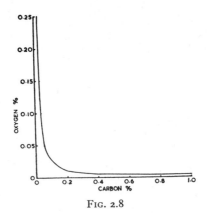

FIG. 2.8

deoxidant added will be correspondingly less than this amount.

2.211 High-carbon steels, medium-carbon steels for forging and steels for sand castings are completely killed, since a structure free from blow-holes is essential, but for many applications, particularly in soft steels, where the quality of the surface of the product is more important than that of the interior, the process called 'rimming' is used. In this process little or no deoxidant is used, and when the melt begins to solidify a layer of almost pure metal first forms at the surface of the mould. This causes the concentration of oxygen in the remaining liquid to increase so that the above reaction (1) begins again, with the consequent evolution of carbon monoxide, which tends to sweep away accumulated impurities from the face of the growing crystals. Thus a shell of very 'clean' metal is produced, and its thickness will depend largely upon the degree of initial deoxidation. When the metal has cooled to the point where solidification begins throughout the remaining liquid much of the evolved gas will be trapped (Fig. 2.9), and porosity in the interior of the ingot will result. Provided that these blow-holes are far enough below the surface, they will weld up effectively when the ingot is heavily worked in a rolling mill. If, however, they are too close to the skin of the ingot they may break through the surface so that they become oxidised, with the result that they do not weld up on rolling. Sometimes the rimming action, that is the reaction between the oxygen and the carbon with the resultant evolution of carbon monoxide, is stopped after the primary stage is over. This is done by deoxidising the partly solid steel in the ingot mould by adding a calculated amount of aluminium.

The main characteristic of rimmed steel is a surface skin which is relatively 'clean' and pure, and this gives a good surface to the finished product. Such

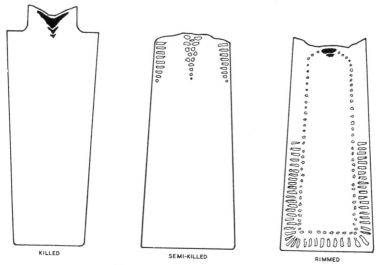

KILLED   SEMI-KILLED   RIMMED

FIG. 2.9—Types of Steel Ingot.

steel is used for deep-drawing processes, tin-plate manufacture, and the production of galvanised sheeting.

In a semi-killed ingot the oxygen content after partial deoxidation is lower than in a rimming steel, so that the evolution of carbon monoxide tends to take place at a later stage in the solidification process. The porosity produced is largely instrumental in eliminating the pipe. Moreover, impurities tend to be 'pushed' nearer to the top of the ingot by the evolved gas, so that much of this impure material is cropped off. Thus some of the useful features of both completely killed and rimming ingots are combined in a semi-killed ingot.

2.212 Some alloy steels and special forging steels are now vacuum de-gassed in order further to improve their soundness. One method of de-gassing is illustrated in Fig. 2.10. Here a stream of molten steel is drawn into a vacuum chamber which contains the ingot mould. Reduction of the internal pressure within the stream leads to its de-gassification. In this way the whole charge is treated successively. Dissolved gases such as hydrogen and nitrogen boil off. This upsets chemical equilibrium within the molten steel so that reactions occur between oxides and silicates and dissolved carbon:

$$\text{Silicates} + C \rightarrow Si + CO \text{ (Boils off)}.$$

Silicon thus liberated dissolves in the steel.

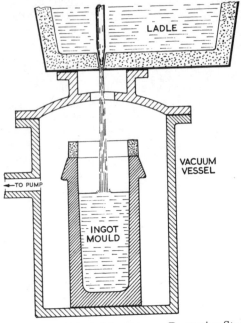

FIG. 2.10—A Method for Vacuum De-gassing Steel.

2.22 Steel Ingot Defects

Defects commonly encountered in steel ingots fall into two main groups: (*a*) those which occur internally; (*b*) those which manifest themselves on or very near to the surface. Some of these defects as, for example, piping, are inherent in any type of cast structure, and can be minimised only by exercising control of the factors affecting their formation. Other faults are the result of bad practice, and can be eliminated completely by correcting errors in the melting or casting processes.

2.221 PIPING. The factors affecting the extent of the pipe in an ingot have already been mentioned here and were explained in some detail in Part I (4.30). In practice, the formation of a pipe is due partly to shrinkage and partly to the evolution of gases from the melt as it solidifies. If the mould is of the big-end-down type secondary piping will be increased by entrapped gases which are evolved after the upper part of the ingot has solidified.

The pipe can be minimised by casting the steel into a big-end-up mould fitted with a hot-top as already suggested, but it can never be completely eliminated. During rolling small cavities comprising the secondary pipe will usually weld up if their internal surfaces are not oxidised. The surface of the primary pipe, however, is heavily oxidised, and it will never weld up success-fully. If an attempt were made to roll the piped portion down to sheet or rod an internal seam would be formed down the centre of the material comprising the original pipe. The piped portion of the ingot is therefore sheared off after the ingot has been rolled to reduce the cross-section sufficiently to make the shearing operation easy. The cropped piece is returned to the refining furnace.

2.222 BLOW-HOLES are formed as a matter of policy in the production of semi-killed or rimmed ingots and do much to reduce the extent of the pipe. In correctly made rimmed ingots the blow-holes are deep under the surface, and since they consist of reducing or inert gases, their internal surface will not be oxidised. They will therefore weld up during rolling.

Blow-holes near to the surface, however, may cause serious difficulties. They may break out during rolling so that their internal surfaces are immediately oxidised, with the result that they will not weld up. Moreover, if they are very near to the surface oxide penetration may reach them when the ingot is being heated for rolling. These oxidised blow-holes are elongated by rolling into long surface 'seams'.

The *quantity* of blow-holes in a steel ingot is a function of the degree of deoxidation employed before teeming the steel, but their *position* depends upon several factors, in particular the teeming temperature, the rate of solidification and the mould design, as well as upon the degree of deoxidation.

2.223 INGOTISM refers to the increase in crystal size from the outer skin to the core of a steel ingot (4.18—Part I). The slower the cooling rate during solidification, the larger will be the individual crystals and the weaker the resulting structure. These 'tender' ingots must be treated carefully during the first few passes through the rolling mill and only small cross-sectional reductions given, or tears will be produced in the ingot surfaces. Once the large crystals have been broken up and recrystallisation has produced smaller ones, weakness due to ingotism vanishes.

Fig. 2.11 shows planes of weakness at the corners of an ingot of square section. Columnar crystals grow perpendicular to the walls of the mould, and those growing from two adjacent faces will meet, forming a plane of weakness or cleavage at an angle of $45°$ to both walls. Therefore sharp corners are usually avoided in the design of ingot moulds as indicated earlier in this chapter.

2.224 SEGREGATION OF IMPURITIES in steel was dealt with in Part I (4.40 and 11.30). In killed steels segregation is less extensive than it is in semi-killed or rimming steels, where evolution of gases tends to carry impurities from the faces of the growing crystals back into the melt so that the most heavily segregated regions are near to and in the pipe of the ingot.

Rimming steel ingots therefore have an outer shell of very pure metal, but the composition changes abruptly towards the core, which contains most of the impurities. In killed steel ingots, however, there is a gradual increase in amounts of impurities from the outside skin to the central pipe.

2.225 NON-METALLIC INCLUSIONS arise mainly from the products of deoxidation, particles of Al_2O_3 and SiO_2 being the most numerous. Both of these oxides are insoluble in molten steel and rise to the surface very slowly following their formation. Since deoxidation is carried out late in the steel-making process, there is a limited period of time for them to float to the surface. This is particularly true when aluminium is used to kill a rimming steel which is already in the ingot mould.

Some of these oxides float to the surface whilst the steel is in the mould and are ultimately cropped off with the pipe, but those which remain as inclusions tend to segregate—often at the planes of weakness—and give rise to internal cracks in the ingot. The incidence of inclusions is reduced by deoxidising the melt as early as possible before teeming so that oxides have a greater opportunity to float to the surface.

Particles of slag may also cause trouble, as will fragments detached from linings of either the furnace or the ladle.

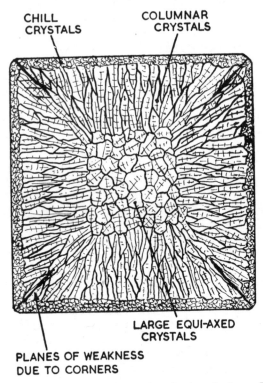

CHILL CRYSTALS   COLUMNAR CRYSTALS

LARGE EQUI-AXED CRYSTALS

PLANES OF WEAKNESS DUE TO CORNERS

FIG. 2.11—The Crystal Structure in a Section of a Large Ingot.

2.226 SURFACE DEFECTS in the finished steel product result from either sub-cutaneous blow-holes, scabs or cracks which have developed in the surface of the ingot. These cracks or tears may be the result of rough handling of the heated ingot in the early stages of rolling, overheating of the ingot during reheating or a rough mould surface which has prevented uniform contraction of the ingot. The cracks open up during rolling and are eventually converted into elongated 'rokes' in the finished material.

Subcutaneous blow-holes which become oxidised are elongated into 'seams' (or 'reeds') which are similar in appearance to shallow rokes. It is possible, however, to determine the origin of each, since rokes are often isolated faults, whilst seams, since they result from blow-holes, are usually distributed over the whole surface of the material.

When ingots are top poured metal may splash on to the sides of the mould, where it solidifies and rapidly oxidises. The rising metal ultimately covers these splashings, which form 'scabs' on the surface of the ingot. These can be chipped out before the ingot is rolled, but occasionally splashings are completely enveloped by the rising metal, which washes them free of the mould surface. They then form subcutaneous discontinuities which give rise to a laminated defect in the final rolled metal.

THE CASTING OF NON-FERROUS METALS

2.30

In chapter one the preparation of a non-ferrous metal bath free from dissolved gases and other undesirable constituents was discussed, and the casting of these metals into ingots of the desired shape will now be considered.

Unlike steel ingots, which are usually of approximately similar proportions, non-ferrous metal ingots may vary in shape between flat slabs approximately 1 m × 0·5 m × 40 mm, and bars 2·25 m long × 50 mm square. The former are used for rolling to sheet and the latter for rolling and drawing to wire. Thus non-ferrous metals are cast into moulds which produce an ingot nearer to the final shape required.

Some non-ferrous metals and alloys are cast into open cast-iron moulds (Fig. 2.12) to produce slabs for subsequent rolling to sheet. Open casting of

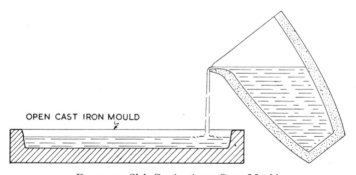

OPEN CAST IRON MOULD

FIG. 2.12—Slab Casting in an Open Mould.

this type is particularly suitable for pure metals, or alloys with a short freezing range which would consequently be prone to extensive piping if cast into a vertical mould. Moreover, a horizontal open mould is cheap to produce and rapid to operate.

The vertical type of cast-iron mould is more often used, however, pouring being effected from the top into the ingot cavity. Moulds of the book type, in which the cover is held in position by means of wrought-iron rings and wedges (Fig. 2.13), are used for casting slabs suitable for rolling to sheet and strip, whilst other forms of split and solid cast-iron mould are also used for casting either bars for rolling and drawing to wire or cylinders for extrusion. In all types of cast-iron mould the volume of iron chill is usually more than double that of the ingot space, in order to obtain uniformly rapid cooling and consequently a fairly uniform fine grain in the resulting ingot.

The molten metal is usually poured into the mould through a tundish. The function of this is not only to direct the stream of metal vertically into the mould so that it does not splash on to the vertical sides but also to regulate

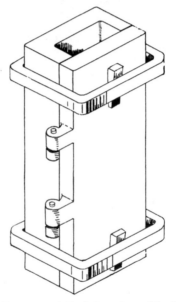

FIG. 2.13—A Book-form Ingot Mould.

the rate at which metal enters the mould. For most non-ferrous alloys the metal should rise in the mould at a rate of about 25 mm per second so that solidification almost keeps pace with the rate of entry of metal into the mould. Molten metal can thus feed into the pipe which tends to form, and this feeding process limits the effects of shrinkage.

The main disadvantage in the use of cast iron as a mould material is its tendency to crack during service. Repeated heating and cooling causes crazy cracking of the mould surface due to the low ductility of the iron. Ultimately these cracks open up as graphite growth (15.50—Part I) occurs, and in consequence the mould must be discarded. These graphite particles would react with the oxide film on the surface of the molten metal, producing carbon monoxide, which would give rise to porosity in the surface of the casting. Moreover, mould-dressing oils tend to collect in these cracks and vaporise a short interval of time later than the dressing oil on the surface, so that gas is forced into the partly solid face of the ingot, forming subcutaneous blow-holes.

Many non-ferrous alloys are cast into water-cooled copper-faced moulds which are either of the book form for casting slabs or of the cannon type for casting cylindrical extrusion billets (Fig. 2.14). The copper surface does not

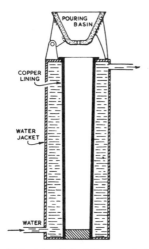

FIG. 2.14—The Principle of the Water-cooled Ingot Mould.

deteriorate as does the cast iron, so that a product with consistently good surface is forthcoming.

2.31 Brasses

Brasses may be cast into any one of the types of mould described above. Slabs destined for hot rolling are often cast into open moulds, but the bulk of slab casting is carried out in vertical cast-iron moulds, the dimensions of the ingot space varying between 60 and 500 mm in width; 25 and 50 mm in thickness; and 0·6 and 2 m in length. Slabs in the larger sizes and up to 75 mm thick are also cast in copper-lined water-cooled book-form moulds. Billets for extrusion are cast both in iron moulds and in copper-lined water-cooled moulds which commonly range in diameter from 75 to 200 mm, and in length from 0·6 to 2·5 m.

The faces of the ingot mould are usually dressed with some substance, the primary functions of which are, first, to prevent adhesion or welding of the ingot to the mould, and secondly, to provide a uniform insulating film which regulates the heat flow from the solidifying metal to the mould. Dressings may be either flaming or non-flaming. Except in cases where tranquil conditions are required in the mould, flaming dressings are generally used, since, in addition to fulfilling the functions mentioned above, they fill the ingot space with a reducing atmosphere which limits the formation of oxides on the surface of the pouring stream of metal. Flaming dressings also appear to have a grain-refining effect on cast brasses.

Non-flaming dressings include such materials as bone ash, kaolin or lamp black in aqueous suspension, whilst flaming dressings consist of powered charcoal mixed with seal oil or rape oil. Various mixtures containing oils, petroleum jelly, tallow, resin, talc, charcoal and kaolin are also used as flaming dressings. A smooth, thin coating of the dressing is applied to the warm mould.

The freezing temperature range of a brass varies with its composition, as will be evident from a study of the thermal equilibrium diagram (Fig. 16.2 —Part I). Therefore pouring temperatures vary between about 1 185° C for

PLATE 2.3—Casting Brass from an Ajax-Wyatt Furnace into Cylindrical 'Cannon' Moulds.

These ingots are subsequently cut into lengths to produce extrusion billets.

a 90–10 gilding metal and 1 050° C for a 60–40 brass. (In each case a super-heat of about 150° C above the liquidus temperature has been allowed.)

In common with other copper-base alloys, a pouring rate which gives a metal rise of 25–30 mm/s in the mould is ideal. When the mould has been filled, further additions of molten metal are made as the level sinks due to contraction on solidification. Skilful feeding in this way can limit the cropped-off pipe to about 50 mm on a 1 m long slab.

2.32 Phosphor-bronzes

Phosphor-bronzes are cast under conditions very similar to those obtained in the case of brasses, cast-iron book-form moulds being used to produce slabs for rolling to sheet, and split moulds about 2 m long and 60 mm square for casting bars for rolling and drawing to wire, rod and turbine blading. Moulds are heated slightly and dressed with seal oil to which has been added a mixture of charcoal and powdered french chalk, though a thin coating of volatile oil without additions is often used. Particular care is necessary to avoid forming a pool of oil in the bottom of the mould, since bronzes are more prone to gassing than are brasses.

Courtesy of Messrs I.C.I. Metals Division.

PLATE 2.4—Water-cooled Book-form Mould for Casting Ingots of Copper Alloys Destined for Rolling to Strip.

Behind the mould is an Ajax–Wyatt furnace used to melt the charge.

Since wrought bronzes have a much higher copper content than do brasses, their freezing temperature ranges are also higher. Pouring temperatures therefore vary between 1 200 and 1 250° C.

In common with many other alloys, both ferrous and non-ferrous, continuous casting methods are used in the case of bronzes. Rods, bars, sections and tubes are produced in high-purity bronze. The molten alloy is stored in a holding crucible furnace from the base of which it feeds into a water-cooled

T.R.I. photograph. Courtesy: T. M. Birkett, Billington and Newton Ltd.

PLATE 2.5—Continuous Casting of Bronze.

Continuous casting units for producing rods, bars, sections and tubes of high-purity bronze, at the Hanley factory of T. M. Birkett, Billington and Newton Ltd. The molten bronze is stored in the crucible on the platform and feeds from an orifice in the base into a graphite die in which it is solidified rapidly (by water cooling) and is then withdrawn steadily in an endless form which is cut into the length required.

graphite die. The bronze solidifies rapidly and is withdrawn steadily from the base of the die. It is then cut to the required length by swinging in a circular saw (Plate 2.5).

2.33 Aluminium Bronze

This alloy presents a special casting problem in view of the rate at which aluminium oxidises at the casting temperature of the alloy. Aluminium oxide forms a thick, tenacious film on the surface of the melt. If the melt is poured into a mould of the type normally used for the production of copper-base alloy ingots this film is broken and pieces of it become entangled in the casting, producing a rough, dirty surface to the ingot, with oxide films and inclusions in the interior.

The problem was tackled in France by P. H. G. Durville, who took out a British patent on his process in 1913. Durville's method, which is something of a classic in metallurgical technology, involves the transfer of the molten bronze from the crucible to the ingot mould without breaking the surface skin of the liquid. The equipment used (Fig. 2.15) consists of a combined

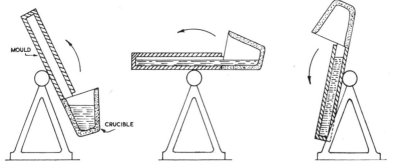

FIG. 2.15—Principle of the Durville Process.

reservoir and mould, the two being connected together in such a way that the pouring-out surface of the reservoir and the pouring-in surface of the mould are in the same straight line. The molten bronze is poured into the reservoir when the apparatus is in position (i) and the bulk of the dross is skimmed from the surface. The cradle containing the apparatus is then tilted through an angle of about 180° so that the liquid bronze is transferred from the reservoir to the mould. When the mould approaches the horizontal position (ii) the speed of rotation is reduced so as to avoid breaking the oxide skin on the surface of the melt as it begins to flow over into the mould. Failure to maintain a steady continuous movement through the horizontal position results in ripple marks on the surface of the ingot.

The cast-iron mould used in the Durville process is preheated to about 200° C and no surface dressing is applied.

2.34 Aluminium-base Alloys

Ingots in aluminium-base alloys are cast in square, oblong or round sections for rolling or extrusion operations.

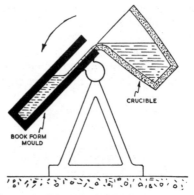

Fig. 2.16—The Tilt Mould for Aluminium
Alloy Casting.

As in the casting of aluminium-bronze ingots the thick oxide skin which forms on the surface of molten aluminium alloys is troublesome, and turbulence must be avoided during pouring, or dross and folds of oxide skin will be incorporated into the ingot. Until recent years the most widely used type of mould for casting aluminium-alloy ingots was the tilt mould (Fig. 2.16). This consists of a heavy cast-iron book-form mould mounted on trunnions so that it can be rotated at a controlled rate. Pouring begins when the mould is in an almost horizontal position, and whilst the mould is being rotated to the

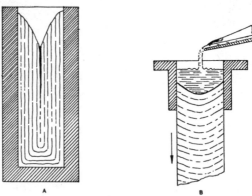

Fig. 2.17

A. Extensive Piping in an Ingot Cast in a Book-form Mould.
B. Piping Eliminated by Progressive Solidification during a Continuous
Casting Process.

vertical position the metal is poured in slowly and with a minimum of turbulence.

This method of casting limits the number of oxide inclusions in the final ingot, but in aluminium-alloy ingots of high-alloy content other faults are also prevalent. Due to the relatively slow rate of cooling which takes place, the crystal structure tends to be rather coarse. Moreover, since heat transfer takes place principally from the sides of the ingot, considerable inverse segregation occurs, resulting in the concentration of the alloying elements (which usually have melting points higher than that of aluminium) towards the outer skin of the ingot. With large ingots feeding must be carried out for a long period after pouring is complete in order to prevent the formation of an extensive pipe.

For these reasons the tilt-mould has lost favour and is now little used except for the casting of ingots of pure aluminium or alloys of low alloy content where

Courtesy of Messrs High Duty Alloys, Slough.

PLATE 2.6—Continuous Billet Casting of Aluminium Alloys.

Here two billets are being cast simultaneously into water-cooled mould heads. The photograph shows the method used to maintain the correct metal level in each of the mould heads.

segration can never be serious. The effects of segregation can be minimised by the use of a continuous casting process in which rapid solidification takes place from the bottom upwards instead of from the sides inwards as indicated in Fig. 2.17.

2.341 The basic principles of a continuous-casting plant are illustrated in Fig. 2.18. Casting begins when the piston is in a position at the bottom of the short thin water-cooled mould. A shell of molten metal freezes very quickly around the sides of the mould and on to the end of the piston, which is then slowly lowered, drawing the solidified shell with it. The movement of the piston is regulated to keep pace with the rate of pouring and the solidification of the shell. A direct water spray on to the casting below the mould itself ensures that solidification will be completed rapidly. By using a system of guide rolls in conjunction with a flying saw the process can be carried out continuously over a long period. Alternatively, the process may be what is usually termed semi-continuous. Here the flying saw mechanism is omitted and the lowering piston moves down into a pit so that ingots of a standard length are cast.

The principal metallurgical advantage of this process is that heat extraction, and hence solidification, takes place vertically rather than laterally. Moreover, solidification occurs very quickly. Both of these factors lead to a minimum of segregation taking place.

Since the level of the molten metal in the mould is kept constant, pouring conditions remain the same throughout the casting period, whereas in ordinary ingot casting the distance between the metal surface in the mould and the

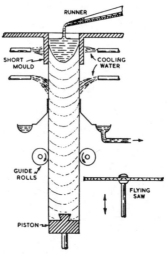

FIG. 2.18—The Principle of Continuous Casting.

pouring spout of the crucible varies during the casting of the ingot. Consequently in continuous casting the pouring mechanism can be designed to give the absolute minimum of turbulence during casting so that the quantity of entrapped oxide is kept low. Further, since the pouring stream is very short, a lower casting temperature can be used, and this, in turn, will mean that less gas is retained in solution at the moment of pouring, resulting in a minimum of gas porosity in the casting.

One obvious advantage of economic importance is the limitation of the pipe to that metal cast right at the end of a run, whilst in individually cast ingots the pipe must be cropped from each ingot.

Continuous-casting processes are used for the production of both round and slab-type ingot sections in aluminium alloys. It should be noted, however, that the process has also been successfully adapted for casting copper alloys, magnesium alloys and both carbon and alloy steels (2.204).

2.342 The present trend is towards the design of *horizontal* layouts for continuous casting plant in general. In some of these a bend-discharge system is used in which the bar leaving the mould is bent in a gentle curve and then straightened again in a horizontal direction (Fig. 2.19). More recently,

Courtesy of Messrs Northern Aluminium Co. Ltd, Banbury.

PLATE 2.7—Continuous Casting of Aluminium Alloys.
Here billets, each 2·5 m long, are being hoisted from the pit
of a 20-billet continuous casting unit.

however, a fully horizontal continuous casting machine has been introduced by Krupps, of Essen. The casting issues from the mould in a horizontal direction and needs only subsequent rolling or forging to its final shape.

In addition to a reduction in the height of the plant and the elimination of the structural problems involved, a greater degree of safety is ensured because it is no longer necessary to hoist ladles of molten metal high above floor level.

In order to obtain a sound product the molten metal must not be exposed to air whilst flowing from the furnace into the mould assembly. In ordinary vertical continuous casting plant suitable runners and down-spouts are

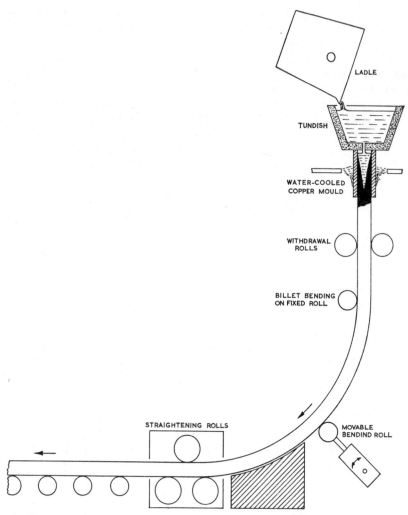

FIG. 2.19—A Continuous Casting Layout using a Bend-discharge System.

necessary to achieve this. Since the down-spouts dip into the head of molten metal in the mould, this limits the size of section which can be cast. In the Krupps process, however, from the moment the metal leaves the tundish it no longer comes into contact with air and this allows much smaller sections to be produced than are possible by the vertical casting process.

2.35 The Continuous Casting of Zinc
The name of Hazlett has been well known for many years in connection with the continuous casting of metals and a modern version of the Hazlett process

has been adopted for the production of continuously-cast stock up to 1·15 m wide and 75 mm thick for the subsequent manufacture of zinc strip and sheet. Part of the production line is illustrated diagrammatically in Fig. 2.20. Here the mould is formed by endless steel belts 7 m long, 1·35 m wide, and 1·25 mm thick and carried on pulleys as indicated. These belts form two sides of the mould, the mould cavity being completed by two sets of small solid steel blocks which are linked together on cables to form two endless chains, sandwiched between the belts. Both belts are driven during casting but the

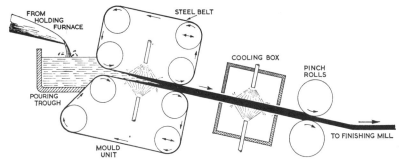

FIG. 2.20—The Hazlett Process for the Continuous Casting of Zinc.

edge dams, formed by the steel blocks (not shown in the diagram), are carried along by friction. The casting cavity is kept flat and parallel by tensioning the belts sufficiently. This is achieved by moving one pulley outwards. Both belts are cooled by a water spray on the inside surface of the belt. Naturally the working life of these belts is limited so that provision is made for their easy replacement.

After leaving the mould, the casting is cooled to a suitable hot-rolling temperature (180 to 240° C) by passing it through a cooling box equipped with water sprays. It then passes, via a stand of pinch rolls, to the finishing mill.

2.36 Defects in Non-ferrous Alloy Ingots

Internal defects in non-ferrous ingots originate in a similar manner to equivalent defects in steel ingots (2.22). Piping and segregation follow the same sort of pattern in both cases as far as formation is concerned, though their minimisation in non-ferrous alloy ingots may be approached in different ways from those used in steel ingots. Gas porosity in steel ingots is generally the result of chemical reactions which take place during solidification, but gas porosity in non-ferrous alloy ingots is invariably the result of hydrogen, which was dissolved during the melting process, being rejected on solidification of the alloy.

Non-metallic inclusions usually consists of particles of the oxide of that component of the alloy which has the highest affinity for oxygen. Thus brasses may contain particles of zinc oxide; bronze threads of tin oxide; and aluminium bronzes and aluminium-base alloys inclusions of aluminium oxide. In each case the incidence of inclusions is reduced by the adequate removal of dross before pouring and the control of turbulence during pouring.

Subcutaneous voids or blow-holes in non-ferrous ingots are less likely to weld up during mechanical working than similar cavities in steel ingots. Their formation during casting and subsequent solidification must therefore be avoided. Voids or blow-holes just beneath the surface of a non-ferrous ingot will produce extensive laminations in the ultimate rolled product. Subcutaneous blow-holes may be formed by the evaporation of dressing compounds which have collected in the cracks on the crazed surface of a cast-iron mould.

Similarly, splashings are a common hazard during the casting of metal into the long, thin slab moulds generally used for non-ferrous alloys. These isolated droplets which freeze on to the mould face are incorporated into the main ingot as in the case of steel ingots. Subsequent rolling of the slab elongates these particles and produces oxidised laminations on the surface of the final strip. This is usually referred to as 'spilly' metal.

ZONE REFINING

2.40

Zone refining is a process whereby a very high purity material is produced from raw material which is already relatively pure. Here the metallurgist encourages the phenomenon of segregation to work for him in 'sweeping' or 'squeezing' out impurities. It was mentioned earlier in this chapter (2.224)

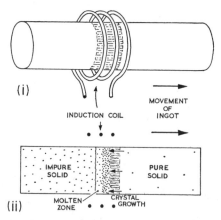

FIG. 2.21—The Principle of Zone Refining.

and also in Part I (4.40), that when a metal solidifies the impurities tend to remain behind in the liquid whilst relatively pure metal forms the growing crystals. Thus a band of molten metal, becoming increasingly impure, is pushed along in front of the advancing crystals.

In zone refining, an ingot of the metal or material is melted progressively along its length, a narrow zone at a time. This is achieved by moving the ingot relative to a narrow heating zone at a speed (usually measured in a few millimetres per hour) which allows crystallisation to follow melting at the desired rate. In this manner the molten zone moves progressively from one end of the ingot to the other and collects within itself much of the impurity which was originally distributed evenly throughout the ingot (Fig. 2.21 (ii)). This concentration of impurity will be deposited in the last portion of the ingot to be melted.

A single 'pass' will reduce the concentration of impurities by a limited amount only, so that a number of such treatments is necessary in practice. In order to speed up the process the ingot can be passed through a chain of heating zones arranged in succession (Fig. 2.22). Much of the impurity is then

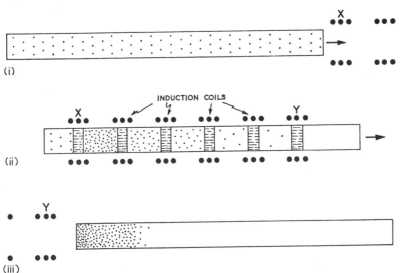

FIG. 2.22—The Function of Successive Zones in a Zone-refining Process.

concentrated in the last 20% of the ingot. This can be cut off, remelted and refined.

The above diagrams show a zone-refining process employing induction heating. The ingot may be supported in a long graphite or ceramic 'boat' which is passed through the series of induction coils. Some materials, particularly those of high melting point or those which are very reactive, are difficult to contain in this way and are held in a vertical plane in slowly rotating chucks whilst the coil system passes along the ingot. The complete system operates inside an enclosed chamber, either *in vacuo* or in an inert gas. In the case of silicon the molten zone is supported mainly by surface tension and this is assisted by electro-magnetic forces which, generated by the induction coil, impart a degree of levitation to the molten film.

Other methods of heating are also employed, the main requirement being that a narrow high-temperature zone be obtained. Thus electron-beam melting (19.40) is used in some systems, whilst in others heat from a carbon arc is focused on the ingot by means of elliptical mirrors. For low melting-point metals like tin, lead, aluminium, antimony and magnesium, resistance heating may be used. A simple apparatus of the type first used for zone-refining lead is shown in Fig. 2.23. Such an apparatus would of course have

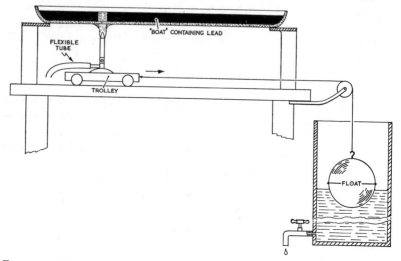

FIG. 2.23—A Simple Arrangement which nevertheless illustrates the General Method of Zone Refining.

a number of shortcomings, not the least being the gradual decrease in speed of the trolley which would result from a progressive fall in the head of water in the cylinder.

2.41

Zone refining was first developed in 1952 and used in the production of high-purity germanium for the manufacture of transistors. Such germanium has an impurity level of less than one part in a thousand million. Since then high-purity silicon and other semiconductors have been refined by this process.

In the field of metallurgy, zone refining has been carried out in connection with the manufacture of high-purity single crystals for use in research. Thus, single crystals of the refractory metals platinum, molybdenum, niobium, tungsten and tantalum have been refined to a purity of 'six nines' (99·9999%). Metals of very high purity often display quite outstanding mechanical properties. For example, high-purity iron is extremely ductile and soft. It also has a high resistance to corrosion due largely to the elimination of the possibility of electrolytic corrosion (22.25—Part I).

The presence of solute atoms in a metal tends to increase its recrystallisation temperature (5.41—Part I). Thus, the recrystallisation temperature of zone refined aluminium is considerably lower than that of ordinary commercial-grade aluminium. It is in fact impossible to work-harden the zone-refined metal since recrystallisation occurs freely below room temperature.

BIBLIOGRAPHY

1 'The Ingot Phase of Steel Production', E. Gathmann (Gathmann).
2 'The Solidification of Castings', R. W. Ruddle (Institute of Metals).
3 'Non-ferrous Foundry Metallurgy', A. J. Murphy (Pergamon Press).
4 'Casting of Brass and Bronze', D. R. Hull (The American Society for Metals).
5 'The Casting of Non-ferrous Ingots', L. Aitchison and V. Kondic (MacDonald & Evans).
6 'Chill-cast Tin Bronzes', D. Hanson and W. T. Pell-Walpole (Arnold).
7 'Symposium on the Metallurgical Aspects of Non-ferrous Metal Melting and Casting of Ingots for Working. No. 6' (Institute of Metals).
8 'Ferrous Metallurgy' (Volume II—'The Manufacture and Fabrication of Steel'), E. J. Teichert (McGraw-Hill).
9 'The Casting of Steel', W. C. Newell (Pergamon Press).
10 'The Making, Shaping and Treating of Steel', J. M. Camp and C. B. Francis (Carnegie–Illinois Steel Corp.).
11 'Casting Pit Practice', J. D. Sharp (Iliffe Books Ltd).
12 'Continuous Casting', D. L. McBride and T. E. Dancy (Interscience Publishers).
13 'Continuous Casting of Steel', M. C. Boichenko (Butterworth).
14 'The Continuous Casting of Steel in Commercial Use', K. P. Korotkov, N. P. Maiorov, A. A. Skvortsov and A. D. Akimenko (Pergamon Press).
15 'Surface Defects in Ingots and their Products', British Iron and Steel Research Association (Iron and Steel Institute).
16 'Zone Refining and Allied Techniques', N. L. Parr (Newnes).
17 'Aluminium', Vol. III–Fabrication and Finishing, Ed. K. R. van Horn (American Society for Metals).
18 BS 1400: 1969—Schedule of copper alloy ingots and copper and copper alloy castings.
19 BS 2970: 1959—Magnesium and magnesium alloy ingots and castings for general engineering purposes.

Chapter three
SAND CASTING

3.10

Apart from those metallurgical materials which are shaped by methods involving powder metallurgy, metals and alloys are first melted and then cast into a mould of predetermined shape. In some cases the mould may be of a simple form giving an ingot which is subsequently shaped plastically by forging, rolling or extrusion. Vast quantities of castings are produced, however, on which no further work is carried out other than cleaning and possibly light machining to accurate dimensions. These are the products of the typical foundry, and generally involve casting the molten metal into a sand mould of the desired shape. Other casting processes similar in principle to sand casting have been evolved in which closer control of dimensions is possible, so that a product is yielded which does not require any finishing operations even when close dimensional accuracy is required; shell moulding and investment casting are examples of such processes.

3.11

Whilst the crystal structure of a casting is often metallurgically less satisfactory than that of a component ultimately produced by a secondary process involving mechanical work (6.22—Part I), many other factors, both technical and economic, have to be considered in deciding what method shall be used to produce an article of given shape. For example, components of intricate shape, both internal and external, may be satisfactorily cast, and as a result subsidiary operations, such as mechanical working and machining, may be minimised or even omitted. Further, construction may be simplified by casting in a single piece and eliminating the necessity of either mechanical or metallurgical methods of joining. Size, too, is an important factor in production, and very large components of several tonnes would be difficult and expensive to produce other than as castings. Again many metals and alloys are both hot- and cold-short, so that they cannot be shaped by either hot- or cold-working processes. Since such materials are often of relatively low cost, their use for casting to shape is important economically. The wide use of cast iron is perhaps the most notable example of this feature of sand casting. Large numbers of any given casting can be produced relatively quickly, so that sand casting is a process amenable to the demands of mass production.

3.12

Many engineering properties are attained more easily in cast metals. Thus, whilst directionality of mechanical properties invariably exists in a wrought material, it is often lacking in a casting. Moreover, a second phase in the microstructure of a cast alloy whose presence may render it unsuitable for mechanical working will nevertheless often improve its machinability (20.20 —Part I). Thus grey cast iron is free-machining because of the presence of graphite particles. A further important feature of cast iron is its capacity for damping vibrations, making it a very useful material for the construction of large frames and housings.

THE BASIC STEPS IN A SAND-CASTING PROCESS

3.20
The production of a desired shape by a sand-casting process first involves moulding foundry sand around a suitable pattern in such a way that the pattern can be withdrawn to leave a cavity of the required shape in the sand. To facilitate this procedure the sand mould is split into two or more parts. With castings of simple shape a two-part mould can be used, each half being contained in a box-like frame. The upper frame is known as the cope and the lower frame as the drag, whilst the two halves fitted together are termed a box or flask. The surface at which the two halves of the sand mould meet when cope and drag are fitted together is called the parting surface.

3.21
Let us now consider the production of a mould for casting a simple gear blank, the pattern of which is shown in Fig. 3.1.

A flat-backed pattern of this type is the simplest possible form of pattern, and can be so moulded that the mould cavity is entirely in the drag, the cope half of the mould merely forming the flat back of the casting.

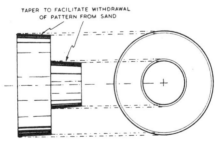

TAPER TO FACILITATE WITHDRAWAL OF PATTERN FROM SAND

FIG. 3.1.

The pattern is first placed on a moulding board along with the drag half of the box (Fig. 3.2 (i)), the box chosen being of adequate size to allow a sufficient volume of sand for effective ramming. Facing sand is now riddled over the pattern and the drag then filled up with ordinary moulding sand, which is then rammed sufficiently over the entire surface to consolidate it. Ramming must not be excessive, or the sand will become so tightly packed that entrapped air and gases cannot escape through the walls of the mould when the molten metal is poured in. At the same time ramming must be carried far enough, or the mould will not be strong enough to withstand handling or the erosive action of the molten metal as it flows through the mould. When the sand has been rammed sufficiently any excess is cut off level with the upper edges of the drag. A small amount of loose sand is now

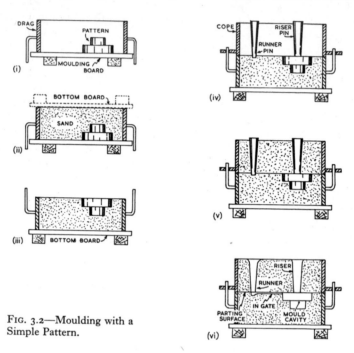

FIG. 3.2—Moulding with a Simple Pattern.

sprinkled on the smoothed surface to provide a bed for the bottom board, which is now placed on top of the drag (Fig. 3.2 (ii)).

3.22

The complete assembly is now turned over and the moulding board removed. After the moulder has brushed away any loose particles of moulding sand, parting sand is sprinkled over the surface of the mould. This parting sand should either be dry clay-free silica sand or burnt moulding sand, its function being to prevent cope and drag halves of the mould from bonding together whilst the cope is being rammed.

The cope box is now placed in position on top of the drag, location being effected by means of the pins on the drag and the holes in the lugs attached to the cope. The runner and riser pins are then placed in position (Fig. 3.2 (iv)) and held so by means of a small amount of moulding sand pressed around them. The purpose of the runner in the finished mould is, of course, to admit the molten metal to the mould cavity, whilst one of the principal functions of the riser is to provide a reservoir from which molten metal can feed back into the casting as it solidifies and shrinks.

3.23

Moulding sand is now riddled into the cope box to a depth of about 25 mm, and in the case of a large mould 'gaggers' would be incorporated in the sand at this stage. Gaggers are suitably shaped wires or rods which are built into the cope to give it strength in much the same way as the steel core operates in reinforced concrete. The cope box is now filled with sand, which is rammed firmly and trimmed off level with the top of the box (Fig. 3.2 (v)). The gate and riser pins are then 'rapped' to loosen them so that they can be withdrawn, and at this stage the cope is 'vented' if this should be considered necessary. Venting consists in making holes through the top of the cope with a piece of thin wire so that air from the mould cavity and any gases evolved from the molten metal can escape quickly. If the moulding sand is sufficiently gas permeable, venting will not be necessary.

The cope is now lifted off and set aside whilst a certain amount of hand work is carried out on the drag. The surface of the sand around the pattern is examined and any minor faults made good. The pattern is then rapped with a rapping bar and hammer so that it can be withdrawn by means of a lifting screw which fits into a threaded hole in the pattern. The ingate is then cut using a specially shaped tool, and sharp corners in the runner, gate and riser channels are chamfered to minimise erosion of the sand during casting.

3.24

All loose sand is now blown out of the mould cavity and gate, and mould dressing (if used) is applied to both cope and drag halves of the mould cavity. Sometimes the cope and drag are then skin dried by playing a gas torch on the mould surface, or completely dried by placing in an oven for several hours.

Finally, the mould is closed by placing the cope on top of the drag, using the pins and lugs to secure correct location. The cope is then either weighted or clamped to the drag in order to prevent any tendency for the cope to be lifted by the hydraulic pressure of the molten metal.

3.25

The foregoing description refers to the manufacture of a sand mould of the simplest type. We will now consider some of the modifications in procedure which are necessary in moulding a somewhat more complicated shape. Assume that a flanged pulley (Fig. 3.3) is to be moulded. In this case several methods would be available to produce the mould, and the process chosen would depend largely upon the number of castings required. If this number was large, then a method involving the production of dry-sand cores might be chosen, since the extra expenditure associated with the provision of equipment for their production would be justified. Fig. 3.4 (i) shows the type of pattern which would be used. This would be moulded in a manner similar to that used for the simple gear blank dealt with above, and the sand mould (with the pattern removed) would then appear as in Fig. 3.4 (ii). The central hole in the pulley and the groove in its circumference are moulded by dry-sand cores, which are placed in the mould after the removal of the wooden

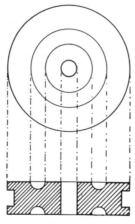

FIG. 3.3.

pattern (Fig. 3.4 (iii)). The dry-sand cores are, of course, produced by a
separate process which is dealt with later in this chapter (3.50).

3.26

If a small number of castings were required it might be more economical to
produce a mould in the manner indicated in Fig. 3.5. Here a three-part flask
has been employed in conjunction with a split pattern in order to dispense
with the relatively expensive dry-sand core used to mould the groove in the
method described above. The central hole is still obtained by using a dry-
sand core, but this will be a simple shape to produce.

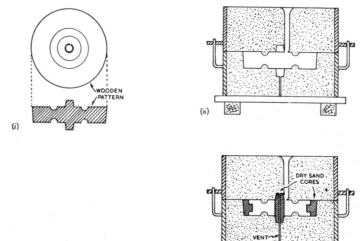

FIG. 3.4—The Use of
Dry-sand Cores.

The two-piece pattern is first rammed up in the middle section (or cheek) of the flask as shown in Fig. 3.5 (i). Next the cope is made in the normal manner (Fig. 3.5 (ii)), a bottom board is placed on top and the assembly then turned over. The third part (Z) is then fixed to the pattern and the drag made up (Fig. 3.5 (iii)). The drag is then lifted off so that the top half of the pattern (Y) can be withdrawn. After replacing the drag a bottom board is placed on top (Fig. 3.5 (iv)) and the whole assembly again turned over so that the cope

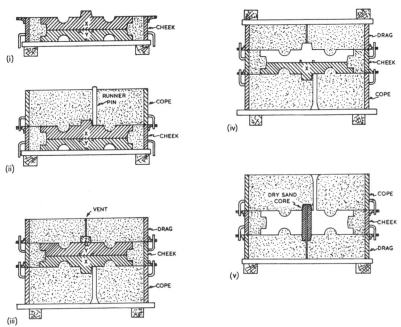

FIG. 3.5—Moulding with a Three-part Flask and a Two-piece Pattern.

can be removed and the remainder of the pattern withdrawn. The dry-sand core is then placed in position and the cope replaced.

These two methods of moulding a flanged pulley by no means exhaust the total numbers of ways of producing such a moulded shape, but are representatives of general moulding practice.

3.27
The cores shown in the mould illustrated in Fig. 3.4 are adequately held in position by the cope and drag. It is sometimes impossible, however, to provide sufficient support for cores in this way, and in such cases the buoyancy of the molten metal would cause the core to move. The core is therefore supported with small metal 'chaplets', which are usually placed between the core and the mould face (Fig. 3.6). As far as is possible, the chaplet is chosen of such a size that fusion between it and the molten metal will be effected.

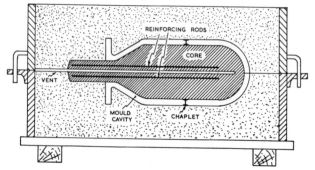

FIG. 3.6—The Use of Chaplets.

The use of chaplets, however, should be avoided when castings which will be subjected to high pressures are being produced.

PATTERNS AND THEIR DESIGN

3.30

The first step in the production of a casting is the manufacture of a suitable pattern. Even when only one casting is required it is necessary to make a pattern, though the choice of material from which the pattern is made will often be governed by the number of castings desired. Thus softwood patterns are only used when a small number of castings is to be produced, whilst for the production of large numbers of castings hardwood or metal patterns may be employed. Alternatively, softwood or plaster of Paris patterns may be metal sprayed or electro-plated in order to make them more durable.

3.31

Patterns should be impermeable to moisture, and for that reason wood and plaster patterns are usually coated with several layers of shellac. They must also remain free from distortion by warping and have a good surface finish to ensure that they can be withdrawn easily from the mould.

3.32

In the construction of a pattern due allowance must be made for the behaviour of a casting during solidification. Metals shrink during solidification, and further contraction of the casting takes place as it cools from the solidus to room temperature. The size of the pattern must therefore be larger than that required in the resultant casting, and in order to avoid the necessity of making due allowance by calculations either at the blueprint stage or in the production of the pattern, the pattern-maker is provided with a special shrinkage rule which is slightly longer than a standard rule bearing similar graduations. For example, the linear shrinkage of cast iron is about 10 mm/metre; therefore the shrinkage rule used to make the pattern for an iron casting is 10 mm longer per metre than a standard rule. Approximate shrinkages for some of the common casting alloys are given in Table 3.1.

TABLE 3.1—*Approximate shrinkages for Some Casting Alloys.*

Alloy	Shrinkage (mm/metre)
Cast iron	10
Steel	20
Brass	15
Aluminium	13
Magnesium base	13

3·33
If parts of a casting are to be machined due allowance for the extra metal necessary must be made when designing the pattern. Similarly, an allowance must often be made for cleaning up a casting, as in the case of large steel castings which cool slowly and therefore tend to oxidise in the mould. Sometimes castings tend to warp or distort as they cool. This is caused by uneven

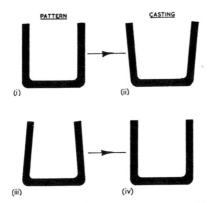

Fig. 3.7—The Pattern Must Be Shaped as (iii) to
Give a Casting of the Required Shape (iv).

shrinkage, and is due to variations in the thickness of cross-section or to one surface being more exposed than the other so that it cools more rapidly. To compensate for this the shape of the pattern is bent in the opposite direction to which the distortion takes place (Fig. 3.7).

3·34
In order that the pattern may be removed from the rammed sand mould without causing damage to the latter it is essential that it shall be tapered sufficiently. Usually a taper of about 5 mm/metre is adequate, though the amount varies according to the type and size of casting and the extent to which the sand has been rammed.

3·35
Patterns may be made in one piece, or they may be split along the parting line of the cope and the drag. They may also be provided with loose sections for

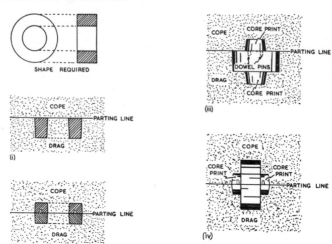

FIG. 3.8—Methods of Moulding a Simple Cylindrical Bush.

moulding undercut or overhanging parts of the casting. Such projections, if attached to the main pattern, would prevent it from being withdrawn from the mould. The loose sections, however, can be withdrawn *inward* into the cavity left after the main pattern has been removed. A simple pattern may often be moulded in a number of ways, as indicated in Fig. 3.8.

If a pattern is split along the parting line between cope and drag each half is moulded separately in cope and drag respectively. Each half is laid on a

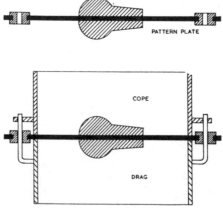

FIG. 3.9—The Use of a Simple Pattern Plate.

flat board and sand rammed around it. Both cope and drag are then turned over, the two halves of the pattern removed and the two parts of the mould brought together. In some cases it is convenient to mount the two halves of the pattern on either side of the bottom board (Fig. 3.9), the complete assembly being known as a pattern plate. This ensures that cope and drag will be located in their correct positions for casting.

Using this type of pattern plate, a moulder usually makes a number of cope halves and then a number of drag halves. Alternatively, a half-match plate may be used in which the two halves of the pattern are on separate plates. The two halves of the mould can be made by different moulders.

3.36
When the pattern is in a single piece and is wholly contoured a 'follower' board must be used. This has a depression made in it to accommodate the contour of the pattern so that a proper parting line can be established between cope and drag. It is essential that the parting line be in the correct position, or the mould may be damaged when the pattern is withdrawn.

MOULDING MATERIALS

3.40
Various types of sand are used in foundries for the manufacture of moulds. Whilst 'green' sand—that is, suitable naturally occurring sand—is the most widely used, other forms, such as dry sand, core sand, cement-bonded sand and shell-moulding sand (5.30) are also employed for specific purposes.

3.41
Sand is formed by the disintegration of rocks under the action of frost, wind and rain, and since rocks vary widely in composition, so also will the resulting sands. A sand suitable for moulding consists largely of grains of silica (SiO_2) together with sufficient clay (usually between 5 and 20%) to act as a binding material. A naturally occurring sand of this type need only be mixed with sufficient water to facilitate moulding. Sometimes two varieties of sand may be blended to produce a mixture with an adequate clay content, whilst the so-called synthetic sands are essentially clean quartz grains (free of clay or organic matter) blended before use with a clay such as Bentonite. Since moisture does not pass readily through these clays, the surface drying of synthetic sand moulds presents a problem, for moisture does not diffuse outwards quickly enough to replace surface moisture removed by evaporation Cereals (fine-ground corn products) may be added to accelerate the passage of moisture through synthetic sands. Sea-sand consists of almost pure silica, and whilst it can be moulded into sand castles of quite intricate design when damp, the reader will know that these castles quickly crumble as the sand begins to dry. This crumbling occurs due to the absence of any form of binder.

A moulding sand must fulfil the following requirements:

(i) it must be sufficiently refractory to withstand the temperature of the molten metal;

(ii) it must contain sufficient bonding material to retain the shape of the mould, and the bonding material itself must be refractory;

(iii) it must be sufficiently permeable to allow gases which are produced to escape.

3.42

The grain size of a moulding sand is also important. For moulding small castings which are not to be machined, a fine-grained sand is used in order to obtain a smooth finish on the surface of the casting. Large castings, however, require a sand of much coarser grain which will be correspondingly more permeable and so permit the escape of the greater volume of gas which may be formed.

3.43

Synthetic sands are now widely used because they are amenable to much closer control, being more uniform in composition than are natural sands. In general, synthetic sands are also more refractory, and consequently have a longer working life. The main disadvantage in their use is that they are mouldable over a narrow moisture range, so that the moisture content must be controlled between closer limits. As a result, synthetic sands dry out more quickly. In addition to the clay binder, some synthetic sands contain a non-thermosetting resin. Not only does this resin act as a binder but also when the molten metal comes into contact with it decomposition occurs so that the sand grains become coated with a layer of soot which effectively prevents the molten metal from welding on to them.

3.44

The moisture content of moulding sands normally varies between 4 and 8%. This is liable to change, and must therefore be checked frequently. Similarly, the clay content of moulding sand falls with repeated use. Each time molten metal comes into contact with the sand a thin layer of clay adjacent to the molten metal is baked so that it loses permanently its plasticity in the manner of pottery clay. Thus the available clay content of the sand diminishes with repeated use, and must be made up by adding new clay.

3.45

The casting temperature of molten iron or steel is high enough to fuse ordinary moulding sand so that it welds on to the surface of the casting. Some form of facing material is therefore generally necessary to prevent sand from sticking to the surface of the casting. The facing material may be mixed with some moulding sand to form a facing sand, or it may be applied directly to the surface of the mould cavity. For example, powdered graphite dusted on to the surface of the mould cavity is a good facing material for iron or steel castings, since it does not melt. Facing sand for iron castings usually consists of equal parts of old and new sand together with a small amount of fine coal dust.

Green-sand moulds are used more than any other type for the manufacture of large numbers of small or moderate-sized castings because of their relatively low cost and the fact that no drying process is necessary before the mould is used, provided that the initial moisture content has been effectively controlled. When a mould with a harder surface which will resist erosion by the molten metal is required, skin-dried moulds are often used. Then an additional binder, such as molasses, resins, linseed oil or cornflour, is either incorporated in the facing sand or sprayed on the surface of the mould cavity. The mould surface is then dried to a depth of about 12 mm by using a gas torch, a current of hot air or infra-red lamps. The mould must then be used fairly quickly, otherwise moisture from the backing sand will begin to soften the dried skin.

Completely dried sand moulds are mechanically stronger than either green-sand moulds or skin-dried moulds, and will therefore stand up to more handling. Additional binders are used as in skin-dried moulds, but in this case they are added to the whole of the moulding sand. Drying is carried out

Courtesy of Messrs The Stanton Ironworks Co. Ltd, Nottingham.

PLATE 3.1—Cores Used in the Casting of Ingot Moulds.
Those shown in the photograph have been 'roughed' with loam.

in ovens at about 240° C. Air-dried moulds are often produced by allowing ordinary green-sand moulds to remain open to the air for some time before use. Some moisture is lost from the mould surface, which consequently becomes harder.

3.46
Loam moulding is used for large moulds which can be produced by mechanical shaping for forming the mould contours and so reducing pattern costs (Fig. 3.10). The rough shape of the mould is built with ordinary bricks and reinforced with iron plates. The loam mixture may consist of coarse silica sand, fireclay, sawdust and sufficient water to produce a mortar-like consistency. Alternatively, mixtures of red sand, horse manure and water are used. The loam mixture is applied to the surface of the brickwork and formed

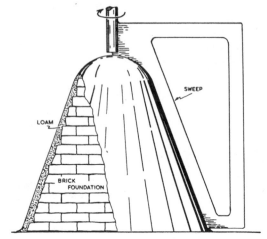

FIG. 3.10—Making the Drag Half of a Mould for a Large
Slag Ladle by Loam Moulding.

to shape by means of a sweep (Fig. 3.10). The surface produced is given a coating of refractory material and the parts then completely dried either in ovens or on the foundry floor.

3·47

The use of Portland cement as a bonding material was first investigated in the U.S.A., and later the Randupson process of cement moulding was introduced in Europe. This process uses as a moulding material clean silica sand mixed with about 10% cement and about 5% water. The damp mixture remains in a condition suitable for moulding for up to 3 hours after mixing. After moulding, the half moulds are stripped and stored in a damp atmosphere for about 24 hours in order to allow them to set, after which they can be assembled ready for casting. The new mixture of sand and cement is generally used for facing, the main body of the mould being composed of crushed used moulds to which a little new cement has been added for bonding.

Cement-bonded sand moulds are useful for the manufacture of larger castings, since the hardened cement–sand mixture has good mechanical strength and allows much thinner mould walls to be used, whilst at the same time a high permeability is maintained. Moreover, since the cement hardens at atmospheric temperatures, no drying ovens are required.

Large steel castings are invariably moulded in what is usually referred to as 'compo'. This mixture consisted originally of crushed used crucibles and firebricks, together with some ganister and bonded with new fireclay. Graphite or powdered coke was also added to increase the refractoriness of the mixture. As the demand for moulding material outstripped the supply of used refractories, calcined fireclays were used as a substitute. A mixture of similar composition is used extensively on the Continent and is known as 'chamotte'.

The main advantage in the use of this type of moulding material is its high refractoriness coupled with good mechanical strength and high permeability, which allows the complete drying of large moulds and also the escape of gases during casting. The coarse nature of compo, however, makes it necessary to use a facing compound of some fine-grained material, usually rich in silica. The moulds are dried in large stoves at a temperature approaching dull-red heat.

3.48

The 'CO₂' process was often regarded as being an entirely new method of bonding both sand moulds and cores when it came into use a few years ago. In fact, the principle of the process was the subject of a British patent taken out by Hargreaves and Poulson in 1898. Little development work seems to have been carried out at the time of the original patent, and the process was forgotten until about 1950, when interest in it was suddenly revived in several places in central Europe. The CO_2 process is now used in steel, iron and non-ferrous foundries.

The principle of the process is that silica sand is mixed with sodium silicate solution so that the individual grains of sand are effectively coated. The required mould or core is then rammed with the mixture, after which the gas carbon dioxide (CO_2) is passed through the rammed sand. Carbon dioxide reacts with sodium silicate to form silica gel and sodium carbonate. The silica gel so formed acts as a strong bond between the silica sand grains, and the process takes place without the application of heat. The absence of a stoving process enables a core to be hardened whilst it is still in the core box, and this in turn results in greater accuracy of dimensions being obtained in the finished core.

When maximum strength is required in the mould or core the sand used should contain no active clay, for whilst the presence of clay increases the *green* strength of the mould, it considerably reduces its *cured* strength. If cured strength is not important a clay-bonded sand may be used so that the green strength of a core is high enough to permit stripping it from the box before gassing. This simplifies the gassing process.

Whatever sand is used it is mixed with about 5% of sodium silicate solution and the mould or core rammed in the usual way, either by hand or mechanically. The rammed sand is then gassed. This can be accomplished in one of two ways:

(1) By introducing carbon dioxide through some form of nozzle to a point well below the exposed surface of the sand. This method is particularly adaptable to the treatment of cores (Fig. 3.11).

(2) By placing the core or mould in an autoclave or gas chamber into which carbon dioxide can be passed.

In addition to the greater dimensional accuracy obtainable in cores bonded by the CO_2 process, there is a considerable reduction in handling because cores are cured in the core box. There is also a greater output per given floor space.

It is claimed that less scabs and hot tears occur in castings made in moulds bonded by the CO_2 process. Moreover, less gas is evolved from the mould

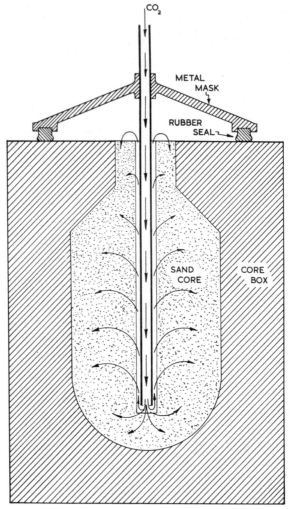

FIG. 3.11—An Example of the Application of the CO_2 Process.

during casting, and there is an absence of obnoxious fumes which often accompany the use of various organic core binders.

The main disadvantage attending the use of cores cured by the CO_2 process is that the bond is not destroyed by heat during the casting operation. Consequently, cores are still strong and therefore difficult to remove from the solid casting. This is particularly true of alloys such as grey iron and steel, which are cast at temperatures high enough to cause further strengthening of the bond. To facilitate the removal of a core, the sand is often mixed with between 3 and 8% of a mixture of coal or coke dust and fireclay, though substances such as wood flour and pitch are also used for this purpose. The organic material burns at the casting temperature, so that the core is weakened sufficiently to facilitate its removal. With low-melting-point alloys, such as those of aluminium, the cores rarely reach a temperature high enough to cause further hardening of the bond, so that additions of organic matter to the sand are unnecessary.

Other disadvantages of the CO_2 process are:

(1) the storage life of the cores is short;

(2) heavy sections are difficult to penetrate efficiently with the gas.

Nevertheless, the process has been adopted in production by many foundries in both the ferrous and non-ferrous trades for the manufacture of many types of casting.

3.49 'cold-setting' processes

Whilst sand moulding is generally an operation where no further treatment is required once the pattern has been removed, many core-making processes involve baking the core (which contains some heat-sensitive binder) in order to give it sufficient mechanical strength to allow handling. The CO_2 process mentioned above can be used both for moulds and cores and is a 'cold' process in that cores made in this way do not require to be baked. Of recent years a number of cold-setting processes have been introduced with varying degrees of success.

3.491 COLD-SETTING SODIUM SILICATE. This process, like the CO_2 process, makes use of sodium silicate as the bonding agent. Here, carbon dioxide is replaced as the 'hardener' by di-calcium silicate, Portland cement or 75% ferro-silicon. The powdered hardener is mixed with the sodium silicate and sand just before moulding. Subsequently the hardener reacts slowly with the sodium silicate to produce a rigid compound which effectively bonds the sand grains.

One particular advantage of this process is that large-size work can be accomplished for which the CO_2 process is unsuitable, though in many other respects the disadvantages of the two processes are similar.

3.492 COLD-SETTING OILS. These materials have offered serious competition to the CO_2 process in recent years, principally because cores manufactured by this process tend to break down more readily than do those bonded by the carbon dioxide/silicate method.

The binder system consists of linseed oil which has been chemically modified so that it will react with certain isocyanates and so harden. The modified oil is mixed with suitable catalysts and accelerators and when brought into initimate mixture with the hardener (for example, 4,4 diphenyl methylene di-isocyanate) solution takes place. Chemical action then begins and 'free radicals', liberated by the isocyanate, cross link the modified linseed oil molecules and build up rigid three-dimensional complex polymers. A firm bond is produced in this way in about sixteen hours at ordinary temperatures, the quantity of binder used being approximately 1·5% of the total sand.

3.493 THE FURRAN PROCESS is a cold-binding method applicable to both moulding and core-making. It is based on the use of furfuryl alcohol along with necessary catalysts and accelerators. A number of advantages are claimed for the process, the chief of which are:

(1) easy breakdown of cores;
(2) improved dimensional accuracy;
(3) increased speed of production;
(4) the possibility of using unskilled labour;
(5) the reduction of obnoxious fume in the foundry.

The principal disadvantage of the process seems to be the relatively high cost of the raw material but this, it is claimed, can be offset by the increased production rate it favours and the fact that reclaimed sand may be used.

CORES AND CORE-MAKING

3·50

Cavities inside a casting are generally formed by using a sand core. When the pattern itself can be shaped so as to form a core as an integral part of the mould this core is termed a green-sand core. Whilst it is an economical

Courtesy of Messrs Fletcher Miller Ltd, Hyde, Cheshire.

PLATE 3.2—The Hand Production of Dry-sand Cores Using a Simple Box.

method of forming holes in a casting, it is limited to holes of short length whose sides are perpendicular to the parting face. Most holes therefore are formed by using sand cores which have been produced separately and are then fitted into the mould when the cope and drag are brought together ready for casting. The core is held in its correct position in the mould cavity by impressions—known as 'core prints'—in the sand mould (Fig. 3.4). These core prints are formed by suitably shaped extensions on the original pattern.

3.51
Most core sands contain special binders, so that the resulting cores have the necessary mechanical strength in order that they can be handled and will resist erosion and the effects of buoyancy when the molten metal is poured into the mould. Dry-sand cores should therefore have the following properties:

(1) *Dry strength* after curing sufficient to withstand handling and transportation to the foundry, and forces exerted by the molten metal which is poured into the mould.

Courtesy of Messrs The Stanton Ironworks Co. Ltd, Nottingham.

PLATE 3.3—Lowering a Finished Core into the Drag Half of a Sand Mould.

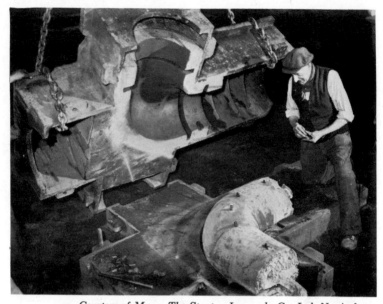

Courtesy of Messrs The Stanton Ironworks Co. Ltd, Nottingham.
PLATE 3.4—The Same Mould as that Shown in Plate 3.3 with Cope about to be
Placed in Position.

(2) *Permeability* in order that gases generated during casting may pass quickly
to the atmosphere. Whilst vents or passages are usually formed in the
core by the core-maker, the layer of sand between the face of the core and
the vent must be sufficiently permeable to allow gas to escape quickly to
the vent passage.

(3) *Collapsibility* after pouring so that the core can be disintegrated rapidly
and without damage to the casting.

The strength of the moulded sand in the green condition, that is, before
being dried, must also be sufficient to enable the moulded core to be removed
from the core box and be transferred to the drying oven.

3.52
Dry-sand cores are produced from synthetic sands, the basis of which is clay-
free silica sand. The sand is thoroughly mixed with the chosen binder and
usually some water to produce a mixture which can be moulded successfully.
The majority of core binders provide both green and dry strength, though
sometimes some bentonite clay may be added to increase the green strength
where necessary. Core binders which have been most commonly used include
core oils, the principal ingredient of which is linseed oil; horse manure;
cereal binders, containing dextrine and casein; resins and pitch; molasses;
bentonite; and thermosetting plastics. These latter possess the following
obvious advantages when used as binders:

Courtesy of Messrs The Stanton Ironworks Co. Ltd, Nottingham.

PLATE 3.5—Pouring the Molten Pig Iron into the Finished Mould Shown in the Two Previous Illustrations.

(1) Cores made from plastic-bonded sand collapse easily, reducing the cleaning time and the number of castings scrapped due to hot cracking (cracks are sometimes formed when the solidifying casting shrinks on to a core).

(2) The baking time is much shorter than that for oil binders, in fact it is measured in minutes instead of hours when dielectric heating is employed.

(3) Thermosetting plastics generate less gas during pouring than do many other binders.

In recent years the use of the CO_2 and other cold-setting processes (3.48 and 3.49) has increased as a means of core binding, with advantages not only in dimensional accuracy but in several other directions.

3·53

Cores are made in wood or metal boxes, the internal cavity being such as to produce a core of the desired shape. The sand is rammed into the core box in much the same way as when making moulds. Core boxes may be of the simple knock-out type, or they may be of split form. In the former the sand is rammed into the box and then trimmed off level along the top face. The core is then turned out on to a flat plate on which it can be dried. A split core box consists of two halves which are clamped together. One or both ends are open in order to facilitate filling with sand and ramming. The book-type of split core box consists of two halves which are usually hinged together. It differs from the ordinary split box in that the core is completely enclosed when the box is shut. With the box open sand is rammed into each half and then sprinkled on one half and the other half closed over it and pressed firmly down. The upper half is then rapped to loosen the core and raised, leaving the complete core in the lower half of the box.

Cores having at least one flat side can be placed on to a flat plate for drying, but other shapes must be supported on a shaped carrier or 'drier' which has a contour similar to that of the box from which the core has been ejected. Drying ovens are either of the batch type or continuous, and usually maintain

Courtesy of Messrs The David Brown Cos, Penistone, nr Sheffield.
PLATE 3.6—The Drag Half (with Cores in Position) of a Large Sand Mould.

a temperature in the region of 260° C. The time necessary for drying usually varies between 2 and 8 hours, depending upon the size of the core. Careful handling of cores is necessary as they are transferred from the box to the drier, and the advantages of the CO_2 process (3.48) and other cold-setting processes (3.49) mentioned above become apparent not only in the maintenance of dimensional accuracy but also in the reduction of handling time which accrues from curing the core whilst it remains in the box.

METHODS OF CONTROLLING SOLIDIFICATION
3.60
The melting of foundry metals was dealt with in chapter one. Here we shall consider some of the practices adopted in controlling the solidification of the metal after it has entered the prepared mould.

3.61
When a metal solidifies it shrinks (4.30—Part I), and this shrinkage may manifest itself in one of the ways indicated in Fig. 3.12 (i) unless modifications to the design of the mould are used with the object of overcoming the effects of shrinkage.

In order to prevent the isolation of pockets of molten metal which will lead to the formation of the type of porosity indicated, 'risers' are incorporated at suitable points in the mould. In addition to providing a reservoir of molten

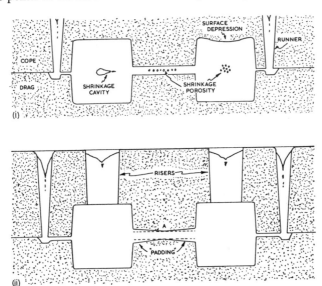

FIG. 3.12.

metal which can feed into the casting and thus counteract shrinkage the riser provides a head of molten metal which will exert hydrostatic pressure and thus improve the impression the metal makes of the mould. The location and dimensions of each riser are important if risering is to be effective, and no pocket of molten metal should be formed which is not connected to a riser, or shrinkage, and its attendant porosity, will follow when the pocket of molten metal ultimately solidifies.

3.62
It may be found that risering does not overcome completely the effects of shrinkage in the central thin section of the casting illustrated in Fig. 3.12 (i). 'Padding' may therefore be used to effect directional solidification from the centre of the section outwards. This entails increasing the thickness of the section, as shown in Fig. 3.12 (ii), so that solidification will begin at A and proceed in both directions away from this point. It is unlikely, in these circumstances, that any pockets of molten metal will become isolated from the heavy sections of the casting, and consequently from the risers.

Sometimes the molten metal in the riser is superheated in order to aid directional solidification and to ensure that the riser remains molten until the remainder of the casting is solid. This is done by adding some exothermic mixture to the molten metal in the riser. The reaction produced is basically similar to that which takes place in the Thermit process (19.30).

Circumstances of design do not always allow the siting of risers at all points where they are desirable. It is then better to induce directional solidification by chilling the metal at those points where it is decided that solidification should begin.

In Fig. 3.13 it is assumed that it is impossible to provide that body of metal at X with a riser. Instead internal chills may be used to effect directional solidification. Similarly, padding of the thin section may not be feasible, and

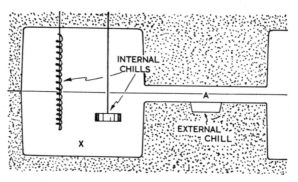

Fig. 3.13—Types of Chill.

an external chill may be used instead at A to promote directional solidification from that point. External chills are generally suitably shaped blocks of copper, iron or steel which are placed at strategic points in the sand mould, whilst internal chills should be of the same composition as the casting itself, since they will eventually become part of it.

3.63

The design of the gate or runner through which the metal enters the mould is also very important. It must be so placed that the mould is completely filled with metal, which should enter the mould with a minimum of turbulence. At the same time slag, dross and loose sand should be prevented from entering the mould cavity, whilst the metal flow should not be so great as to cause any appreciable erosion of the sand.

The simplest type of gate is one sited at the parting line. This is cheap to produce, since it can be cut by hand when the cope and drag are separated for the removal of the pattern. Alternatively, the gate can be formed by an integral part of the pattern. Sometimes the gate is situated in the cope half of the mould so that it will function as riser during solidification, whilst in some cases the gate is built into the drag, particularly when moulding for light alloys. Any loose sand, which sinks in molten light alloys, then tends to

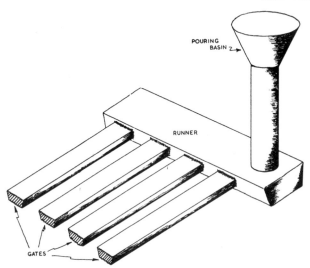

POURING BASIN

RUNNER

GATES

FIG. 3.14—A Multiple Gate.

be trapped in the bottom of the gate instead of being carried into the mould. With large castings in light alloys, it is often necessary to use a multiple gate (Fig. 3.14) in order to achieve controlled solidification and avoid the formation of 'hot spots' which would probably form if only one gate were used. The sand in the region of a single gate would become very hot, so that solidification at that point would be retarded and shrinkage cavities ultimately form there.

3.64

In some cases a splash core may be incorporated in the gate (Fig. 3.15). This is a dry-sand core placed where erosion of ordinary moulding sand would be likely. A further refinement to the gate may be the addition of a skim bob (Fig. 3.15), the function of which is to reduce the rate of metal flow so that

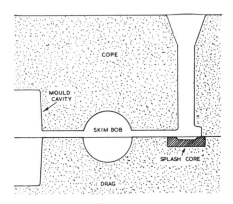

COPE

MOULD CAVITY

SKIM BOB

SPLASH CORE

DRAG

FIG. 3.15.

Courtesy of Messrs The David Brown Cos, Penistone, nr Sheffield.

PLATE 3.7—General View of a Steel Foundry.
A charge is being poured from an electric furnace into a ladle for transfer to the waiting sand moulds.

foreign matter, such as slag and dross, are trapped and prevented from entering the mould cavity.

CLEANING AND INSPECTION

3.70
Prior to cleaning, the gates and risers of the casting are removed. In iron castings this can often be done by means of a sledge hammer, but steel castings are usually trimmed by oxy-acetylene cutting or sawing with a metal-cutting saw. This latter method is also invariably used to remove gates and risers from non-ferrous castings. Sometimes a nick is cast in the gate in order to facilitate its removal by hammering.

In the case of large castings a pneumatic chisel is often used to remove small pieces of gates, fins and the projecting stems of chaplets.

3.71
Sand still adhering to the casting is then removed. This is sometimes achieved by vibrating the castings in special fixtures or by sand-blasting or shot-blasting. Non-ferrous castings can conveniently be treated by 'hydro-blasting', in which process a high-velocity stream of water impinges upon the castings,

washing away much of the sand. Iron castings are less suitable for this treatment because they tend to rust.

3.72
Some castings can be cleaned economically by tumbling. The tumbling barrel consists of a cylindrical steel shell, closed at its ends by cast-iron heads and mounted on horizontal trunnions. Sufficient castings are charged to prevent breakage by excessive movement as the barrel rotates. In addition to cleaning the casting, this process also polishes the surface and removes fins and sharp edges, but it is obviously unsuitable for fragile castings.

3.73
Grinding wheels may be employed to cut off gates and risers as well as for the removal of fins, parting-line impressions and other unwanted attachments. Such wheels are carried in either fixed or portable grinding machines, and usually run at peripheral speeds of between 25 and 50 m/s. The abrasives most commonly used are silicon carbide or aluminium oxide. These are bonded with shellac, resinoid, vulcanised rubber or vitrified bonding materials according to the combination of hardness and toughness required in the resulting wheel.

3.74
Visual examination of castings will reveal many of the more common surface defects. Sometimes the defect will be obvious as soon as the casting is shaken out of the sand, but small defects may be discovered only after the casting has been cleaned. Visual inspection will also reveal incompletely chipped fins and chaplets, whilst hard spots, which in iron castings might lead to high machining costs, are often revealed by means of a simple file test.

3.75
Internal cavities in a casting can be revealed by the use of X-rays (3.82—Part I), whilst surface cracks and fissures can often be detected by the magnetic dust method (3.81—Part I) or by the use of penetrants (21.81—Part I). Supersonic testing is, however, becoming increasingly popular for detecting cavities and other discontinuities in castings. This method is based on the length of time it takes a high-frequency sound wave to travel from its source through a section of the casting and back again to its source. If a cavity or flaw is present in the metal section the wave is reflected from the surface of the defect, and thus returns in a shorter period of time. The wave is plotted and measured on an oscillograph, and by this method the location and approximate size of the defect can be determined.

3.76
Pneumatic or hydraulic pressure tests can be employed to test those castings, such as valves and cylinders, where pressure-tightness is important. If the casting is liable to shatter, hydraulic testing is safer, since water undergoes a negligible reduction in volume under pressure. Small castings can be tested with air pressure whilst submerged under water, so that leaks are readily indicated by the formation of air bubbles.

DEFECTS IN SAND CASTINGS

3.80

In the melting and casting of metals many variable factors have to be considered in order to reduce the incidence of defects. In general, defects may arise from faults in technique which can be classified under the following headings:

(1) bad melting practice;
(2) bad pouring practice;
(3) poor moulding practice;
(4) poor pattern design;
(5) incorrect metal composition;
(6) moulding sand and cores of incorrect composition or poor condition;
(7) bad placing of gates and risers.

If a casting has been inadequately risered the effects of *shrinkage* may manifest themselves as internal porosity or cavities, or in the form of depressions in the surface of the casting as indicated above (Fig. 3.12 (i)).

3.81

Blow-holes, on the other hand, are due to the presence of gas in the original molten metal. As this solidifies gas is rejected from solution and forms gas-filled cavities in the casting. Under the microscope it is often possible to distinguish between shrinkage cavities and small blow-holes by studying their shape and location (4.17—Part I).

Whilst blow-holes are usually situated well below the surface of a casting, what are called '*blows*' often exist at or near to the surface. These subcutaneous cavities are formed by gases emanating from the mould itself and which have been unable to escape due to lack of permeability of the moulding sand or to poor venting. Gases causing these 'blows' may originate from moisture in the sand; from corrosion products on chills or other inserts; or from organic core binders.

3.82

Inclusions may be due to the presence of slag or oxide particles in the molten metal. They may also consist of sand particles washed from the surface of a mould which has been poorly made or in which inferior sand has been used. A clean melt can be obtained by proper attention to fluxing and skimming prior to casting, whilst faulty moulds can be avoided by better inspection and adequate sand control.

3.83

'Cold Shuts' result mainly from lack of fluidity of the molten metal. They appear as seam-like discontinuities which are formed when two metal streams meet inside the mould but have insufficient fluidity to allow them to break the oxide films which separate them. '*Misruns*' are also due to lack of fluidity in the metal, and refer to castings which are of incomplete impression, the molten metal not having penetrated to all recesses of the mould. Apart from bad pattern design in the form of very thin sections which chill the metal, such defects are due almost entirely to pouring metal which is too cold, and which therefore lacks fluidity.

3.84
A number of defects may arise from faults in mould construction or from poor-quality sand. If the sand has been loosely rammed, or if it does not contain sufficient binding material, sections of the mould may be eroded by the stream of molten metal, giving rise to rough lumps of excess metal on the casting. These are usually called '*scabs*'. If coarse sand has been used in the preparation of the mould surface molten metal may penetrate the spaces between the grains without detaching them. The obvious remedy is to use finer facing sand. Excessive *fins* on the casting are due to loosely fitting cores or to the cope and drag not fitting closely together at the parting line.

3.85
Hot Tears are cracks which are formed by contraction stresses in a casting, just as solidification is complete and whilst the metal is still relatively weak or 'tender'. Such cracks are typified by an irregular fractured surface which is heavily oxidised. They may be due to faulty design of the pattern, as is indicated in the frequently quoted example shown in Fig. 3.16 (i). Here the outer rim of the wheel is likely to solidify before the central hub, and as the spokes cool and shrink hot tears may develop where they join the hub, since

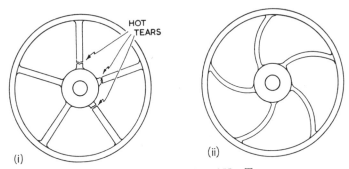

FIG. 3.16—The Formation of Hot Tears.

the metal there is still in a plastic state. If the design is modified as indicated in Fig. 3.16 (ii) the spokes will tend to be pulled straight by contraction rather than to develop hot tears. Hot tears may also be formed by cores which are too hard and which do not collapse easily enough under the pressure of the solidifying and contracting metal. Poor design of castings causing internal stresses to be set up during cooling may also lead to *warping*.

BIBLIOGRAPHY
1 'A Manual of Foundry Practice', J. Laing and R. T. Rolfe (Chapman and Hall).

2 'Modern Foundry Practice', E. D. Howard (Ed.) (Odhams Press).

3 'Principles of Metal Casting', R. W. Heine and P. C. Rosenthal (McGraw-Hill).

4 'Casting in Steel', The British Steel Foundries Association (Pitman).

5 'A Practical Guide to the Design of Grey Iron Castings', The Council of Iron Foundry Associations.

6 'The Metallurgy of Steel Castings', C. W. Briggs (McGraw-Hill).

7 'Typical Microstructures of Cast Metals', Institute of British Foundrymen.

8 'The Solidification of Castings', R. W. Ruddle (Institute of Metals).

9 'Analysis of Casting Defects', American Foundrymen's Association.

10 'Cores and Coremaking', F. D. Roper (Allen and Unwin).

11 'Non-ferrous Foundry Metallurgy', A. J. Murphy (Pergamon Press).

12 'Small Scale Aluminium Casting', L. O. Joseph (Macmillan and Co.).

13 'Aluminium Alloy Castings', E. Carrington (Griffin).

14 'Magnesium Casting Technology', A. W. Brace and F. A. Allen (Chapman and Hall).

15 'The Casting of Steel', W. C. Newell (Pergamon Press).

16 'Steel Foundry Practice', J. H. Hall (Penton Publishing Co.).

17 'Fundamentals of Metal Casting', R. A. Flinn (Addison–Westley Publishing Co.).

18 'Densing and Chills in Foundry Work', E. Longden (Griffin).

19 'Foundry Sand Control', W. Davies (United Steel Companies).

20 'Foundry Moulding Sands of India', Jatinder Mohan et al. (Council of Scientific and Industrial Research, New Delhi).

21 'A Guide to the Engineering Properties of Iron Castings', Joint Iron Council.

22 'Aluminium', Vol. III—Fabrication and Finishing, Ed. K. R. van Horn (American Society of Metals).

23 'Principles of Magnesium Technology', E. F. Emley (Pergamon Press).

24 'The Design of Steel Castings', The British Steel Castings Research Association.

25 'British and Foreign Specifications for Steel Castings', The British Steel Castings Research Association.

26 'Foundry Core and Mould Making by the CO_2 Process', A. D. Sarker (Pergamon Press (U.K.); Macmillan (U.S.A.)).

27 BS 1400: 1969—Schedule of copper alloy ingots and copper and copper alloy castings.

28 BS 2094: Glossary of terms relating to iron and steel. Part 9: 1964—Iron and steel foundry.

29 BS 2970: 1959—Magnesium and magnesium alloy ingots and castings for general engineering purposes.

30 BS 3511: 1962—Hand-operated geared ladles for steel foundries.

31 BS 4080: 1966—Methods of non-destructive testing of steel castings.

Chapter four
DIE-CASTING

4.10

At the beginning of the present century the only metals being die-cast on a commercial scale were tin and lead, and their alloys, and it was not until the First World War that aluminium alloy die-castings were produced in any quantity. Earlier attempts at die-casting zinc-base alloys had proved fruitless because of the intercrystalline corrosion experienced in such alloys during their subsequent use (18.20—Part I), but in the years following the First World War the introduction of high-purity zinc-base alloys lead to their wide application in die-casting.

In this type of process, molten metal can be transferred to the metal mould with or without the use of externally-applied pressure. In the process originally termed 'gravity die-casting' but now often called 'permanent mould casting', the molten metal is generally poured into the mould so that the latter is filled under gravity. The title 'die-casting' is now nearly always used to describe the process in which pressure is used to inject molten metal into the die cavity.

4.11

Principal advantages accruing from the use of pressure in a die-casting process are twofold. First, the rapidity of transfer of the molten metal from the bath to the die cavity results in little loss of heat during injection. Consequently, very thin wall sections can be cast, since the injected metal flows quickly between the closely adjacent die surfaces without appreciable chilling taking place. Secondly, since pressure is maintained *during* solidification, the effects of shrinkage are largely eliminated. When a metal or alloy solidifies it occupies less volume, and this phenomenon results in the formation of a 'pipe' in an ingot cast at atmospheric pressure. Moreover, very rapid cooling may lead to the formation of a secondary pipe (4.30—Part I), since solidification proceeds too quickly for molten metal to be able to feed into the interstices between the growing crystals so that shrinkage cavities are produced. In the die-casting process, however, the maintenance of pressure during solidification forces molten metal into such shrinkage cavities as they begin to form.

FACTORS AFFECTING THE CHOICE OF THE PROCESS

4.20

The proposal to use a die-casting process involves the consideration of economic as well as technical factors. The initial cost of a metal die is high compared with the cost of producing a wooden pattern and a small number of sand moulds, so that a die-casting process will be economically possible only if a large number of castings are required. At the same time, although initial tool costs and maintenance costs are high in the production of a die-casting, machining, finishing and assembly costs of the product (where these apply) are much lower than is the case with sand castings, so that it is possible to 'break even' on the production costs of a die-cast component when a large number of them is to be produced.

4.21

Obviously technical considerations will also have to be met, and die-casting may prove to be an unsuitable process for technical reasons. Some alloys, for example, have high shrinkage coefficients which would lead to the development of cracks in the die-cast product, whilst in some cases very intricate shapes could be produced only if, as in sand casting, the mould can be destroyed

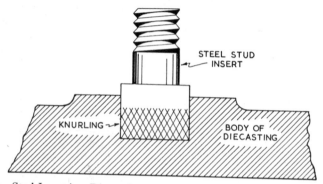

FIG. 4.1—Stud Insert in a Die-casting.
The part of the head which protrudes forms a step which prevents cast metal from reaching the threaded portion.

in order to facilitate extraction of the resultant casting. Moreover, considerations of mechanical strength may dictate that the component be produced by a combination of hot-forging and machining.

The technical advantages of die-casting are many. The process produces a structure which is superior to that of a sand casting. The speed of solidification results in a very fine grain, and this in turn leads to a higher strength than is generally obtainable in a sand casting. Greater dimensional accuracy is possible, and this results in smaller machining costs. Superiority of finish is also a feature, and this reduces finishing costs, as already mentioned.

4.22

A special feature in the application of the die-casting process is the possiblity of using 'inserts'. These may be employed to increase the strength of the component, but are more often used to include some feature which would be difficult to mould or which can be produced more cheaply by the use of an insert. Possibly the most common use of inserts is the inclusion of a threaded steel portion (Fig. 4.1) in the component. Other applications include the production of rotor elements for small electric motors, in which the copper commutator sections are die-cast into a zinc-base alloy body. In each case the insert is correctly 'located' in the die cavity and the molten metal then injected.

4.23
If any one of the above advantages of die-casting is considered singly it may be argued that better properties could be obtained by the use of some other shaping process. This may be true, but when a certain optimum association of properties is desired, die-casting may well prove to be the best method of production to employ.

DIE-CASTING METHODS

4.30
Most of the early machines used for die-casting were of the 'gooseneck' type, in which the alloy to be cast was melted in a pot which actually formed part of the machine itself. Injection into the die cavity was accomplished by means of a plunger or by the use of compressed air, and it was upon the latter method that one of the earliest die-casting machines used on an industrial scale was based. This was the 'direct-air' gooseneck machine (Fig. 4.2). In this

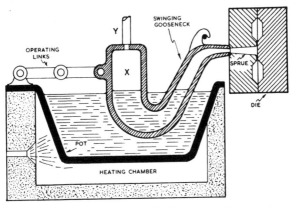

FIG. 4.2—The 'Direct Air' Die-casting Machine.

machine the nozzle of the gooseneck was made to dip beneath the surface of the molten metal as the die opened, thus filling the chamber (X). The die was then closed and the nozzle brought up into the horizontal position, in contact with the die opening or 'sprue'. Pneumatic pressure applied via the pipe (Y) then injected molten metal into the die cavity.

The direct-air submerged gooseneck machine has become largely obsolete. This is due partly to porosity introduced into the casting by the pneumatic pressure system, but mainly because of the prolonged contact between the chamber of the machine and the molten metal charge leading to serious contamination of the latter by iron. Even with relatively low-melting-point zinc-base alloys this contamination was considerable, but with the higher-

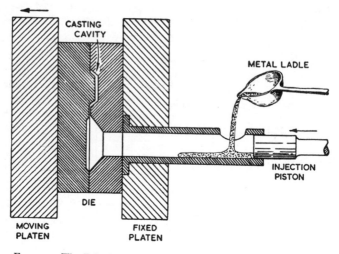

FIG. 4.3—The Principle of the Cold-chamber Die-casting Machine.

melting-point aluminium-base alloys the iron 'pick-up' was as much as 4·0% during a day's working. This led to the development of the 'cold-chamber' die-casting machine, the principle of which is shown in Fig. 4.3.

4.31

In this machine a charge of metal sufficient for a single casting is poured into the sleeve adjoining the die. The plunger then forces the charge through the runner channels into the die cavity itself. Not only is the superficial area of the machine exposed to the molten metal much less than it is in the submerged gooseneck machines, but the temperature of the surface and time of contact between the molten metal and parts of the machine are much lower. All of these factors will reduce contamination of the charge by iron.

4.32

Most of the cold-chamber machines make use of a horizontal sleeve as shown in Fig. 4.3. There exists, however, a number of modifications of this type of machine. An example is furnished by the Polak machine, the principle of which is shown in Fig. 4.4. Here the metal, in a state of incipient fusion, is ladled into a well (A), the bottom of which is formed by a spring-loaded counter-plunger (B). The plunger (C) is brought down so that the charge is displaced into the die cavity as shown, leaving a metal residue, or 'slug', separating the plunger and counter-plunger. As the plunger is withdrawn again the counter-plunger follows it to shear the slug from the tapered sprue* and so eject it from the metal well. Machines of the Polak type are used quite widely for the manufacture of large die-castings.

---

* This term is used to denote both the opening leading into the die and the metal 'get' which fills it during casting.

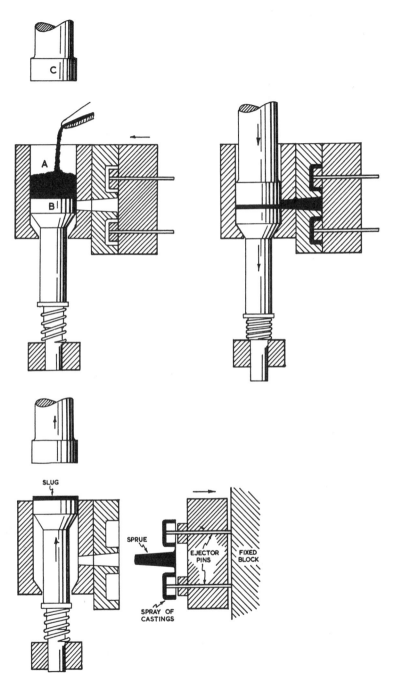

FIG. 4.4—The Principle of the Polak Die-casting Machine.

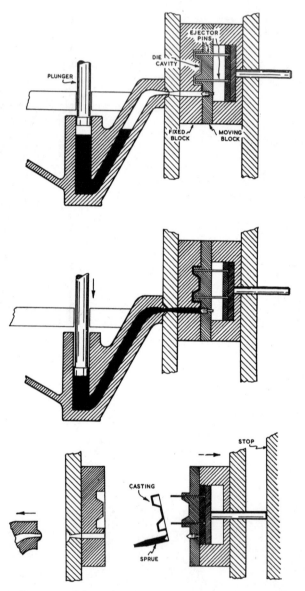

FIG. 4.5—Sequence of Operations in the Gooseneck Die-casting Machine.

4·33

Such gooseneck machines as are now used are of the plunger type. These are employed mainly for die-casting zinc-base and other low-melting-point alloys in which contamination by iron will be less extensive. The operational sequence of a typical machine of this kind is shown in Fig. 4.5.

Many die-casting machines now produced are convertible to either cold-chamber or gooseneck systems of injection, thus making them adaptable to the economical production of either zinc-base or aluminium alloy die-castings.

Courtesy of Messrs High Duty Alloys Ltd, Slough, Bucks.

PLATE 4.1—A Buhler '800' Pressure Die-casting Machine.
This horizontal machine is fully automatic with the exception of pouring in the molten aluminium alloy. It produces pressure die-castings up to 10 kg in mass.

SOME POINTS TO BE CONSIDERED IN THE DESIGN OF DIES

4·40

It is impossible in a book of this type to do more than mention a few elementary principles of die design. Such work is of a nature which must be adapted to individual problems, and can therefore only be undertaken adequately by a man with practical experience.

4·41

Factors both metallurgical and mechanical must be taken into account when designing a die. Shrinkage porosity, for example, is a fault likely to prevail if abrupt changes in section occur in the die-casting. Consequently, such changes should be avoided as far as possible in die design. The location of the gate may also affect internal soundness. In Fig 4.6 the position of the gate is unsatisfactory. Since the casting consists of two fairly heavy sections connected by a narrow channel, there is a chance that metal will become chilled, and hence solidify, in this narrow channel before the right-hand section is filled, thus causing shrinkage porosity in the core of this section. By locating

Courtesy of Messrs High Duty Alloys Ltd, Slough, Bucks.

PLATE 4.2—A Large Pressure Die-casting Machine of the Polak Type.

The operator on the right is transferring molten metal from a ladle to the holding furnace, which is near to the die assembly.

the gate somewhere in the centre of the narrow channel molten metal would be fed simultaneously to both heavy sections, thus reducing the risk of porosity.

4.42

Provision must be made for air to escape from the die cavity as the molten metal is injected. Adequate 'venting' is therefore necessary. The parting line of the die can be adapted to provide air vents by cutting shallow grooves about 25 mm wide and 0·12 mm deep on the face of the die member containing the cavity. Such vents allow air to escape, but molten metal freezes immediately it enters the narrow orifice. In some cases venting at the parting line is insufficient, particularly where air is likely to be trapped in deep recesses of the die cavity. Then, venting can often be arranged at the side of an ejector pin.

4.43

Ejector pins are used to push the casting out of the die. Generally, the die is so designed that the casting is carried away by the moving half of the die, the ejector pins being located in recesses in this half. As the die opens and the half carrying the casting moves away the ends of the ejector pins come up against a fixed block, so that the pins are pushed forward, thus ejecting the casting (Figs. 4.4/5). Since it is difficult to ensure that the ends of the ejector pins shall always lie flush with the surface of the die, it is considered best practice to arrange for them to terminate about 0·12 mm *below* the die surface.

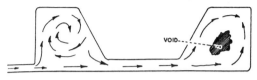

FIG. 4.6.

This means that small bosses will be formed on the surface of the casting. (Plate 4.3) These can subsequently be ground off before the casting is 'finished'.

4·44
The position of the parting line must be carefully considered when designing a die. The ejection of the casting must be possible, and here the general principles governing the removal of a wooden pattern from a sand mould may be followed. In some cases the use of cores is inevitable, and these are generally removed from the casting after it leaves the die. As the die wears the mark

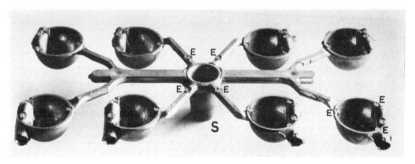

PLATE 4.3—A 'Spray' of Die Castings used in the Manufacture of Furniture Castors. These are shown still attached to the 'runner' system and the central 'sprue' (S). The marks (E) formed by the ejector pins, both near the sprue and on each individual casting, are clearly seen.

due to the parting line will become more evident on the casting. It should therefore be in a position where it can easily be removed if necessary by grinding.

Wherever possible two features (such as holes), which must be maintained at an accurate distance apart, should be cored in the *same* half of the die— usually the moving half. If they are separated by the parting line dimensional variation may occur in the distance separating them, since small particles of grit may lodge between the die faces and prevent the die from being completely closed.

DIE STEELS

4.50

Steels suitable for the manufacture of die-casting dies range in composition from medium plain carbon steels for use with low-temperature alloys to chromium–molybdenum–tungsten–cobalt steels for die-casting copper-base alloys.

In addition to working temperature, other factors, such as the expected length of run and the intricacy of the die cavity, must be taken into account when choosing a die steel. Thus a low chromium–molybdenum steel may be regarded as being a general-purpose die alloy for the casting of zinc-base alloys, whilst for short runs in such alloys a plain–carbon steel may be adequate as a die material. On the other hand, where conditions of service are severe or where a particularly long run is envisaged, a chromium–vanadium steel might be used as a die steel for the casting of zinc-base alloys.

4.51

A few of the more popular steels suitable for the manufacture of die-casting dies are shown in Table 4.1. The heat-treatments mentioned are those necessary to obtain the required degree of hardness in the working die. In addition, large die blocks should be stress-relieved after rough machining in order to prevent subsequent distortion. The rough-machined block is heated to 560° C soaked for a short period dependent upon the size of the block and then cooled in still air. Very large blocks are best cooled in the furnace.

DIE-CASTING ALLOYS

4.60

Of recent years the numbers of alloys which are die-cast on a commercial scale has been considerably reduced. Both the low-temperature alloys based on tin and lead and the high-temperature copper-base alloys now find very limited application, and the bulk of die-casting is carried out in zinc-base and light alloys.

Moreover, the number of alloys in these two groups has diminished. For example, only two zinc-base ('Mazak') alloys are in frequent use, as indicated in Table 4.2, whilst not more than five aluminium-base alloys are commonly employed. Of these latter, the alloy covered by Specification 4L33 and containing 10–13% silicon has by far the widest application.

4.61

The dangers attendant in melting magnesium-base alloys make them somewhat unpopular with many die-casters in view of the controlled melting practice which must be used (18.13—Part I). Of these magnesium-base alloys one containing 9–10% aluminium and 1% zinc ('Elektron') is the most popular. It is characterised by good fluidity and is less prone to the formation of 'seams' at points where two metal streams merge than are some other magnesium-base alloys.

TABLE 4.1—*Die Steels*

Composition (%)									Applications	Suggested heat-treatment
C	Mn	Si	Ni	Cr	Mo	V	W	Co		
0·45	0·6	—	—	—	—	—	—	—	Tin and lead alloys or short runs on zinc-base alloys	Not generally necessary
0·3	0·7	0·5	—	0·8	0·25	—	—	—	General-purpose steel for zinc-base alloys	(Often supplied heat-treated and can be machined in this state.) Heat to 860° C and oil-quench. Temper between 420 and 650° C according to required hardness
0·4	0·7	0·15	—	2·0	—	0·2	—	—	Long-run production of zinc-base alloys. Short runs on aluminium-base alloys (5 000–8 000 castings)	Heat to 850° C and oil-quench. Temper between 420 and 480° C according to hardness required
0·5	0·5	0·25	0·2	0·75	0·75	—	—	—	General-purpose alloy for light-alloy casting	Heat slowly to 750° C in a non-decarburising atmosphere. Then raise temperature to 850° C and oil-quench or cool in air. Temper at 600° C for several hours, depending upon size of die
0·4	—	1·0	—	5·0	1·3	1·1	—	—	Long-run production of aluminium-base alloys	(An air-hardening steel which can also be nitrided.) Heat slowly to 750° C packed in non-decarburising material. Raise to 1 000° C soak and cool in air. Temper for several hours at 550° C cool and repeat tempering process
0·35	0·45	0·35	—	1·3	0·4	—	4·5	5·0	Copper-base alloys and arduous service with aluminium alloys	Air harden to makers' instructions
0·35	—	—	—	5·0	1·5	—	1·5	1·5	Copper-base alloys	Case-harden at 925° C for 8 hours; cool in air. Temper at 570° C

TABLE 4.2—*Zinc-base*

BS Specification (Castings)	Composition (%)							
	Zn	Al	Cu	Mg	Fe (max.)	Pb (max.)	Cd (max.)	Sn (max.)
1004A	Rem.	3·8–4·3	0·10 max.	0·03–0·06	0·10	0·005	0·005	0·002
1004B	Rem.	3·8–4·3	0·75–1·25	0·03–0·06	0·10	0·005	0·005	0·002

TABLE 4.3—*Aluminium-base*

BS1490	Composition (%) (Maximum values unless otherwise stated)								
	Al	Cu	Mg	Si	Fe	Mn	Ni	Zn	Other elements
LM2-M	Rem.	0·7–2·5	0·3	9·0–11·5	1·0	0·5	1·0	1·2	Ti 0·2 Sb 0·2 Pb 0·3
LM4-M	Rem.	2·0–4·0	0·15	4·0–6·0	0·8	0·3–0·7	0·35	0·5	Ti 0·2 Sn 0·05 Pb 0·1 Mn, Fe 1·3
LM6-M	Rem.	0·1	0·10	10·0–13·0	0·6	0·5	0·1	0·1	Sn 0·05 Pb 0·1
LM18-M	Rem.	0·1	0·1	4·5–6·0	0·6	0·5	0·1	0·1	Sn 0·05 Pb 0·1
LM20-M	Rem.	0·4	0·15	10·0–13·0	0·7	0·5	0·1	0·2	Ti 0·2 Sn 0·05 Pb 0·1
LM24-M	Rem.	3·0–4·0	0·1	7·5–9·5	1·3	0·5	0·5	3·0	Pb 0·3 Sn 0·2

For other die-casting alloys

4.62

When mechanical properties have to be taken into account in selecting an alloy it will be found that, under normal working conditions, there is little to choose between zinc-base and aluminium-base alloys as far as tensile strength and % elongation are concerned. In respect of the Charpy impact value, however, zinc-base alloys show a clear advantage over the aluminium-base alloys.

FAULTS IN DIE-CASTINGS

4.70

Die-castings can suffer from both internal and external defects which are produced during manufacture. Most surface defects are readily apparent on visual examination, but internal defects manifest themselves only as a result of failure or microscopical examination of a suitable section.

Die-castings

Mechanical properties				Characteristics	Trade alloys
Tensile strength		% elongation	Impact (Charpy)		
N/mm²	tonf/in²				
293	19	4	32	Used for applications requiring dimensional precision. Stable in strength and dimensions at normal and elevated temperatures	Mazak 3
355	23	3	34	Stable under normal conditions, but subject to dimensional increase and loss of strength at elevated temperatures	Mazak 5

Die-castings

Minimum mechanical properties (Chill cast)						Dura-bility	Machina-bility	Related specifications
0·1 % Proof Stress		Tensile strength		% Elonga-tion	Impact (Charpy)			
N/mm²	tonf/in²	N/mm²	tonf/in²					
—	—	147	9·5	—	—	Good	Fair	—
69	4·5	154	10	2	3·2	Good	Good	BS L 59
69	4·5	185	12	7	6·5	Very good	Fair	BS 4L33
62	4	139	9	4	—	Very good	Fair	—
62	4	185	12	5	—	Good	Fair	—
—	—	177	11·5	1·5	—	Good	Fair	—

see Table 18.1 (magnesium-base)—Part I.

4.71

The most common internal defect is porosity. This generally arises from shrinkage during solidification, and is consequently prevalent where there is a sudden change in the thickness of the section. Such porosity can often be minimised by modification in the design of the casting as indicated in Fig. 4.7.

Porosity may also be due to air entrapped during the casting process, and is most often found in long, thin, channel-shaped sections in which the metal tends to chill rapidly. It is usually possible to distinguish between these two types of defect, since shrinkage porosity always occurs at the core of a heavy section and consists of many finely dispersed cavities, whilst blow-holes occur singly and are not necessarily found in the core of the casting.

4.72

Surface defects in die-castings arise from a number of causes, and consequently vary considerably in nature. Moreover, the nomenclature used to describe these defects is by no means precise. The term 'fins', for example, may refer to the 'flash' or thin film of metal coincident with the parting line of the die when the latter has not closed completely. It may also refer to the minute ridges which are formed in the casting when a die begins to be affected by heat cracks. Under the influence of repeated heating the die surface cracks into irregular polygons (rather like crazy paving). This is called 'heat-checking', and the resultant casting may be said to be 'checked'.

4·73
The term 'ejector mark' also has a dual meaning. It may be used to describe the cast impression (either a depression or a protuberance) produced when the end of an ejector pin does not lie flush with the die surface but it is more

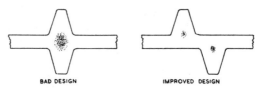

BAD DESIGN   IMPROVED DESIGN

FIG. 4.7.

often used to describe a mark produced on the surface of the casting as the ejector pins come into action in stripping it from the die. Such marks are usually a sign that the pins have become a loose fit in their housings due to wear. 'Drags' are suface defects introduced during stripping, and refer to very light score marks produced on the surface of the casting by some slight imperfections in the die surface. Deeper marks so produced are known as 'scores'.

4·74
The formation of 'sinks' or 'hot spots' is basically due to contraction of the metal as it solidifies. If chilling is not sufficient, as, for example, in the region of an isolated boss (Fig. 4.8), to produce a rigid shell, contraction of the metal

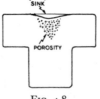

SINK

POROSITY

FIG. 4.8.

in the core will draw in the surface, usually producing a small depression the surface of which is bright.

4·75
'Hot tears' are caused by uneven contractions, and usually manifest them-selves as cracks in thin-sectioned areas of large castings. Similar cracks may also be formed due to hot-shortness of the alloy itself. Such hot-shortness is

usually due to the presence of an impurity which has the effect of increasing the liquidus–solidus range of the alloy. Zinc-base alloys contaminated with tin tend to be hot-short.

PERMANENT MOULD CASTING

4.80

In its simplest form, permanent mould casting employs a two-part metal mould which is filled from a hand ladle so that the mould cavity receives its charge under the action of gravity. As with other processes the demands of modern high-speed production have led, in many cases, to a degree of automation being adopted. For example, automatic pouring may be introduced in several ways. In one of these the mould is attached to the lip of a tilting furnace so that a gradual transfer of metal from furnace to mould takes place without turbulence (Fig. 4.9). A much sounder casting, free of entrapped oxides and gas, is thus obtained. Moreover, the head of molten metal in the furnace acts as a riser and when the casting is solid, the liquid head runs back into the furnace as the assembly returns to its vertical position. In many processes mould movement, core retraction and casting ejection are carried out with manually-operated lever systems.

4.81

Moulds and large cores are generally of cast iron, high-duty or high-temperature irons containing small amounts of nickel, chromium and molybdenum being widely used. Smaller moulds and cores are often of hot-working die steels of the chromium–molybdenum type (Table 4.1). Steel dies are appropriate when water cooling is adopted in order to increase production rates, since they will resist thermal shock more readily.

4.82

Cores of complex shape must be split in order to allow their removal from the finished casting. When this is impossible, sand cores must be used. These must have properties similar to those used in sand-casting processes (3.50) and are commonly made from sands bonded with oils, resins or by the CO_2 process (3.48). In order to dispense with the use of cores in the manufacture of lead toy soldiers, tea-pot spouts and other articles where dimensional accuracy was not required, a process known as 'slush' casting' was used at one time. Here a shell of metal was allowed to solidify in the mould and the still molten core then poured out, a hollow casting with a wall of fairly uniform thickness being the result. Since toy soldiers are now made largely of plastics, the process is now little used.

4.83

A typical two-part die assembly, utilising a sand core is shown in operation (Fig. 4.9). Here the mould is slowly tilted into the vertical position during the pouring operation in order that splashing and turbulence will be avoided and that no air will be entrapped. If molten metal were poured into the mould whilst it was standing in the vertical position, air would most certainly be drawn into the casting, whilst splashing of the molten metal within the die cavity would cause 'cold laps' due to adherence of particles of metal to the mould surface.

4.84

Permanent mould castings are superior in most respects to sand castings. They are generally sound and fine-grained in structure. Their surfaces are smoother than those of sand castings, whilst closer dimensional tolerance can

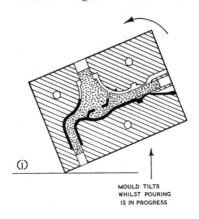

MOULD TILTS
WHILST POURING
IS IN PROGRESS

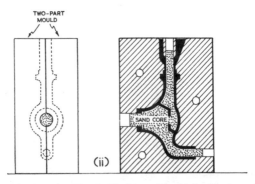

Fig. 4.9—The Operation of a Simple Two-part Mould for Casting a Brass Tap. The interior cavity of the tap is obtained by using a sand core.

also be maintained. At the same time they are less likely to contain entrapped gas than pressure die castings.

The choice between die casting and permanent mould casting for any particular article is governed by a number of factors both technical and economic. Technical considerations include mechanical properties, dimensional accuracy, complexity of shape and surface finish; whilst economic factors are concerned mainly with the number of castings to be manufactured and the time required to produce each one.

BIBLIOGRAPHY

1 'The Die Casting Process', H. K. Barton (Odhams Press).
2 'Die Casting', H. H. Doehler (McGraw-Hill).
3 'A Handbook of Die Casting', F. D. Penny (Her Majesty's Stationery Office).
4 'Designing for ALCOA Die Castings', Aluminium Co. of America.
5 'Magnesium Casting Technology', A. W. Brace and F. A. Allen (Chapman and Hall).
6 'Practical Considerations in Die-casting Design', Imperial Smelting Corporation (New Jersey Zinc Company).
7 'Aluminium', Vol. III—Fabrication and Finishing, Ed. K. R. van Horn (American Society for Metals).
8 'Principles of Magnesium Technology', E. F. Emley (Pergamon Press).
9 BS 1004: 1955—Zinc alloys for die casting and zinc alloy die castings.
10 BS (C.P. 3001): 1955—Zinc alloy pressure die casting for engineering.
11 BS 1400: 1969—Schedule of copper alloy ingots and copper and copper alloy castings.

Chapter five
OTHER CASTING PROCESSES

5.10
There are many casting processes of specialised application. Here we shall attempt to deal with only four which are important in the engineering sense. It is interesting to note that whilst the full-mould process is of comparatively recent origin, being dependent upon the use of expanded polystyrene as a pattern material, investment casting probably has its foundations in pre-history and was 'rediscovered' during the nineteenth century as a means of producing castings of great precision.

CENTRIFUGAL CASTING
5.20
It was not until the turn of the century that centrifugal casting became fully established as an industrial process. Mention of centrifugal casting usually brings to mind the casting of pipes without the use of a central core. It should be realised, however, that this is not the sole application and that some modifications of the process do not produce hollow sections at all. One principle which all centrifugal casting processes have in common is to increase the gravitational force upon the molten metal when it is cast and so ensure that it find its way more completely into the recesses of the mould cavity.

Modifications of centrifugal casting can be classified under three main headings: (1) true centrifugal casting; (2) semi-centrifugal casting; (3) centrifuging.

5.12 True Centrifugal Casting
This process is employed in the manufacture of hollow cylindrical products. When the length of the product is great compared with its diameter the mould is rotated about a horizontal axis. Thus gun barrels, cast-iron pipes, hollow propeller shafts and many other types of tubular product with diameters up to 1·25 m have been made by this method. In the production of centrifugal castings in which the diameter is greater than the length the mould is usually rotated about a vertical axis.

Two methods for the production of tubular products by the horizontal process are shown in Fig. 5.1. In (i) a sand-lined mould is being used for the manufacture of cast-iron pipes. The cast-iron flask containing this sand lining is carried on four driving rollers and is held in position by guide rollers above. These upper guide rollers may be raised at the end of the spinning operation so that the flask may be replaced by another carrying a new sand lining. The increased diameter at the left-hand end of the pipe can only be produced by the use of a sand core as shown.

The use of a sand mould is to be preferred when the casting is a long one, otherwise the metal would be chilled before it reached the farthest end of the mould. Moreover, if the casting is of such a shape that the mould must be broken in order to remove it, then obviously a sand mould would have to be

Courtesy of the Stanton Ironworks Co. Ltd, Nottingham.

PLATE 5.1—A General View of a Shop Producing Centrifugally-cast Iron Pipes.

used. Metal moulds can, however, be employed when the number of castings required justifies the cost of such a mould, and when the outside shape of the casting is such that it can be withdrawn from the mould. Castings made in a metal mould will have a much finer-grained structure, and therefore tend to give rather better mechanical properties.

In this process metal is fed in at one end of the mould, which is spun at high speeds during casting so that centrifugal force spreads the molten metal evenly along the entire length of the mould and holds it there until solidification is complete.

Fig. 5.1 (ii) shows an alternative method of centrifugal casting which is useful when pipes up to 6 m long are being made or when casting conditions are likely to lead to very rapid solidification. Here the pouring trough is equipped with a long spout which reaches to the farthest end of the mould. As casting begins the rotating mould is moved along a track away from the

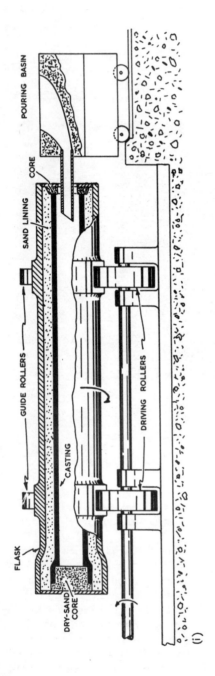

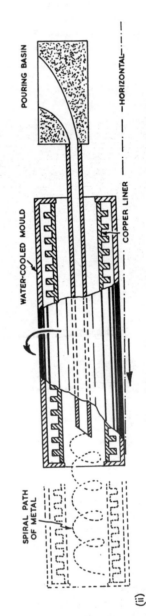

Fig. 5.1—The Production of Pipes by Centrifugal Casting in a Horizontal Mould.

stationary end of the pouring spout so that molten metal is deposited in a helical path along the whole length of the mould. In this way the serious chilling effect which would otherwise affect that metal which would need to flow the whole length of the mould is avoided.

In these true centrifugal casting processes no core is required. The external shape may be a plain cylinder; a fluted cylinder; a hexagonal section; or even a square section, but the internal bore will, of course, always be cylindrical. The use of a correct spinning speed is important. If it is too low the metal may 'slip' relative to the wall of the mould and produce laps or

Courtesy of The Stanton Ironworks Co. Ltd, Nottingham.

PLATE 5.2—Centrifugal Casting.
The operator on the right is skimming the molten metal as it runs from the ladle to the mould which is on the left.

folds in the surface of the finished casting. If, on the other hand, the speed is too high, then excessive pressure of the molten metal at the inner surface may cause hot tears to form in the thin shell which has already solidified and which has consequently shrunk away from the mould face. Speeds used for most processes are such as will produce centrifugal accelerations of between 60 and 80 times the value of 'g'.

Although centrifugal casting is limited in its application to a small number of shapes, its use is advantageous in respect of the elimination of cores. Moreover, since gates and risers are unnecessary, there is much less casting waste, and in some cases a consequent yield of almost 100% on metal melted. Since centrifuging increases the apparent relative density of the metal compared with other materials, such as gas bubbles, sand and slag, these impurities tend to come more rapidly to the surface and are less likely to become trapped as inclusions. Impurities of this nature therefore collect on the inner surface from which they can easily be removed by machining.

White-metal bearings may be cast centrifugally using an ordinary lathe arranged to give superficial speeds between 4 and 6 m/s. Two tinned and preheated half shells are clamped together in a simple jig and rotated in the

Courtesy of The Stanton Ironworks Co. Ltd, Nottingham.

PLATE 5.3—Centrifugal Casting.
Extracting a large cast-iron pipe from the mould.

lathe chuck. Molten Babbitt metal is then poured in. If a lead-base bearing metal is used the SbSn cuboids, being lighter, tend to migrate towards the centre (18.42—Part I). This is advantageous since the inner surface will ultimately be the bearing surface.

5.22
Centrifugal casting is also used in the manufacture of bearings in phosphor-bronze, leaded bronze and copper-lead alloys. An interesting method has been developed recently for the production of copper-lead bearings. These are made from an alloy containing 75% copper, 24% lead, 1% tin, and since lead is insoluble in copper, difficulty is always experienced with segregation.

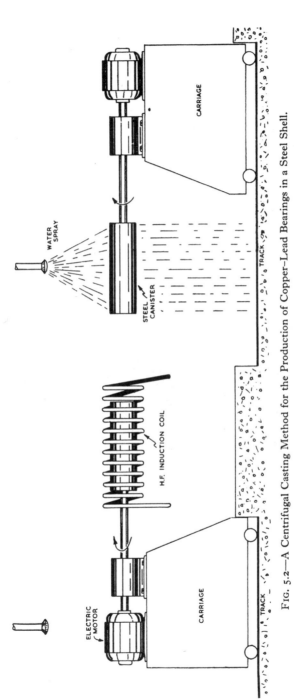

WATER SPRAY

STEEL CANISTER

TRACK

CARRIAGE

H.F. INDUCTION COIL

ELECTRIC MOTOR

CARRIAGE

TRACK

Fig. 5.2—A Centrifugal Casting Method for the Production of Copper-Lead Bearings in a Steel Shell.

The bearings in question are for diesel engines used in heavy road vehicles, and are cast on to a steel shell.

A steel canister which will ultimately form the bearing shell is filled with the required amount of swarf obtained by milling a rod of the composition stated above. The swarf is compressed around a core, and the canister is then loaded on to a heat-resisting chromium-steel mandrel which can be rotated at speeds of several hundreds of revolutions per minute, depending upon the size of the canister. The assembly is mounted on a carriage as shown in Fig. 5.2, so that the rotating canister can be moved axially into a high-frequency induction coil which raises the charge to casting temperature in a few minutes. The canister is then withdrawn, still rotating and quenched by a water spray. A loading and quenching station is provided on either side of the high-frequency coil so that whilst a canister is being fitted to one mandrel a similar canister can be heating on the other.

5.23 Semi-centrifugal Casting

Semi-centrifugal casting is employed in the production of shapes which are symmetrical about a central axis, as for example the wheel shown in Fig. 5.3. Here a sand mould of almost orthodox pattern is used, the metal being poured into a central runner whilst the mould rotates about a vertical axis. As the

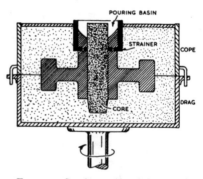

FIG. 5.3—Semi-centrifugal Casting.

molten metal enters the hub part of the mould cavity it is thrown outwards by centrifugal force through the spoke cavities and into the rim cavity. Since there is always a danger of molten metal being forced out through the parting line of the mould, speeds of rotation are usually lower than those used in true centrifugal casting. Consequently if a central hole is required it must be obtained by the use of a dry-sand core as indicated.

5.24 Centrifuging

This process is similar in application to semi-centrifugal casting, but in this case the casting is not necessarily symmetrical in shape, and its centre is not the centre of rotation. The object of centrifuging is to produce dense castings in intricate shapes. The principle of a centrifuge machine is shown in Fig 5.4. Here a number of moulds—in this case investment moulds—are placed around the central pouring basin, to which they are connected by horizontal runners. The complete assembly is rotated at a sufficiently high speed, and when molten metal is poured into the basin it is thrown outwards by centrifugal forces so that it finds its way via the horizontal runners into the moulds. This type of process has been used for many years in the dental profession in the manufacture of gold inlays.

Courtesy of Messrs John Holroyd & Co. Ltd, Rochdale.

PLATE 5.4—Centrifugal Casting of Phosphor-bronze Tubes.
Here the mould rotates about a vertical axis.

SHELL MOULDING

5.30
This is a relatively new process for the manufacture of moulds, and was in fact developed by Johannes Croning in Hamburg during the latter part of the Second World War. When the War ended it was estimated that one factory in Germany was producing over 6 000 hand-grenade cores per day by this new method. During the immediate post-war years the process was introduced into the U.S.A., and was adopted in England subsequently.

Shell moulding involves the use of resinous materials of the phenol–formaldehyde or urea–formaldehyde type as bonding agents for silica sand, and in this respect is akin to the application of bonding agents in cores used in orthodox sand-casting processes. Basically the process consists of making a thin shell of resin-bonded sand around a metal pattern, separating the shell from the pattern and clamping it to a mating shell to form a complete mould into which metal can be cast.

5.31 Outline of the Process

Fine sand of high silica content is generally used in shell-moulding processes. Since resinous materials are used as bonding agents for the sand, the presence of clay is unnecessary, and in fact tends to reduce the flow of the sand–resin mixture during moulding. The sand is intimately mixed with about 5% by weight of the plastic bonding agent, though the proportion of the latter which is necessary depends largely upon the particle size of the sand being used.

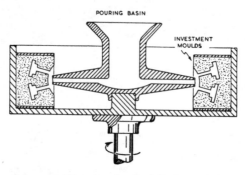

FIG. 5.4—Schematic Diagram of a Centrifuge-type Multiple-mould Casting Machine.

The use of fine sand promotes a much better finish in the casting, but makes necessary a higher proportion of bonding agent than is required when coarser sand is used.

Each half of the shell mould is made on a pattern plate, which must be of metal, usually carbon steel, because of the relatively high temperature at which moulding is carried out. This plate is first heated to between 200 and 250° C and is then sprayed or brushed with silicone oil in order to facilitate the subsequent stripping of the shell from the pattern. The pattern plate is then placed on top of a dump box containing the sand–resin mixture (Fig. 5.5 (i)) and the dump box inverted so that the pattern becomes covered by the sand–resin mixture (Fig. 5.5 (ii)).

The resin melts, and in about 30 seconds the pattern has become coated with a shell of resin-bonded sand. The shell is soon quite hard, because the formaldehyde-type resins used are of the thermo-setting variety. The dump box is turned back to its original position so that the surplus of sand and resin falls back into the bottom of the dump box (Fig. 5.5 (iii)).

The pattern plate is then removed, and with the shell still adhering to it is transferred to an oven where the shell is hardened still further by curing it for about 2 minutes at 315° C. The shell is then stripped from the pattern plate by means of ejector pins built into the plate. Normally these pins bear on the

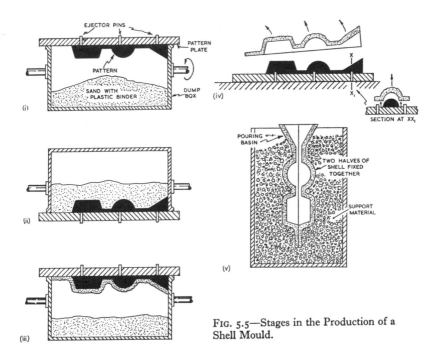

FIG. 5.5—Stages in the Production of a Shell Mould.

Courtesy of Messrs John Holroyd & Co. Ltd, Rochdale.

PLATE 5.5—The Production of a Shell Mould.

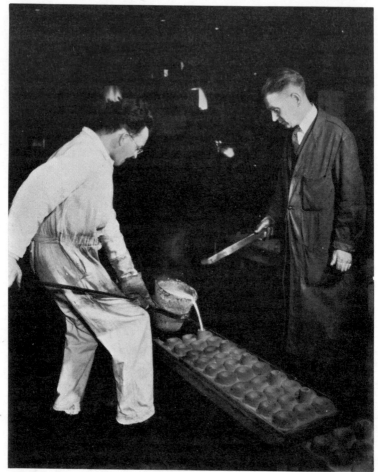

Courtesy of Messrs John Holroyd & Co. Ltd, Rochdale.
PLATE 5.6—Casting into a Shell Mould.

surface of the shell at the edges of the mould cavity (Fig. 5.5 (iv)), and usually do not need to bear on any of the surfaces of the mould cavity itself.

Two halves of the mould so produced are then joined together either by adhesives, bolts, clamps or—in the case of small moulds—by spring paper clips. Sometimes the mould is supported with metal shot, coarse sand or gravel (Fig. 5.5 (v)), and is then ready to receive the molten metal.

5.32 Advantages and Limitations of the Process
The main advantage attendant upon the use of shell moulding lies in the high quality of the product obtained, particularly in respect of accuracy of dimensions. Tolerances of the order of 5 mm/metre are claimed to be common practice as compared with about 4 mm/metre in the average pressure die-

casting. Accuracy is often of such a high order as to obviate subsequent machining.

The incidence of surface defects is very small as compared with sand castings. Loose sand and sand inclusions are absent, and due to the high permeability of the shell mould, surface blows are almost non-existent. Surface cleaning of the casting is reduced to a minimum and in some cases eliminated.

Since a shell mould has a small capacity for heat as compared with a sand mould, the casting cools much more slowly. Consequently, gates and risers can be much smaller, so that less metal need be melted. Moreover, since metal can be cast at a lower temperature into a shell mould, lower oxidation losses and gas absorption are encountered. However, because of the slower cooling rate of the shell-mould casting, it is likely to be coarser grained than a similar casting produced in an orthodox sand mould.

Shell moulds store well and are quite rigid, so that mould making need not be sited adjacent to the metal-melting plant, as is necessary in the case of green-sand moulding. Relatively unskilled labour can be employed in the manufacture of shell moulds, and labour costs are only a fraction of what they are in green-sand moulding. At the same time there is an enormous improvement in working conditions in so far as the volume of sand and the dust it generates are reduced. Shell moulding can be mechanised to the extent where sand handling is almost eliminated and where dirt and dust are practically absent.

One of the main disadvantages of the process lies in the high cost of producing the metal patterns, since these need to be of considerable dimensional accuracy. Obviously this disadvantage is largely offset by the greater dimensional accuracy obtained in the resultant casting.

Most foundry metals and alloys can be cast quite successfully into shell moulds, and it would seem that the process has a very promising future.

INVESTMENT CASTING

5.40

Investment casting came into public eminence quite recently in connection with its application in the production of the turbine blades used in jet-engine construction. It is also generally known that the process was used in the manufacture of precision castings during the Second World War. This has led many to assume that the investment casting process was discovered during the War. In fact, it is known that investment casting was practised in Ancient China and also in pre-Christian Egypt. It is thought that craftsmen in those early times carved their design in wax and then kneaded a clay mould around it. The mould was then hardened by firing, a process which also melted out the wax pattern and left a mould cavity without cores or parting lines.

The rediscovery of the process cannot be attributed to twentieth-century metallurgists, but to Benvenuto Cellini, who, during the sixteenth century, used it in the production of many of his works of art in gold and silver. Like other craftsmen, such as Stradivarius—and later metallurgist Huntsman —Cellini kept his process secret so that it was lost again, and did not reappear until towards the end of last century when the 'lost wax' or 'cire perdue' process was adopted in dentistry. In the 1930s it was used for the casting of parts for surgical repair work in a cobalt alloy which is chemically inert when encased in human flesh.

5.41 An Outline of the Process

In making a gold 'filling' the dentist first removes all decayed portions of the tooth and then presses wax into the cavity. After shaping the exposed surface approximately he removes the wax pattern thus produced. A plaster mould is then cast around this wax pattern, the wax melted out and a casting which is an exact replica of the tooth cavity then produced by casting gold into the mould. Investment casting as used in industry today follows the same general outline in that a wax or plastic pattern is coated or 'invested with some refractory material which acts as a mould into which metal may be cast.

Since an expendable wax pattern is required for the production of each mould, it follows that a permanent mould must first be produced for the manufacture of the wax patterns. For casting a simple shape, such as is shown in Fig. 5.6, the master mould could be machined in two steel plates as indicated in (i). In some circumstances, however, it might be desirable to produce first a master pattern in brass and then to cast a two-piece metal mould from this.

The brass master pattern is first embedded in plaster of Paris up to a desired parting line, the plaster of Paris being contained in one half of a two-part flask. The other half of the flask is placed in position and molten low-melting-point, tin–lead–bismuth alloy, poured into it. When the alloy has solidified the two halves of the flask are separated and the plaster of Paris removed from the first half. The cast half of the die is then polished and the brass master pattern carefully replaced in its impression. Before the flask is reassembled the parting surface of the cast half is coated with a parting compound. Alternatively, a sheet of very thin rubber is stretched over the parting surface. Molten alloy is then poured into the other half of the flask, so producing a two-part die in low-melting-point alloy. Although it is soft, the die will be serviceable for several thousands of injections of wax. In fact rubber dies are used where detail is of more importance than dimensional accuracy as, for example, in the jewellery trade.

To produce the wax patterns the two halves of the die are clamped together and molten wax injected into it at a pressure of 3·5 to 7 N/mm². When the wax pattern has solidified it is removed from the die and the end of the wax gate suitably trimmed (Fig. 5.6 (iii)) so that it can be attached, using a heated hand tool, to a central runner (Fig. 5.6 (iv)). The assembled runner with its 'tree' of patterns is then fixed on to a flat bottom plate by a blob of molten wax. A metal flask lined with waxed paper and open at each end is

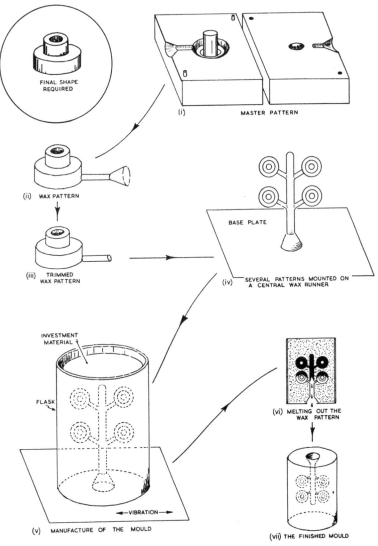

FINAL SHAPE
REQUIRED

(i) MASTER PATTERN

(ii) WAX PATTERN

(iii) TRIMMED
WAX PATTERN

BASE PLATE

(iv) SEVERAL PATTERNS MOUNTED ON
A CENTRAL WAX RUNNER

INVESTMENT
MATERIAL

FLASK

←—VIBRATION—→

(v) MANUFACTURE OF THE MOULD

(vi) MELTING OUT THE
WAX PATTERN

(vii) THE FINISHED MOULD

FIG. 5.6—Stages in the Production of an Investment Mould.

placed over the assembly. The gap between the end of the flask and the bottom plate is sealed with wax and the investment material then poured into the flask. This stage of the process is carried out on a vibrating table so that any air bubbles and excess moisture are brought to the surface whilst solidification is taking place (Fig. 5.6 (v)).

For castings made at low temperatures an investment material composed of powdered silica and plaster of Paris is still sometimes used. Here the plaster of Paris acts as a binder and the silica as a refractory aggregate. A more refractory investment material is based on sillimanite* bonded with silica. The wax pattern is given a primary coating about 1·25 mm thick by dipping it in a slurry containing fine sillimanite sand and a silicon ester (usually ethyl silicate) containing 2% piperidine. This coating is then dusted with a coarse-grained refractory in order to produce better bonding between the primary coating and the investment backing. The backing consists of coarser sillimanite sand and ethyl silicate.

The bonding action of ethyl silicate depends upon its being hydrolysed to *ortho*-silicic acid by the presence of moisture:

$$Si (OC_2H_5)_4 + 4H_2O = H_4SiO_4 + 4C_2H_5OH$$
Ethyl ortho-Silicic Alcohol
silicate acid

When the mould is heated the *ortho*-silicic acid is calcined to silica, which acts as a very refractory bond to the sillimanite sand:

$$H_4SiO_4 = SiO_2 + 2H_2O$$

Sometimes a little hydrochloric acid is added to the investment mixture to accelerate the hydrolysis of the ethyl silicate.

The investment is allowed to dry in air for about 8 hours. The base-plate is then removed and the inverted flask passed through an oven at about 100–150° C so that the wax melts and runs out, leaving a mould cavity in the investment material (Fig. 5.6 (vi)). When most of the wax has been removed the mould is preheated prior to receiving its charge of molten metal. The preheating temperature varies with the metal being cast, but is usually between 700 and 1 000° C. The object of preheating is to remove the last traces of wax by volatilisation, convert the ortho-silicic acid to silica and also to ensure that the cast metal will not be chilled but will flow into every detail of the mould cavity.

Molten metal may be cast into the mould under gravity, but if thin sections are present this will only be satisfactory if the investment material has a high permeability. Consequently, it is usual to inject the molten metal by air pressure or by the use of a centrifuge (Fig. 5.4). For air-pressure injection a furnace of the rocking-arc type may be used (Fig. 5.7). When the charge is ready for pouring the mould is clamped in position on top of the furnace as shown. The complete assembly is then inverted on the trunnions provided and an air pressure of 35–100 kN/m² applied simultaneously, thus forcing the molten metal into the mould cavity. Whilst an air-tight seal between the mould and the furnace is necessary, the permeability of the mould must be sufficient to allow the escape of air through it.

Sillimanite is a naturally occurring alumino-silicate mineral of the composition $Al_2O_3.SiO_2$. It is found principally in the Khasi Hills, Assam, and at Pipra, Rewa, India. It is characterised by a low coefficient of expansion and is used widely as a refractory material after being ground and calcined.

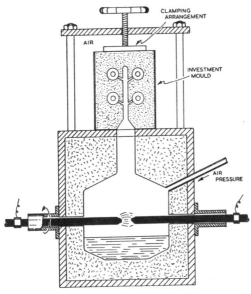

FIG. 5.7—Indirect-arc Furnace Assembly for Investment Casting under Pressure.

PLATE 5.7—Some Small Precision Investment Castings Used in Textile Machinery.
These castings are made in the extremely hard alloy 'Stellite' (14.22—Part I).

5.42 The 'Mercast' Process

An interesting development in the investment casting process is the use of mercury instead of wax in the production of the expendable pattern. Liquid mercury is poured into the master die, which is then submerged in refrigerated acetone at about −60° C. In this temperature range mercury soon freezes and produces a solid metal with roughly the same mechanical properties as solid lead. A piece of wire is frozen into the gate of the mercury pattern to facilitate handling it.

A mould is then made by dipping the frozen mercury pattern into an investment slurry several times until the desired thickness of coating is obtained. When the slurry has hardened the temperature is allowed to rise so that the mercury melts and runs out. The mould so produced is dried at about 100° C, placed in a flask and invested with coarser backing material. The completed mould is then further preheated before the molten metal is cast into it.

It is claimed that mercury produces a pattern of greater accuracy of detail than can be otained with wax.

5.43 Advantages and Limitations of Investment Casting

The investment casting process is particularly useful in the manufacture of small components from those metals and alloys which cannot be shaped by forging and machining operations. Among the best-known examples of this type of application are the blades for gas-turbine and jet engines.

Tolerances in the region of ±3 to ±5 mm/metre are commonly obtained industrially by the investment casting process. It can therefore be used for the production of complicated shapes in which extreme dimensional accuracy is not required. A further advantage, from the aesthetic point of view at least, is the absence of a disfiguring parting line which will always appear on castings made by any process involving the use of a cope and a drag.

The principle disadvantages of the investment casting process are its relatively high cost and the fact that the size of castings produced is normally limited to an average of less than 0·5 kg in mass. Although castings up to 15 kg have been made, the majority of castings produced commercially are of a mass of 0·03 kg or less.

In addition to its use in the manufacture of jet-engine blades, other typical products of the investment casting process include:

(1) special alloy parts for use in chemical engineering processes;
(2) valves and other fittings in oil-production and refinery plant;
(3) parts for machines used in the production of modern textile fabrics; (Plate 5·7).
(4) tool and die applications, such as milling cutters, precision gauges, forming and swaging dies;
(5) parts for miscellaneous industrial and domestic equipment, such as glass moulds, dairy equipment, cams, levers, spray nozzles, food-producing equipment, parts for sewing machines and washing machines.

THE FULL MOULD PROCESS

5.50

This process resembles investment casting in that a single-part flask is used, so that no parting line—and hence, no fins—appear on the resultant casting. The *consumable* pattern is of expanded polystyrene, with which material readers will be familiar in the form of ceiling tiles. Polystyrene is an organic substance of the formula:

$$\left[\begin{array}{c} \cdots \!-\! \underset{\underset{H}{|}}{\overset{\overset{H}{|}}{C}} \!-\! \underset{\underset{H}{|}}{\overset{\overset{H}{|}}{C}} \!-\! \cdots \\ \underset{H}{\overset{C}{}} \underset{\underset{C}{}}{\overset{C}{}} \underset{H}{} \\ H \end{array}\right]_n$$

where 'n' is between 1000 and 2000. It is a polymer (1.84—Part I) derived from benzene and ethylene and, in its expanded form, contains only 2% of actual solid polystyrene, which accounts for its extremely low relative density. It melts at just above 100° C and consequently shrivels up to 2% of its original volume. On burning it produces a mixture of carbon dioxide and water vapour but no solid residue.

5.51

An expendable pattern, complete with the necessary runners and risers attached, is cut from expanded polystyrene and completely surrounded with sand. The molten metal is then poured *on to the pattern* which immediately burns, leaving a cavity which is almost immediately occupied by the molten metal (Fig. 5.8). Carbon dioxide and water vapour which are released do not dissolve in the molten metal but disperse through the sand mould, which must therefore be sufficiently permeable to allow this. Since polystyrene is a fragile material the pattern is easily damaged during the moulding process if the sand is rammed too hard. It has been found, however, that moulding can be carried out by pouring ordinary sea sand around the pattern. Presumably the burning polystyrene produces a tacky bond between the sand grains for just long enough for a skin of metal to form. Alternatively the CO_2 process (3.48) can be used, to produce a more stable mould.

5.52

Expanded polystyrene does not cut cleanly. Hence it is difficult to obtain a good surface finish to the pattern and, consequently, to the resultant casting. Initial shaping can best be accomplished by the use of sharp knives and heated stainless-steel wires, whilst optimum surface finish is obtained by using a high-speed sanding disc. Flat surfaces can be faced with tissue paper (stuck on with wall-paper adhesive), or mould dressing can be applied to the surface of the pattern.

5.53

The obvious advantages of the process are that fewer design limitations are imposed by the combination of expendable pattern and one-part flask, whilst

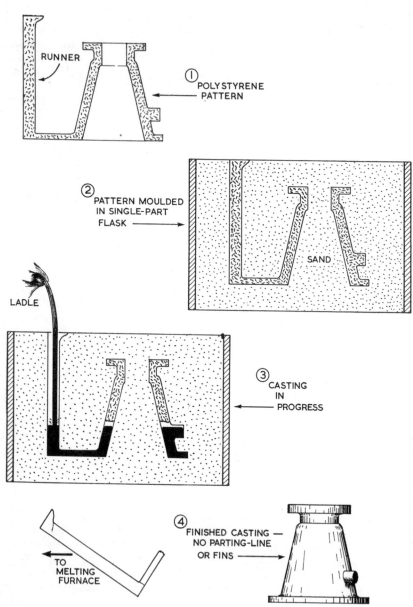

RUNNER

① POLYSTYRENE PATTERN

② PATTERN MOULDED IN SINGLE-PART FLASK

SAND

LADLE

③ CASTING IN PROGRESS

TO MELTING FURNACE

④ FINISHED CASTING — NO PARTING-LINE OR FINS

Fig. 5.8—The 'Full-Mould' Process using an Expendable Polystyrene Pattern.

less skill is required in moulding. The cost of producing individual patterns must of course be taken into account so that the process lends itself particularly to the manufacture of individual castings or prototypes.

5·54
A notable example of a full-mould casting in Britain is Geoffrey Clarke's cross which originally adorned the summit of Coventry Cathedral. In this case the polystyrene pattern was coated with wax and the polystyrene then dissolved by perchloroethylene to leave a hollow wax pattern in the sand. In the engineering industries the process is used in the manufacture of large press tool die holders and similar components.

BIBLIOGRAPHY
1 'Cast Iron Pipe (Centrifugal Casting)'. P. Longmuir (Griffin).
2 'Shell Moulding', Machinery's Yellow Back No. 34 and 34A.
3 'Investment Precision Casting', Machinery's Yellow Back No. 35.
4 'Precision Investment Casting', E. L. Cady (Reinhold Publishing Corp.).
5 'Investment Casting for Engineers', R. W. Wood and D. von Ludwig (Reinhold Publishing Corp.).
6 'Non-ferrous Foundry Metallurgy', A. J. Murphy (Pergamon Press).
7 'The Casting of Steel', W. C. Newell (Pergamon Press).
8 BS 1211: 1958—Centrifugally cast (spun) iron pressure pipes for water, gas and sewage.
9 BS 3146: Investment castings in metal. Part I: 1959—Carbon and low-alloy steels. Part II: 1961—High-alloy steels, nickel and cobalt alloys.

Chapter six
POWDER METALLURGY

6.10
Initially powder-metallurgy processes were used to replace casting for those metals which were difficult to melt industrially because of their high melting points. In fact, early iron manufacture was dependent upon the use of pressure to weld together the particles of solid iron produced by reduction in a primitive hearth. The first direct application of powder metallurgy appears to have been in the manufacture of platinum ingots during the last century, but it was not until the early years of the present century that serious development of the process took place in the production of sintered tungsten ingots for the manufacture of wire for electric-light filaments. Subsequently the manufacture of sintered-carbide materials was introduced in 1914, and today the number of powder-metallurgical products is so great that this branch of metallurgy can be regarded as an industry in itself.

6.11
Powder-metallurgy processes are no longer confined to the treatment of very refractory materials, but have been extended to include the manufacture of alloys which can also be produced by more orthodox methods. Thus 'Alnico' magnets (14.35—Part I) can be manufactured by casting them to shape, but a magnetically superior alloy can be produced by powder metallurgy. Whilst in cast metals the presence of any internal porosity would be regarded as a serious defect, a *controlled* degree of porosity in many powder-metallurgical products is utilised as, for example, in oil-less bronze bearings. Powder-metallurgical products can thus be divided into two main groups: (*a*) dense materials, in which the porosity is reduced to a minimum, as in tungsten and tungsten carbide; (*b*) porous materials, such as are used in bearings. At present the range of powder-metallurgical products includes components and ingots in the refractory metals tungsten, molybdenum, tantalum and niobium; the hard carbides of tungsten and tantalum; magnets ('Alnico' and iron powder cores); self-lubricating bearings; welding electrodes; filters; and various other sintered components in both ferrous and non-ferrous materials.

6.12
If a metallic powder is subjected to a sufficiently high pressure a degree of bonding takes place between the particles even at room temperature, and a coherent mass is produced. Heating the compacted mass improves the coherence between the particles by promoting inter-granular grain growth

and diffusion. The temperature used is usually somewhere above the recrystallisation temperatures of the metals but below their melting points, though in some cases the sintering temperature exceeds the melting point of one of the metals so that it melts and consequently becomes a bonding matrix for the particles of the other metal.

6.13

The principal stages in a powder-metallurgy process therefore include:

(1) obtaining the metal powders in a suitable degree of fineness and purity;
(2) subjecting them to a sufficient pressure in a suitable mould to cause cohesion to occur between the particles;
(3) sintering the compacted mass at a temperature high enough to cause diffusion and inter-granular crystal growth to occur;
(4) finishing, sizing and inspecting the product.

The manufacture of a typical powder-metallurgy product will now be considered in outline.

6.14 The Manufacture of Cemented Carbides

The cemented carbides used in making cutting tools and drawing dies consist of the carbides of tungsten, titanium, molybdenum and tantalum bonded with ductile cobalt or nickel. The carbides used, and the proportions in which they are employed, are chosen to suit the particular application for which the carbide is intended.

Assuming that tungsten carbide bonded with cobalt is to be manufactured, the raw materials will consist of carbon (in the form of lampblack), tungsten oxide and cobalt oxide powders. The tungsten oxide and cobalt oxide are first heated separately in a current of hydrogen in order to reduce them to the metallic state. The particle-size of the resulting metallic powders is to some extent controlled by the time and temperature of the reducing process.

6.15

The tungsten powder is then ground and mixed with lampblack in the correct molecular proportions to provide tungsten carbide, and the mixture heated to about $1500°$ C for 2 hours in a neutral atmosphere. The mass of tungsten carbide which is produced is then ground in a ball mill so that the resultant particle-size is of the order of 20×10^{-6} m.

The ground tungsten carbide is intimately mixed with cobalt powder so that the particles of carbide become coated with a film of cobalt powder which provides the necessary bond during the subsequent sintering stage. Camphor or paraffin wax (in an organic solvent) is added to the mixture so that, after the solvent has evaporated, about 0·5 to 2·5% of the solid remains to act as a lubricant.

6.16

The compacting of the mixture is carried out in hardened steel dies at a pressure of 75–450 N/mm^2; a pressure of 150 N/mm^2 being usual. The resulting volume of the compact is about two-thirds that of the mixed powders.

At this stage of the process the compacted units are sufficiently robust to be handled if reasonable care is exercised.

A preliminary sintering treatment at 850–1 000° C in a controlled atmosphere is then given, and the components are then strong enough to be shaped by ordinary machine-tool processes, adequate dimensional allowance being made for alternation in size during the final sintering operation. Final sintering is generally carried out in tubular electric furnaces through which a stream of dry hydrogen passes, the time of treatment being upwards of 90 minutes according to the thickness of the section. The temperature used is in the region of 1 350–1 550° C. Distortion during this high-temperature operation is minimised by loading the components on to special supports which follow their contours. After sintering, the components are allowed to cool slowly to room temperature.

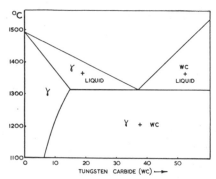

FIG. 6.1—Part of the Pseudo-binary Equilibrium Diagram
of Cobalt and Tungsten Carbide.

As is indicated in the pseudo-binary equilibrium diagram (Fig. 6.1), sintering actually takes place above the eutectic temperature of the cobalt–tungsten carbide system. Hence some liquid, consisting of a solution of tungsten and carbon in cobalt, is present, and this infiltrates during the sintering process, thus producing a denser structure. As the sintered compact cools again tungsten carbide precipitates from the solid solution, γ, and is deposited upon the particles of undissolved tungsten carbide already present. The final structure consists of particles and dendrites of tungsten carbide with an interlocking network of cobalt-rich solid solution, γ. Since the solid solution of tungsten carbide in cobalt is very small—approximately 1% at 0° C— the resultant γ remains very ductile and so resists the formation and propagation of cracks during service.

THE PRODUCTION OF METAL POWDERS

6.20

In the manufacture of sintered carbides outlined above one method for the production of metallic powders was mentioned. Other methods, however, are also used, the more important being:

6.21 Mechanical Pulverisation

This method is particularly suitable for brittle metals, though crushing and milling of steel scrap and swarf can also be employed. The finely divided metal so produced is carried from the mill in a gas stream to a cyclone separator, where the metal powder is removed and the gas returned to the input side of the compressor.

6.22 'Atomising'

This process and its modifications have been used to prepare powders of a number of metals, including copper, zinc, lead, aluminium and iron. A stream of the molten metal is sprayed into a current of compressed air or inert gas, the powder so formed being collected in a dust-collector system.

In the production of iron powders by this method it is desirable for the raw material to contain some carbon. This not only prevents oxidation of the iron by contact with the air stream, but as carbon monoxide is formed by contact of the carbon with the air this carbon monoxide helps to cause disintegration of the iron particles into tiny cups and hollow spheres. The iron powder is usually cooled in water and then heated in hydrogen to remove residual carbon and so produce a soft iron powder.

6.23 Condensation of Metal Vapours

This can be applied in the case of metals, such as zinc, cadmium and magnesium, which can be boiled, the vapour being condensed in a powder form.

6.24 Electrolytic Deposition

Electrolytic deposition is used principally for the production of copper powders employed in the manufacture of oil-less bronze bearings. Electrolysis of an acidified solution of copper sulphate is carried out between a copper anode and an aluminium cathode. The conditions of current density and electrolyte composition are adjusted so that instead of a coherent coating being obtained the deposit is dendritic and spongy. This deposit is scraped off the aluminium cathode; the copper deposit is removed periodically from the bottom of the electroysis tank, centrifuged to remove excess electrolyte and then washed in water. After being dried in an oven the powder is screened, any oversize material being ground.

Electrolytically produced copper powder is used more widely in the manufacture of oil-less bearings than powder produced by any other process. The particles of electrolytic copper are dendritic in shape, and thus lend themselves admirably to the compacting and sintering process, in which the tin becomes molten and thus infiltrates into the dendritic form of the copper.

6.25 Chemical Reduction

This process has already been mentioned in connection with tungsten and other refractory metals, the oxide powders of which are reduced by heating them in a current of hydrogen.

The most important powder used in the large-scale production of iron-base components is Swedish sponge iron. It is of low cost, reasonable purity and good compacting properties. High-purity magnetite ore (2.20—Part I) is ground to a suitable degree of fineness, mixed with powdered charcoal and heated. The iron oxide is reduced to iron powder which is fine enough for direct compacting.

$$Fe_3O_4 + 4C = 3Fe + 4CO$$
$$Fe_3O_4 + 4CO = 3Fe + 4CO_2$$

The large quantities of iron oxide scale from rolling mills can be pulverised and treated in a similar manner.

Copper powder can be produced by the same method, that is, by heating copper oxide in a stream of hydrogen or one of the hydrocarbon gases.

$$Cu_2O + H_2 = 2Cu + H_2O$$

6.26 Hydride and Carbonyl Processes

Some metals can be made to combine with hydrogen, forming hydrides. The hydrides of tantalum, niobium and zirconium are stable at room temperatures, but begin to dissociate into hydrogen and the pure metal powder when heated to about 350° C.

Similarly, nickel and iron can be made to combine with carbon monoxide, forming volatile carbonyls. The carbonyl vapour is then decomposed in a cooled chamber so that almost spherical particles of very pure metal are deposited.

$$Ni + 4CO \underset{\longleftarrow}{\longrightarrow} \underset{\substack{\text{Nickel} \\ \text{carbonyl}}}{Ni(CO)_4}$$

This method is useful in producing very pure nickel and iron.

POWDER MIXING

6.30

The choice of powder-mixing plant depends very largely upon the types of powder being combined. Simple paddle- or blade-type mixers are generally used for copper and tin powders in the manufacture of sintered-bronze bearings, whilst for some metals the tumbler mixer is more efficient. This consists of a metal drum which rotates on a horizontal axis. In most rotary mixers a slow speed is necessary to prevent particles of different densities being separated by centrifugal force.

6.31

Where work-hardening of the particles is unlikely to take place, as in the case of tungsten carbide, and where a very intimate admixture of a fine powder with a coarse powder is required the use of a ball mill is preferable. This is a horizontal-drum type of mixer which carries a quantity of metal balls which assist in pulverising and mixing the charge. The balls are separated from the mixed powders by means of a close-mesh screen.

For high-speed compacting internal lubrication of the powder mix is the best way of preventing excessive friction between the powder and the walls of the compacting tools. Surface lubrication of the tools under such conditions would be impracticable. Lubricants used include stearic acid, various metallic stearates, such as zinc stearate; graphite; oils; paraffin; glycerine; camphor; and a solution of paraffin wax in benzol. Failure to lubricate the tools would, of course, lead to excessive wear in them.

BONDING AND COHERENCE OF METAL POWDERS

6.40

When clean metallic particles are pressed together cold welding occurs at the surfaces of contact. The pressure used shapes the contacting surfaces to each other and enables welding to occur across a large area of common surface which disappears when welding is complete.

That cold welding does take place is proved by the fact that compacts of soft copper particles produced by moderate pressure will possess considerable strength and show no friability.

6.41

The bonding of metallic particles in intimate contact occurs at room temperature and is not dependent upon using a high temperature. The more malleable metals are easy to compact, but the harder metals are not so readily deformed to enlarge the surface common to two adjacent particles. Hence metallic powders must be obtained in their softest state, for whilst a pressure of 4 N/mm^2 may be sufficient to compact tin, a pressure of up to 775 N/mm^2 may be required for tungsten.

If the metal particles are not clean coherence will not occur. Moreover, the shape and size of particles determine to a large extent the total surface area of contact between them. After the pressing operation many small cavities remain, resulting in a porosity in the metal parts. These cavities are often utilised, as in the production of oil-less bearings and filters.

THE COMPACTING OPERATION

6.50

Presses used for compacting metal powders are of two types, i.e. mechanical or hydraulic. Mechanical presses are generally operated by rotating-cam movements, and double-end compression (see Fig. 6.2) is usually possible with this type of press. The capacity of a mechanical press varies widely with the application. It is usually of the order of 100–400 kN for the manufacture of sintered-bronze bearings, though capacities of 1 MN or even 5 MN are used for other metals. Even higher capacities are possible with hydraulic presses.

The wear on dies used for the compacting of metal powders is considerable. When the output of components justifies the high cost the most satisfactory material from which to make the dies is tungsten carbide, since it possesses good resistance to wear and has relatively low friction properties. High-speed steels are also very useful materials in these respects. However, unless large quantities of components are required it may not be economical to use these expensive materials, and in such cases either a high-chromium high-carbon die steel, or a carbon steel hard-coated with chromium, may be used.

6.51

A set of press tools of the type used for making bronze-bearing bushes is shown in Fig. 6.2. In Fig. 6.2 (i) the feed hopper has distributed metal powder into the die cavity. The hopper then moves aside, trimming the powder level with the top of the cavity (Fig. 6.2 (ii)), and at the same time the top punch

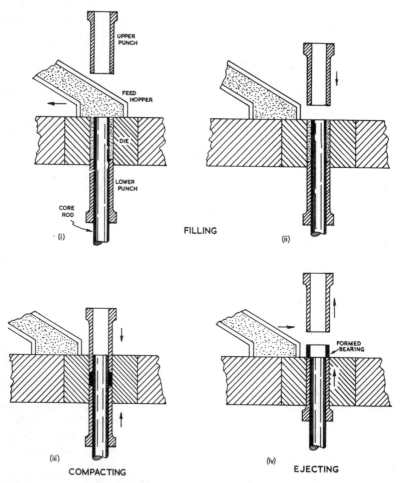

FIG. 6.2—Compacting a Bronze Bearing Bush.

begins to move downwards. As it makes contact with the surface of the powder the bottom punch moves upwards, so that the powder is squeezed into a compact of the desired size (Fig. 6.2 (iii)). The top punch is then withdrawn and the bottom punch continues its upward stroke to eject the compact (Fig. 6.2 (iv)).

6.52

Rotary table presses with twelve or more die cavities are often used, and the speed of operation is such that outputs of between 300 and 3 000 compacts per hour are common. The feeding of powder, and the forming and ejection of compacts become virtually continuous.

SINTERING
6.60

After being compressed into a briquette of the shape required in the finished component the agglomerated metals are sintered. Sintering operations really fall into two groups:

(1) Those processes in which neither of the compacted metals melt and in which grain growth and diffusion, taking place across the cold-weld surfaces, lead to the adequate cementing of the particles into a cellular type of structure. The sintering of pure tungsten is an example of this type of operation.

(2) The processes in which one of the metals melts and infiltrates between the particles of the other metal, alloying with their surfaces, and thus producing a continuous metallic bond. The manufacture of sintered bronzes is typical of this section of powder metallurgy.

6.61

Sintering temperatures and times vary considerably with different materials. Porous bronze bearings require treatment for only a few minutes at 800° C, whilst iron-base compacts and cemented carbides require treatment for up to 2 hours at 1 200–1 250° C. The refractory metals platinum and tungsten need even higher temperatures in the region of 1 300–2 500° C.

6.62

Sintering is usually carried out in electric-resistance furnaces, though gas- or oil-fired furnaces are sometimes used. For the treatment of bronze bearings and similar components the mesh-belt conveyor-type of furnace (Fig. 14.7 and Plate 6.1) is very widely used. Both in respect of cost of operation and technical performance, this type of furnace is superior to others for this class of work. A conveyor furnace is most suitable from the economic point of view, since it achieves a fairly short heat-treatment cycle for large numbers of items. The sintering process requires careful technical control, and continuous equipment is more likely to produce uniformity in heat-treatment.

6.63

Sintering atmospheres of the exothermic type can often be made sufficiently reducing to prevent oxidation of the components, but in electric furnaces some form of controlled atmosphere must be supplied. Indeed, it is generally desirable to use a strongly reducing atmosphere, so that any oxide present will be removed and so ensure a strong bond between the metal particles being sintered. For brass and bronze partially burnt coal-gas can be used, whilst for iron–carbon alloys a carbon-enriched cracked ammonia atmosphere (14.52)

Courtesy of Messrs Birlec Ltd, Birmingham, 24.

PLATE 6.1—Mesh-belt Conveyor Furnace Used for Sintering Bronze and Similar Components.

This illustration shows the delivery end. Immediately behind this is the cooling tunnel and in the rear the heating chamber.

is employed in order to prevent decarburisation. Tungsten and tungsten carbide are usually sintered in an atmosphere of dry hydrogen.

SIZING AND IMPREGNATION

6.70

A high degree of dimensional precision is generally required in bronze bearings, as well as in many other components produced by powder-metallurgical methods. The sintering process, however, inevitably produces some distortion and alternations in size, and it is therefore usual to apply a sizing operation after sintering in order to achieve the required dimensional precision and to improve the surface finish of the component. Only a slight change in density will occur during sizing.

6.71

Sizing is carried out on mechanical or hydraulic presses, the sizing tools being basically similar to forming tools and, in the case of bronze bearing bushes, comprising die, core rod, top punch and bottom punch. Even with oil lubrication, wear on sizing tools is considerable, and since dimensional tolerances, of 1 mm/metre are often required, it is obvious that permissible tool wear must not exceed this level. The most satisfactory material for sizing tools is tungsten carbide, though high-carbon high-chromium die steels and hard-chromium plate are often used as a compromise on costs.

6.72

After sizing, oil-less bearings are impregnated with lubricating oil, absorption being accelerated by the application of both vacuum and heat. Oil fills about 90% of the pores of the bearing. It is not possible to fill all pores, since a small number are 'blind', that is they do not inter-communicate with neighbouring voids.

THE MANUFACTURE OF STRIP AND SECTION FROM METAL POWDER

6.80 Continuous Roll Compacting

As long ago as 1843 Henry Bessemer (2.71—Part I) produced brass strip by rolling a mass of fine turnings, whilst in 1902 a patent for the roll-compacting of high-melting-point metal powders was granted to Siemens and Halske. In this process, metal powder was fed from a hopper into a horizontal rolling mill, that is, a mill in which the axes of the rolls are in a single horizontal plane (Fig. 6.3 (i)).

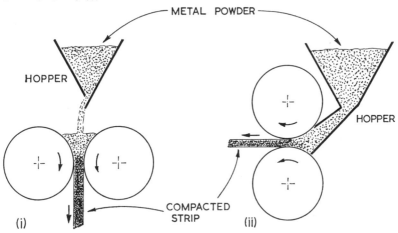

FIG. 6.3—The Compacting of Metal Powders by Rolling.

Little further progress was made until in recent years, and now compacting of powders in both horizontal and vertical mills (Fig. 6.3 (ii)) has become well established.

6.81

Once a suitable relationship between the quantity of powder, roll dimensions, roll gap and speed has been arrived at which will produce a satisfactory compacted material, a continuous process may be established as outlined in Fig. 6.4.

6.82

One of the main disadvantages of such a system would seem to be that a very long sintering furnace would be needed, or alternatively, a very low roll speed and production rate, in order that satisfactory sintering of the compacted material would take place. Consequently the process can be of a batch type in which 'green' (that is, unsintered) strip can be cut into lengths as it leaves the compacting rolls and subsequently sintered as flat stock. Alternatively, the operation can be a continuous one in which the compacted strip is partially sintered, followed by either hot- or cold-rolling and then further sintering as required.

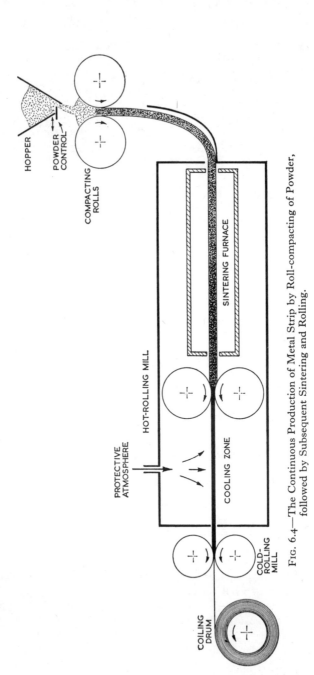

FIG. 6.4—The Continuous Production of Metal Strip by Roll-compacting of Powder, followed by Subsequent Sintering and Rolling.

6.83

Until recently this method of producing strip from metal powder was economical only on a small scale due to the high cost of metal powders, as well as slowness of the sintering process. It was used, therefore, only for very pure or very high-melting-point metals. However, in Canada, where nickel, copper and cobalt are produced as powders direct from the ore, sheet is now being rolled by this method. Such a process would also appear to be potentially useful in the compacting and rolling of mixtures—including metals with non-metal powders—and for dealing with alloys which show excessive segregation or brittleness in the cast form.

6.84 Extrusion of Metal Powders

Both hot and cold extrusion of metal powders is carried out, generally for the shaping of special materials. Components of uniform cross-section such as cemented carbide drills and cutters can be made by cold extrusion. The main disadvantage of the process is that considerable amounts of a suitable

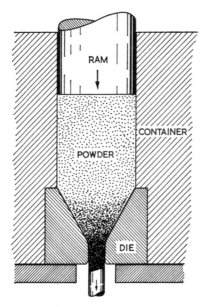

Fig. 6.5—The Cold Extrusion of Metal Powder.

binder must be added to the powder, not only to bond the particles but to act as a lubricant without which wear on the die and container would be excessive. This binder must be removed before or during sintering and since, in some cases, it amounts to nearly 50% of the total bulk of material, its removal results in considerable shrinkage of the product.

The most common binder is paraffin wax which is introduced to the metal powder in the molten state or, alternatively, in solution in a suitable organic solvent such as benzol. The solvent is allowed to evaporate before extrusion is carried out. The mixture is often compressed before being extruded. This reduces its volume and so increases the extrusion pressure by increasing the area of contact between the particles.

A typical cold-extrusion operation, using a hydraulic press, is indicated in Fig. 6.5. The powder(s), mixed with the binder, is charged to the container and then forced through the die by means of the ram. The cross-section of the product depends upon the shape of the aperture in the die.

6.85

The hot extrusion of powders is useful in the manufacture of rods, tubes and other shapes, since the amount of deformation in a single process is high and consequently a product of high density is obtained. Foremost amongst powder materials which are treated in this way are refractory metals, beryllium, cermet reactor fuel materials (uranium oxide in a stainless-steel matrix) and various dispersion-strengthened materials (8.62—Part I) such as SAP.*

Since the extrusion temperatures of refractory metals are generally high (sometimes above 1 400° C) it is often necessary to 'can' the material in mild steel. This is done either by packing the refractory powder into a support can or by compacting it and then, after heating it to the extrusion temperature, encasing it in a stout outer container of mild steel heated to 1 100° C. The composite billet is then extruded as indicated in Fig. 6.6, the die and container being protected from extremes of temperature in much the same way as in the extrusion of steel (9.65) when using glass as a lubricant.

6.90 Advantages and Limitations of Powder Metallurgy

The powder-metallurgy process is of particular interest to the metallurgist, since it frees him from the limitations imposed by phase equilibrium. Useful alloys cannot be produced from the liquid phase unless the metals concerned are mutually soluble in the liquid state. For example, it is difficult to produce copper–lead bearing alloys containing large amounts of lead, since the two metals are insoluble as liquids. Mixed powders of copper and lead can, however, be successfully compacted and sintered.

6.91

The addition of non-metallic substances which would be insoluble in the liquid alloy—and consequently would not be incorporated into its structure —can also be made to powder-metallurgical products with the knowledge that they will be evenly distributed throughout the structure. Thus, graphite

---

* 'Sintered aluminium powder'—a dispersion-strengthened material. Aluminium is milled to a fairly coarse powder size, the particles of which become coated with a natural oxide film (22.71—Part I). This powder is then compacted and sintered or extruded. The most important property of SAP is that the dispersed oxide particles in the aluminium matrix promote considerable strength at high temperatures, e.g. 108 N/mm² at 500° C. This value will be obtained even after a month at temperature, whereas under similar circumstances most aluminium *alloys* have a strength of only 15 N/mm². An obvious disadvantage of SAP is that it cannot be joined by *fusion* welding since any melting process destroys the dispersion pattern of the oxide particles.

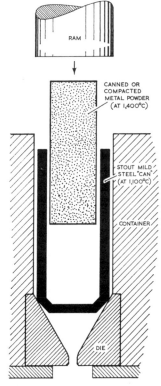

FIG. 6.6—The Hot Extrusion of a 'Canned' Refractory Metal Powder.

and copper can be compacted for the manufacture of dynamo brushes, whilst small additions of thorium oxide can be made to tungsten destined for the production of electric-lamp filaments (5.50—Part I). Recently the incorporation of organic lubricants into compacts for the production of bearings has been developed.

6.92

A further special application of powder metallurgy is in the manufacture of laminated bimetallic strips, whilst porous metals for filters and the like can only be made from powders. Mention has already been made of the importance of powder metallurgy in the production of those metals and alloys which present melting or casting difficulties.

6.93

Although the cost of metal powders is high, this is largely offset by the absence of process waste. In melting and casting processes waste occurs in the form of losses by volatilisation, slagging, oxidation, metal splashing, gates and risers. Powder losses, however, are usually less than 0·5%. More important still is the accuracy with which composition and purity can be controlled in powder-metallurgical processes, there being no appreciable changes in composition and no risk of contamination by sulphur or oxygen. In addition, physical faults, such as blow-holes and slag inclusions, will not be encountered.

6.94

Powder-metallurgical processes lend themselves to high production rates and automation. Thus highly skilled labour is not necessary to the extent which is required in a casting process, where skill and experience are generally important attributes. Consequently these processes have moved into fields normally covered by casting and forging and are no longer confined to those materials requiring special treatment or in which special properties are sought.

6.95

As with many new processes, over-enthusiastic claims were made in the early days of its development regarding the universality of application of powder metallurgy, but fortunately a better appreciation of its advantages and limitations now prevails.

Foremost amongst the limitations of powder-metallurgical processes is the fact that complicated shapes, such as are produced by casting, cannot be made by compacting, since metallic powders lack the ability to flow to the extent of molten metals. It is, however, economical in many cases to produce a simple blank by powder metallurgy and then machine it to some more complicated shape.

Other limitations of the process can be classified as follows:

(1) The strength and toughness of parts produced by powder metallurgy are usually inferior to those parts produced by casting or forging. The brittleness encountered is a function of the porosity associated with sintered products.

(2) The initial costs of dies and tools are high, and these must be offset by mass-production methods. Wear on tools also involves high maintenance costs.

(3) The size of products is limited because of the large presses and expensive tools which would be required for compacting. Nevertheless, components up to 12 kg in mass have been produced.

(4) Due to friction and the tendency for metal powders to stick to the sides of the die, there is often some lack of homogeneity in the physical properties of the compact. Thus, compacts pressed from the top tend to be less dense at the bottom.

(5) Some metals are difficult or impossible to compress, since they tend to cold-weld to the walls of the die, and thus to cause excessive wear on the die.

(6) Several metal powders present serious fire and explosion risks, and precautions must be taken to prevent such powders from becoming air-borne.

6.96 Some Noteworthy Applications of Powder Metallurgy

Initially, powder-metallurgical methods were restricted to the compacting of the refractory metals and the manufacture of porous bronze bearings and cemented carbide tools. During the Second World War and in the post-war years, however, the field of application of powder metallurgy has been considerably extended. One interesting use of the process which was made in Germany during the War was in the production of shell-driving bands, shortage of supply of other metals forcing the Germans to make these bands from sintered iron.

In addition to those materials mentioned above, the metals and alloys used for the production of sintered components include copper; bronze; 90–10 and 70–30 brasses; iron; iron–copper mixtures; infiltrated iron; and various iron alloys.

6.97

Although iron is not regarded as a good bearing material, the relative cheapness of porous sintered-iron bearings has led to their popularity in suitable applications. Improved properties are obtained by the addition of from 2 to 10% copper, higher copper contents now having been discontinued. A sintered porous 10% copper–iron alloy may develop a tensile strength of 247 N/mm^2 after sintering for 15 minutes at 1150° C.

Another technique of recent development is the manufacture of infiltrated iron. A fairly lightly compacted 'skeleton' of iron powder is placed in contact with copper powder and heated at 1150° C in a reducing atmosphere. The copper melts and is drawn by capillary action into the voids in the iron skeleton. Erosion of the iron skeleton at the point of entry of the molten copper would be liable to take place and lead to the formation of a surface layer deficient in iron. This is prevented by using as the infiltrant copper which is already saturated with 2·5% iron.

6.98

Sintered metal filters are used in the filtration of oils; petroleum liquid; water; and many chemical liquids. Since good corrosion resistance is obviously called for, 89–11 bronze; 18–8 stainless steel; Monel and nickel filters have been produced, but of these bronze and stainless steel are at present the most important. Porosity is controlled by selection of particle size in the original metal powders. No compacting process is used, the powder being sintered in a suitably shaped mould, and in the case of alloys a pre-alloyed powder is employed. Bronze filters may have a porosity of 30–40%. Nevertheless, the mechanical strength may be as high as 60 N/mm^2. The main difficulty in producing stainless-steel filters is in attaining the necessary sintering temperature of 1300° C under suitable conditions on an industrial scale.

6.99

An interesting example of a product associated with the use of metal powders is the manufacture of magnetic cores for transformers and the like. Iron powder coated and bonded with plastic is used, the iron particles thus being insulated from each other so that eddy currents are reduced.

By using powder-metallurgical methods, friction material for heavy-duty brakes can be compounded to give the following properties:

(a) suitable dynamic and static coefficients of friction;
(b) friction which is reasonably constant with time and temperature;
(c) adequate durability;
(d) adequate heat capacity;
(e) low cost.

Recent research suggests that powder-metallurgical processes may be useful in producing and increasing the range of materials which rely for their mechanical properties on dispersion hardening (8.62—Part I) and upon fibre-strengthening mechanisms.

BIBLIOGRAPHY

1 'Powder Metallurgy in Practice', Machinery's Yellow Back No. 23.
2 'Treatise on Powder Metallurgy', Vols. I, II, III and IV, C. G. Goetzel (Interscience Publishers, Inc.).
3 'Powder Metallurgy', P. Schwarzkopf (The Macmillan Co., N.Y.).
4 'Powder Metallurgy', O.E.E.C. Publication, Paris.
5 'Practical Course in Powder Metallurgy', D. Yarnton and M. Argyle (Cassell).
6 'Fundamental Principles of Powder Metallurgy', W. D. Jones (Arnold).
7 'Powder Metallurgy', S. A. Tsukerman (Pergamon Press).
8 'Powder Metallurgy', R. L. Sands and C. R. Shakespeare (Newnes).
9 BS 3029: 1958—Method for the determination of compressibility of metal powders.

Chapter seven
THE ROLLING OF METALS

7.10
From the days of Tubal Cain until the Renaissance, hand-forging was the principal method used for shaping metals. Indeed, one of the earliest references one can find to the rolling of metals is that in 1550 a Frenchman named Brulier 'first rolled sheets of metal to uniform thickness for the purpose of making coins of equal weight'. In 1624 Philip IV of Flanders issued an edict which limited the exodus of Walloon craftsmen to Sweden, where they had introduced amongst other metallurgical processes that of rolling. A little later a flattening and slitting mill was introduced into England for use in the nail-making trade. The popular story is that one Richard Foley gained access to a Walloon foundry disguised as a musician for the alleged purpose of performing in a sort of seventeenth-century 'Workers' Playtime'. Whilst there he obtained sufficient information about the process to return to England and develop a slitting mill of his own.

It was soon realised that in addition to flattening metal sheet the rolling mill could also be used for reducing its thickness, and by 1680 a sheet mill was in use in Staffordshire. Although tin-plate manufacture began in South Wales at an earlier date, a rolling mill was first established there in 1697 for the production of iron sheets for tinning. Previous to this the sheets had been made by hammering.

7.11
Henry Cort, however, is popularly regarded as being the father of the modern rolling mill. In 1783 he took out British Patent No. 1315 to cover his introduction of grooved rolls for the manufacture of iron bars. Already possessed of a considerable fortune acquired in other directions, Cort spent most of it on a small mill which he built at Fontley in Hampshire in his efforts to develop the iron trade in England. It is a far cry from the days of Cort to the present, when a very large proportion of the 25 million tonnes of steel cast in Britain alone each year passes through a rolling mill in at least one stage in its fabrication.

7.12
Modern rolling mills fall into two main groups, those which produce flat shapes, such as plates, sheets and strip, when the rolls are smooth and run parallel to each other; and those designed to produce shaped sections, such as squares, rounds, rails and joists, when suitably grooved rolls are used. Rolling

also figures in the field of chipless machining in so far that components of changing cross-section can be produced by transverse-rolling processes (7.70).

Obviously a mill used for rolling flat products can be employed in the manufacture of material of different thickness by altering the gap between the rolls, but for the production of sections, grooves must be machined in the roll surface for the manufacture of each shape.

ROLLING-MILL CONSTRUCTION

7.20

The main parts of a typical rolling mill are shown in Fig. 7.1. The *rolls* themselves are contained in a *housing* which is usually of cast steel, and the *necks* of the rolls run in bearings which are supported in *chocks*. These chocks

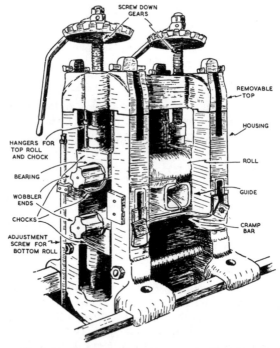

FIG. 7.1—The Main Parts of a Simple Two-high Non-reversing Mill.

can be moved up or down in the framework of the housing in order to regulate the gap between the rolls. Only a small movement of the lower chock is generally possible in order to allow for compensation for wear, but the top roll is capable of considerable movement.

7.21

To prevent the neck of the top roll from coming into violent contact with the upper chock when a work-piece is fed into the roll gap the neck is kept in contact with the upper chock, under conditions of non-load, by hydraulic pressure applied to another chock *beneath* the neck of the upper roll. This hydraulic pressure also keeps the upper chock in contact with the *screw-down gear* end and prevents damage to it at the same time. The screw-down gear is used to adjust the roll gap and in a large plate mill it is generally mechanically operated.

When a mill is used for rolling sections *guides* must be fitted to lead the work-piece into the correct grooves in the roll gap.

7.22
Since the rolls are capable of independent vertical movement, it is necessary to use flexible couplings between the roll ends and the drive. Extending beyond the roll necks are *wobbler ends* which engage in loosely fitting cast-steel couplings known as *wobbler boxes*. These couplings fit over the ends of connecting *spindles*, which are shaped in a similar manner to the wobbler ends of the rolls. A typical rolling mill connecting drive is shown in Fig. 7.2. The

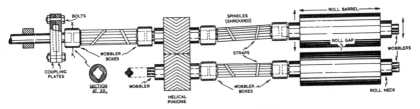

Fig. 7.2—A Typical Rolling Mill Drive.

coupling system between mill and driving motor is usually made the weakest part of the drive, so that it will break during a possible over-load and thus protect the driving motor.

THE ROLLING OPERATION

7.30
Rolling provides the cheapest and most efficient method of reducing the cross-sectional area of a piece of material in such a way that the final thickness is uniform throughout great lengths of the product.

The plastic flow of metal which takes place in a work-piece as it passes between a pair of rolls can be investigated by drilling a series of holes equally spaced along the length of the work-piece and then plugging these holes with pins of some other metal. If the mill is stopped when the work-piece has been only partly rolled a section through the piece will indicate the extent to which plastic flow has taken place at various points in the section of the work-piece (Fig. 7.3).

7.31
If we assume that the strip is wide compared with its thickness, then lateral spread can be neglected. Thus, since metals are relatively incompressible:

$$\text{Area } ABDC = \text{Area } A_1B_1D_1C_1.$$

Since the work-piece is being elongated by the rolling process, it follows that its velocity on leaving the roll gap is greater than its velocity as it enters the roll gap;

i.e.

$$\frac{V_1}{V} = \frac{A_1B_1}{AB}.$$

Consequently, at only one point in the arc of contact (XY) between the rolls and the work-piece will the peripheral speed of the roll surface be the same as the forward velocity of the work-piece. This point is called the neutral point or the point of no slip. Where the ingot enters the rolls its forward velocity

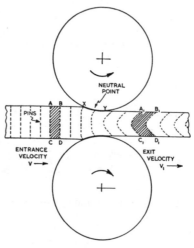

FIG. 7.3.

will, of course, be less than the speed of the rolls, whilst as it leaves the rolls its forward velocity will be greater than the peripheral speed of the rolls. Therefore at all points, except the neutral point, on the arc XY slip between the rolls and the work-piece must occur.

7.32

Since slip is taking place between the rolls and the work-piece, it follows that frictional forces will come into action (Fig. 7.4). As the rolls rotate they exert a frictional force, F, drawing the metal between them and a corresponding frictional resistance, F_1, to the work-piece leaving them. The friction of the rolls against the work-piece also produces relative movement between the surface layers and the interior of the material, leading to the type of plastic flow which is indicated by the bending of the pins as shown in Fig. 7.3. Deformation during rolling is caused by a combination of compressive and shear stresses. The compressive stresses are, of course, due to the squeezing action applied by the rolls and the shear stresses by the friction between the rolls and the work-piece.

If the coefficient of friction between the rolls and the work-piece is reduced,

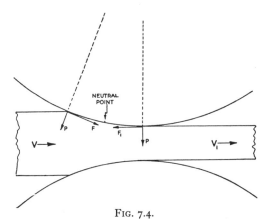

FIG. 7.4.

then the force tending to separate the rolls will also be reduced, i.e. the roll pressure will be reduced. This is shown diagrammatically in Fig. 7.5. Therefore the provision of smooth surfaces on the work-piece and the roll surfaces will reduce friction between the two. This will lead to a reduction in the separating force between the rolls, which in turn will result in a smaller energy consumption by the rolling process. In cold-rolling operations friction can be reduced by using highly polished rolls and adequate lubrication.

7·33
The position of the neutral point is determined by the balance of the horizontal components of all forces acting on the work-piece. It can be shown that when the coefficient of friction increases the neutral point moves in the direction of the entrance to the roll gap, whilst if the degree of reduction increases the neutral point moves towards the exit. The maximum reduction possible in a single pass through a pair of rolls (always assuming that the separating force involved does not exceed the capacity of the mill) is that produced when the neutral point reaches the exit, but since no frictional force (Fig. 7.5 (iii)) is then available to draw the metal through the rolls, the latter will begin to slip over the surfaces of the work-piece. Therefore when the coefficient of friction between the rolls and the work-piece is low only small reductions in thickness will be possible, and attempts to increase output by reducing the separating

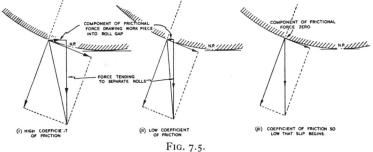

FIG. 7.5.

force via improved lubrication are frustrated by a movement of the neutral point towards the exit.

7·34

If a simple two-high mill with parallel roll surfaces were used to reduce the thickness of metal strip, elastic deformation of the rolls would lead to the faces of the emergent work-piece becoming cambered as indicated in Fig. 7.6. (i). Thus the work-piece would be thicker at the centre (X) than at the outer edges (Y). Moreover, since the edges were being extended more than the centre during rolling, strip with wavy or rippled edges would be produced.

FIG. 7.6—Illustrating the Need for Roll Camber.

Not only would the quality of such finished material be poor but the actual rolling process would be impeded.

It is therefore necessary to grind the surface of the rolls to some pre-determined camber (Fig. 7.6 (ii)) which will bear a relationship to the roll pressures employed such that the resultant strip shall have parallel faces. Having established this relationship the rolling loads must be kept constant to ensure that the rolls always flex to the required amount and so produce the result shown in Fig. 7.6. (iii). Too great a roll pressure will lead, though to a lesser degree, to the result already mentioned (Fig. 7.6 (i)); whilst too small a roll pressure will produce the result shown in Fig. 7.6 (iv). In the latter case the *central* portion of the material will be rippled or wavy due to the greater amount of elongation it has undergone.

7·35

A thick piece of soft metal obviously has a greater capacity for deformation than a thin piece of hard metal, and with the latter a point may be reached where no further reduction in thickness is possible by passing the work-piece through a given pair of rolls. This state of affairs obtains when the force necessary to produce only *elastic* strain in the work-piece is so great that it also produces elastic distortion in the rolls themselves or in their bearings or housings, so that the roll gap opens sufficiently for the work-piece to pass through without any plastic deformation taking place. The effects of increasing roll pressures and lubrication have already been discussed. Hot-rolling or annealing prior to cold-rolling may be employed to reduce roll pressures, but these methods are not applicable when the object of cold-rolling is to obtain a certain degree of hardness in the product.

Consequently two possibilities remain:

(1) Tension may be applied to the work-piece at both sides of the roll gap, as shown in Fig. 7.7. Here T_2 is the tension tending to pull the work-piece through the rolls, whilst T_1 is the force tending to hold it back. These forces, working in opposition to the frictional forces which are in operation, tend to reduce the separating force between the rolls.

(2) Rolls of smaller diameter may be used. This has the effect of reducing the area of contact between the work-piece and the rolls, and so reducing the total separating force. The obvious disadvantage of this method is that the rigidity of the rolls is reduced assuming that their length remains the

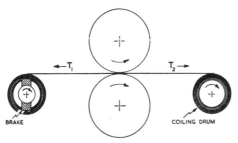

FIG. 7.7—A Method for Cold-rolling Thin Metal.

same. It is therefore necessary to back up the small-diameter working rolls with idling rolls of large diameter, thus forming a four-high mill (Fig. 7.8 (iii)). With even smaller working rolls it may be desirable to prevent distortion in both horizontal and vertical directions, in which case a six-high mill (Fig. 7.8 (iv)) may be used. For rolling very hard thin materials it may be necessary to employ rolls of very small diameter but of considerable length. In such cases adequate support of the working rolls can only be obtained by using a cluster mill (Fig. 7.8 (v)). Here each working roll is supported by two intermediate rolls, which in turn are reinforced by three backing rolls.

MICROSTRUCTURAL CHANGES DURING ROLLING

7.40

In addition to the production of useful shapes, the object of rolling is to obtain a metallurgically satisfactory structure in the finished material. During rolling a considerable redistribution of impurities takes place, and the effects of segregation which were present in the original ingot are reduced. At the same time residual coring is eliminated and a more homogeneous product is a result of the mechanical mixing action of rolling. Moreover, there is always a considerable reduction in grain size of the finished material as compared with the original ingot.

7.41

Cold-rolling as a primary forming process is applied only to very malleable metals and alloys. It is often used as a finishing process, however, in order to

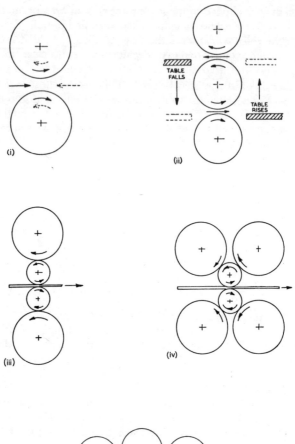

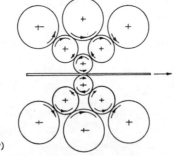

FIG. 7.8—The Arrangement of Rolls in Various Types of Rolling Mill. (i) and (ii) are used mainly for hot-rolling processes, whilst (iii), (iv) and (v) are used only for cold rolling.

obtain hardness, strength or a good surface finish in an alloy which otherwise has been shaped by hot-rolling. During cold-rolling the as-cast crystals are distorted as mechanical slip takes place (5.11—Part I) and become work-hardened in the process. The capacity for further cold work must then be restored by an annealing process, the temperature during annealing being so controlled as to give a grain size commensurate with optimum mechanical properties (Fig. 7.9 (i)). The degree of cold work in the final pass through the rolls is controlled to give the desired combination of work-hardening, strength and ductility in the product.

Hot-rolling is nearly always used in the initial shaping or 'breaking down' of cast ingots, since at elevated temperatures malleability is generally high, allowing most metals to be deformed with ease. The process of hot-rolling is carried out well above the recrystallisation temperature of the material being rolled, so that as deformation of the crystals takes place in the roll gap recrystallisation begins almost at once (Fig. 7.9 (ii)). If a continuous train of rolls is being employed in a rolling process the initial temperature of the ingot will need to be high. Consequently, grain-growth will follow recrystallisation. Further distortion of the crystals will take place in the next set of rolls, and will again be followed by recrystallisation. This process is repeated along the succession of roll gaps, but provided that the finishing temperature is not too high, the final grain size will be satisfactory.

TYPES OF ROLLING MILL AND THEIR APPLICATION

7.50
It was mentioned earlier in this chapter that the rolling of thin, hard materials generally demands the use of small-diameter rolls in order that the arc of contact between roll and work-piece is small. Conversely, big thicknesses of soft material can be rolled easily, and this is accomplished more quickly by the use of large-diameter rolls, so that a big 'draft' or reduction in thickness can be taken in a single pass. Consequently, steel ingots are hot-rolled in massive two-high mills of the reversing type. It is interesting to note that the first mill of this kind was constructed by John Ramsbottom, manager of the Crewe works of the London and North-Western Railway Company, in 1866. It is reported that his reversing drives were powered by a spare locomotive engine and that when the engine was run at a speed equivalent to 26 m/s a plate was successfully rolled.

7.51
Modern two-high reversing mills used for primary reduction are referred to as slabbing mills when the product is a slab destined for the manufacture of flat sheet, plate or strip; and cogging mills when the product is a rectangular-sectioned 'bloom' for the subsequent manufacture of bar, rod, rail or joist sections. The rolls used in these primary reduction mills are of cast or forged steel, and are between 0·8 and 1·25 m in diameter, and up to 20 tonnes each in mass. They are driven by a reversing electric motor of up to 12 MW capacity, and in order to facilitate rapid reversing, the whole structure of the mill and its drive must be massive.

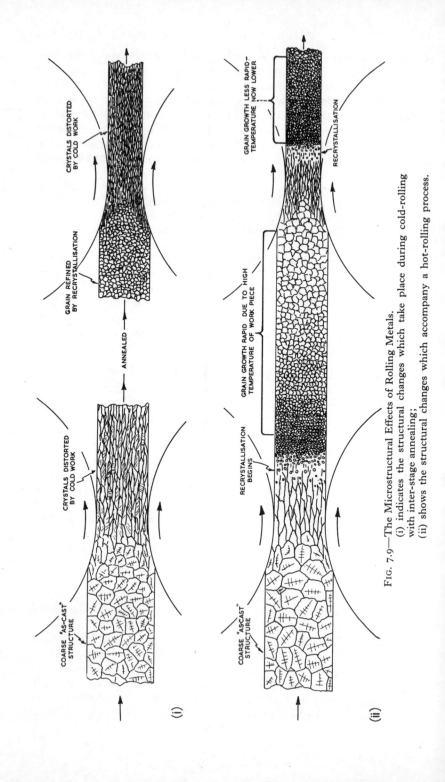

COARSE "AS-CAST" STRUCTURE

CRYSTALS DISTORTED BY COLD WORK

ANNEALED

GRAIN REFINED BY RECRYSTALLISATION

CRYSTALS DISTORTED BY COLD WORK

(i)

COARSE "AS-CAST" STRUCTURE

RECRYSTALLISATION BEGINS

GRAIN GROWTH RAPID DUE TO HIGH TEMPERATURE OF WORK PIECE

GRAIN GROWTH LESS RAPID—TEMPERATURE NOW LOWER

RECRYSTALLISATION

(ii)

FIG. 7.9—The Microstructural Effects of Rolling Metals.
(i) indicates the structural changes which take place during cold-rolling with inter-stage annealing;
(ii) shows the structural changes which accompany a hot-rolling process.

Before being fed into a mill of this type the ingot is heated in a soaking pit to a temperature in the region of 1300° C. It is then deposited on to one end of a live-roller table which is situated on either side of the roll stand (Fig. 7.10), and these live rollers introduce the ingot into the roll gap. As it passes through to the other side the other set of live rollers (which can be reversed along with the rolling mill itself) carry the ingot back into the roll gap, which in the meantime has been reduced. Before each pass through cogging rolls the work-piece is turned on to its side. This is achieved by the use of finger-type manipulators, which rise up between the live rollers (Fig. 7.10). Moveable

Courtesy of British Iron and Steel Federation.

PLATE 7.1—'Breaking Down' a Large Steel Ingot in
a Cogging Mill.
Note the table of live rollers in the foreground.

guides are used to push the work-piece laterally and so direct it into the appropriate groove in the roll gap.

It may appear that production would be stepped up if a train of primary reduction rolls of the non-reversing type were used instead of a single two-high reversing mill. It must be remembered, however, that when the bloom or slab leaves the primary-reduction mill it passes through further sets of rolls, so that if its final cross-section is small its length will be correspondingly very great. In these circumstances, even if the work-piece leaves the final

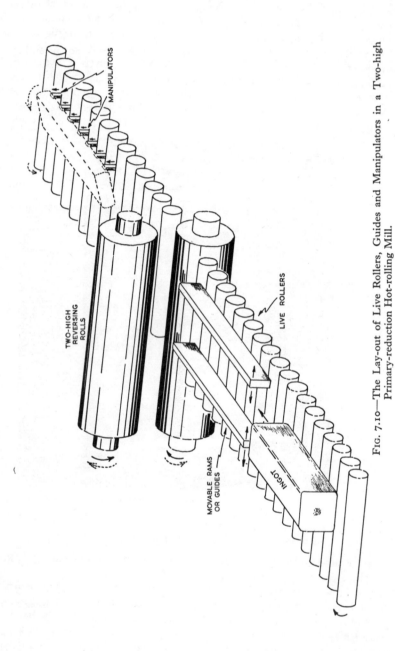

MANIPULATORS

TWO-HIGH
REVERSING
ROLLS

LIVE ROLLERS

MOVABLE RAMS
OR GUIDES

INGOT

FIG. 7.10—The Lay-out of Live Rollers, Guides and Manipulators in a Two-high
Primary-reduction Hot-rolling Mill.

mill at a speed of 18 m/s the bottle-neck will remain at that end of the production line rather than at the slabbing or cogging end. Moreover, since heat is lost only very slowly from the heavy sections during slabbing and cogging stages, there is little incentive to speed up the process at this end for such reasons.

7.52
The first Bessemer steel rail was rolled at Dowlas, Glamorganshire, in 1857, the rolls being driven by an engine which had been built in 1830 and was still running in 1905. The three-high mill was introduced in both Britain and America in the same year in order to speed up the production of rolled-steel products by keeping pace with the large output from the Bessemer converters. Until then only two-high non-reversing rolls had been used, and the work-piece had to be passed back over the rolls in order to receive further reduction.

Courtesy of Northern Aluminium Co. Ltd.

PLATE 7.2—The First Stage in the Production of Rolled Rod and Wire at the Rogerstone Works of the Northern Aluminium Co. Ltd.
An aluminium billet being rolled down to size in the bar mill

With the three-high mill, however, the work-piece is rolled on both the forward and return passes (Fig. 7.8 (ii)).
The mill consists of three rolls of equal diameter mounted one above the other, the work-piece passing first between the lower and middle rolls, and then returning between the middle and upper rolls, so that the thickness is reduced at each pass. Since the mill is kept running in one direction only, a much less powerful motor and transmission system is required, and a large flywheel can be incorporated between the motor and the rolls in order to help

maintain a steady speed when the work-piece enters the roll gap. These three-high mills are equipped with tables which move vertically on either side of the stand, so that the work-piece is fed automatically into the roll gap and a fast method of working maintained. The rolls employed are either plain or grooved to produce plate or section respectively.

The construction of a three-high plate mill is naturally more complicated than that of a two-high mill, since three pinions are required, and both the middle and upper rolls must be capable of vertical adjustment.

7·53

The reasons for using four-high and cluster mills have been mentioned already. The mills are used principally in the cold-rolling of thin material, where heavy draughts are required. Often a four-high stand will be an

Courtesy of Messrs Robertsons, Bedford; and Messrs Reynolds T.I. Aluminium Ltd, Tyseley, Birmingham.

PLATE 7.3—A Three-stand Tandem Hot-finishing Mill for Aluminium and Light-alloy Strip up to 1·3m Wide.
Speed 2·5 m/s.

integral part of a continuous mill which consists of a number of non-reversing stands. In most cases only the working rolls are driven, the heavy backing rolls being turned by friction.

Fig. 7.11 illustrates the lay-out of a typical continuous mill for the hot-rolling of steel strip. In a mill of this type a single housing containing two, three or four rolls is generally referred to as a *stand*, and when the stands are arranged in the manner shown they are said to be in tandem. Three stands of two-high rolls are shown comprising the finishing train. It is obvious that the roll

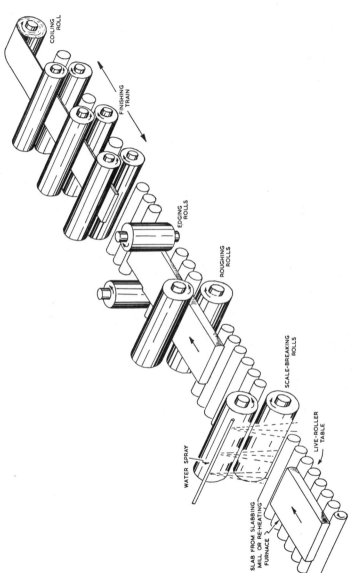

COILING
ROLL

FINISHING
TRAIN

EDGING
ROLLS

ROUGHING
ROLLS

SCALE-BREAKING
ROLLS

WATER SPRAY

LIVE-ROLLER
TABLE

SLAB FROM SLABBING
MILL OR RE-HEATING
FURNACE

FIG. 7.11—A Schematic Layout of a Continuous Hot-rolling Strip Mill.

Courtesy of Messrs Sendzimir Ltd, London, W.1.

PLATE 7.4—The Arrangement of Backing Rolls in the Sendzimir Mill. This type of mill has advanced far beyond the cluster mill and the use of such small diameter working rolls enables tungsten carbide to be employed for this purpose.

speeds in each stand must be carefully controlled to accommodate the increase in length of the work-piece as it gets thinner. Thus, the final pair of rolls must rotate at a considerably greater speed than the first pair of the train.

7.54

An alternative type of continuous mill is one in which the stands are placed side by side so that a common drive can be used for all of them. The drive passes from one stand to the next by means of wobbler boxes, which connect the wobbler of one roll to its neighbour in the next stand via an intermediate spindle. Such a train is generally driven by a single non-reversing motor, therefore it is necessary to use a series of three-high stands but containing

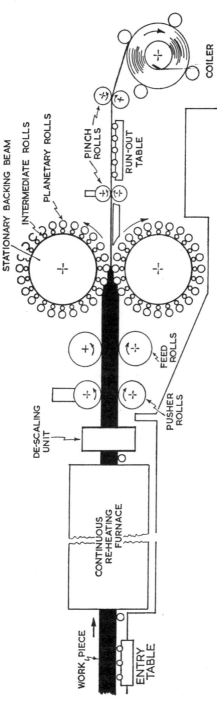

Fig. 7.12—The Principle of the Krupp–Platzer Planetary Mill.

only two rolls in each. The work-piece passes through the first stand, where the rolls are driven from the lower and middle pinions, and is then looped round through the second stand, where the rolls are driven from the middle and upper pinions and are consequently rotating in the opposite direction to those in the first stand. Such a mill is generally referred to as a bastard three-high mill, and is suitable for rolling small sections, such as wire or rod.

7·55

Substantial development of the 'planetary' mill has taken place in recent years. The original idea was introduced by Platzer in 1938 and successfully operated about three years later by Messrs Ductile Steels of Willenhall, Staffs. Fig. 7.12, however, illustrates the principles of a modern Krupp–Platzer planetary mill used for hot-rolling steel strip up to 400 mm wide.

In this mill the backing beams are *stationary* whilst the intermediate rolls and work rolls rotate around them, as do the planets around the sun. The intermediate and work rolls, which are carried in cages, are driven by gears. The work-piece is pushed by feed rolls into the roll gap. First, a thin layer of the surface is rolled wedge-shaped, the thickness of this layer depending upon the feed rate. Each successive pair of work rolls gradually reduces the angle of the 'wedge' until, on leaving the last pair of rolls, a perfectly flat strip is produced. By this method reductions of 90 to 98% can be produced in a single pass.

In addition to the hot-rolling of flat strip this mill can be adapted to produce material of square, round or other section, whilst its characteristic features favour its use in conjunction with a continuous-casting unit (2.204). Moreover, it would be economical in use where outputs are small and a changing rolling schedule is necessary, as, for example, in the non-ferrous industries. The cold-rolling of ductile materials is also feasible.

7·56

Grooved rolls are used in the manufacture of both simple and more complex sections, such as round, square, half-round and hexagonal rod, as well as rails and joists. A typical sequence of grooves used in the production of wire rod starting from a 100-mm square billet is shown in Fig. 7.13. Here alternate oval and diamond-shaped grooves are used in order to produce the maximum plastic flow in the metal during rolling, and so increase the uniformity of the product. In order to produce maximum uniformity by plastic flow the work-piece is turned through 90° before each pass. It should be appreciated, of course, that the initial 100 mm square billet used here has already undergone some twenty passes through primary-reduction rolls in order to reduce it from an ingot of possibly 500 mm square.

Each set of grooves must be carefully designed. If, for example, an excessive 'fin' was formed in one pass, as shown in Fig. 7.14 (i), this would buckle and be rolled in during the following pass and lead to the formation of a *seam* in the final product. By adequately splaying out the edge of the groove, as shown in Fig. 7.14 (ii), the fin which is formed is of such dimensions that it will be flattened during the subsequent pass through the next groove.

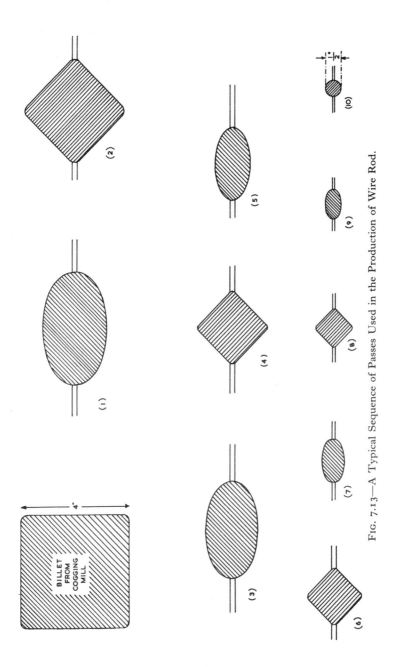

BILLET FROM COGGING MILL

4"

(1)

(2)

(3)

(4)

(5)

(6)

(7)

(8)

(9)

(10)

$\frac{1}{2}$

Fig. 7.13—A Typical Sequence of Passes Used in the Production of Wire Rod.

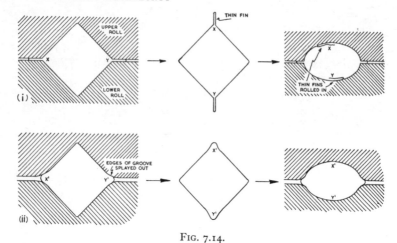

FIG. 7.14.

Typical roughing (Fig. 7.15 (i)) and finishing (Fig. 7.15 (ii)) passes are shown for the manufacture of a rolled-steel joist. In the finishing pass the grooves are so designed that no fin of variable dimensions can be formed, whilst other important dimensions are maintained with accuracy.

7·57
In many instances management of the rolling operation has passed under the control of the electronic computer which can determine the pass required at each stage for a particular work-piece. Such a computer will provide the best programme for each work-piece from:

(i) equations relating reduction to roll pressure and torque; and which are deduced partly from rolling theory and partly from previous practical data analysed by the computer;

(ii) other information about composition, size and temperature of the work-piece;

(iii) data accumulated and stored when a similar work-piece was last rolled.

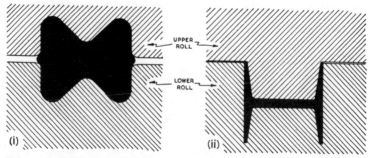

FIG. 7.15—(i) Roughing and (ii) Finishing Passes Used in the Manufacture of a Rolled Steel Joist.

Data relating to the size and composition of the work-piece to be processed are fed into the computer by the operator, whilst temperature information is supplied by a pyrometer suitably sighted on the work-piece. Similarly, instruments which measure roll pressure, torque, speed and roll gap also feed in their necessary information.

Automatic control of continuous strip mills has been in operation for some years. An on-line digital computer is employed, setting up the mill and controlling it during production. In such a mill, control of inter-stand tension in the work-piece is most important since excessive tension causes the strip to decrease in width. Control is exercised by regulating the speed of individual stands by reference to instruments as indicated in Fig. 7.16.

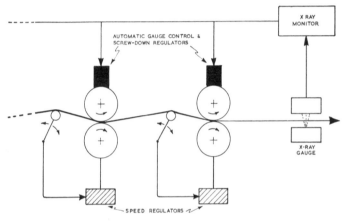

FIG. 7.16.

Work-piece thickness is controlled by automatic regulation of the screw-down gears of stands by reference to suitable instruments which measure the out-going gauge. Such instruments are based on the absorption or scattering of X-, β-, or γ-rays transmitted through or reflected by the strip. They feed their information back to the control mechanism of the screw-down gears which increase or decrease the roll gap accordingly (Fig. 7.16).

TUBE-MAKING PROCESSES INVOLVING ROLLING OPERATIONS
7.60

The year 1885 saw the publication of some of Professor Henry C. Sorby's more important work on the metallography of iron and steel. About the same date, in Germany, Gottlieb Daimler had invented a small single-cylinder engine which he used to propel a bicycle. In the same year at Remschied in Germany the Mannesmann Brothers perfected a method for the production of tube shells by the rotary piercing of solid metal billets.

Two processes for the manufacture of seamless tubes which rely essentially upon rolling operations are the Pilger Process and the Plug Rolling Process. In either of these processes the initial shell from which the tube is made is produced either by the original Mannesmann process or by modern three-roll rotary piercing.

7.61 The Mannesmann and Rotary-piercing Processes

In the Mannesmann Process a heated cylindrical steel billet is rotated between two slightly tapered barrel-shaped rolls (Fig. 7.17). The axes of rotation of the rolls are inclined at a small angle either side of the axis of rotation of the billet; both rolls rotating in the *same* direction at about 130 rev/min. The spinning action of the rolls tends to increase the periphery of the original billet so that metal is drawn from the centre of the billet, thus leading to the formation of a cavity there. However, whilst the spinning action of the rolls is fundamentally the cause of the cavity being formed independently of the action of the mandrel tip, in practice the latter projects farther into the 'gorge' than is shown in Fig. 7.17 (which illustrates only the principle of the process). This

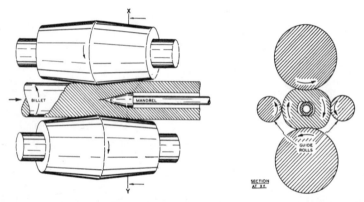

FIG. 7.17—Rotary Piercing in the Mannesmann Mill.

ensures that the cavity will form axially at the piercing point. It must be emphasised, however, that the functions of the mandrel are to ensure the formation of the bore axially and also to 'clean up' the internal surface of the bore. The spinning action of the rolls is the underlying cause of the formation of the bore. There is, of course, a natural tendency for the hole to open up along the central pipe of the ingot, since this region contains the bulk of the impurities, and is therefore weakest.

Whilst the spinning action produced by the rolls and leading to the formation of an internal cavity is an essential feature of the Mannesmann Process, it can also cause some difficulty. For example, the internal crack may form in an irregular manner, whilst the tendency of the billet to 'tear apart' means that the setting of the rolls is extremely critical. Moreover, the Mannesmann Process can only be used to pierce a limited range of steels.

The three-roll piercer, recently established by the Tube Investment organisation, differs fundamentally from a two-roll piercer in that the centre of the billet ahead of the plug is in a uniform state of lateral compression and is not subjected to alternating tensile and compressive forces such as are generated by the spinning action of the two rolls in the Mannesmann Process. Elimination of this tendency to tear open the centre of the billet makes the process less demanding in terms of mill setting and quality of raw material. However, since the pressure exerted by the plug is now instrumental in forming the bore, higher axial loads must be carried both by the plug and its water-cooled support bar.

The three rolls are orientated at 120° (Fig. 7.18) round the piercer centre line and with their axes inclined to the horizontal pass line. The angle of

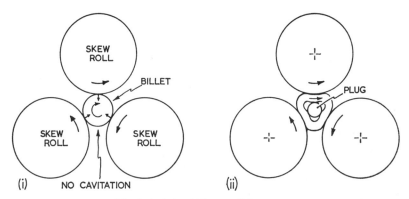

FIG. 7.18—The Principle of Three-roll Rotary Piercing.

inclination (or 'skew') of the roll axes can be varied from 0 to 15°. With modern three-roll piercers it is possible to produce seamless tube from continuously-cast steel, as well as to pierce a wider range of compositions. Such a mill can handle billets up to 3·8 m long and 0·2 m diameter and with this process the incidence of internal defects is reduced.

7.62 The Pilger Process

This process is used for the manufacture of seamless tubes in a very wide range of sizes. Possibly the most spectacular application is the production of large-diameter pipes which are used to carry oil from the wells to the refineries.

The Pilger Mill is a two-high mill fitted with rolls of the type shown in Fig. 7.19. Each roll has cut in it a semicircular groove. This groove tapers over a short distance from a large to a small diameter which remains constant for the rest of the circumference. Thus, as the rolls rotate, the circular roll gap is first large, then becomes small and then large again.

A bloom, produced either by the Mannesman Process or by three-roll piercing, is threaded on to a mandrel which ultimately protrudes into the mouth of the rolls. The mandrel itself is attached to a pneumatic cylinder and piston, and a mechanism which turns the mandrel and bloom through 90° at each 'step' of the process.

When the rolls rotate into the 'open' position (Fig. 7.20 (i)) the pneumatic pressure in the cylinder forces the piston forward so that the bloom and mandrel are thrust into the roll gap. Continued rotation brings the narrower section of the rolls into contact with the bloom so that they 'bite' into it and isolate a small collar of metal XY (Fig. 7.20 (ii)). This is then rolled on to the mandrel, and in consequence the whole mandrel assembly is forced backwards against the pressure in the pneumatic cylinder (Fig. 7.20 (iii)). The

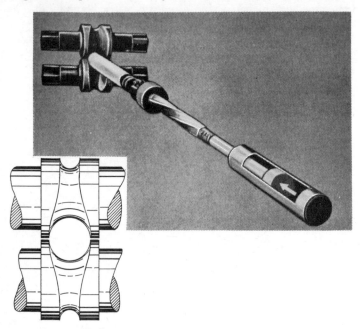

FIG. 7.19—Pilger Rolls in the 'Open' Position.

last part of the stroke (Fig. 7.20 (iv)) is for the purpose of 'ironing out' that portion of tube which was reduced in the previous rotation cycle, and so removing the ridges left by the gaps between the rolls. (The bloom rotates through 90° between each successive cycle.) The rolls finally turn into the open position again, so that the pressure in the pneumatic cylinder forces the bloom forward a further step, and at the same time the mandrel assembly turns through 90°.

The name 'pilger' is derived from the forwards and backwards progress of the bloom. 'Pilger' is in fact German for 'pilgrim', the reference being to the fact that a pilgrim approaches a holy place by taking two steps forward and one backwards. As the pilgered tube becomes longer it moves off the end of the mandrel on to a bed of rollers. Finally, when rolling is completed, the small rim which remains of the original bloom is cut off by a hot saw and the tube passed several times through a pair of sizing rolls, being turned through 90° between each pass. This ensures uniformity in the outside diameter of the tube.

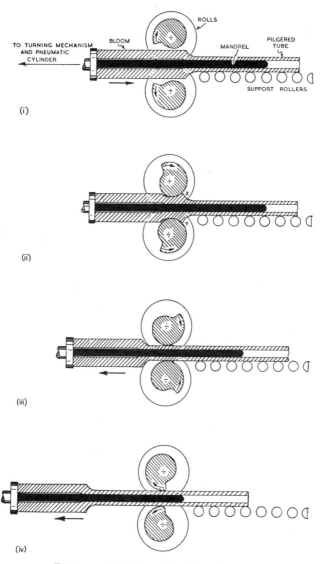

FIG. 7.20—Principles of the Pilger Process.

7.63 The Plug Rolling Process

After leaving the Mannesmann Mill the bloom may be elongated into tube form by the Plug Rolling or Automatic Mill Process. The mill used in this process consists of a two-high stand with rolls in which regular semicircular grooves have been machined in order to provide a circular roll gap of the required diameter. Just behind the rolls is a long bar which carries at its end a pointed plug on to which the bloom is rolled. The upper roll is then raised and the tube returned towards the operator by means of two small grooved rolls situated either side of the plug. Another plug about 2 mm larger in diameter than the first is now fitted behind the rolls and the tube rolled on to this after first being turned through 90°.

7.64
The surface of the tube is now smoothed by a *reeling* process. This involves rotating the tube between two slightly conical rolls, the inside of the tube being supported with a mandrel. The action of reeling is therefore very similar in principle to the Mannesmann Process, since not only is the surface of the tube smoothed but its diameter is also increased by about 6 mm. At the same time the cross-section of the tube is made perfectly circular.

Courtesy of Messrs Robertson Ltd, Bedford; and Messrs The Weldless Steel Tube Co. Ltd, Wolverhampton.

PLATE 7.5—A Pilger Mill for the Manufacture of 240 mm-diameter Tubes.

The tube is now finished in a sizing mill, which consists of several pairs of circular-grooved rolls, each pair being set at 90° to the previous pair (Fig. 7.21). The final pass through this mill reduces the outside diameter of the tube by about 6 mm.

The manufacture of tubes by the Push Bench Process is not generally classified as depending upon the action of rolling. However, the modern push bench nearly always makes use of roller dies (Fig. 7.22) instead of the older ring dies, so that the process can be regarded as one of rolling in which the motive force is applied to the work-piece instead of to the rolls. In conjunction with those processes dealt with above, the Push Bench Process comprises one of the most important methods of producing seamless steel tubes with diameters between 75 and 200 mm.

7.65 The Push Bench Process

The billet stock used in this process is usually square in section and is broken whilst still cold into pieces of a length sufficient for the length of tube being made. The billets are then heated in a continuous furnace to a temperature of about 1300° C, a process which takes up to 4 hours.

When the billet has reached the required temperature it is placed in the container of a quick-acting hydraulic press (Fig. 7.22 (i)). Here a stout cylindrical punch operated by a hydraulic ram forces a hole to a predetermined depth into the billet. At the same time the billet assumes the cylindrical shape of the container and is also elongated somewhat (Fig. 7.22 (ii) and (iii)). The operation is known as 'punch piercing'.

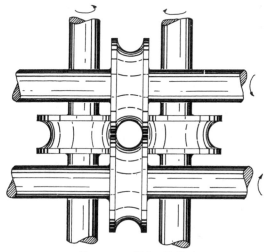

Fig. 7.21—Sizing Rolls.

The 'bottle' or 'thimble' from the punch-piercing operation is then slipped on to the end of a long round steel mandrel bar which is used to force the bottle through a series of roller dies of progressively smaller aperture. In this way the bottle is elongated along the mandrel during its passage through the dies, so thinning the wall of the shell and correspondingly increasing its length.

The first die in the train may be of the ring type in order that the bottle shall be squeezed firmly on to the end of the mandrel and that most of the scale shall be removed from its surface. Each of the roller dies which follow consists of four concave-surfaced rollers arranged as shown in Fig. 7.22. These dies are fixed so that the axes of the rollers in each die are at 45° to those in the preceding die. This ensures that 'scrubbing' marks caused by the junctions of adjacent rollers in a die are immediately ironed out in the die which follows.

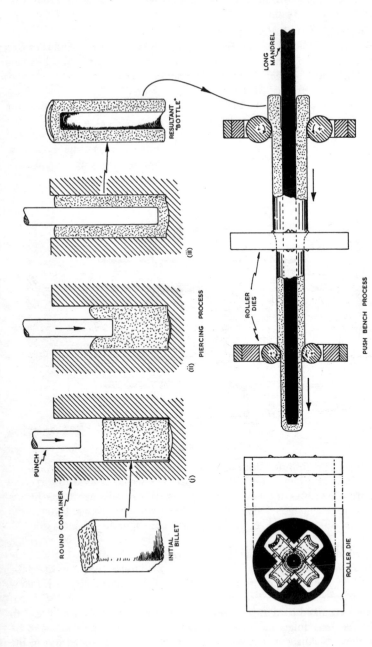

FIG. 7.22—Principles of the Push Bench Process for the Manufacture of Seamless Tubes.

After leaving the last die the tube is tight on the mandrel from which it is removed by passing through a reeling mill. The closed front end and the ragged back of the tube are then trimmed off and the tube passed through sizing rolls (Fig. 7.21). Finally, the tube is straightened by a further reeling process.

Push benches may have as many as thirty dies and the mandrel, which may be 7·5 m or more in length, may reach speeds of 2 m/s. Consequently, the process is a very rapid one.

TRANSVERSE ROLLING

7·70

A number of processes have been developed which feature transverse rolling. Unlike formal rolling all of these processes have the object of producing a component of changing cross-section. Thus they can be classified as chipless machining operations in the full sense of the term.

Courtesy of Messrs Accles and Pollock Ltd, Oldbury.

PLATE 7.6—Tube Reeling.

Some of these processes make use of two rolls in which the direction of both roll rotation and work-piece feed are similar to those in the Mannesmann Process (7.61). In other processes three rolls are used in a manner similar to those employed in three-roll rotary piercing.

7.71 Three-roll Profile Shaft Rolling

The method of control in this process resembles that in conventional hydraulic copy turning. Shaping is achieved, however, by the use of three skew rolls with a variable roll gap instead of a cutting tool (Fig. 7.23). The use of three rolls instead of two, and the fact that a small contact area is employed, helps to produce considerable deformation in an axial direction. This eliminates the main defect of ordinary cross rolling—the tendency to form cavities in the central zone (the Mannesmann effect). Moreover, in common with many other chipless machining processes, continuity of 'fibre' is maintained and this brings obvious advantages.

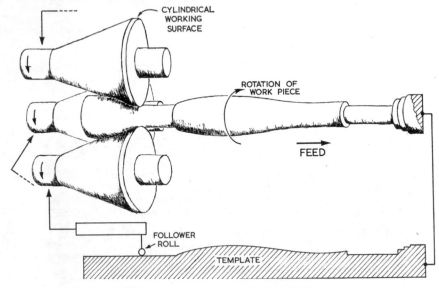

FIG. 7.23—Three-roll Profile Shaft Rolling.

Typical products of this type of process include stepped and tapered shafts and axles for electric motors; armatures; textile spindles; main shafts and half-shafts.

7.72 Wedge Rolling is a process suitable for the production of simple shapes which can then be finished by orthodox drop forging. The process employs two suitably grooved rolls which rotate Mannesmann-fashion, the work-piece being fed in a similar manner to that in the Mannesmann Process. Naturally only shapes which are circular in cross-section can be formed in this way.

7.73 Rolling Circular Components with a Small Length/Diameter Ratio

This process has been used extensively in the manufacture of steel balls and rollers, but particularly for crusher balls (40 to 120 mm diameter) used in ore grinding.

The heated bar is fed in a direction parallel to the axes of two fixed-centre rolls (Fig. 7.24). These rolls have a special helically-grooved form and the process of deformation is effected by 'screwing' the bar into the space formed between the rotating rolls. The original cylindrical bar is progressively deformed on a small advancing section with the result that a string of balls joined end-to-end in successive stages of manufacture is produced. With each revolution of the rolls an amount of metal with a volume equal to that of the part being produced, is gripped by the helical groove and formed to a

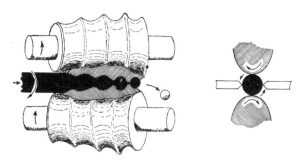

FIG. 7.24—Process for Rolling Steel Balls.

component of correct shape. The final shoulder of the rolls has sharp edges which separate the component from the string which follows.

The helical groove is calculated such that the total volume of metal in the groove remains constant whilst the change in profile and dimensions of the groove give the effect of stretching that part of the bar. In this way the necessary tensile stress is maintained so that the formation of internal cavities (the Mannesmann effect) is eliminated.

BIBLIOGRAPHY

1 'The Rolling of Metals', L.R. Underwood (Chapman and Hall).
2 'The Rolling of Strip, Sheet and Plate', L. C. Larke (Chapman and Hall).
3 'The Theory and Practice of Rolling Steel', W. Tafel (Penton Publishing Co.).
4 'Elements of Rolling Practice', The United Steel Companies.
5 'Ferrous Metallurgy' (Volume II—'The Manufacture and Fabrication of Steel'), E. J. Teichert (McGraw-Hill).
6 'The Cold Working of Non-ferrous Metals and Alloys', Symposium (Institute of Metals).
7 'The Hot Working of Non-ferrous Metals and Alloys', Symposium (Institute of Metals).
8 'Manufacture of Seamless Tubes (Ferrous and Non-ferrous)', G. Evans (H. F. and G. Witherby).
9 'The Control of Quality in the Production of Wrought Non-ferrous Metals and Alloys. II—The Control of Quality in Working Operations', Symposium (Institute of Metals).
10 'The Making, Shaping and Treating of Steel', J. M. Camp and C. B. Francis (Carnegie–Illinois Steel Corp.).

11 'Fundamentals of the Working of Metals', G. Sachs (Pergamon Press).

12 'Rolls Pass Design', The United Steel Companies Ltd.

13 'The Physical Metallurgy of Rolling', F. H. Scott (Arthur H. Stockwell).

14 'Deformation of Metals during Rolling', I. Y. Tarnovskii, A. A. Pozdeyev and V. B. Lyashkov (Pergamon Press).

15 'Rolling Mill Practice', P. Polukhin, N. Fedosov, A. Korolyov and Y. Matveyev (Peace Publishers, Moscow).

16 'The Theory and Practice of Flat Rolling', C. W. Starling (University of London Press).

17 'Rolls and Rolling', E. E. Brayshaw (Blaw–Knox Co.).

18 'Rolling Mills', A. I. Tselikov and V. V. Smirnov (Pergamon Press).

19 'Research on the Rolling of Strip (1948–58)', British Iron and Steel Research Association.

20 'Aluminium', Vol. III—Fabrication and Finishing, Ed. K. R. van Horn (American Society for Metals).

21 'Principles of Magnesium Technology', E. F. Emley (Pergamon Press).

22 BS 2094—Glossary of terms relating to iron and steel.
      Part 3: 1954—Hot rolled steel products (excluding sheet, strip and tubes).
      Part 4: 1954—Steel sheet and strip.
      Part 5: 1954—Bright steel bar and steel wire.
      Part 8: 1954—Steel tubes and pipes.

23 BS 2870: 1968—Schedule of rolled copper and copper alloys—sheet, strip and foil.

24 BS 2874: 1969—Schedule of copper and copper alloys—rods and sections (other than forged stock).

25 BS 2875: 1969—Schedule of wrought copper and copper alloys—plate.

26 BS 3370: 1970—Wrought-magnesium alloys for general engineering purposes—plate, sheet and strip.

27 BS 4391: 1969—Recommendations for metric basic sizes for metal wire, sheet and strip.

Chapter eight
FORGING PROCESSES

8.10
The decrease in the number of horses in the twentieth century has resulted in the village blacksmith becoming a much less familiar figure than the one our Victorian forebears liked to sing about. In fact, where the village smithy still exists it is generally hidden behind a garage with its inevitable array of petrol pumps. At the same time it is true that the blacksmith may have increased his scope for metallurgical processes by including some welding apparatus amongst his equipment in order to be in a position to cope with the running repairs to modern farm machinery.

8.11
The village blacksmith's industrial counterpart is still an important member on the payroll in most engineering establishments, and many readers will be familiar with his methods of working. He first heats his work-piece in a forge which employs a coke fire burning in an open hearth. The necessary high temperature is maintained by the use of forced draught. In the old days this was obtained by means of bellows, but a modern hearth is equipped with an electrically driven air blower.

When the work-piece, which has been surrounded by hot coke, attains the forging temperature the smith forges it by hammering it on an anvil. The anvil is a heavy steel casting with a flat top, a horn which has a curved surface for producing curves of different radii and a square hole in the top to accommodate various anvil tools. A stout pair of tongs are used to hold the work-piece whilst it is being forged. The various formers used in smithy work are fitted at the end of slender handles, but, whilst they may resemble hammers, they are not used for striking. Instead, the smith holds the forming tool in position on the work-piece whilst his mate strikes the end of the tool with a sledge. The working faces of the forming tools are shaped differently according to the impression they are required to impart to the forging. Fig. 8.1 shows a fuller being used. This tool has a rounded, chisel-shaped working edge and is used to draw out work more quickly than is possible by using the flat surfaces of hammer and anvil. The fuller concentrates the force of the hammer blow, and its action may be compared with that of small-diameter rolls, which 'bite' more easily into a work-piece than large-diameter rolls used in a similar rolling mill. A similar fuller is also used as an anvil fitting, so that the metal is drawn out on both sides. When the reduction produced is

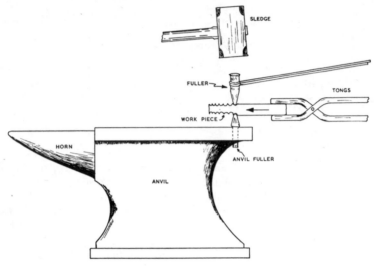

FIG. 8.1—The Blacksmith's Equipment.

sufficient the grooves which have been formed can be smoothed out by hammering the work-piece on the flat anvil. The smith can also cut metal by using hot chisels, whilst holes can be formed by using a punch in conjunction with an anvil block having a suitably sized hole in it.

8.12

In addition to shaping metals by the methods mentioned above, the blacksmith can weld pieces of iron together. He first cleans the surfaces to be joined by the application of a flux (often fine sand), and then hammers the pieces together so that welding takes place across the mating surfaces.

8.13

Genesis (IV, 22) describes Tubal Cain, who was seven generations from Adam, as 'the forger of every cutting instrument of brass and iron', and it seems almost certain that hand forging remained the only method of working solid metals and alloys until the thirteenth century. Possibly the earliest documentary evidence of the use of water power for such purposes is that in 1323 a forge near Moyeuvre, in Lorraine, introduced the water wheel to work bellows and possibly also to drive forging hammers. The old ship's anchor shown in Plate 8.1 is a relic of the days when the principal ferrous product was wrought iron, shaped by a combination of hand- and power-assisted forging.

The advent of steam power saw its application to forging early in the nineteenth century. At first the hammers were raised by cams, which in turn were driven by steam engines, but in 1838 James Nasmyth, a Scots engineer, perfected the double-acting steam hammer, in which the hammer or tup was connected directly to a piston working in a steam cylinder.

Until the middle of the nineteenth century most forging had been done with a flat hammer and anvil or with simple impressions in a die face. At about this time, however, came the introduction of metal dies of sufficient accuracy to permit the production of parts closer to required dimensions. Little further fundamental change took place in forging processes until the significance of high-energy rate forming was appreciated in recent years.

8.14
Thus in contrast to the hand work done by blacksmiths from the time of Tubal Cain onwards, modern forgings are generally made by squeezing heated metal into a specific shape produced by a cavity in two matching die blocks.

PLATE 8.1—This ancient anchor on view on the quayside in Donegal Town is popularly supposed to have belonged to the French war ship *Romaine*, one of the vessels sent by the French to assist Wolfe Tone in his struggle towards Irish Independence.

It is a relic of the days when the bulk of ferrous production was carried out in wrought iron by a combination of hand- and power-assisted forging. Corrosion due to the action of salt water (the anchor was not raised to its present position until 1951) has revealed in the ring (inset) the fibrous structure typical of wrought iron.

Such a forging is called a closed-die forging, and its production entails the use of machined dies and massive power-transmitting equipment. It will generally only be economically possible when large-scale production is contemplated of components in which a minimum of further work is necessary. At present both impact and compression methods are in use for the manufacture of closed-die forgings. Falling hammers of up to 250 kN are employed whilst hydraulic presses of as much as 500 MN capacity have been operated.

When production runs are small or when very large components are to be manufactured semi-hand forging may be employed. Here the hammers or presses are fitted with flat faces rather than contoured dies, and the shaping of parts relies entirely on the skill of the operator.

THE METALLURGICAL PRINCIPLES OF FORGING
8.20
During any hot-working process a redistribution of the impurities present in the work-piece takes place. Most of the stock material used in forging operations will have been rolled down from the ingot stage and will be supplied as billets or bars. Any impurities present in the original ingot will have become elongated along the length of the piece in the direction of rolling.

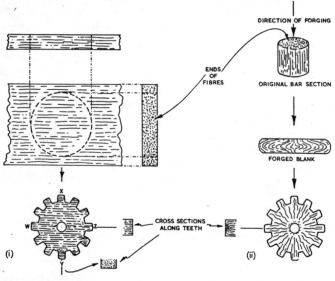

FIG. 8.2.
(i) Gear Machined from Rolled Strip showing particular weakness of teeth in the region of X and Y due to direction of fibre. The teeth at W and Z will be correspondingly strong.
(ii) Gear Machined from a Forged Blank.
The fibre flow lines give maximum strength in the teeth.

In this way the impurities assume a fibrous distribution similar in directionality to the grain in wood. As with wood, the mechanical properties are better in the direction of the fibres, whilst across the fibres the mechanical properties are at their poorest.

It is therefore important in the design of a forging to ensure that the fibres flow in the direction in which maximum strength is required. Fig. 8.2 (i) illustrates the effect of machining a small gear-wheel from a flat piece of rolled steel. Here the fibres run in one direction only, that of the direction of rolling in the original strip. Obviously the teeth in the regions of X and Y

will be relatively weak, since the machining process has cut through the fibres so that they 'outcrop' to the surface, and pressure on the sides of the teeth will tend to cause failure by shear along the exposed fibres. If, however, the blank from which the gear is machined is produced by upset forging, as indicated in Fig. 8.2 (ii), a satisfactory structure will be produced. Here a piece of rolled bar has been forged end-on so that, in the disc produced, the fibres are distributed radially as shown. When the teeth are subsequently cut the fibres will pass along them, and maximum strength and toughness will be achieved. As the stresses a gear-wheel has to meet consist mainly of a pressure across the teeth, the gear made from an up-ended bar will be more satisfactory, as the fibres are in intimate and interlocking contact.

Fibre, if badly disposed, may give rise to distortion during heat-treatment, since imperfectly arranged fibre sets up unequal stresses on cooling.

Thus in any forging process it is important to control the plastic flow of metal in order to obtain fibres, and consequently maximum strength, in the required direction. The distribution of flow lines can be examined macro-scopically as described in 10.40—Part I. Photographs of macro-sections of typical forgings are shown in Plates 8.8 and 8.9.

8.21

Broadly speaking, the best mechanical properties obtainable in a material are those associated with a fine-grained structure. It is therefore important to control the forging process in such a way that a fine-grained structure is produced. This usually means that the completion of forging should coincide with the work-piece reaching a temperature only just above that of recrystal-lisation. Crystals will have become considerably distorted by the forging process, and when forging is complete recrystallisation will immediately take place and a large number of small crystals be produced. If the finishing temperature is high above the recrystallisation temperature of the metal, then there will be ample opportunity for grain growth to occur as the temperature falls to the recrystallisation temperature. Consequently, the final grain will be coarse. By finishing the forging process only a little above the recrystallisation temperature, however, grain growth will be restricted, since the temperature soon falls below that at which crystal growth can take place.

TABLE 8.1—*Minimum Recrystallisation Temperatures* (° *C*)

Pure iron	.	.	.	.	450
Nickel .	.	.	.	.	600
Copper .	.	.	.	.	190
Aluminium	.	.	.	.	150
Zinc	.	.	.	.	20
Tungsten	.	.	.	.	1200

Table 8.1 gives recrystallisation temperatures for some of the commoner metals. In cases where grain growth is sluggish it is possible to heat the metal considerably in excess of the recrystallisation temperature without excessive grain growth taking place, but in other cases the finishing temperature needs

to be accurately controlled, as grain growth at temperatures much in excess of that of recrystallisation is rapid.

Fig. 8.3 shows diagrammatically the relationship between the finishing temperature and the final crystal size of a 0·45% carbon steel after forging. Although recrystallisation of a mechanically worked ferrite-pearlite structure takes place between 450 and 650° C, the phase changes which take place between the upper and lower critical temperatures also influence the structure of a steel (11.53—Part I). In Fig. 8.3 it is assumed that hot-rolled stock material of medium grain size is used. If this is heated to above the upper critical temperature the initial ferrite-pearlite structure will have changed to fine-grained austenite, and as this is heated to the forging temperature (in the

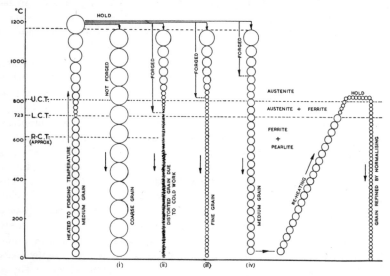

FIG. 8.3—Effects of Finishing Temperature on Grain Size During Forging
(0·45% Carbon Steel).

region of 1 100° C) grain growth will occur. Naturally if the steel is now allowed to cool without any mechanical work being applied a coarse-grained ferrite-pearlite structure will be produced (i). If, however, the work-piece is forged so that forging finishes well *below* the upper critical temperature (ii), then the steel will have insufficient opportunity to recrystallise, even though the finishing temperature is still above that of recrystallisation. Recrystallisation becomes increasingly sluggish as the recrystallisation temperature is approached on cooling, and the work-piece may cool sufficiently rapidly to prevent significant recrystallisation from taking place. A cold-worked type of structure may then prevail in the finished forging.

If forging ceases at a high temperature (iv), then the newly formed austenite grains will grow rapidly, so that medium or coarse grain will result. This coarse grain can be refined by a subsequent normalising treatment as indicated, but generally it is more satisfactory to control the forging temperature to produce a fine grain on recrystallisation (iii).

8.22

The behaviour of metals under different rates of stress application was mentioned briefly in connection with the significance of impact testing (3.52—Part I). During recent years a number of techniques for the forming of metals and alloys have been introduced under the general description of high-energy rate forming, for which phrase 'HERF' is the generally-accepted acronym (19.50). In all of these processes the necessary energy is released during a very short period of time and it is the *rate* of energy release rather than its total quantity which is the significant factor. In HERF processes energy is released at such a rate that *local deformation occurs before energy can be dissipated* by 'plastic waves' through the material. In addition to various other advantages arising from the use of such a process, mechanical efficiency is also thus increased.

When applied to forging processes, HERF can produce significant plastic flow even in materials which are relatively hard, tough and brittle when studied under conventional conditions. Hence work can be forged to precise limits, smaller radii, thinner cross-sections and with a superior finish. Moreover work is shaped in a fraction of the time required by the established processes. Hence dies heat up to a lesser extent so that die wear is reduced and less energy is lost as heat.

TYPES OF FORGING HAMMER AND PRESS

8.30

Modern forging processes employ both hammers and presses to exert the necessary force. The hydraulic press is particularly useful where large items are to be forged, but it is slow in operation, and the work-piece must sometimes be reheated several times. An important advantage of the press, however, is that, since the flow-resistance of a metal is less if the deformation is slow, deformation takes place more uniformly throughout the metal. The hammer, on the other hand, with its rapid succession of blows, tends to affect the surface more than the interior of the work-piece.

Forging hammers are very versatile and relatively quick in action. They are mechanical versions of the blacksmith's hammer and anvil, and differ very little in fundamental operation. Every forging hammer consists basically of a heavy mass or tup, which is allowed to fall or is driven down on to the work-piece; and an anvil on which the work-piece is placed. In drop (or closed-die) forging one half of the die is attached to the tup and the other half to the anvil.

8.31

The earliest type of forging hammer, known as the *helve* or *tilt-hammer*, consisted essentially of a tup attached to the end of a pivoted beam. The beam was raised by a cam mechanism which was driven by water power. Modern tilt-hammers are still used for light work, but water power has been replaced by an electric motor for their operation. In the *double-acting steam hammer* (Fig. 8.4), which is widely used for the manufacture of medium-sized steel forgings, the tup is connected directly to a piston working in a steam cylinder so that it can be both raised and then driven downwards by steam pressure. In single-acting steam hammers, which are now rarely used, the tup is raised by steam and then allowed to fall under gravity. The movement of the

Courtesy of Messrs B. & S. Massey Ltd, Manchester, 11.

PLATE 8.2—A Typical Drop Hammer—the 20 cwt. Massey 'Marathon'.

tup in a double-acting steam hammer is controlled either by a handle or by a foot pedal, and the blow which is delivered can be varied from a mere tap to a fall from the maximum height assisted by the full pressure of the steam.

8.32

In order adequately to absorb the force of the blow transmitted by the tup in hammer forging the anvil must be about twenty times as massive as the tup. Additionally, the anvil must be supported on a steel base, which in turn is usually carried by oak supports in massive concrete foundations. The *duplex hammer* is designed to absorb the shock in the machine itself. In this hammer the anvil is no more massive than the tup, and as the latter descends the anvil rises to meet it, so that the shock is absorbed internally. Since both the tup and the anvil move, it is impossible for the operator to hold a work-piece on the anvil, so that the use of the duplex hammer is limited to closed-die forging.

8.33

Similar in principle to a single-acting steam hammer is the *air-lift gravity hammer*. Here a piston working in a cylinder with compressed air is used to raise the tup to the required height, after which the tup is allowed to fall under gravity. Capacities are usually much smaller than for the double-acting steam hammer.

8.34

In the *board drop hammer* (Fig. 8.5) the tup is mounted on a wooden or steel board which passes between two pinch rolls which are in continuous motion.

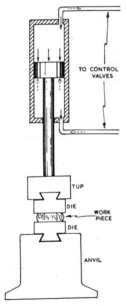

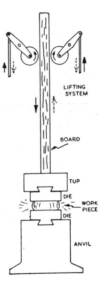

FIG. 8.4—Double-acting Steam Hammer.

FIG. 8.5—Board Drop Hammer.

To raise the tup the rolls are moved inwards by a control mechanism so that they grip the board and move it upwards. At a pre-set height the board is released automatically so that the tup falls under gravity.

8.35

Forging presses are of either hydraulic or mechanical operation. The *hydraulic press* is used for the heaviest work, and capacities of up to 150 MN are in general use, whilst capacities of 500 MN have been employed. The principle

Courtesy of Messrs Austin Motor Co., Birmingham.

PLATE 8.3—A Massey Double-acting Drop hammer.

of the hydraulic press is shown in Fig. 8.6. The press is usually operated by pumps which increase the pressure in oil or water, this pressure then being transmitted to the cylinders in order to raise the ram or force it downwards. The forging pressure can usually be varied, either continuously or in increments up to the rated capacity of the press.

8.36 Mechanical Presses are widely used for the manufacture of impression-die forgings up to about 55 kg in mass. Such presses are quick-acting, the ram being forced down by a crank and toggle-joint mechanism, which is usually electrically driven. Thrusts of up to 70 MN are obtained with this type of press.

8.37
The application of high-energy rate forming (HERF) to the forging process has already been mentioned (8.22). The release of energy at a high rate is achieved in some forming processes by the use of explosives (12.91), by spark discharge (12.92) or by electro-magnetic methods (12.93). In forging, how-ing, however, pneumo-mechanical machines are generally used as in the

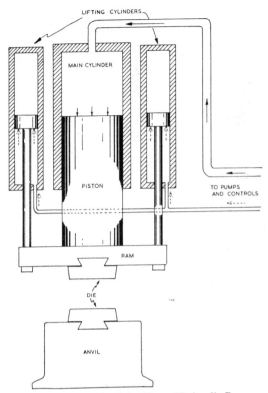

FIG. 8.6—Principle of the Heavy Hydraulic Press.

'dynapak process'. The principle of the dynapak machine is shown in Fig. 8.7. Both halves of the cylinder are filled with nitrogen such that the pressure, P_1, is approximately 14 N/mm², whilst the pressure, P_2, is only about 1·4 N/mm². If the area of the piston face exposed by the orifice is 'a_1' whilst the area of the other piston face exposed to the pressure, P_2, is 'a_2', then, for the piston to be in a state of equilibrium:

$$P_1 a_1 = P_2 a_2$$

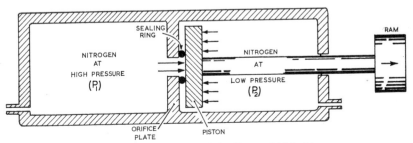

FIG. 8.7—The Principle of the 'Dynapak' Machine.

If now a 'controlled imbalance' is introduced by means of a small increase in P_1 the seal is broken and a very large increase in the total force acting on the piston is produced *instantaneously*. Hence the piston is subjected to great acceleration since much of the expansive energy from the gas is converted into kinetic energy of the ram.

Most machines of the type used for closed-die forging incorporate a pair of opposed rams, each of which carries half of the die. This reduces shock on the machine frame so that beaten-earth foundations are no longer required. Moreover since a much higher proportion of the available kinetic energy is now absorbed by the work-piece, the mechanical efficiency is increased.

FORGING PROCESSES

Modern forging operations can be classified under three main headings: (1) smith forging; (2) closed-die forging; (3) 'upset' or machine forging.

SMITH FORGING

8.40

Modern smith forging is in many ways an extension of the art practised by the blacksmith, in that various hand tools are used for producing the desired shapes in the work-piece. The forging force, however, is supplied by helve hammers, by steam or air hammers or by hydraulic presses, so that forgings varying in size from less than 0·5 kg up to 200 tonnes can be produced. The

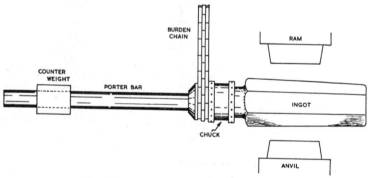

FIG. 8.8—'Blooming Down' a Large Ingot.

shaping of the component relies entirely upon the manipulative skill of the smith, and the method is used where small quantities of forgings are required or for preliminary shaping prior to drop forging.

When using a power hammer the smith is helped by one or more workers —the number depends upon the magnitude of the work. Generally, the smith himself holds the work-piece in a pair of tongs, and the hammer operator works under his directions. If the work-piece is large it may be supported in a chain sling (Fig. 8.8) suspended from an overhead crane, which will be operated by another worker. Other helpers are employed to hold fullers.

cutters and other tools, which are mounted on long steel handles. If it is desired to forge the work to a specified thickness a hardened steel gauge block mounted on a long handle is placed on the lower die block so that it prevents the hammer from forging the work-piece beyond that thickness.

Courtesy of Northern Aluminium Co. Ltd, Birmingham.

PLATE 8.4—A Large Forging Press Used for Shaping Aluminium Alloys.

An experienced smith can produce circular, rectangular, hexagonal and octagonal sections, as well as steel rings, with smooth surfaces, and to quite close dimensional accuracy. Large forgings are often produced direct from an ingot, whilst ingots are sometimes reduced to blooms or billets by this method. Fig. 8.8 illustrates the process of 'blooming down' a large ingot on a hydraulic press. If the finished forging is to be of circular cross-section an octagonal ingot will be used. A chuck and porter bar are fitted to the feeder head of the ingot, which can then be rotated by the mechanical action of the burden chain. When high-capacity presses or hammers are used and the work is correctly manipulated during forging more uniform mechanical working may be achieved than in a hot-rolling process.

CLOSED-DIE FORGING

8.50

Closed-die forging processes include both drop forging, in which some form of hammer is used, and press forging, in which a mechanical or hydraulic press is employed. In each process a closed impression die is used to shape a piece of heated metal. In such a die the metal is totally enclosed in the die cavity, one half of the die being attached to the tup or ram and the other half to the anvil. The impact of the tup or the pressure of the ram on the heated work-piece forces it into every part of the mating dies.

Drop forging can be used to produce parts from a few grams up to several hundred kilograms in mass and it is a very suitable process for the mass production of forgings. A forging is usually processed through a series of impressions made in a single pair of die blocks, but sometimes it is necessary to use more than one pair of die blocks and, consequently, more than one forging hammer. In such circumstances the hammers are arranged close to each other so that the forging can be finished without the necessity of reheating the work-piece.

Since it is important for the two halves of the die to align correctly in a drop-forging process, the guides must be more accurately constructed than they are in a hammer used for smith forging. Board drop hammers or double-acting steam hammers are commonly used for the manufacture of drop forgings, but air- or steam-lift drop hammers are also employed. Both mechanical and hydraulic presses are used for press forging, though the former are in more general use.

8.51 Dies and Die Blocks

The die blocks which contain the shaped impressions (or dies) are attached to the tup and anvil respectively by dovetails and keys. Since these dies must withstand severe stresses, resist wear and have a long life under conditions of mass production, nickel–chromium–molybdenum steels containing about $1 \cdot 5\%$ nickel, $0 \cdot 75\%$ chromium, $0 \cdot 3\%$ molybdenum and $0 \cdot 5\%$ carbon are generally used for the production of steel forgings. For forging non-ferrous alloys or for steel forgings where lower temperatures are encountered, a chromium-molybdenum–vanadium steel containing $5 \cdot 0\%$ chromium, $1 \cdot 25\%$ molybdenum, $0 \cdot 3\%$ vanadium and $0 \cdot 4\%$ carbon may be employed.

8.511 The die block is generally produced by forging an ingot, in the manner shown in Fig. 8.9, in order to obtain flow lines in such a direction as will give maximum impact resistance to the die block. After being forged the die blocks are hardened and tempered and the die impressions then 'sunk' in them with the aid of milling cutters of various shapes. The milling cutter may be guided manually, in which case the operator follows marking-out lines on the block; or it may be guided by a stylus which traverses the profile of a master pattern. After the impression has been milled out some hand finishing may be necessary, and the whole of the die impression is then polished so that the plastic flow of the work-piece will not be impeded unduly during forging.

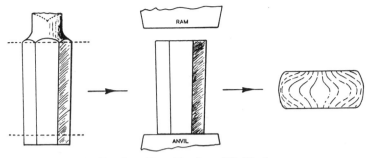

FIG. 8.9—Press Forging a Die Block.

8.512 The walls of the die cavity for drop forging are tapered, usually at an angle of 7°, in order to facilitate the removal of the finished forging from the die, in the same way that a wooden pattern is shaped so that it can be withdrawn from the sand in a sand-moulding process. Sharp corners are avoided as far as possible in die impressions, since such corners lead to stress concentrations and premature cracking of the dies.

To keep within the dimensional tolerances for thickness of parts, the dies are brought together face to face during the finishing stage of forging. It is obvious that to ensure complete filling of all parts of the die during forging a

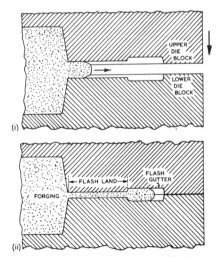

FIG. 8.10—The Formation of Flash.

blank which is heavier than the finished forging must be used. The excess metal is forced out of the die cavity, and would prevent the die from closing properly unless steps were taken to accommodate it. Therefore the die faces around the impression are recessed sufficiently (see Fig. 8.11) to form a *flash gutter* into which the excess metal can flow (Fig. 8.10). The thickness of the *flash land* which connects the flash gutter with the main body of the forging

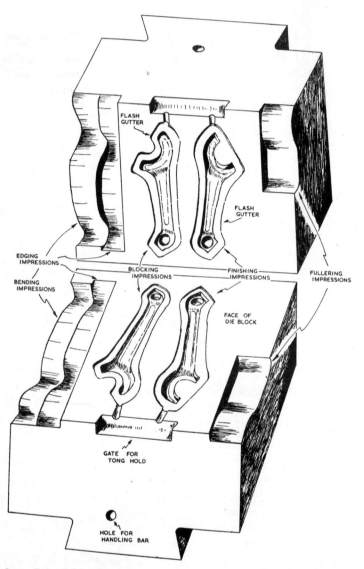

FLASH GUTTER

FLASH GUTTER

EDGING IMPRESSIONS

BENDING IMPRESSIONS

BLOCKING IMPRESSIONS

FINISHING IMPRESSIONS

FULLERING IMPRESSIONS

FACE OF DIE BLOCK

GATE FOR TONG HOLD

HOLE FOR HANDLING BAR

FIG. 8.11—Pair of Die Blocks Used in the Drop Forging of a Connecting-rod for a Well-known Make of Car.

is important. If the flash land is too thin the metal may chill to such an extent that it will not flow into the gutter. The dies may then be damaged due to the extra resistance which must be overcome in closing the dies sufficiently. Too great an allowance, however, might mean that metal flows into the flash gutter so easily that the more intricate parts of the die are not filled properly. An additional function of the flash land is that it serves as a buffer or pad between the die faces and absorbs part of the hammer blow. Direct impact between the relatively cold die faces would give rise to stresses which might cause cracking or fracture of the hardened faces. When forging is complete the flash is sheared off in a mechanical press, which is fitted with a trimming tool and corresponding punch, having an outline similar to that of the forging at the flash plane.

8.513 When the die-sinking operations have been completed it is usual to clamp the die blocks together and pour molten lead or some other low-melting-point metal into the die through the gate provided (Fig. 8.11). The casting thus obtained can then be checked for dimensional accuracy before the die blocks are put into use.

8.514 The dies used for press forging are similar to those used for drop forging. Since the heated work-piece is placed in the lower die with tongs, the gate for the tong hold (Fig. 8.11), which is necessary in a drop forging die, can be omitted here; ejector pins are fitted to the lower die block to push the forging out of the die cavity. In these circumstances the taper on the die walls can be reduced to about $3°$.

As with drop-forging dies, flash is formed, but press forging is quicker than drop forging, since only one pressure application by the ram is necessary at each die cavity instead of the succession of blows usually needed in drop forging. Moreover, highly skilled operators are not needed in press forging, since the forging pressure and die travel are regulated automatically.

8.52 Drop-forging Operations
Fig. 8.11 shows a typical drop-forging die used in the manufacture of a connecting-rod for a popular automobile. In addition to the production of the finished shape, the preliminary operations of fullering, edging, bending and blocking are carried out in this type of die.

8.521 To produce a forging of the connecting-rod in question a section of stock bar (Plate 8.5 (i)) is first heated to the forging temperature. The die itself is also heated to about 200° C in order to reduce thermal shock. Preliminary forging operations are then carried out on the work-piece, using the appropriate sections of the die, the aim being to obtain a work-piece of roughly the correct proportions for the final shaping of the connecting-rod. The fullering operation reduces the cross-section of that portion of the work-piece which will ultimately be between the big-end of the rod and the small-end of the rod. The work-piece is rotated in the die whilst being hammered in order to obtain the section shown (Plate 8.5 (ii)). Edging is then carried out in order to gather the metal in the required bulk for the production of other sections of the rod (Plate 8.5 (iii)), whilst the bending process which follows forms the work-piece asymmetrically to prepare it for the forging of the finished shape (Plate 8.5 (iv)).

8.522 The blocking operation then follows. This forms the work-piece into its first definite shape (Plate 8.5 (v)) and involves hot working the metal by a succession of blows in the appropriate die impression. The metal flows

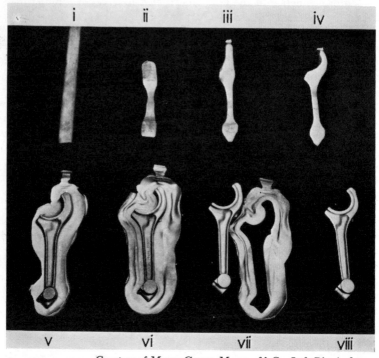

PLATE 8.5—Stages in Drop Forging a Connecting-rod for a Popular Make of Car.

plastically and completely fills the blocking die, excess metal flowing to form flash. All details which might impede this plastic flow are omitted from the blocking die, and corners are also rounded for the same reason.

8.523 The finished shape (Plate 8.5 (vi)) is obtained by several successive blows of the hammer upon the work-piece placed in the final impression in the die blocks. Plastic flow necessary during finishing is much less than during the fullering and blocking processes, and finer details are therefore introduced at this stage. When hammering is finished the forging is surrounded by flash, as shown.

Whilst the forging is still hot the flash is trimmed in a press fitted with a tool and punch which conform to the shape of the connecting-rod. The centres in the big-end and small-end of the rod are sometimes punched out at the same time. The finished forging (Plate 8.5 (vii)) is then returned to the finishing die and re-struck lightly in order to realign it, an operation aptly described as 'tapping'. The connecting-rod (Plate 8.5 (viii)) is then ready for heat-treatment.

8.53 High-energy Rate Forging

The principles of HERF as applied to forging have already been mentioned in this chapter (8.22 and 8.37). Die design as compared with that for orthodox drop forging is modified to some extent. For example, a forging produced by a series of eight operations in the orthodox manner may be made by a single blow in the dynapak process. Moreover it is often possible very significantly to reduce the amount of 'flash' required. Very fine detail is reproducible in the finished forging due to more accurate filling of the die recess. This results from the very high *local* pressures which are transmitted. In general work can be forged to more precise limits, smaller radii, thinner cross-sections and with a superior finish.

High-energy rate forging was developed largely in the U.S.A. for shaping the more exotic materials for space-craft components, but its use has since spread to carbon and alloy steels. Since dynapak machines can generally be worked successfully by less skilled operators, some *users* of forgings have recently installed these machines in their own factories to eliminate the need for buying-in forgings.

8.54 Forging Rolls

A variety of shapes with straight or tapered sections can be forged with the aid of rolls. These rolls are semi-cylindrical and are grooved to conform to the shape of the component being forged. Each roll may carry a number of grooves according to the complexity of the shape being produced.

The rolls rotate continuously and the work-piece is placed in the roll gap when they are in the open position (Fig. 8.12 (i)). As the rolls rotate they grip the work-piece and roll it back (Fig. 8.12 (ii)) towards the operator, who then places it in the appropriate position for the next pass.

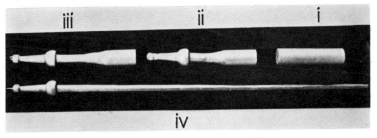

PLATE 8.6—Stages in a Roll Forging Process.

8.541 Forging rolls are used principally to draw out short, thick sections of metal into long, slender sections of non-uniform diameter (Plate 8.6). Components such as knife blades, automobile drive shafts, axles and gear-shift levers are made in this way, but the more general application is the preliminary forging of components which will ultimately be finished by a drop-forging operation.

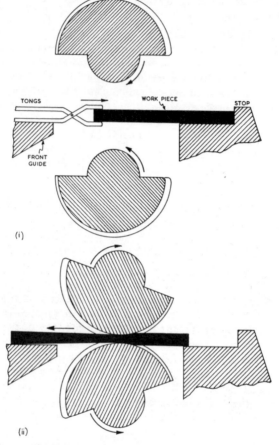

FIG. 8.12—The Action of Forging Rolls.

UPSET FORGING

8.60

This process was originally developed for heading bolts but today its scope has been widened to produce a large variety of components, the mechanical properties of which benefit considerably from the forged structure obtained (6.34—Part I).

The type of forging machine employed is essentially a double-acting press, but its dies move in a horizontal instead of a vertical plane. Moreover, the forgings are produced whilst still attached to the ends of the stock bars. The fixed half of the die, which corresponds to the anvil in a forging hammer, consists of a pair of gripping jaws which have semicircular grooves machined in their meeting surfaces. These grooves are so dimensioned that when the two halves of the fixed die close they grip the stock bar firmly.

The length of bar to be headed is first heated at the end and then inserted between the jaws of the fixed die until it meets a 'stop'. This stop is so placed that the required amount of metal to produce the head protrudes beyond the jaws of the fixed die. The machine is now set in motion, usually by depressing a foot pedal. The gripping die closes, and immediately the moving die strikes the heated end of the rod, so forging it to shape. The moving die is shaped to produce a head of the required dimensions. After heading has taken place the machine continues its cycle and the moving die retracts as the gripping die opens.

8.61

For complex upset forgings a sequence of different dies may be necessary, the bar being placed in each die in turn until the forging process is complete

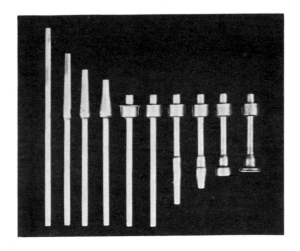

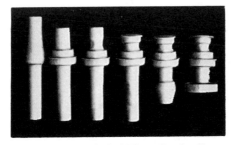

PLATE 8.7—Stages in Typical Upset Forging Processes.

(Plate 8.7). Similarly, if the production of a large head is contemplated this may have to be carried out in several stages to avoid buckling the bar which would result from attempts to upset a length which was too great relative to its diameter.

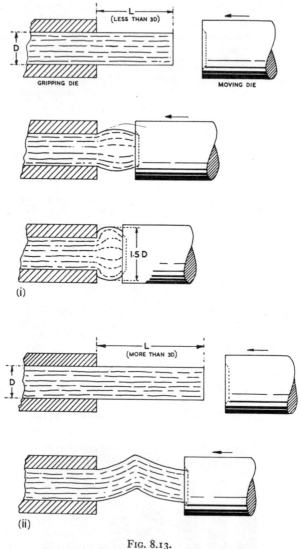

FIG. 8.13.

8.62

In the design of dies for upset forging three rules, formulated originally by E. R. Frost, are followed:

(1) The length, L, of unsupported metal which can be upset at one stroke without risk of serious buckling must not be more than three times the diameter, D, of the bar (Fig. 8.13). In practice, L is usually kept below $2 \cdot 5D$.

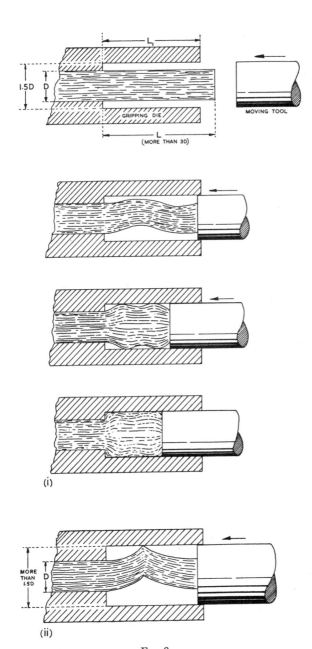

FIG. 8.14.

(2) Where the length, L, of unsupported metal is not greater than three times the diameter, D, of the bar, the maximum increase in cross-section obtainable at a single stroke is $1\frac{1}{2}$ times the diameter of the bar. Again, in practice a lower figure of $1 \cdot 4D$ is generally used.

(3) A length of metal more than three times the diameter of the bar can be upset in one stroke provided that a die of the type shown in Fig. 8.14 (i) is used. Here the diameter of the die impression must not exceed $1 \cdot 5D$ and the length of bar $(L - L_1)$ projecting beyond the die face must be less than the diameter of the bar, D.

$$\text{In practice, } L_1 > L - \frac{D}{2}.$$

Working stock longer than three diameters can also be supported against serious bending by a heading-tool recess as indicated in Fig. 8.15. Since this die does not open (as does the gripping die), the recess must be tapered as shown so that the upset portion can be withdrawn at the end of the stroke.

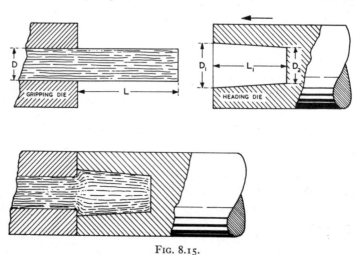

FIG. 8.15.

The diameter must not exceed $1\frac{1}{2}D$ at the mouth (D_1) of the recess and $1\frac{1}{8}D$ at the bottom (D_2), and the length of the recess must be at least $\frac{2}{3}$ the length of the working stock. In practice, the following working recommendations are generally followed:

$$D_1 \leqq 1 \cdot 4D$$
$$L_1 \leqq \frac{2L}{3}$$
$$D_2 = 1 \cdot 1D$$
$$L_1 \geqq L - 2 \cdot 5D.$$

Upset forgings from $0 \cdot 025$ kg to as much as 250 kg in mass can be produced. As suggested earlier in this chapter, it is advantageous to produce many components, such as gears, by this process, since the radially distributed fibres often give maximum strength in the direction in which it is required.

8.63 Cold Heading

Cold heading is a process used mainly in the manufacture of nails and small bolts from wire. It is essentially an up-setting operation carried out on a cold material, and consequently the extent to which the material may be headed is restricted by its capacity for cold work. Accordingly, nails are generally produced from dead-mild steel.

The machine used for nail-making consists essentially of a cold-heading tool similar in principle to an upsetting die, a cutting tool to produce the nail point and a mechanism to feed the wire automatically into the heading die. Wire is fed into the gripping die so that just sufficient protrudes to form the head of the nail. The heading tool then strikes this protruding end to form the nail head, and immediately the gripping die opens so that the wire is fed forward by an amount appropriate to the required length of the nail. The gripping die closes again and a pair of cutter jaws close on the wire, cutting it and at the same time forming the nail point. Immediately the finished nail falls away the heading tool strikes the protruding end of the wire to form the next nail head. The cycle repeats rapidly to give a constant flow of nails from the machine.

METALS AND ALLOYS SUITABLE FOR FORGING

8.70

Whilst the range of metals and alloys which can be forged successfully is very large, the ease with which hot forging can be carried out does vary considerably from one alloy to another. Thus, whilst a given shape might be obtained by a single hammer blow in a piece of mild steel, to produce the same shape from a similar piece of 'Nimonic' alloy (18.32—Part I) might require many hammer blows and intermediate reheating operations. This is, of course, an extreme case, since 'Nimonic' alloys are difficult to forge by virtue of the very properties which make them useful, namely their retention of mechanical strength at high temperatures.

In closed-die forging the life of the die is related to the type of alloy being forged. Generally speaking, high-carbon steels, and those with additions of chromium, vanadium and tungsten, will reduce the life of a die because of the abrasive action which hard carbides have on the die surfaces.

8.71

In addition to plain carbon steels, large quantities of low-alloy steels of the nickel–chromium and nickel–chromium–molybdenum types are shaped by closed-die forging processes for the production of highly stressed parts such as axle-shafts and other automobile parts. Stainless steels also forge quite successfully, though wear on the dies is high.

8.72

Many non-ferrous alloys are also suitable for shaping by forging. In particular, wrought aluminium alloys of the heat-treatable type (Table 17.3—Part I) find

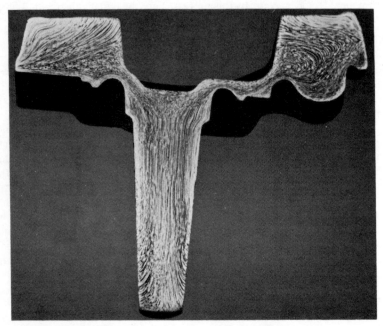

PLATE 8.8—Macro-section of a Forging Showing the Flow Lines.

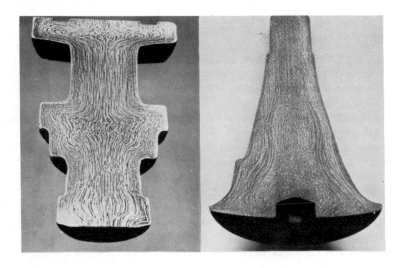

PLATE 8.9.
(i) A Macro-section of the Upset Forging shown in Plate 8.7 (ii).
(ii) Macro-section showing the Flow Lines in a Large Railway Buffer.

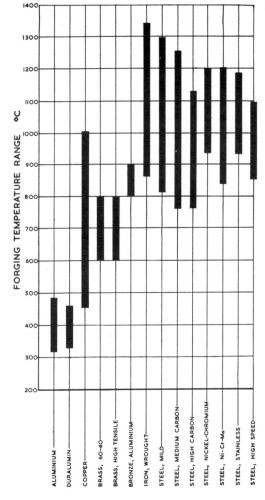

FIG. 8.16—Forging Temperature Ranges of Common Forging Alloys.

wide application in the aircraft industries for many components associated with engine construction. Since the strength–weight ratio is so important in aircraft construction, forgings in magnesium-base alloys are also used (Table 18.2—Part I).

Of the copper-base alloys, the best-known forging alloys are in the 60–40 range of brasses, though 95–5 aluminium bronze, cupro-nickel and pure copper can all be forged successfully.

FORGING DEFECTS

8.80

Defects which occur in a forging may be due to faults in the structure or composition of the alloy from which it was made, or they may arise during the heating process before the work-piece is taken to the forging hammer. Alternatively, defects may be produced due to poor forging technique or to the use of badly designed die equipment.

8.81

Faults in the structure of the stock material include surface defects in bars, such as seams which have been introduced during the original rolling process, heavily segregated or piped areas (Fig. 4.14—Part I) and inclusions of various types. Such faults and also variations from specification in respect of composition can be checked by adequate inspection of the incoming stock.

8.82

Overheating or soaking the metal for too long at a high temperature, prior to forging, may lead to excessive oxidation of the surface. This may manifest itself in the form of pieces of scale which are driven into the surface of the work-piece during forging operations. Subsequent cleaning processes may remove the pieces of scale from the surface, leaving shallow surface depressions in the forging.

8.83

The more serious defects which may arise during the actual forging operations are:

(1) The formation of cold shuts. These are usually caused by poor die design or sometimes by the incorrect positioning of the work-piece in the die cavity. The effects of one aspect of bad die design are shown in Fig. 8.17. The sharp corner at X causes the metal to flow across the die rather than follow its contours, and as the die closes a fold is produced in the metal, giving rise to a cold shut as indicated.

(2) Coarse grain, which may be present in the final forging due to the finishing temperatures being too high. This will be less important in the case of steel if a normalising treatment is to follow forging.

(3) A poor impression. This may be caused by the metal not filling the die cavity correctly, and may be due to the work-piece being of inadequate size or being forged at too low a temperature. Alternatively, the die design may be poor, so that the metal has been unable to flow sufficiently.

(4) Breaking of the fibre flow. This will be revealed when a macro section of a forging is examined. Broken fibre results in poor mechanical properties, and is caused by the metal flowing too rapidly at right angles to the original direction of the fibres during forging.

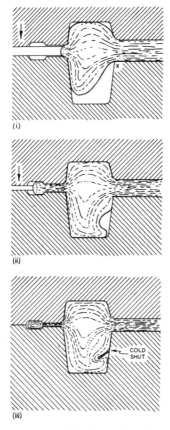

FIG. 8.17—The Formation of a
Cold Shut.

(5) Mismatched forgings, which are produced when the upper and lower die blocks are out of alignment during the hammering process.

(6) Flash-line cracks sometimes develop if the reduction in thickness during forging is excessive. Flash cracks in steel forgings (Fig. 8.18) may develop after forging or even after subsequent heat-treatment. The flash of a forging which undergoes considerable reduction in thickness during the process develops, as a result, a fibre structure which is weak in the normal direction. Any undue strain in this direction may therefore cause fracture. If a forging tends to develop flash cracks these may be prevented by

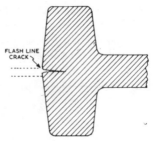

FIG. 8.18—The Formation of a
Flash-line Crack.

reducing the amount of metal in the forging or limiting the reduction which takes place in the flash itself.

BIBLIOGRAPHY

1 'Drop, Press and Machine Forging', J. C. Sharman (The Machinery Publishing Co.).
2 'The Closed Die Forging Process', P. E. Kyle (The Macmillan Co., N.Y.).
3 'Forging and Forming Metals', S. E. Rusinoff (American Technical Soc.).
4 'Forging Handbook', W. Naujoks and D. C. Fabel (American Soc. for Metals).
5 'Ferrous Metallurgy' (Vol II—'The Manufacture and Fabrication of Steel'), E. J. Teichert (McGraw-Hill).
6 'The Hot Working of Non-ferrous Metals and Alloys', Symposium (Institute of Metals).
7 'The Making, Shaping and Treating of Steel', J. M. Camp and C. B. Francis (Carnegie-Illinois Steel Corp.).
8 'Fundamentals of the Working of Metals', G. Sachs (Pergamon Press).
9 'Cold Forging of Steel', H. D. Feldmann (Hutchinson).
10 'Aluminium', Vol. III—Fabrication and Finishing, Ed. K. R. van Horn (American Society for Metals).
11 'Principles of Magnesium Technology', E. F. Emley (Pergamon Press).
12 BS 224: 1938—Steel for die blocks for drop forging.
13 BS 944: 1941—Cast leaded brass bars (suitable for forgings) and forgings.
14 BS 1001: 1960—High-tensile brass forging stock and forgings.
15 BS 2094: Glossary of terms relating to iron and steel. Part 6: 1954—Forgings and drop forgings.
16 BS 2872: 1968—Schedule of copper and copper alloys—forging stock and forgings.
17 BS 3372: 1970—Wrought-magnesium alloys for general engineering purposes—forgings.
18 BS 4124: Non-destructive testing of steel forgings. Part 1: 1967—Ultrasonic flaw detection.
19 BS 4670: 1971—Alloy steel forgings.

Chapter nine
EXTRUSION

9.10

The term 'extrusion' is used in the metallurgical sense to describe several processes which include both the impact method of producing tooth-paste and similar tubes and the manufacture of solid and tubular stock in relatively complex sections. These latter products are made by heating a cast billet to a suitable temperature, placing it in a container and then forcing it through a die by the application of pressure from a hydraulically driven ram to produce

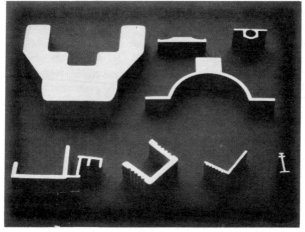

PLATE 9.1—Some Extruded Sections.
The upper four are in 60/40 type brass and the lower four in aluminium alloys.

a bar or tube of the required cross-sectional dimensions. Since the final wrought shape can be obtained in a single process from the cast billet, it is obvious that extrusion is a very attractive proposition, provided that the required output of material is large enough to justify the rather big financial outlay on plant.

Nevertheless, almost a hundred years elapsed between the earliest perception of the fundamentals of extrusion and its establishment as a process for the shaping of metals and alloys other than lead. In 1797 the well-known hydraulic engineer Joseph Bramah was granted patents in respect of a press for the manufacture of lead pipe, which, it is suspected, was to be used for the transfer of beer. However, lead pipe continued to be made by the older process of rolling a hollow cylindrical billet on to a mandrel (16.40) until in 1820 Thomas Burr, a Shrewsbury plumber, constructed a hydraulically operated extrusion press for the production of lead piping. In the early presses lead was poured into the container of the machine, but in 1863 Shaw designed a press in which solid cylindrical shells of lead were forced through a suitable die.

9.11

The development of the electrical industries in the latter half of the nineteenth century engendered a demand for a covering for cables which would protect them from the effects of moisture. Lead was recognised as being the most useful material for the purpose at that time, both on account of its corrosion resistance and its pliability. At first strip lead was wound spirally around the cable and then soldered along the seam. This method was replaced by the use of 15m lengths of lead pipe into which the cable was threaded, the lengths of pipe then being soldered end to end. In 1879, however, Wesslau in Germany and Borel in France were the first to devise methods by which a lead covering could be extruded directly on to cables.

9.12

The experience gained in the extrusion of lead encouraged other workers to investigate the possibilities of extruding harder metals, and in particular the alloys of copper. The main difficulties encountered were not only those associated with the provision of much greater pressures but also with the design of dies which would withstand these pressures. In 1894 Alexander Dick, German-born of British parentage, obtained his first patents for a press for the extrusion of brasses of the 60–40 type, and within a short time his Delta Metal Company was producing extruded brass at the factories in Birmingham, London and Dusseldorf. The extrusion process has since been developed to deal with a considerable range of alloys, and in recent years the shaping of steel by this method has been carried out successfully on an industrial scale.

EXTRUSION BY THE 'DIRECT' METHOD

9.20

Extrusion is accomplished by either the 'direct' or 'indirect' process (Fig. 9.1). In the former a heated billet of the metal (M) is placed in the container (C) of

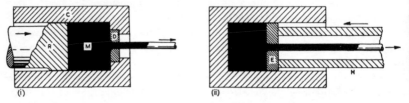

FIG. 9.1—The Principles of (i) Direct and (ii) Indirect Methods of Extrusion.

the press and then forced through the die (D) by the ram (R), which advances into the container. In the indirect process, however, the die (E) is carried by the hollow ram (H), which causes extrusion to take place in a direction opposite to that of the movement of the ram. It is generally more satisfactory in practice when using the indirect process to employ a fixed ram and move the container and billet. The principle remains the same, however, in that no relative motion between the billet and the container occurs.

9.21

Since there is no relative movement between the billet and the container in the indirect process, less mechanical energy is used in overcoming frictional forces between the two. Nevertheless, this does not mean that the indirect process has been universally adopted, and for a number of technical reasons the direct method is still the more widely used.

9.22

Extrusion presses may be mounted so that they extrude the metal either vertically or horizontally, though the latter method is the more general. For the extrusion of copper-alloy billets of about 0·15 m diameter a press employing a ram force of between 10 MN and 15 MN is commonly used; but for the

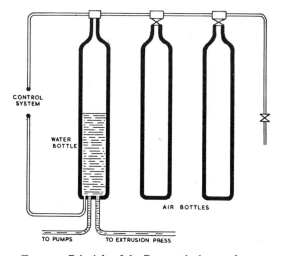

FIG. 9.2—Principle of the Pneumatic Accumulator.

extrusion of aluminium alloys presses of up to 120 MN capacity capable of receiving billets up to 0·75 m diameter are in use; the reason being the difficulty of extrusion of aluminium alloys coupled with the demand for a great diversity in cross-sectional dimensions in products in these alloys.

The ram pressure is obtained from a hydraulic system operated by motor-driven pumps. Since the power necessary to effect extrusion varies from alloy to alloy, and is in any case generally in excess of the capacity of the pumps, it is usual to employ some form of high-pressure accumulator. Both dead-weight and pneumatic accumulators are in use. The former consists essentially of a vertical steel cylinder containing water which is loaded by a piston carrying on its head-plate cast-iron discs or scrap to a total mass of several hundred tonnes. As pressure water is used, the piston falls and is raised again by the delivery of water from the pumps. Of recent years the dead-weight accumulator has lost ground in favour of the pneumatic system, which consists essentially of a forged-steel water bottle into which water is delivered by the pumps, and from which it can be withdrawn as required by the extrusion press (Fig. 9.2). To provide the necessary storage of energy the water bottle is connected to a series of air bottles containing compressed air which applies the necessary force to the water.

9.23

The elements of design of a typical horizontal press for the extrusion of solid sections by the direct process are shown in Fig. 9.3. The arrangement consists essentially of the container (C), which is a massive steel shell fitted with an

Courtesy of Messrs I.C.I. Metals Division.

PLATE 9.2—25-MN Press for the Extrusion of Copper and Copper-alloy Rods and Sections.

alloy steel liner (L); the extrusion ram (R), which exerts pressure on a disc or 'pad' (P) usually about 6 mm smaller in diameter than the bore of the container; and the die assembly (E, B, H and D), which is kept in close contact with the container during extrusion by the wedge (W). The die assembly usually consists of the die (D) retained in a die-holder (H), which in turn is supported by the bolster (B) fitted in the die-head (E). Accurate fitting between the die-holder and the container is assured by the use of a

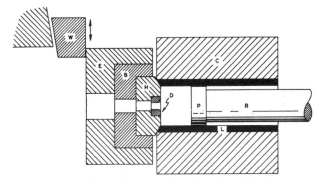

FIG. 9.3—Typical Construction of an Extrusion Press.

conical seating as shown. The parts which come into contact with the hot metal during extrusion, viz. the pad (P), the liner (L) and the die (D), must be able to withstand severe conditions of high temperature, stress and abrasion, and are usually made from a suitably heat-treated 10%-tungsten-type steel (Table 13.8—Part I).

9.24
The cycle of operations of a press such as that described above is illustrated in Fig. 9.4. A hot billet (B) is fed to the cradle (T), from whence it is pushed into

Courtesy of Messrs Northern Aluminium Co. Ltd, Banbury.

PLATE 9.3—75-MN Press for the Extrusion of Aluminium Alloys.
The operator is checking the temperature of a billet prior to its transfer to the container.

the container by the advancing ram, the pad (P) first being interposed between the billet and the ram (Fig. 9.4 (i)). As the billet is brought into contact with the die it is first upset and then extruded under full pressure from the accumulator (Fig. 9.4 (ii)). As will be seen in Fig. 9.4 (iii), the billet is never completely extruded. Instead a small piece (X), known as the 'discard', is allowed to remain in the container, the ram being halted at a predetermined point by the stop (S).* The wedge (W) and the stop (S) are then raised so that the ram pushes the discard and die assembly clear of the container. A hydraulic reciprocating gear attached to the die-head then draws it away from the main body of the press and into a position where the discard (with the pad partly embedded in it) can be cut off by means of mechanical shears, a circular saw (Fig. 9.4 (iv)) or even a hand-driven chisel. The end of the extruded bar is then dislodged from the die by moving the die-head back against a small ejector mandrel which has been swung into position. It is common practice to use a pad which is about 6 mm smaller in diameter than the bore of the container. In this way much of the surface scale present on the original billet is retained as a sleeve (known as a 'skull' or 'canister') in the container. This canister may withdraw along with the discard, or it may stick in the container, in which case it is pushed out by using a fairly tight-fitting disc in conjunction with the ram. The die assembly is then moved back into contact with the container ready to receive the next billet for extrusion.

9.25
It is important to consider the manner in which the plastic metal 'flows' in the container during the extrusion stroke. Different alloys behave in different ways, but in all cases the temperature gradient which exists between the core of the billet and its outside skin affects the result similarly. Let us assume that a billet has been heated to a temperature higher than that normally required for the successful extrusion of the alloy. When it is placed in the container its outside skin becomes chilled relative to its core, due to contact with the walls of the container. The core of the billet is therefore more easily extruded than the outside skin, which has become relatively hard and which, therefore, tends to remain in the container (Fig. 9.5 (i)). As extrusion proceeds, the outside skin begins to buckle or 'concertina' (Fig. 9.5.(ii)), and is ultimately drawn into the stream of extruded metal (Fig. 9.5 (iii) and (vi)), so that the resultant rod is badly 'piped' over a considerable portion of its rear length.

9.26
It has already been suggested that one factor which influences the production of this defect, commonly known as the 'extrusion defect' or 'back-end defect', is that of temperature control, and it is important to avoid the use of too high an extrusion temperature. Nevertheless, although the control of temperature will reduce the proportion of metal which suffers from the extrusion defect,

---

* Although it would be difficult to extrude this final piece of the billet by reason of the extremely high pressure required, there are other reasons, which will be dealt with later in this chapter, why it is desirable to discard a portion of the billet.

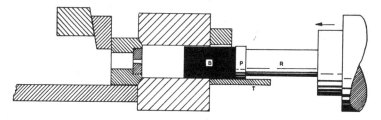

(i) – BILLET (B) IS FED FROM CRADLE (T) INTO CONTAINER

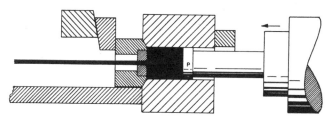

(ii) – THE EXTRUSION STROKE IN PROGRESS

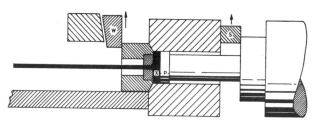

(iii) – THE END OF THE STROKE.

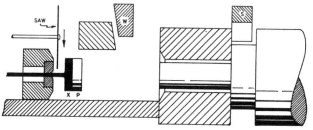

(iv) – CUTTING OFF THE DISCARD (X).

FIG. 9.4—Extrusion Cycle Using a Horizontal Press.

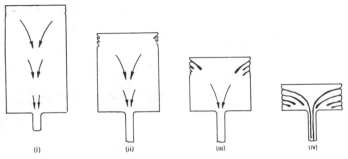

FIG. 9.5—Formation of the Extrusion Defect.

it will not eliminate this defect entirely, and other methods must also be adopted to reduce the incidence of waste.

9.27
It was mentioned earlier in this chapter that extrusion is usually stopped whilst a portion of the original billet remains in the container. This discard contains the bulk of the rumpled skin of the billet, and it is general practice to reject a discard amounting to 10 or 15% of the weight of the original billet. This figure varies, however, with the type of alloy being extruded. As a further means of reducing the amount of skin which enters the extrusion stream, an extrusion pad which is somewhat smaller in diameter than the bore of the container is employed. Thus a 'skull' of material, consisting mainly of the outer chilled and oxidised skin of the billet, remains in the container and does not therefore enter the extrusion stream (Fig. 9.6).

9.28
Among the well-established methods of extrusion, possibly the most effective way of reducing the extent of the extrusion defect, however, lies in the use of the indirect or 'inverted' process. Here there is no relative movement between the billet and the container, and hence less tendency for the outer skin to be drawn into the extrusion stream by turbulence in the metal which has not yet

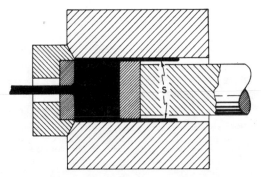

FIG. 9.6—Formation of a 'Skull' (*S*) During Extrusion.

been extruded. The development of hydrostatic extrusion (9.40) may lead to the virtual elimination of the extrusion defect.

EXTRUSION BY THE INDIRECT OR INVERTED METHOD

9.30

Many extrusion presses are of the 'universal' type, that is they can be adapted for operation by either the direct or indirect methods. The elements of design of such a press are indicated in Fig. 9.7.

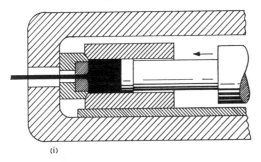

(i)

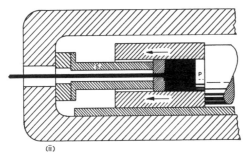

(ii)

FIG. 9.7.
(i) Press Set up for Extrusion by the Direct Process.
(ii) Press Adapted for Extrusion by the Indirect Process.

9.31

The upper sketch shows the press set up for extrusion by the direct process. Here the die and container are fixed, and the moving ram extrudes the billet through the die in the manner already dealt with in this chapter (Fig. 9.4). Fig. 9.7 (ii) shows the press adapted for extrusion by the indirect process. In this case the die-holder is replaced by a die-stand (S) and the extrusion ram is replaced by a closure plate (P) attached to the main ram cross-head. A billet is placed in the container, which is pushed along by the ram cross-head so that the billet is extruded through the die. The billet and container move along together, and there is no relative movement between the two.

9.32

The absence of movement between the billet and the container results in less turbulence in that part of the billet not yet extruded (Fig. 9.8) as compared

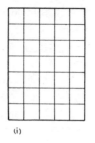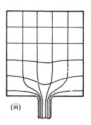

FIG. 9.8.
(i)   Billet before Extrusion.
(ii) Billet during Extrusion by the Direct Process.
(iii) Billet during Extrusion by the Indirect Process.

with that which prevails in the direct process. It is generally considered that this factor leads to a reduction in the incidence of the extrusion defect.

9.33

It was mentioned earlier in this chapter that less energy is required to effect extrusion by the indirect process than by the direct process. In the latter the total pressure necessary is that required to bring about deformation at the die together with the pressure required to cause deformation in the residual length of the billet and also overcome friction between the outer skin of the billet and the walls of the container. Consequently, as the length of the billet decreases, the total pressure required to cause extrusion also diminishes

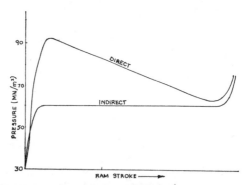

FIG. 9.9—The Variation in Pressure during the Extrusion of an Aluminium Alloy by both the Direct and Indirect Methods.

(Fig. 9.9). With the indirect process, once a zone of deformation has been created and extrusion has commenced, the pressure remains virtually constant during the stroke of the ram. This pressure is smaller than that required in the direct process, because there is no relative movement—and hence no frictional forces to oppose motion—between the billet and the container, and no internal movement of the metal except at the die face. In both cases the extrusion pressure increases as the length of billet approaches zero at the end of the stroke.

HYDROSTATIC EXTRUSION

9.40
The extrusion defect can be eliminated and the billet extruded completely, that is, without the formation of a discard, in a method developed in recent years at the National Engineering Laboratory. In this process, termed 'hydrostatic extrusion', the billet is surrounded by a liquid on all sides except at its front end which is pointed and which bears against a cone-shaped die

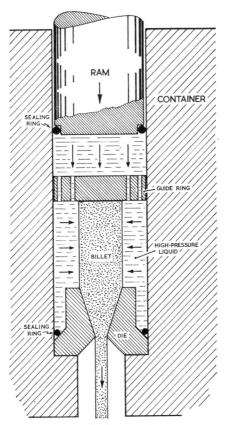

FIG. 9.10—Hydrostatic Extrusion.

(Fig. 9.10). The liquid transmits pressure applied to the ram. This pressure not only forces the billet forward into the die but also compresses the billet circumferentially. Since there is no friction between billet and container much lower working loads are required than in normal direct extrusion processes and it is this absence of friction which is responsible for eliminating the extrusion defect. Moreover, since friction is absent, *cold* extrusion of mild steel can be accomplished without the need for a phosphate coating which is necessary when cold forging a similar material.

Various liquids have been tried but possibly the most successful is mineral oil to which 10% of the well-known high-pressure lubricant, molybdenum disulphide, has been added. Although at present most work has been carried out on cold materials, it seems likely that hydrostatic extrusion may be developed for use at elevated temperatures.

9.41

A very significant advantage of the process is that many materials of limited ductility, which could not be extruded successfully by conventional methods, can be extruded by the hydrostatic process. Frictional forces between die and billet often cause cracking to occur before extrusion can begin, due to secondary tensile stresses which they set up. In hydrostatic extrusion the use of small-angle dies and the absence of contact between billet and container lead to a decrease in redundant work and friction and so make possible the cold extrusion of difficult materials such as high-speed steel. Some materials, even less ductile, may still crack as they emerge from the die if hydrostatic extrusion is employed as outlined above. They can, however, be dealt with successfully if the extrusion is allowed to emerge into a chamber containing a suitably pressurised liquid. This balances to some extent the secondary tensile forces present in the die region and prevents cracking of the section as it emerges from the die. This device makes use of the fact that, for many materials, malleability under compression is greater than ductility in tension (3.20—Part I). Cast iron may be successfully cold-extruded in this way, in addition to zirconium, beryllium, tool steels, titanium alloys, nickel alloys and even some brittle intermetallic compounds.

THE EXTRUSION OF TUBES

9.50

Prior to the introduction of the extrusion process, tubes in many non-ferrous alloys were produced by the relatively expensive method of cold drawing them from a hollow-cast shell. The manufacture of tubes now constitutes an important branch of extrusion, and of recent years the production of steel tubes by this process has become a commercial undertaking.

In order to extrude a tube it is necessary that some form of mandrel should be passed axially through the billet so that its tip lies in the aperture of the die thus forming an annular gap through which the metal is extruded. Fig. 9.11 (i) shows how this can be achieved using a hollow-cast or bored billet. Here the mandrel is fixed to the end of the ram and passes through a hole in the pressure pad. When the extrusion stroke begins the tip of the mandrel moves into the mouth of the die just before pressure is exerted on the billet. An alternative method of fitting the mandrel is shown in Fig. 9.11 (ii). In this instance the mandrel is floating and, generally, better concentricity of the resultant tube is obtained by this method. Provided that the billet has been accurately bored and is uniform in its plasticity, the mandrel will centre itself with accuracy if

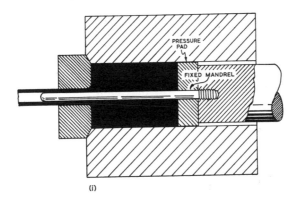

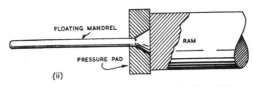

FIG. 9.11—The Extrusion of Tubes from Hollow Billets.

Courtesy of Messrs High Duty Alloys Ltd, Slough, Bucks.

PLATE 9.4—Extruded Light-alloy Tube Emerging from the Container of a 50 MN Press.

it is allowed to float in this manner. Conversely, attempts to fix the mandrel centrally usually fail, particularly if the pressure varies from point to point in the container.

9.51
The production of hollow billets, whether by casting or by boring, is relatively expensive. Moreover, during preheating for extrusion the internal bore becomes oxidised, and this may lead to the formation of inaccessible and

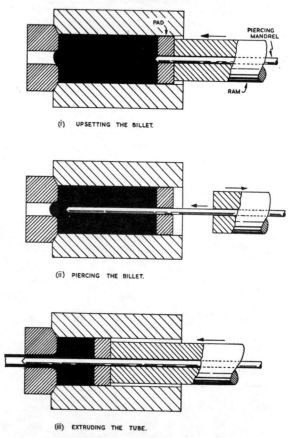

(i) UPSETTING THE BILLET.

(ii) PIERCING THE BILLET.

(iii) EXTRUDING THE TUBE.

FIG. 9.12—The Extrusion of Tubes from Solid Billets.

invisible defects on the inside surface of the finished tube. Many alloys therefore are cast as solid billets, which are then preheated, followed by piercing and extrusion as a single operation (Fig. 9.12).

The diameter of the billet is somewhat smaller than the bore of the container. Consequently, when the billet is charged to the container it will lie on the bottom of the container, and attempts to pierce a concentric hole would fail, so in order to ensure concentricity of the extruded tube the billet is first upset so that it fills the bore of the container. The mandrel is therefore made to move independently of the ram, so that the latter can first be used to upset the billet (Fig. 9.12 (i)). The ram is then withdrawn and the mandrel driven forward, so that it pierces the billet and advances into the mouth of the die (Fig. 9.12 (ii)). Pressure is then applied by the ram so that extrusion of the tube is affected (Fig. 9.12 (iii)).

The foregoing diagrams illustrate the extrusion of tubes by the direct process in horizontal presses. Vertical presses working on the indirect principle are also used, and are particularly useful for the extrusion of high-quality tubes of small thickness and outside diameter in brasses and other copper-base alloys. By using an accurately bored billet in conjunction with a floating mandrel, tube of the highest concentricity can be produced in the vertical press.

9.52
The necessity of maintaining uniform wall thickness makes it difficult to extrude long lengths of small-diameter or thin-walled tubing in aluminium alloys. The high local stresses encountered cause deflection of the long, unsupported mandrel and produce eccentricity in the tube. It is therefore customary either to extrude thick-walled tube stock in short lengths which are subsequently cold drawn or to use a die of the 'porthole' type.

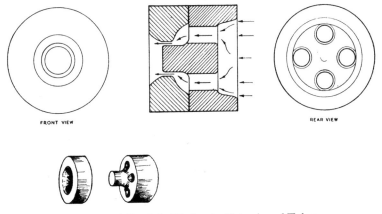

FRONT VIEW   REAR VIEW

FIG. 9.13—A Porthole Die for the Extrusion of Tubes.

The 'porthole' die (Fig. 9.13) employs a short stub mandrel which can be accurately centred and profiled to produce the necessary interior shape in the resultant hollow section. As indicated in Fig. 9.13 the die first causes the metal to divide into several streams—in this case four—which then pass into a mixing chamber, where they become pressure-welded together before being extruded over the short stub mandrel as a tubular section.

The use of this process is naturally restricted to those alloys of aluminium which can be pressure-welded successfully. Hollow sections of complex profile, such as architectural members and heat-exchanger tubes (finned both externally and internally) in pure aluminium and fairly soft aluminium–magnesium–silicon alloys, can be manufactured by this process. By extruding a sufficiently large billet a small-diameter tube nearly four hundred metres long can be produced in a single operation

ALLOYS SUITABLE FOR EXTRUSION

9.60

The suitability of a metal or alloy for extrusion depends upon three main factors:

(1) the temperature range over which extrusion is possible;
(2) the stiffness of the metal or alloy at the extrusion temperature;
(3) the abrasive action of the metal or alloy on the die and other press tools.

The range of temperature at which a metal can be extruded lies between, at the lower limit, that temperature where the metal becomes too stiff for extrusion or, alternatively, begins to work harden and, at the upper limit, that temperature at which it becomes hot short and cracks as it leaves the die. For metals which have a small extrusion temperature range, and particularly if that is at a high temperature, it is important to be able to work rapidly and so to offset the effects of chilling. The capacity of the press must accordingly be adequate. Rapidity of working at high temperatures is also important in so far as the life of the dies and press tools is concerned, in order to prevent excessive exposure of the tools to conditions of high temperature and pressure. As the temperature of the tools rises above 600–700° C the hardness of the steels from which they are made falls considerably, and the tools undergo serious abrasion.

9.61

The stiffness of the alloy at the extrusion temperature will obviously determine the capacity of the press in terms of pressure required. Whilst pressures of more than 1 150 N/mm² exerted by the ram are unusual, pressures of up to 1 600 N/mm² are sometimes used for the harder metals and alloys.

9.62

Amongst the first of the harder alloys to be extruded were the brasses. In fact, leaded brasses containing 55–60% copper are still loosely described in the Birmingham area as 'Delta metals', by virtue of their having been first extruded on a commercial scale by the Delta Metal Company of Alexander Dick. Such brasses still constitute the most adaptable group of alloys available for extrusion in a great variety of shapes from tubing to curtain rail. Whilst the extrusion of α brasses of the 70–30 type presents some difficulty on account of their rather narrow extrusion temperature range, those brasses of α + β compositions containing between 55 and 65% copper are excellent extrusion alloys because of their reversion to an all-β structure at the extrusion temperature (16.31—Part I). Large quantities of free-cutting brass containing 56–60% copper and 2·5–3·5% lead are extruded in the form of round- and hexagonal-section rod, whilst hot-stamping brass containing rather less lead is also an important product. High-tensile brasses (16.37—Part I), too, are generally shaped by extrusion.

Whilst pure copper is considerably stiffer than the brasses mentioned, it can be extruded over a wide range of temperatures, and is therefore a very suitable material for shaping by this process. Amongst other copper-base alloys which can be extruded are aluminium bronze, tin bronze, phosphor-

Courtesy of Messrs The Loewy Engineering Co. Ltd, Bournemouth.

PLATE 9.5—A 14–30 MN Press for the Extrusion of Tubes and Sections in Stainless Steel, Nickel Alloys and Brass.
This press was recently installed in a German factory by a British firm.

bronze, nickel silvers and cupro-nickel. (In addition to cupro-nickel many of the nickel-base alloys can also be shaped by extrusion.)

9.63

It is difficult to specify an extrusion temperature for any particular alloy, since this varies with such factors as the speed of extrusion and the complexity of the section produced. For copper alloys extrusion temperatures vary from 650° C for the $\alpha + \beta$ brasses to as high as 1050° C for 70–30 cupro-nickel.

9.64

The production of aluminium-base and magnesium-base alloy extrusions was stimulated by war-time demands. In order to provide long lengths in the bulky sections often required in aircraft spars and similar sections, it was necessary to install very heavy presses. It was therefore common to encounter presses with total capacities of 50 MN force and extruding billets of up to o·5 m diameter and 1·25m long, whereas in the brass trade presses of 10 MN capacity extruding billets of 0·15 m diameter are general.

The commercial grades of aluminium and some of the softer aluminium–manganese, aluminium–silicon and aluminium–silicon–magnesium alloys extrude readily at temperatures between 450 and 500° C, but many of the high-strength alloys, such as duralumin, present difficulty, and the extrusion conditions must accordingly be strictly controlled.

Courtesy of Messrs The Loewy Engineering Co. Ltd,
Bournemouth.

PLATE 9.6—Tube Manufacture in the Extrusion Press Shown in Plate 9.5.
The heated billet, together with a pad is about to be pushed into the container. Note the mandrel projecting from the end of the ram. A swinging circular saw (top left) is used for cutting off the finished extrusion.

9.65

Whilst in connection with the shaping of steels several press-forging operations are loosely referred to as extrusion, the present meaning of the term will be confined to the type of operation dealt with in the foregoing pages of this chapter. The shaping of steel by extrusion methods of this type did not begin industrially until 1937, when the process was used for the manufacture of seamless tubes. Since extrusion temperatures in the region of 1 100–1 250° C are necessary, it follows that wear on tools and dies is very high. Consequently, the process was mainly of interest in the manufacture of tubes in the more expensive austenitic stainless steels, particularly since the smaller amount of oxide produced when alloy steel billets are heated minimises wear on the dies. However, large quantities of tubes have been produced in carbon and low-alloy steels.

Presses are similar in general design to those used in the extrusion of non-ferrous metals and alloys. One modification adopted was the use of conical

Courtesy of Messrs The Loewy Engineering Co. Ltd, Bournemouth.

PLATE 9.7—The Delivery End of the Extrusion Press Shown in Plate 9.5. Note the quenching tank for cooling the finished sections. The bin (bottom left) contains 'discards' from tube extrusion.

dies in order to reduce friction, and consequently abrasion, on the die faces. Attention was also paid to the lubrication of the die, mandrel and container in order to reduce the tendency of hot steel to seize on to these parts.

Possibly the most important advance in the extrusion of steel was made possible by the use of glass as a lubricant during extrusion. Before being extruded the heated billet is rolled in a glass-fibre mat, whilst a glass-fibre pad is also placed against the face of the die. Similarly, in the extrusion of steel tubes from bored billets a glass-fibre sock is placed over the mandrel. The hot billet is thus completely isolated from the press tools by the glass, which flows under the action of heat and pressure and acts as a lubricant which protects the press tools from excessive abrasion.

9.66 Defects in Extruded Sections

The well-known 'extrusion defect' which is, a fault peculiar to this type of process has already been dealt with in this chapter. It may occur in the latter part of an extruded section, and its elimination calls for a carefully planned procedure which is strictly controlled at all stages of production.

Other internal flaws in an extruded section are generally attributable to the existence of defects in the original cast billet. Thus gas porosity in a cast billet may manifest itself in the form of blisters on the surface of the extruded

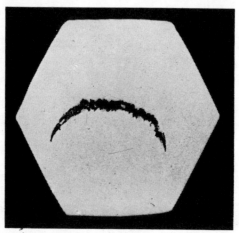

PLATE 9.8—The 'Extrusion Defect' in a Section of Hexagonal Brass Rod Approx. 12·5 mm Across the Flats.

metal, either immediately on extrusion or, in the case of aluminium alloys, during a subsequent heat-treatment operation. Particles of oxide and dross which occur in the leading half of the extrusion are nearly always due to inclusions trapped in the billet and originating from bad melting or pouring conditions during the casting process.

9.67

Transverse cracking (Plate 9.9) in an extruded section is nearly always caused by extruding the alloy at too high a temperature, at which tensile strength is low. Frictional forces between the die and the work-piece give rise to secondary tensile stress in the work-piece which cracks due to its reduced tensile strength. The same effect may be obtained by extruding it too rapidly, so that excess heat generated from frictional forces within the container does not have an opportunity to dissipate, and so raises the temperature of the metal passing into the die. The cracks may not be obvious on inspection, and if incipient they will manifest themselves in failure of the section during service or by opening up and becoming oxidised in the case of extruded stock upon which subsequent hot or cold work is carried out.

With aluminium alloys indication that the rate of extrusion is too high is first given by a scored, broken surface on the product. This is possibly due to the fouling of the die as a result of the extrusion metal alloying with it at a critical temperature.

9.68
Though it should be considered as a characteristic rather than a defect of extrusion, there is likely to be some variation in grain size along the length of an extruded section. The leading end of the rod, which has undergone little mechanical deformation, may be quite coarse grained as compared with the back end of the rod, which has suffered considerable plastic flow in the

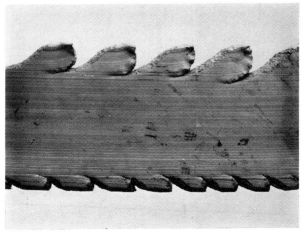

PLATE 9.9—Transverse Cracking in the Leading End of an
Extruded Brass Strip.

container, and has, moreover, been extruded at a lower temperature. In the case of $\alpha + \beta$ brasses used for subsequent forging operations difficulty is often experienced with the metal from the back end of a bar, since on reheating for forging grain growth is very rapid, leading to cracking and splitting during the forging operation.

THE EXTRUSION OF LEAD CABLE-SHEATHING

9.70
As was stated earlier in this chapter, one of the earliest applications of extrusion was in the production of the lead sheathing for cables used in electrical industries. Lead possesses excellent corrosion-resisting properties and is still unsurpassed as a protective covering for cables used underground or in other situations where they are exposed to conditions promoting corrosion. Whilst pure lead is more corrosion resistant than its alloys, additions of 1·0% antimony or 0·25% antimony and 0·25% cadmium are sometimes made in order to increase the strength and hardness of the covering.

The press most widely used for the extrusion of lead cable-sheathing was hydraulically operated and of the vertical type. The principal features of such a press are shown in Fig. 9.14. In all processes for the extrusion of lead the initial billet-casting operation is eliminated by casting the molten lead direct into the container. After removing the bulk of the dross from the surface of the metal in the container the ram is allowed to come into contact with the molten lead, under light pressure, in order to prevent the formation of a shrinkage pipe as the metal solidifies. The lead solidifies and is allowed to cool to 250° C which is a suitable temperature for extrusion. Cooling may be

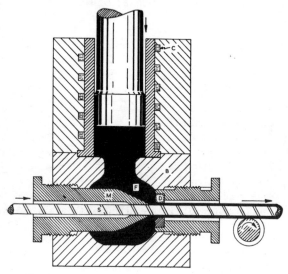

FIG. 9.14—The Extrusion of Lead Cable Sheathing.

accelerated by passing steam or water through the helical channel C (Fig. 9.14) between the liner and the main body of the container.

The solid lead is then subjected to the full pressure of the ram, which forces it through the cavity in the die-block B and into the forming chamber F. This chamber surrounds a hollow mandrel M, which carries the cable S to be sheathed, the lead dividing into two streams as it passes round the mandrel. These two streams meet and weld together on the other side of the mandrel and flow, in the form of an annulus of decreasing diameter, towards the die D. In the mouth of the die the lead is forced on to the cable in the form of tubular sheathing, the cable acting rather in the manner of a moving mandrel of the type used in tube drawing (10.44). The pressure which the lead sheath exerts on the cable is sufficient to draw it through the hollow mandrel and off a drum situated behind the press. As the finished cable leaves the press it is usually cooled by passing it through a trough of water and is then coiled on a drum.

When the bulk of the lead charge has been extruded the ram is raised and a new charge of lead cast on top of the remainder of the previous charge. The extrusion cycle is then repeated, and in this way continuous sheathing may be obtained on great lengths of cable.

9.71
One of the principal defects in lead cable-sheathing made by the process outlined above lies in the inclusion of dross and oxide at the interface between the residue of one charge and the charge which follows. Research carried out on methods of reducing the amount of entrapped oxide entering the extrusion stream falls under three main headings:

(1) The limitation ōf oxidation of the lead during pouring.

(2) The removal of dross or oxide once they are formed.

(3) The delivery of lead from the melting unit in a clean condition. In one very comprehensive system used at one of the G.E.C. works in America lead is kept out of contact with the air from the time it becomes molten until it emerges in the form of cable sheathing.

In one continuous extrusion machine the orthodox ram used in other extrusion processes is dispensed with and instead a screw-type of mechanism rotating around the hollow mandrel delivers lead from a feeder-head into the forming chamber at sufficient pressure to extrude it through the die. Molten lead can be added to the feeder head as required to maintain the level of molten metal. Since dross remains on the surface, little if any is carried down into the forming chamber. The outside surface of the container below the feeder-head is cooled by water sprays so that the lead reaches the screw-feed mechanism in a pasty condition and is solid before it reaches the forming chamber. The method of feeding the cable through the hollow mandrel into the mouth of the die is still used, however, in a manner similar to that shown in Fig. 9.14. Only the method of delivery of the lead to the forming chamber is basically different.

EXTRUSION-FORGING

9.80
This is basically a forging process which is allied to extrusion in so far as part of the component is extruded whilst hot through a die. An example of this type of process is the manufacture of poppet valves for internal-combustion engines. These valves can be made in a single operation from a heated steel slug in a press, the principle of which is shown in Fig. 9.15. The heated steel slug is partly extruded through the die by application of pressure from the punch to form the shank of the valve, but sufficient metal is retained in the die to form the head. The punch is then raised and the valve ejected from the die by a tool in the lower half of the die-holder. Such valves are generally made from a heat-resisting chromium steel and are extruded at about 1100° C.

IMPACT EXTRUSION

9.90
The production of collapsible metal tubes by impact extrusion began as long ago as 1841, when John Rand introduced the process in order to manufacture lead tubes as containers for artists' colours. A few years later tubes of tin were

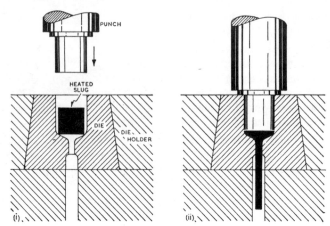

FIG. 9.15—Extrusion-forging a Poppet Valve.

made by the same process, but the extrusion of aluminium by impact methods did not begin on a commercial scale until 1920.

Most impact extrusion processes are cold-working operations. In discussing the effects of the rate of application of mechanical forces on a metal (3.60—Part I) it was pointed out that the mechanical properties are often relative to the rate of loading. During the impact extrusion of copper, for example, reductions in thickness of the order of 95% are possible, and this is far in excess of that which can be given by other cold-forming processes without the

Courtesy of Messrs Betts & Co. Ltd, Colchester.

PLATE 9.10—The Impact Extrusion of Collapsible Tubes.

The photograph shows slugs, impact extruded tube and finished machined tube. (Note that the thread is machined after extrusion.)

introduction of inter-stage annealing. Moreover, if attempts are made to extrude the metal slowly in an impact machine the high pressures necessary to effect extrusion are usually sufficient to cause collapse of the tools. It seems therefore that there is a small time-lag between the commencement of deformation of a metal and its beginning to work-harden, and that during this small time interval considerable cold work can be effected before hardening asserts itself (8·22).

9.91 The Production of Collapsible Tubes

Disposable tubes in lead, tin and aluminium are used as containers for a wide range of domestic materials, such as shaving cream, tooth paste, medicines, greases, shoe polish and condensed milk. Sometimes lead lined with tin is used in order to provide a cheaper tube which is nevertheless suitable for containing foods and medical products. The tin used for disposable tubes is occasionally stiffened by the addition of 0·5% copper, whilst lead for the same purpose is hardened by adding 0·5% antimony.

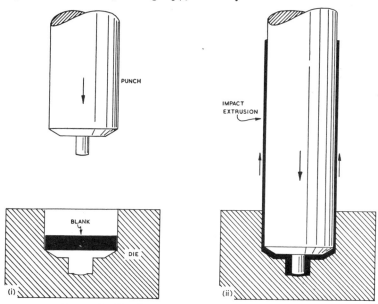

Fig. 9.16—The Impact Extrusion of Collapsible Tubes.
(a)   (b)

In addition to the manufacture of collapsible tubes, aluminium is used for the production of many other articles in the form of deep shells by impact extrusion methods. These articles include canisters and capsules for food and medical products; shielding cans for radio components; and electric torch cases.

Heavily constructed mechanical presses are generally employed in the impact extrusion of these collapsible tubes. The principles of die and punch arrangement in such a press are shown in Fig. 9.16. A small unheated slug of metal is placed in the die cavity, and as the ram descends it drives the punch rapidly into the die cavity and transmits a very high pressure to the metal, which immediately fills the cavity. Since there is no other method of egress, the metal is forced upwards through the gap between the punch and the die so that it travels along the sides of the punch, forming a tube-shaped part. As the punch is raised the extrusion is removed by an automatic stripping mechanism. The wall thickness of the tube is determined by the amount of clearance between the punch and the edges of the die cavity. The threaded nozzle of the collapsible tube may be formed during the impacting operation, but it is more usual to form the thread in a subsequent process.

Courtesy of Messrs Betts & Co. Ltd, Colchester.

PLATE 9.11—Older Type of Vertical Impact Extrusion Press Used for the Manufacture of Collapsible Tubes. (*a*) During the extrusion stroke; (*b*) withdrawal of the extruded tube.

Whilst the impact extrusion of tin and lead is carried out on cold metal, aluminium slugs may be heated up to 250° C for forming. Zinc, alloyed with 0·6% cadmium, used for the impact extrusion of dry battery shells, is first heated to 150–180° C since in this temperature range zinc is very plastic.

9.92 The Hooker Process
This process resembles closely that of hot extrusion by the direct method in so far as the flow of metal in relation to the die and punch is concerned. The Hooker process, however, employs impact extrusion under cold-working conditions, and its products include small brass cartridge cases, copper tubes for radiators and heat exchangers, and other short tubular components. Whilst tin and lead can be extruded by the Hooker process, it is more often used for the cold extrusion of copper and its alloys, particularly when the resultant component is required in the work-hardened condition.

Hooker extrusion is generally carried out in a crank press, the tool arrangement of a typical form of the process being shown in Fig. 9.17. Flat slugs are sometimes used in the Hooker process, but cupped blanks are usually considered to be more satisfactory and economically worth while, despite the

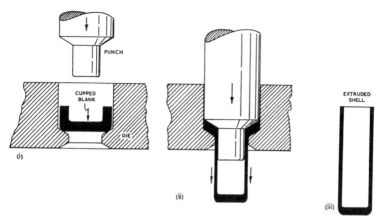

FIG. 9.17—Impact Extrusion by the Hooker Process.

Courtesy of Messrs Betts & Co. Ltd, Colchester.

PLATE 9.12—A Modern Horizontal Impact Extrusion Press for the Manufacture of Collapsible Tubes Note the automatic feed of slugs

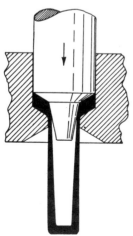

FIG. 9.18.

extra forming cost involved. The blank is placed in the die, and as the punch descends, metal is forced down between the body of the punch and the die, producing a tubular extrusion as shown. If the body of the punch is tapered (Fig. 9.18) so that as it descends into the die opening the annular gap between the punch and the die diminishes, then a tube of tapering wall thickness can be produced.

BIBLIOGRAPHY

1 'The Extrusion of Metals', C. E. Pearson and R. N. Parkin (Chapman and Hall).

2 'The Hot Working of Non-ferrous Metals and Alloys', Symposium (Institute of Metals).

3 'Rod and Wire Production Practice', Institute of Metals Division (American Institute of Mining and Metallurgical Engineers).

4 'Tube Producing Practice', Institute of Metals Division (American Institute of Mining and Metallurgical Engineers).

5 'The Manufacture of Seamless Tubes (Ferrous and Non-ferrous)', G. Evans (H. F. and G. Witherby).

6 'Extrusion of Plastics, Rubber and Metals', H. R. Simonds, A. J. Weith and W. Schack (Reinhold Publishing Corp.).

7 'The Control of Quality in the Production of Wrought Non-ferrous Metals and Alloys. II.—The Control of Quality in Working Operations', Symposium (Institute of Metals).

8 'Fundamentals of the Working of Metals', G. Sachs (Pergamon Press).

9 'The Mechanics of Metal Extrusion', W. Johnson and H. Kudo (Manchester University Press).

10 BS 2006: 1966—Metal collapsible tubes. Amendment 1971.

11 BS 2094: Glossary of terms relating to iron and steel. Part 8: 1956— steel tubes and pipes.

12 BS 3373: 1970—Wrought-magnesium alloys for general engineering purposes. Bars and sections.

Chapter ten
DRAWING ROD, WIRE AND TUBES

10.10

Metals and alloys which are ductile will always be found to be malleable, but the converse is not necessarily true. Many metals which are very malleable possess low ductility because they are not sufficiently strong in tension to withstand the stress which is necessary to cause deformation. Moreover, the malleability of a metal generally increases as the temperature rises, whilst ductility is less at a high temperature. Again this is consequent on the reduction in tensile strength of a metal at an elevated temperature. Drawing and deep-drawing processes demand high ductility in the stock being used, and are therefore cold-working operations.

Most of the early metals and alloys to be used by man included those of relatively high ductility, such as gold, silver, copper and bronze. It is therefore not surprising to learn that drawing processes appear comparatively early in the history of metallurgical operations. Whilst it cannot be stated with any accuracy when drawing was introduced as a manufacturing process, it is known that some time between the sixth and tenth centuries the Venetians and Italians began drawing wire by hand through holes in draw plates. However, wire continued to be made by the older method of hammering the metal into plates and then cutting these into narrow strips until well into the sixteenth century; and although a water-powered wire-drawing machine was installed in Nuremburg in 1351, it is possible that the draw plate may not have reached England until 1565, when it was introduced by a Saxon, Christopher Schultz, by permission of Queen Elizabeth I.

10.11

An important feature of cold-drawing operations is that ductile material can be drawn down to very small diameters and to exact sizes. The surface finish of a cold-drawn product is also superior to that of a hot-rolled or extruded material, and the mechanical properties of the resultant section can be varied by controlling the degree of cross-sectional reduction in the final cold-drawing operation. Cold-drawing is used extensively in the production of rods of various cross-section, as well as of wire; and is one of the principal processes used for the manufacture of high-quality tubes and other hollow sections.

As compared with either hot rolling or extrusion, cold drawing is a slow process, since the metal being drawn must undergo intermediate annealing operations between successive drawing stages in order to restore the capacity of the metal for further cold work. With suitable alloys hot rolling or extrusion is often employed to produce stock of a cross-section very near to that required in the final product, so that a single cold-drawing operation is sufficient to attain the necessary combination of good finish, accuracy of dimensions and adequate strength.

ROD DRAWING

10.20

As already indicated, rods in both ferrous and non-ferrous alloys are formed in the initial stages of production, either by hot-rolling or by extrusion: the main purposes of cold drawing are to straighten the resultant rod, size it accurately, give it a smooth, bright surface and in some cases to control the degree of strength and hardness in the resultant product.

10.21

Since rod is drawn in straight lengths, the operation is carried out on a draw-bench which must be long enough to accommodate the length of rod required. Such a draw-bench (which is similar in construction to the one used for drawing tubes shown in Fig. 10.8) consists essentially of a die held rigidly in a stout steel frame and a 'dog' which grips the end of the rod and pulls it through the die. The dog runs on rails, which constitute part of the main frame of the draw-bench, and the motive power is transmitted by means of the chain-and-sprocket system indicated in Fig. 10.8. The chain resembles a very large bicycle chain, and is moving continuously.

10.22

To operate the bench the end of the rod, which has been pointed or 'tagged' as described later, is pushed through the die and then between the grips of the dog. The hook-shaped projection at the end of the dog is then pushed down so that it engages in the moving chain. This automatically tightens the grip of the dog on the end of the rod, which is thus pulled through the die.

10.23

Before the bar is drawn its surface must be clean. With many non-ferrous alloys the surface which results from the previous hot-rolling or extrusion process is adequate in this respect, but steel rods need to be cleaned by pickling before they can be drawn. This involves immersing the rods in a solution containing from 3 to 10% sulphuric acid (sometimes hydrochloric acid is used) in water. The pickling solution is heated to between 60 and 70°C and its function is to detach the oxide scale present on the hot-rolled stock without causing undue pitting of the surface of the metal beneath. In order to reduce the tendency of the pickling bath to pit the metal surface, an inhibitor (usually an organic compound containing nitrogen) is added. This not only minimises attack by the acid on the metal surface but also leads to economy in the amount of acid used by reducing waste in the formation of ferrous sulphate.

$$Fe + H_2SO_4 \longrightarrow FeSO_4 + H_2$$

After being pickled, the bars are washed in water to remove the bulk of the acid solution. In order to remove the last traces of acid the rods are immersed in an emulsion of slaked lime and water. In addition to neutralising remnant acid, the excess lime dries on the surface of the rods and forms a base which will absorb the mineral oil or grease which is generally used as a lubricant in

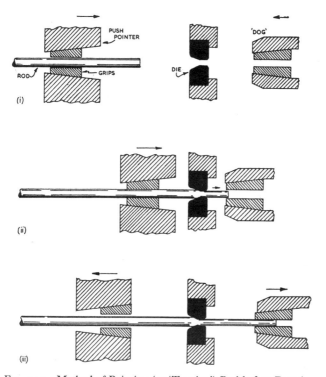

FIG. 10.1—Method of Pointing (or 'Tagging') Rod before Drawing.

the production of bright-drawn steel rods. Some rods are drawn with soap as a lubricant, but this generally leads to the production of a rather dull surface on the finished rod.

10.24

Pointing of the rod so that it may be threaded into the die may be affected mechanically in a rotary swaging machine which reduces the diameter of the rod by about 1·5 mm over a length of about 200 mm from its end. An alternative method of pointing the end, which is particularly useful when a more complicated cross-section is being dealt with, is to immerse the length required for the tag in hot 50% sulphuric acid. This dissolves away some of the metal and reduces the cross-sectional thickness so that the end of the rod can be pushed through the die into the jaws of the dog.

In most modern machines equipment for tagging the rod is included in the draw bench itself in the form of a push pointer. The push-pointer jaws grip the rod (Fig. 10.1 (i)) and force it for a short distance through the die, so that the resultant tagged portion passes between the jaws of the waiting dog.

WIRE DRAWING

10.30

Hot-rolled or extruded stock from about 5 mm diameter up to as much as 25 mm diameter is used in the manufacture of wire. In general, of course, the smallest diameter which will give the required properties in the final product is used. In the case of steel the stock material is usually coiled whilst it is still hot and is delivered to the wire-drawing plant in the black or unpickled state.

For pickling, the loosely coiled stock is loaded on to hooks suspended from an overhead crane so that it can be dipped in a succession of tanks containing progressively stronger acid solutions. Either hot sulphuric acid solutions or cold hydrochloric acid solutions are used, though solutions containing ferrous sulphate or ferrous chloride and sulphuric acid or hydrochloric acid are sometimes preferred. The scale on this stock is much thinner than on the heavy rods used for rod drawing, and can therefore be removed without excessive acid attack, but on the other hand, its complete removal is even more important than in the case of rod drawing.

After being pickled, the coils are washed thoroughly and then 'sulled' by allowing them to remain wet for about 20 minutes, so that a film of iron hydroxide (rust) forms on the surface of the metal. This rust film is soft, and will therefore not abrade the die surfaces; in fact, it acts as a primary lubricant. The coils are then dipped in an emulsion of slaked lime and water and dried* in an oven so that the film of lime left on the surface acts as a bond for the lubricant proper. This is usually dry soap. The subsequent operation is called 'dry drawing', the surface of the resultant wire being rather dull and dirty due to the presence of the lime and soap.

10.32

'Wet drawing' may be used if a bright finish is required on the wire. In this process the pickled wire is immersed in an inhibited solution of copper sulphate or tin sulphate to give it a firmly adherent coating of copper or tin. The metal-coated wire is then prepared for the wet-drawing operation by immersing the coils in a tank of fermented liquor made from rye-meal, yeast and water. An alternative wet lubricant consists of an emulsion of fats and soap in water, along with additions of anti-foaming substances.

The amount of cross-sectional reduction per pass in a wet-drawing process is usually less than that possible in dry drawing. In dry drawing between 35 and 45% reduction in cross-sectional area is possible in a single pass, as against 10–20% in wet drawing. The *total* amount of reduction which can be

---

* The heating process is also beneficial in that it helps to remove dissolved hydrogen from the stock. During the pickling process some of the hydrogen which is formed (10.23) dissolves in the surface of the steel and would give rise to brittleness during drawing were it not removed.

Courtesy of British Iron and Steel Federation.

PLATE 10.1—A Single-die Wire-drawing Machine.
Note the 'dog', which is attached to the block by means of the
stout chain.

given before annealing becomes necessary is, however, greater with wet drawing. The above figures refer to the drawing of mild-steel wire; steels of higher carbon content will tolerate much less reduction than this.

10.33
Hot-rolled or extruded copper rod destined for drawing is usually quenched in water whilst still hot in order to break off most of the oxide scale. It is then lightly pickled in hot 10% sulphuric acid and washed thoroughly before drawing. Since copper is very ductile, a greasy lubricant is all that is required to assist drawing. Brass rod from which wire is drawn is first pickled in 10% sulphuric acid or in a chromic acid–sulphuric acid solution if a particularly bright finish is required. After being washed the coiled rod may be lubricated by immersion in hot soap solution so that a film of soap dries on the surface. Alternatively, a greasy lubricant may be flushed on to the rod as it enters the die.

10.34

For drawing large-diameter wire (6–12 mm) and coiled strip in rectangular and other sections the 'bull block' (Fig. 10.2) is often used. This consists of a heavy steel drum or 'block' (A) which rotates about a horizontal axis and behind which is situated a die (D), held in a stout frame (H). The end of the work-piece is first swaged, then threaded through the die and gripped by the dog (C), which is attached to the block by means of a short length of riveted-link chain. As the block rotates the wire is pulled through the die and winds on to the block. The drawn wire is work-hardened, and therefore somewhat springy, so that as the free end of the coil is pulled through the die the wire

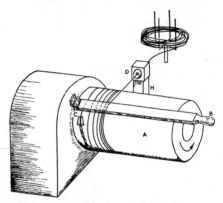

Fig. 10.2—A 'Bull Block' for Drawing Strip or Wire.

tends to uncoil itself from the block. In order to prevent this some form of brake (B) is brought into action by the operator so that the drawn wire is clamped firmly to the block.

The method just described is called a 'single-holing' process, since the wire is drawn through only one die. Smaller blocks for drawing finer wire are usually mounted so that they rotate about a vertical axis, the complete machine being mounted on a stout bench-like frame. (As in the multiple-die machine in Fig. 10.3.)

10.35

The amount of reduction which can be achieved in a single pass through a die is, of course, limited by the tensile strength of the drawn wire (maximum tensile force = cross-sectional area of drawn wire × yield strength after drawing). Consequently, to take advantage of high ductility without breaking the wire, and at the same time avoid having to set up the coil of wire on a fresh machine for a further pass, multiple-die wire-drawing machines are employed (Fig. 10.3). In such machines a driven block is placed in front of each die. As the wire is pulled through the first die it is wound two or three turns on to the first block, from which it automatically uncoils and passes to the next die. Obviously as the length of wire increases every time it passes through a die, each successive block must rotate more quickly than the previous

Courtesy of British Iron and Steel Federation.

PLATE 10.2—A Multiple-die Wire-drawing Machine for the Production of Steel Wire.

The wire is being drawn on to the block on the extreme right.

Courtesy of Messrs I.C.I. Metals Division.

PLATE 10.3—A Multiple-die Wire-drawing Machine for the Production of Brass Wire.

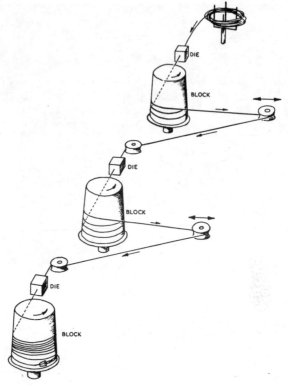

FIG. 10.3—Diagrammatic Representation of a Multiple-die Wire-drawing Machine.

one. Since it is difficult to control the speed of each block accurately enough to avoid slack wire accumulating between one block and the entrance to the next die, some method of taking up the slack is generally required. This is shown schematically in Fig. 10.3.

10.36 Dies

The total tensile force necessary to draw wire through a die is the sum of the force needed to cause deformation of the metal by transverse compression and shearing and the force required to overcome friction between the wire and the surfaces of the die. Consequently, any increase in friction diminishes the amount of reduction which can be given to the wire in a single pass, and it is therefore important that friction be reduced to a minimum by efficient lubrication and correct die design.

A wire-drawing die consists of a tapered hole, the working surface of which must be smooth, sunk in a material of considerable strength and wear resistance. Much of the bell-mouthed entrance AB of the die (Fig. 10.4) is never in contact with the work, but serves as a reservoir for lubricant which is carried in by the work. The tapered portion BC is the actual working surface where plastic deformation takes place, and is therefore the part of the die which must be most carefully designed and prepared. The angle of taper is critical, and depends both upon the metal to be drawn and the material from which the die is made. Its surface must be polished to reduce friction to a minimum so that the required reduction can be obtained with the least possible tensile force. The section *CD* is usually cylindrical, and must be of adequate length, so that as the working part of the die wears and, in fact, *C* moves nearer to *D*, the diameter of the wire will remain within specification.

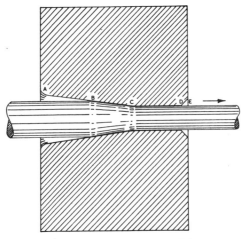

Fig. 10.4—A Wire-drawing Die.

The function of the part *DE* which is countersunk in the back of the die is to provide reinforcement for the working section of the die and prevent the circular edge from breaking or pulling away.

10.37

Dies can be made from a variety of materials, including chilled cast iron, high-carbon steels and alloy steels (Table 13.5—Part I). Carbon and alloy steel dies have the advantage that they can be forged so that as the die hole wears to an extent where the resulting wire is oversize the hole can be hammered up and then reamered out to the correct dimensions. Chilled-iron dies are generally limited in their application to the production of low-quality materials.

Since its introduction as a die material some years ago, increasing use has been made of tungsten carbide (6.14) because of the long life its very hard surface offers. It is now the most widely used die material. As tungsten carbide is expensive and also somewhat brittle, only the working part of the die is made from tungsten carbide, and this is held in a mild-steel block as shown in Fig. 10.5.

In addition to long life between resetting operations, much less power is consumed when using tungsten carbide dies, due to less friction; a better surface finish is also obtained in the resultant wire. The initial cost of the

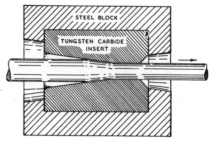

FIG. 10.5—A Tungsten Carbide Die for
Wire Drawing.

tungsten carbide die, however, is considerably higher than that of a steel die
and holes cannot be hammered as they wear. Instead they must be opened
up to the next working size.

10·38

Modern high-speed production of wire depends mainly upon adequate
lubrication of the die/work-piece interface. In 'hydrodynamic lubrication'
die and wire are completely separated during drawing by a film of lubricant.
To achieve this it would be necessary to feed in the lubricant at a pressure
equal to that prevailing at the die/wire interface but, in a method devised by
Christopherson, the actual motion of the wire helps to force lubricant into
the mouth of the die (Fig. 10.6).

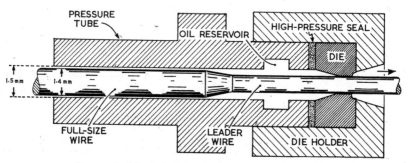

FIG. 10.6—The Principle of the Christopherson Tube.

The wire passes through a pressure tube fixed to the face of the die and,
since there is only a very small clearance between the tube and the wire, the
flow of lubricant is constricted. As the 'leader' wire passes through the tube
this causes lubricant to pile up into the mouth of the die and, by the time the
full-sized wire has reached the die face, the pressure in the lubricant may be
of the order of 80 to 310 N/mm² *assuming a wire speed of some* 3 *m/s.* Such
pressures will provide a film of lubricant $2 \cdot 5 \times 10^{-6}$ m thick and at the same
time cause some reduction in the diameter of the wire even before it enters
the die. Under production conditions, however, the small clearance necessary
between tube and work-piece introduces problems and, since the method

depends upon the wire moving at a fairly high speed, lubrication is inefficient and erratic during starting and stopping.

For these and other reasons the original Christopherson method has been replaced by a similar process which, however, uses dry soap as the lubricant (Fig. 10.7). In this process the tube has been replaced by a short nozzle (zone 1) in which dry soap, picked up as the wire passes through a soap box, is compressed so that it liquifies. In zone 2 the pressure of this liquid soap is increased to about 450 N/mm^2 as it passes through a short cylindrical

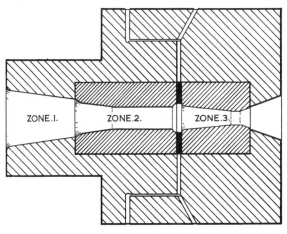

FIG. 10.7.

section of tube having a clearance of the same order as that in the Christopherson tube. Zone 3 consists of the actual die where drawing of the wire occurs in the presence of a film of lubricant some $2 \cdot 5 \times 10^{-5}$ m thick. In steel-wire drawing mills this process is effective in prolonging die life by up to twenty times.

10.39 Patenting of Steel Wire

As has already been indicated, the amount of reduction which can be given to a wire in a single pass is governed by the relationship between tensile strength and ductility. Higher-carbon steels in the hot-rolled condition generally possess insufficient ductility for drawing to small wires, and if drawn the resultant wire is too brittle to be of use. A heat-treatment process known as 'patenting' is therefore often used, both before drawing and as a final treatment for the drawn product.

The object of patenting is to increase the yield strength of high-carbon steel wire and at the same time retain sufficient ductility to allow considerable deformation. Patenting is essentially a high-temperature austempering process (12.47—Part I), in which the wire is heated to above its upper critical temperature and then cooled rapidly in a lead bath. In the double-lead-bath patenting process the wire passes continuously through a lead bath maintained above the upper critical temperature of the wire, then through a second cooler lead bath. This method of quenching effectively austempers the wire to give a tough bainitic structure.

Wires for pianos, guitars and other musical instruments contain 0·75–0·85% carbon, and a combination of patenting and drawing produces in them tensile strengths in excess of 2300 N/mm². Wire containing 0·20–0·90% carbon for the manufacture of wire ropes is also patented; and this process is also used during the drawing of many spring wires.

TUBE DRAWING

10.40

Several methods for the manufacture of seamless tubes and pipes have already been described elsewhere in this book (7.60 and 9.50). The main object of some of these processes is to form the actual tube shape from the initial ingot or billet and, whilst the product may be suitable for many applications, for

Courtesy of Messrs Accles & Pollock Ltd, Oldbury.

PLATE 10.4—Tube Drawing.
This photograph shows the 'dog' gripping the 'tagged' end of the tube and drawing it through the die.

others it is necessary to carry out subsequent cold-drawing or cold-rolling operations on the tube shape in order to obtain in it the accuracy of dimensions or quality of finish required. For example, extruded tubes often suffer from some degree of eccentricity, and this can be reduced to some extent by cold drawing. Moreover, extruded tubes may be too soft or not sufficiently straight. In either case the required properties can be obtained by cold drawing the extruded tube shell.

Small-diameter tubes are in any case taken through their final forming stages by means of cold-drawing operations, since only by such methods is adequate accuracy of dimensions obtained. The manufacture of very fine tubing for hypodermic needles illustrates this point. Some alloys which are not amenable to hot-working operations may be cold drawn as tubes direct from a cast tube shell, intermediate annealing stages being employed to restore the capacity of the alloy for further cold work. Although cold-drawing is most often applied to tubes of small diameter, the process can be used for tubes up to 0·3 m diameter.

Before being drawn the tubes are pickled; and in general, similar solutions to those employed in rod and wire drawing are used. Steel tubes are first dried after pickling and then lubricated by being dipped into some mixture, such as palm oil and tallow. Alternatively, they may be lubricated by power-pumped oil. Copper-alloy tubes, after pickling and washing, are often dipped into hot soap solutions, so that a coating of soap dries on to both the internal and external surfaces and acts as a lubricant.

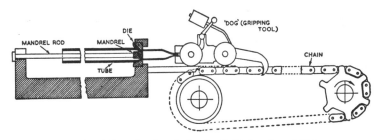

Fig. 10.8—A Drawing-bench for the Cold-drawing of Tubes.

The draw-bench and die assembly (Fig. 10.8) used for the cold-drawing of tubes is very similar in design to that used for drawing rods. Tube drawing differs from rod drawing, however, in that it is generally necessary to support the walls of the tube as it passes into the die by the use of a mandrel situated inside the tube.

10.41 Drawing without a Mandrel

Tubes in which the wall thickness is great in relation to the diameter can be drawn without the use of a mandrel. Reductions of up to 35% can be obtained in steel tubes by this method, which is generally known as 'sinking'. One end of the tube is swaged so that it can be threaded through the die and drawn in a similar manner to a rod.

The process is also used for relatively thin-walled tubes provided only a small reduction is contemplated or if the internal dimensions of the tube are of minor importance. Moreover, long tubes which can be handled in coil form for redrawing may be drawn by this method. Internal lubrication of the tube is, of course, not necessary.

Since the internal surface of the tube is unsupported and drawing forces are acting only upon the outer surface, sinking tends to increase the magnitude of unbalanced internal stresses and frequently raises them close to a point where failure is likely to take place.

10.42 Drawing with a Fixed Mandrel

In this method the mandrel, or 'plug' as it is often called, is short in length and is held in position in the mouth of the die by means of a tie rod attached to it and to a fixed support at the opposite end of the draw-bench (Fig. 10.8). The rod is detachable at its fixed end so that it can be drawn backwards and aside in order that the tube shell can be threaded over it. The tagged end of the tube is then pushed through the die and gripped by the dog whilst the back end of the mandrel rod is anchored to its support. The tube is then drawn through the annulus formed between the die opening and the mandrel as shown in Fig. 10.9.

Whilst this method of drawing tubes is characterised by accuracy of internal diameter and uniformity of wall thickness, it has the disadvantage that friction

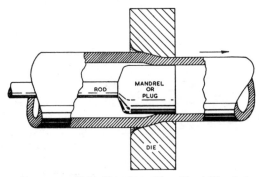

FIG. 10.9—Tube Drawing with a Fixed Mandrel.

forces between the tube walls and the die and mandrel are great. The surface area of the tube in contact with the faces of the die and mandrel is much larger than is the case when drawing solid rod. At the same time the sectional area of the tube is correspondingly small, so that the magnitude of the tensile pull which can be applied is limited. Consequently, the amount of reduction in a pass by this method is limited to about 40% for steel tubes.

Frictional forces between the tube and the die decrease as the die angle is increased. Consequently, large die angles are frequently used in drawing with a plug. Friction between the plug and the internal surface of the tube may be reduced to a minimum by efficient lubrication. This can be effected by using a hollow tie rod through which the lubricant is forced.

Only tubes above 6 mm diameter are generally drawn by this method since in addition to the disproportionately large frictional resistances encountered when drawing small-diameter tube, mechanical difficulties are encountered in fixing so small a mandrel to the necessary tie rod.

10.43 Drawing with a Floating Mandrel

As mentioned above, the production of small-diameter tubes entails the use of a very fragile mandrel rod if the fixed-mandrel method is used. Moreover,

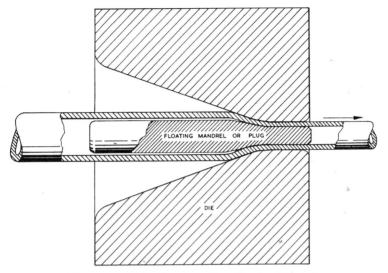

FIG. 10.10—Tube Drawing with a Floating Mandrel.

the length of tube which can be drawn is limited by the length of mandrel rod which can be accommodated in the draw-bench. Sometimes, however, a floating mandrel (Fig. 10.10) can be employed, and there is then virtually no limit to the length of tube which can be drawn. The contour of the plug is so designed that the plug adjusts itself to the correct position during drawing. Its maximum diameter is, of course, greater than the smallest diameter of the die.

This method is particularly suitable for the manufacture of small-diameter tubes in which the wall thickness is great in relation to the bore. Tubing produced in this way can be wound on to a drum, thus enabling great lengths to be manufactured.

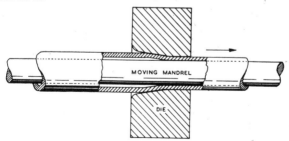

FIG. 10.11—Tube Drawing with a Moving Mandrel.

10.44 Drawing with a Moving Mandrel

In this method the mandrel consists of a heat-treated alloy steel rod equal in length to the finished tube and of a diameter equal to the bore of the finished tube. The rod is not fixed to the draw-bench, but moves through the die along with the tube to which it acts as mandrel (Fig. 10.11).

An obvious advantage of this method is that there is little relative movement between the internal surface of the tube and the mandrel rod—and consequently little frictional loss—since the two are moving through the die at almost the same speed. The mandrel rod is in fact moving at the same speed as that portion of the tube leaving the die. Therefore it must move into the die mouth at a somewhat greater speed than the tube being drawn. This actually has a lubricating effect, as the internal walls of the tube as they pass through the die encounter a continually new surface of mandrel.

Courtesy of Messrs Accles & Pollock Ltd, Oldbury.

PLATE 10.5—A Preliminary Stage in the Production of Tubing for Hypodermic Needles (10.45).
The tubing is supported by a continuous wire mandrel and is drawn through the die and on to the block, which is rotating about a horizontal axis (see Fig. 10.2).

A disadvantage of the process is that the drawn tube must be stripped from the mandrel. In order to do this, the diameter of the tube must be increased slightly, and this is usually effected by some form of swaging or reeling operation. Reeling is similar in principle to the Mannesmann rotary piercing process (7.61), in that the tube, whilst still on its mandrel, is fed axially between two rolls which are slightly askew, as indicated in Fig. 10.12. The combination squeezing and spinning operation tends to increase the diameter of the tube slightly, so that it will slide off the mandrel.

The moving-mandrel process is used mainly for tubes below 6 mm diameter and also for larger sizes where the wall is so thin that it would be damaged by friction if a fixed mandrel were used. Very-large-diameter tubes, however, are not drawn with a moving mandrel because of the difficulty in handling the bulky rods necessary and the very high cost of attaining adequate hardness and straightness in them. The impact strength of tubes drawn by this method is superior to those drawn by the plug processes, whilst tubes made by sinking are generally the most brittle.

10.45
Small-diameter stainless-steel tubing used in the manufacture of hypodermic needles is drawn by the moving-mandrel method. In the final operation of the process a hard steel wire constitutes the mandrel. The finished tubing is stored

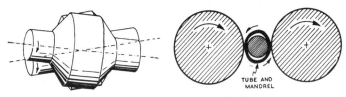

TUBE AND
MANDREL

FIG. 10.12—The Principle of Reeling.

with the wire still in position so that it serves as a support for the very thin walls.

The smallest size tube of this type in normal production has an outside diameter of 0·4 mm and a bore of 0·19 mm, but tubes as small as 0·04 mm outside diameter have been produced. A well-known Midland firm of tube manufacturers once received from an American competitor what the latter described as 'the smallest diameter tube in the world'. This sample was duly returned to its American manufacturers after a tube made in the Midlands had been threaded inside it. Long may such rivalry between old friends continue.

BIBLIOGRAPHY
1 'Rod and Wire Production Practice', Institute of Metals Division (American Institute of Mining and Metallurgical Engineers).
2 'Tube Producing Practice', Institute of Metals Division (American Institute of Mining and Metallurgical Engineers).
3 'The Manufacture of Seamless Tubes (Ferrous and Non-ferrous)', G. Evans (H. F. and G. Witherby).
4 'Steel Wire (Stahldraht)', A. Pomp (Trans. C. P. Bernhoeft) (The Wire Industry).
5 'Ferrous Metallurgy' (Vol. II—'The Manufacture and Fabrication of Steel'), E. J. Teichert (McGraw-Hill).
6 'The Cold Working of Non-ferrous Metals and Alloys', Symposium (Institute of Metals).
7 'The Control of Quality in the Production of Wrought Non-ferrous Metals and Alloys. II.—The Control of Quality in Working Operations', Symposium (Institute of Metals).
8 'The Making, Shaping and Treating of Steel', J. M. Camp and C. B. Francis (Carnegie-Illinois Steel Corp.).

9 'Fundamentals of the Working of Metals', G. Sachs (Pergamon Press).
10 'Aluminium, Vol. III—Fabrication and Finishing', Ed. K. R. van Horn (American Society for Metals).
11 BS 980: 1950—Steel tubes for automobile purposes.
12 BS 2017: 1963—Copper tubes for general purposes.
13 BS 2871: 1970—Schedule of copper and copper alloys—tubes.
14 BS 2873: 1969—Schedule of copper and copper alloys—wire.
15 BS 4391: 1969—Recommendations for metric basic sizes for metal wire, sheet and strip.

Chapter eleven
DEEP DRAWING AND ALLIED PROCESSES

11.10

The forming and manipulation of sheet metal into a variety of complex shapes has been practised for centuries by craftsmen using various hand tools. Eventually, however, the art of these craftsmen began to be challenged by machines, and manual skill has now been largely replaced by the accumulated experience of the designing engineer. It is now generally agreed that the limiting factor in the development of deep-drawing processes lies in the mechanical properties of the materials available rather than in the methods of manipulation devised by the engineer. When the metallurgist produces a higher-quality material the press-work technologist quickly develops more efficient ways of shaping it.

11.11

The object of deep drawing is to form a cup-shaped component from a piece of flat sheet metal by a process of shaping followed by drawing. Deep-drawn components range in size from small cartridge cases to aluminium milk churns, washing-machine tubs and even larger articles. The process is usually associated with the more ductile metals and alloys, such as 70–30 brass, cupro-nickel, copper, aluminium and some of its alloys, various nickel alloys and mild steel. Of necessity, however, stronger and less ductile alloys, such as those of the 'Nimonic' series, must often be shaped by modified deep-drawing operations. Such work has been assisted by the adoption of lubricating oils to which small additions of molybdenum disulphide, now well known as a high-pressure lubricant, have been made.

11.12

We will now consider briefly some of the principles of manipulation in a simple deep-drawing process. Fig. 11.1 (i) illustrates an attempt to form a cup by locating a suitable metal blank over a die opening and then forcing it through the die by means of a punch which has a rather smaller diameter than the die opening. Let us assume that the operation has been successful. In the original metal blank (Fig. 11.1 (ii)) a circle of radius OY is in contact with the bottom of the punch during drawing, and the metal there will therefore be in tension during the whole of the process. Thus in the finished cup (Fig. 11.1 (iii)) the length of the arc YY' is the same as it was in the original blank. The length of the arc XX' on the original blank, however, has been reduced so that it is the same as YY'. Therefore, during drawing, that part of the blank between YY' and XX', and in particular that near XX', will be in compression, and consequently there will be a tendency for it to buckle. If the blank is unsupported, as indicated in Fig. 11.1 (i), wrinkling of the rim will undoubtedly occur, and in order to prevent this some form of blank-holder is generally used, as shown in Fig. 11.2.

Here the outer rim of the blank is clamped by the blank-holder until the compressive forces in the blank are gradually dissipated as drawing nears completion and XY (Fig. 11.1 (iii)) becomes elongated in the final cup. The

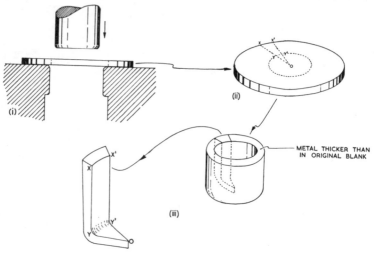

METAL THICKER THAN IN ORIGINAL BLANK

Fig. 11.1—Metal Flow during the Formation of a Cup.

pressure of the blank-holder must be sufficient to prevent wrinkling, but it must not be so great as to prevent the movement or flow of the metal towards the edge of the die as drawing takes place.

11.13

The depth of shell which can be drawn in a single operation depends upon the tensile strength and thickness of the metal. The maximum drawing force which can be employed will obviously be the product of the tensile strength and the annular cross-sectional area of the wall. Factors impeding metal flow during drawing include excessive pressure by the blank-holder and friction between the metal and the punch or die. Holder pressure must therefore be kept to the minimum necessary to prevent wrinkling, whilst friction must be minimised by using dies and punches with the smoothest possible surfaces and by adequate lubrication where possible. Drawing is facilitated when the edges of the punch and die have large radii and generous clearance through which flow of metal can take place.

11.14

Generally when the depth of draw exceeds 60% of the outside diameter of the cup one or more redrawing operations will be necessary, though the extent to which cold deformation can occur depends obviously upon the metal being drawn. Due to cold-working, the metal hardens, and this limits the amount of work which can be applied during a single drawing operation. Before being redrawn the cup must be annealed, then pickled to remove scale and finally washed, dried and lubricated.

REDRAWING

11.20

In many cases redrawing is made necessary by the complex shape of the finished component rather than by cold-working of the metal having taken place. For example, if the finished component has sharp corners the metal

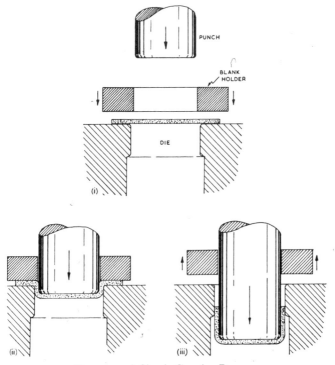

FIG. 11.2—A Simple Cupping Process.

would possibly rupture at these points if an attempt was made to draw the component to its final shape in a single operation. In such a case redrawing operations would be applied to shape the metal step by step, each step approaching more closely the final shape of the component.

11.21

In single-action redrawing (Fig. 11.3 (i)) no blank-holder is used. Consequently, the process requires a low drawing force, and it can be used to produce considerable reduction in thick material. If the material is so thin

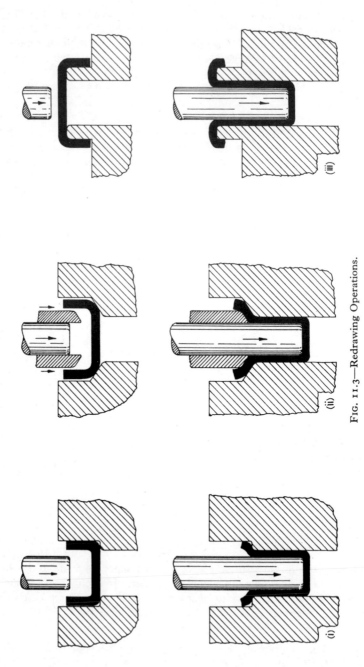

FIG. 11.3—Redrawing Operations.

that it tends to wrinkle, then double-action redrawing (Fig. 11.3 (ii)) may be used, employing a blank-holder as indicated. Reverse redrawing (Fig. 11.3 (iii)) is particularly useful in the avoidance of wrinkling, since its use tends to cause the replacement of tangential compressive forces in the rim by tensile forces. The redrawing of rectangular sections is often best accomplished using reverse redrawing since the tendency of rectangular sections to wrinkle is even greater than with cylindrical shells.

11.22
It was demonstrated earlier that when the metal is drawn the top rim of the shell tends to become thicker than the bottom of the shell. Consequently, if the wall is required to be of uniform thickness in the final product some degree of wall thinning or 'ironing' will have to be carried out. This is effected by making the clearance between the die and the punch less than the smallest wall thickness in the shell to be drawn, as indicated in Fig. 11.3 (i), (ii) and (iii). It should be noted, however, that redrawing can be employed without any wall thinning taking place by making the clearance between the die and the punch greater than the wall thickness of the cup which is to be redrawn.

MACHINES AND TOOLS FOR CUPPING AND REDRAWING OPERATIONS

11.30
The simplest and oldest method of producing cups is to employ a single-acting machine which is fed, either by hand or mechanically, with blanks which have been produced in a separate process. Modern cupping machines, however, may be either single-, double- or triple-acting presses which blank out and cup from metal strip which is fed in by mechanical or manual means. There are three essentially different types of operations in these presses.

11.31
In the first, which employs a double-acting press, the cupping punch operates concentrically within the blanking punch, the die being of the compound type designed to perform first the shearing and then the cupping operations (Fig. 11.4). The stroke of the blanking punch must be capable of accurate adjustment, since it is required to act as blank-holder during the subsequent cupping stage. In this type of machine the punches usually work along a vertical axis, the products being pushed through the cupping die and stripped from the cupping punch by the bottom face of the die or by using an extraction box. Often the machine is designed to blank and cup several components at a single stroke by providing multiple punches and dies. Not only does this speed up production but it also allows the multiple punches to be so spaced as to reduce the amount of webbing scrap to a minimum. Such a practice is only possible where very large-scale production is undertaken, and difficulty often arises in securing satisfactory synchronisation of the multiple tools.

11.32
The second method uses a single-acting press, but since the tools are of the combination type, thin metal can be blanked and cupped in a single stroke.

The blanking punch shown in Fig. 11.5 is recessed to form the actual cupping die. During a complete stroke of the machine this tool first cuts the blank, and then in conjunction with the blank-holder and the stationary cupping punch forms the cup. The blank-holder moves down with the die, and is therefore mounted on a spring-loaded or pneumatically actuated base, which is

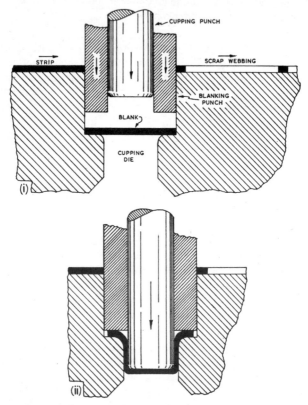

FIG. 11.4—Double-acting Press with Combination Tool.

depressed when the blanking punch descends. The cup so formed is usually pushed out of the die by a spring-loaded ejector, and the machine is generally set at an angle so that the resultant cups slide away under gravity. Combination tools find wide application for thin-gauge material, since their operation is quite simple.

11.33

The third principal method employs a triple-acting machine, by the use of which blanking, cupping and embossing can be carried out at each stroke. Its functions are similar to those of a double-acting machine, but the cupping punch carries the cup through the die and into contact with another punch moving in the opposite direction. The end of the cup is thus squeezed between the two punches, and so receives the desired impression. Triple-acting machines are also generally set at an angle to the vertical, so that the cups produced fall away under gravity.

11.34

Only the essential principles in the design of cupping presses have been outlined above. Such presses invariably possess a number of refinements, such as provisions for trimming the end of the flange on the cup produced. This can be achieved by means of a cutting ring fitted under a shoulder of the cupping punch, this causing the flange of the cup to be pinch-trimmed at

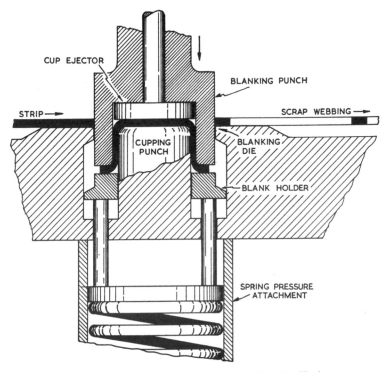

Fig. 11.5—Single-acting Press with Combination Tool.

the end of the cupping stroke. By the adoption of other refinements which facilitate rapid and smooth production, modern machines can be operated at speeds up to 200 strokes per minute, whilst in some of the ultra-high-speed presses speeds in excess of 1 000 strokes per minute can be attained.

11.35

Various types of machine are used in redrawing operations. These may work in either vertical, horizontal or inclined positions. Much of the recent development in press design has been in the provision of feeding mechanisms which facilitate rapid production. Multi-stage presses are often used for the production of small articles which are required in very large numbers, such as the brass caps for electric lamps. These presses often incorporate in a single unit tools for blanking, cupping, drawing, threading and other operations. Since the setting of tools for such an operation is expensive, a production run of at least 50 000 parts is generally required to make it economically worth while. The machines used are usually of the single-acting camshaft type, carrying a number of vertical push rods to which the punches are fixed. The

Courtesy of Messrs The London Aluminium Co. Ltd, Witton, Birmingham, 6.

PLATE 11.1—A 4-MN Hydraulic Press Used in the Deep Drawing of Aluminium Washing-machine Bowls.
The operator can be seen feeding a blank into the press.

dies are located in line in a horizontal die bolster to correspond with the punches, and the product in its intermediate stages is generally transferred along the series of dies by a reciprocating feed mechanism which consists essentially of actuated fingers.

LUBRICATION

11.40

The principal function of a lubricant in a drawing operation is to prevent metal-to-metal contact between the tools and the work-piece. One of the main problems associated with the increase in speed of modern presses has been the tendency of lubricant films to break down, and thus permit actual contact between the tools and the work-piece. Not only does this state of affairs lead to wearing of the tools but, equally serious, 'fouling' of the tools may also occur. 'Fouling' of the tools is caused by the building up of particles of metal from the work-pieces on both the punch and the die and leads to scoring of the surface of the product. When such fouling of the tools has taken place it is necessary to strip down the press, clean the tools and reset them. Naturally this adds to production costs, and alloys, such as brasses, which have low fouling tendencies are consequently popular alloys for presswork.

11.41
In addition to its lubricating action, the agent used must also serve as a coolant in modern high-speed processes. For this reason soap solutions find wide application as lubricants in the pressing and deep drawing of copper alloys. Some authorities favour the addition of animal and vegetable oils to these soap solutions in order to form emulsions, a popular lubricant consisting of 100 dm³ of water 3 kg soap and 3 kg soluble oil. Other lubricants used in the deep drawing of copper and its alloys include lard-oil blends (10–20% lard oil in mineral oil), and mineral oils containing additions to improve both the film strength and the lubricity.

11.42
Under severe conditions of deep drawing, liquid lubricants are inadequate since they tend to break down. In such cases solid lubricants are often used, including graphite in tallow; or dry soap. Alternatively, additions may be made to liquid lubricants in order to improve their film strengths. Such additions include french chalk; organic phosphorus compounds; and sulphur compounds. Many motorists will be familiar with the extreme-pressure lubricant, molybdenum disulphide, MoS_2, introduced some years ago. This compound was successfully added to various liquid-drawing compounds, particularly for drawing alloys of the 'Nimonic' series (18.32—Part I). Much more severe reductions can be obtained by the addition of 2% molybdenum disulphide to an otherwise orthodox drawing oil, provided that the surface of the 'Nimonic' alloy is first given some form of surface treatment, such as by the proprietary 'oxylating' process.

SOME DEFECTS ENCOUNTERED IN DEEP-DRAWING PROCESSES

11.50
Wrinkling or puckering of the metal undergoing deep drawing has already been dealt with. There are, however, several other faults which may develop due either to defective material or the use of incorrect drawing techniques.

Fig. 11.6 shows a cup which has failed at the punch radius. This occurs when thinning of the wall in that region has taken place to such an extent that the stress set up in the metal has exceeded its tensile strength. Clearly the maximum drawing force must not exceed the tensile strength of the material multiplied by the annular area of the shell at its thinnest section. Excessive blank-holding pressure, which has restricted the flow of metal in the blank and caused it to thin drastically at the punch radius, may cause failure in this way. Alternatively, insufficient clearance between punch and die or inadequate radius of punch or die may also lead to failure of this type.

11.51

'Earing' of a drawn cup (Fig. 11.7) may sometimes be encountered. Such 'ears' are caused by directional properties in the sheet from which the cup was drawn. Cold-working tends to produce preferred orientation in sheet materials, and this leads to varying properties in different directions, so that

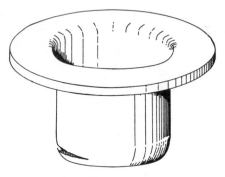

FIG. 11.6.

the metal deforms more easily in some directions than in others, thus forming ears on the deep-drawn parts. Research has shown that the conditions which tend to increase directionality in metal sheet are heavy penultimate reductions, low penultimate annealing temperatures and a high final annealing temperature.

Earing can be minimised by avoiding excessive deformation in the deep-drawing process. Further, the shape and size of the ears can be controlled to

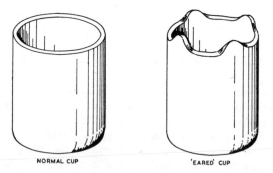

NORMAL CUP   'EARED' CUP

FIG. 11.7.

some extent by varying the shape of the blank (to oval or even square instead of circular) and by providing increased local clearance on the tools. It is generally necessary to find by test the most suitable orientation of the major axes, relative to the sheet, in order to reduce earing to a minimum.

11.52

The surface quality of the deep-drawn component depends very largely on the grain size of the sheet from which it is blanked and drawn. Coarse grain will often manifest itself as a rough or rumpled surface on those parts of the component which have undergone the greatest amount of deep drawing and which have not been in contact with the die face (Fig. 11.8). This roughness resembles to some extent the surface of an orange, and is commonly referred to as the 'orange-peel effect'.

In order to avoid this unpleasant surface condition, adequate control of grain size in the sheet to be drawn is necessary. This means that a standardised routine must be followed in the final annealing process, since annealing at too high a temperature or for too long a period leads to the formation of coarse

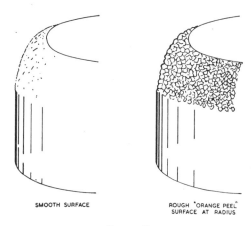

SMOOTH SURFACE   ROUGH 'ORANGE PEEL' SURFACE AT RADIUS

FIG. 11.8.

grain. Grain size, which is estimated in 'mm average grain diameter', can be determined quite easily by metallographic examination. Although ductility is higher in the case of relatively large grain sizes of 0·06–0·07 mm, when surface smoothness is of paramount importance it is better to restrict grain size to a maximum of 0·04 mm at the expense of a slight drop in ductility. When ironing takes place in the deep-drawing process the polishing action of the tools prevents the formation of 'orange peel' on the surface, and it is then advantageous to use material having a larger grain size in the region of 0·07 mm.

11.53

When a cup is deep drawn the metal forming the bottom of the cup undergoes no deformation, but the cylindrical wall is subjected to an increasing amount of cold work from the bottom to the upper rim. Near the bottom (at C) the amount of cold deformation may be so small that, on annealing the cup, very few nuclei are formed in this region when the recrystallisation temperature is reached. Consequently, the grain at C may be very coarse, and on redrawing will show up as 'orange peel' (Fig. 11.9).

In the case of mild steel this effect can be overcome by normalising the drawn cups at 910° C instead of giving them a recrystallisation anneal at 650° C. Normalising leads to complete recrystallisation of the material as fine-grained austenite, which, on cooling, transforms to similarly fine-grained

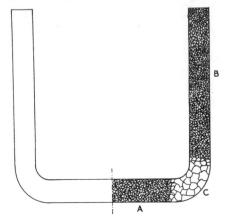

FIG. 11.9—The Effects of Critical Deformation on the Structure during Subsequent Annealing.
At *A* the fine-grained structure of the original blank is retained. At *B* the grain is fine due to recrystallisation following cold work. In the region of *C* the grain is coarse due to very light deformation before annealing.

ferrite and pearlite. No such normalising process is, of course, possible in the case of non-ferrous metal cups, and it is important to ensure that all parts of the cup receive more than the critical amount of cold-work which would produce coarse grain on annealing.

11.54
The need for assessment of the suitability of a metal for deep drawing led to the establishment of the Erichsen cupping tests. In this test a specimen of the sheet to be drawn is clamped between what are in effect a blank-holder and a die face, as shown in Fig. 11.10. A load is then applied to the sheet by means of a standard steel ball so that the sheet is drawn downwards through the die aperture until failure, in the form of a small crack in the cup, occurs. The test thus simulates a deep-drawing operation, and can therefore be considered as giving a reasonably good assessment of a material's capacity for being deep drawn. The Erichsen Number is in fact the depth (in mm) of the cup which is formed when failure begins.

It should be appreciated that the results obtained from the Erichsen cupping test depend largely upon the thickness of sheet which is tested and upon the blank-holder pressure employed, as well as upon the surface quality of the sheet. Moreover, the results obtained upon any particular machine cannot with certainty be related to those obtained from another machine, even if it is of similar design. The test therefore serves rather as a guide to the quality of sheet than as a test upon which specifications can be formulated.*

In addition to indicating the depth to which material may be drawn, the Erichsen test will reveal the presence of coarse grain as evidenced by 'orange

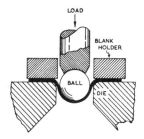

FIG. 11.10—Principle of the Erichsen Cupping Machine.

peel' on the surface of the cup (Fig. 11.11). Possibly the most reliable criteria on which to base an assessment of a material's suitability for deep drawing are hardness determinations coupled with an examination of grain size.

MARFORMING

11.60

One of the most expensive items in a deep-drawing operation is the cost of the tools, and in particular the die. A few years ago therefore research began into the possibility of using much cheaper tools and if possible eliminating completely the need for a die. The Guerin process had already found application in the production of aircraft fuselage parts in light alloys. In this process

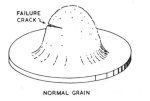 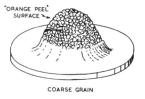

FIG. 11.11—Erichsen Test Pieces.

the displacement of a rubber pad under extremely high pressures, so that it conformed to the contour of a die block placed between it and the table of the press, enabled shallow forms to be manufactured cheaply from sheet metal. Drawing operations, however, were only partially successful, as lack of control over the metal surrounding the punch led to considerable wrinkling.

The cheapness with which tools could be made for use in conjunction with a 'rubber press' was a great incentive to the development of the process for deep drawing. In order to overcome wrinkling or puckering of the metal at

---

* The Erichsen test has since been covered by a BSI specification (see Bibliography) in which blank-holder clamping pressure is standardised.

the edges of drawn cups due to lack of support, a steel pressure plate P (Fig. 11.12) was used to surround the punch, pressure being applied to this plate from a hydraulic cylinder.

11.61

'Marforming', as the process was called originally, is illustrated diagrammatically in Fig. 11.12. The rubber pad is in effect a universal die which shapes itself to the punch as drawing proceeds and pressure is applied. Thus, the tools required are cheap and simple to manufacture. Moreover, for

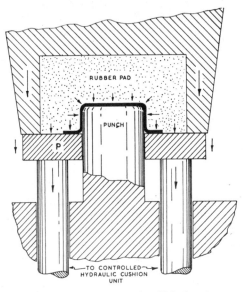

FIG. 11.12—The Principle of Marforming.

products of the same internal dimensions but made from different gauges of sheet only one punch and pressure ring are required, since the rubber automatically compensates for the different gauges of material. A rubber pad and a hydraulic unit can be fitted to any ordinary single-acting hydraulic press of adequate duty.

HYDROFORMING

11.70

In the 'hydroform' process the solid rubber block of marforming is replaced by a rubber diaphragm supported by hydraulic pressure. This diaphragm is sealed into the press head in order that it will withstand the very high hydraulic pressures used when the press is working under full load. Obviously when the diaphragm is not in contact with a working surface the pressure must be released, otherwise the rubber diaphragm would be blown out balloon fashion and burst. During forming, the pressure developed in the press head is due partly to that applied initially by the external pumps and partly to the compression produced by the advancing punch. Thus pumping may build up a pressure approaching 60 N/mm² after the rubber diaphragm has been brought into contact with the work blank, and as the forming punch is driven upwards this may raise the pressure by compression to a maximum of 100 N/mm².

11.71

The forming cycle is illustrated in Fig. 11.13 In Fig. 11.13 (i) the blank to be formed has been placed on the blank-holder ring and the press head has begun to descend. This press head, containing the hydraulic fluid at zero pressure, grips the blank between the edges of the diaphragm and the blank-holder, and the press head is then locked in position. The hydraulic pressure is then raised in the press-head cavity by means of pumps to a value determined by a pre-set control (Fig. 11.13 (ii)). As soon as this pressure is attained the punch is driven upwards, so forcing the metal against the diaphragm, which acts as a universal die (Fig. 11.13 (iii)). As the punch travels upwards it exerts a great compressive load on the hydraulic fluid in the press head, and so increases the pressure in it. This pressure is controlled to a predetermined value by a system of bleeder valves which permit the escape of fluid from the press head. When the punch reaches its required height it is locked in position. The pressure is then neutralised in the press head, which is raised, and the punch then withdrawn from the finished product, which is left standing on the blank-holder ring (Fig. 11.13 (iv)).

11.72

An outstanding feature of this process is that tools are cheap to produce, and depending upon the shape of the component and the material from which it is to be made, tools can be manufactured in resin-impregnated timber, plastic materials, mild steel and cast iron. Obviously in the drawing of hard alloys such as Nimonic, plastic punches would be inadequate, since they would begin to deform before the work blank. In such cases mild-steel punches would be employed.

Another advantage gained by using the hydroform process is that very little local thinning of the work-piece takes place. As the pressure increases in the press head the blank is gripped tightly between the diaphragm and the head of the punch, this setting up frictional forces which prevent sliding, and consequently limit stretching of the metal over the punch. Because of this 'locking' of the metal to the punch, bigger reductions per draw are possible so that one or two operations only are necessary as compared with four or five to produce the same degree of drawing in a conventional deep-drawing process.

Further, in hydroforming the 'die' is flexible, so that returned forms and undercut forms can be produced readily. The production of undercut necessitates fitting the punch with detachable pieces which can be lifted clear with the pressed part and then removed for reassembly on the punch ready for the next cycle. A novel feature of the process is that by feeding two blanks into the press together mating parts can be produced with a good sliding fit

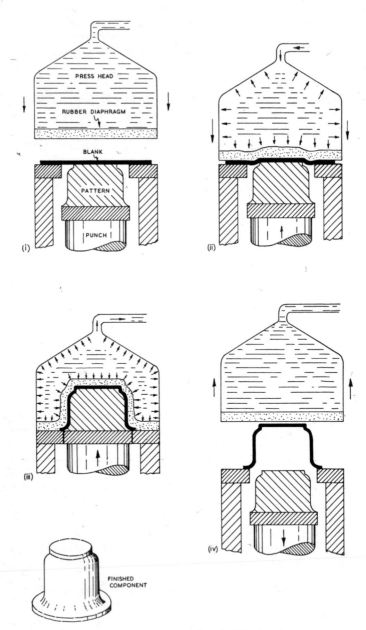

PRESS HEAD

RUBBER DIAPHRAGM

BLANK

PATTERN

PUNCH

(i)

(ii)

(iii)

(iv)

FINISHED
COMPONENT

FIG. 11.13—The Principles of Hydroforming.

At present hydroforming is used for the manufacture of many aircraft parts in various aluminium alloys. Components are also made in mild steel and stainless steel, whilst considerable development of the process is taking place with many of the harder non-ferrous alloys in the Nimonic series.

BIBLIOGRAPHY

1 'The Metallurgy of Deep Drawing and Pressing', J. D. Jevons (Chapman and Hall).

2 'Brass Pressing', Copper Development Association.

3 'The Cold Working of Non-ferrous Metals and Alloys', Symposium (Institute of Metals).

4 'The Final Forming and Shaping of Wrought Non-ferrous Metals', Symposium (Institute of Metals).

5 'Presswork and Presses', J. A. Grainger (Machinery Publishing Co.).

6 'Fundamentals of the Working of Metals', G. Sachs (Pergamon Press).

7 'Pressworking of Metals', C. W. Hinman (McGraw-Hill).

8 'Techniques of Pressworking Sheet Metal', D. F. Eary and E. A. Reed (Staples Press).

9 'Aluminium, Vol. III—Fabrication and Finishing', Ed. K. R. van Horn (American Society for Metals).

10 BS 3855: 1965—Modified Erichsen cupping test for sheet and strip metal.

Chapter twelve
MISCELLANEOUS COLD-WORKING PROCESSES

12.10
The fundamental mechanical properties of malleability, ductility and toughness (3.20—Part I) govern the suitability of a metal for deformation by particular cold-working processes. Such processes involve deformation of the metal by compression, stretching, shearing and bending. Generally those metals and alloys which are both malleable and ductile will be amenable to deformation by processes based on any of these methods. Those metals, however, which are malleable but at the same time are weak in tension can be deformed successfully only by processes which are based on the use of compression. In recent years it has been realised that the properties of a material are closely related to the *rate* at which it is deformed. This fact forms the basis of modern high energy rate forming processes.

12.11
Many industrial cold-working processes involve deformation of the work-piece by a combination of stretching, compression and bending. Several of these processes have been dealt with in foregoing chapters. For example, deep drawing proceeds in the main by bending and stretching actions, though some compression of the metal takes place at the upper rim of the cup (11.12). Though wire- and tube-drawing processes may seem to consist entirely in stretching operations, compressive forces are exerted on the metal by the die.

12.12
Shearing is an operation which is preliminary to many processes. Whilst hard metals can generally be sheared more easily than soft ductile ones, the bulk of metallurgical material which is sheared is ductile metal for the production of blanks for pressing, deep drawing, coining, embossing and allied operations. But in addition to the production of blanks, shearing is the basis of other processes, such as piercing, trimming, notching and parting, whilst milling, drilling and other metal-cutting processes find their origin in shearing.

12.13
Bending operations are many and varied, and their success depends upon the toughness of the material to be used. In a simple bending operation to produce a straight flange, one side of the work-piece is deformed in tension and the other side in compression, but in industrial processes the operation of bending is often combined with compression and stretching. Thus in bending a curved flange the flange may be either in compression or in tension, depend-

ing upon whether it is on the inside or the outside of the curved surface. In addition to simple bending operations on sheet, strip, rod and tube, the elements of bending are involved in such cold-working processes as spinning, cupping, rubber-pad forming and stretch forming.

12.14

Processes in which simple stretching is employed are not numerous, since soft metals are often weak in tension and therefore greater control of deformation is necessary if rupture of the material is to be avoided. The drawing of wire and tubes has already been mentioned as a process where stretching occurs, whilst deep drawing also involves a measure of stretching. Amongst those processes in which stretching action predominates are stretch-forming, spinning and embossing.

12.15

As was mentioned earlier in this book, malleability generally increases with temperature. Consequently, most processes which depend mainly on compression are hot-working processes, such as rolling, press and hammer forging and extrusion. A few cold-working processes rely upon the application of almost pure compression to effect deformation; coining, which is dealt with in this chapter, and cold-heading are typical examples. Cold-forging processes such as these are used when it is necessary to develop strength and hardness in a component or when a bright, clean finish is required. Many other cold-working processes rely for their operation on the action of compressive stresses which are brought into play indirectly and which are complementary to stretching or bending forces, as in drawing, deep drawing and many bending operations.

SHEARING OPERATIONS

12.20

Shearing operations can be classified into two groups: (1) in which a guillotine or similar type of universal shearing machine is used to cut metal to any desired shape or size; (2) in which single-purpose tools or dies are used to cut a single shape in sheet metal. When, in the latter type of process, the end product is the piece of metal which is detached from the strip or sheet, as, for example, in the production of a disc for a deep-drawing operation, the process is usually called *blanking*; whilst when the piece which is cut out is scrap material, then the operation is called *piercing*.

12.21

Blanking operations are used to produce work-pieces in many different shapes for subsequent cupping, deep drawing, cold forging, simple bending and several allied processes. Sometimes the product of blanking is a finished component, as in the manufacture of brass plates and wheel blanks for time switches and cheap clocks.

12.22

The mechanism of a shearing operation is shown in Fig. 12.1. As pressure is applied to the work-piece by the punch, maximum stress concentration occurs where the sharp edges of the tools make contact with the metal. Cracks therefore start from these points, and if the clearance between the punch and the die is correct the cracks will meet near the centre of the metal thickness, thus producing a clean cut with a minimum of expended energy. The effects of incorrect clearance between punch and die are indicated in Fig. 12.2. Whether excessive or inadequate clearance is allowed, the cracks propagated by the tool edges will not meet, and a clean cut will not be obtained. When

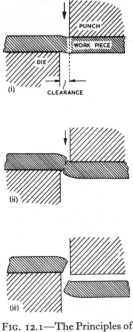

FIG. 12.1—The Principles of
Shearing.

excessive clearance is allowed a greater amount of metal comes under the influence of plastic deformation before fracture takes place, and undue distortion of the edges of the metal occurs. A rough, ragged edge is likely to be produced, and a sliver of metal of section $ABCD$ may become detached between the punch and the die, constituting a possible source of damage to the surface of the blank.

The clearance allowed between punch and die is dependent largely upon the mechanical properties of the metal to be sheared, but is usually in the region of 5–10% of the metal thickness. Hard, brittle alloys tend to crack after only a small amount of plastic deformation has taken place, so that small tool clearances are used when shearing such materials. Ductile alloys, however, undergo more plastic deformation before fracture occurs, and the tool clearance must be correspondingly large. Although the force required for shearing hard materials is greater than that for shearing soft, ductile materials, the total amount of energy used is generally less because the working stroke is shorter (Fig. 12.3). Moreover, the edges provided by the shearing operation are much smoother and less distorted in the case of a hard metal than with a soft ductile metal.

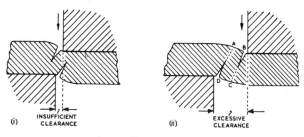

FIG. 12.2.

12.23

The force required to effect shearing when the complete cut is made at the same instant is given by

$$F = L \times d \times s$$

where F is the force required, L is the length of cut, d the thickness of the metal and s its shear strength. A smaller cutting force is required if the tool

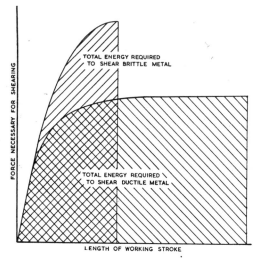

FIG. 12.3—Energy Required to Shear Ductile and Brittle Metals.

edges are brought together progressively instead of instantaneously, so that the cutting action becomes analogous to that of a pair of scissors, in which a cut is propagated through the material in the direction of the cut as the blades are closed. This can be effected quite easily in universal shears, such as an ordinary guillotine, by slanting the cutting edge of the upper blade at an angle to the lower one. A similar effect can be obtained in blanking and piercing tools by providing either the punch or the die with an angle (Fig. 12.4), usually referred to as 'shear'. This cutting angle is usually quite small (about 10°), since the useful length of the stroke is only equal to the thickness of the metal being sheared. The decision as to whether the 'shear' shall be on the punch or on the die will depend whether the tools are used for piercing or blanking. In a piercing operation, where the resultant perforated strip is required in a flat state, the shear will be on the punch (Fig. 12.4 ii)), but in a blanking process, where the blank is required to be flat, the shear will be on the die

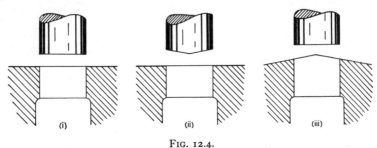

FIG. 12.4.

(Fig. 12.4 (iii)). In either case the work-piece will remain flat, whilst distortion occurs in that part of the material to be scrapped. For thin materials it is usual to leave the faces of both punch and die flat (Fig. 12.4 (i)).

12.24
The mechanical properties of a material depend very largely upon the rate at which it is deformed. If a very high tool speed is used in a blanking operation the rate of local hardening *overtakes* the rate of plastic flow in the material. Consequently, if the stress concentration is high enough, cracks are propagated in the locally hardened region because, in effect, the tool speed is above the speed of the 'plastic waves' in the material and fracture occurs before the material can begin to absorb the energy injected locally.

In high-energy rate blanking, tool speeds of 10 m/s are used as compared with speeds of 0·6 m/s in conventional blanking processes. Rubber cushions are generally employed as shock absorbers. Moreover, in the high-energy rate process much greater tool clearances can be used and a very clean cut still obtained.

BENDING OPERATIONS

12.30
A large number of cold-working processes involve some bending of the work-piece during the forming operation. Thus deep drawing proceeds by a combination of bending, stretching and compression. There are several processes, however, in which deformation is effected almost entirely by simple bending.

We will first consider the way in which deformation occurs during a simple bending process in a bar of square cross-section (Fig. 12.5). If AXA_1

becomes the inside edge of the bend it will become shorter in length, and will consequently be in a state of compression, whilst BZB_1, which has become the outside edge, will increase in length and be in a state of tension. Between AXA_1 and BZB_1 a plane through NYN_1 and perpendicular to AA_1B_1B will exist in which no alteration in length has taken place and which is in an unstressed state. This is called the neutral plane. Metals, like other crystalline solids, are virtually incompressible. Therefore no volume change will accompany bending, and since the cross-sectional area of AXA_1N_1YN decreases, the cross-sectional area of CUC_1M_1VM must increase correspondingly. Similarly, since the cross-sectional area of NYN_1B_1ZB increases, the

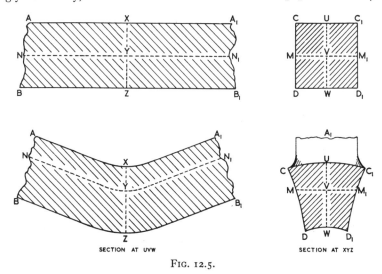

SECTION AT UVW   SECTION AT XYZ

FIG. 12.5.

cross-sectional area of MVM_1D_1WD must decrease. A cross-section through the bent bar at XYZ is therefore of the shape shown.

Since the cross-sectional area CUC_1M_1VM is increasing, it offers greater resistance to compression, whilst the area MVM_1D_1WD is decreasing, so that it offers less resistance to the tensile forces acting on it. Therefore the length of BZB_1 is increasing far more quickly than the length of AXA_1 is decreasing, and ultimately the material will fail in tension at Z. As the metal in area NYN_1B_1ZB is increasing in length more quickly than the metal in AXA_1N_1YN is decreasing in length, that metal in AXA_1N_1YN which is near to the neutral plane NYN_1 changes from a state of decreasing compression to one of increasing tension, and consequently as bending proceeds the neutral plane NYN_1, which was originally mid-way between AXA_1 and BZB_1 in the unbent bar, begins to move nearer to AXA_1.

Because stretching is taking place more rapidly than compression, it follows that after bending the length of the bar, $\dfrac{AXA_1 + BZB_1}{2}$, is greater than it was in the original piece. It also follows that the area of cross-section at XYZ has decreased due to bending so that the work-piece will now be weaker. These, and other, factors must all be considered when a blank is to be cut for use in any bending operation.

The deformation which has been accompanied by bending is part plastic and part elastic. Consequently, when the bending force is removed the *elastic* compression which was present in the metal in the region of X disappears and expansion takes place there. Similarly, the *elastic* tension which was present in the metal in the region of Z also disappears, so that the metal there contracts. The resultant 'spring back' causes the bend to open to a degree which is dependent upon the initial proportion of elastic to plastic deformation. In bending operations a number of methods are used for reducing spring back. If we assume that the bar (Fig. 12.5) is put into tension before the bending force is applied such that the whole of the section $CUC_1M_1D_1WDM$ is in tension during bending, then less spring back will occur when the forces are released. This is the basis of stretch-forming (12.60). The type of distortion which takes place when a bar is bent is exaggerated when a tube is bent (Fig. 12.6). Here the amount of metal

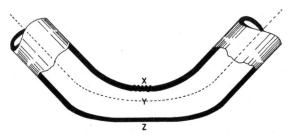

FIG. 12.6.

between X and Z is very small, so that the metal at Z distorts more readily in tension than does that at X in compression. Therefore the walls of a tube are usually supported during a bending operation by filling the tube with sand or a quantity of fusible alloy, or by using a stout spiral spring of a diameter similar to the bore of the tube.

12.31
For the manufacture of a multitude of small components, such as brackets, picture hooks, hinges, switch contacts, etc., small power or hand presses are frequently used. These presses are fitted with suitable form tools. A tool suitable for making a simple right-angled bend in mild-steel strip is shown in Fig. 12.7. Here the effects of spring back are overcome by bending the blank to a more acute angle than is required in the final component. The die angle required is generally found by trial and error, and it follows that once this has been established raw material of uniform temper must be forthcoming if a constant angle of bend is to be attained in the components on a production run. Fig. 12.8 shows a tool arrangement suitable for producing a series of

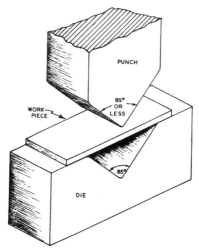

FIG. 12.7—Typical Tool for Making
Right-angled Bends in Mild Steel.

bends or corrugations at a single stroke. Here some stretching will occur in
the work-piece in addition to simple bending.

12.32

In some bending operations the type of distortion obtained in section
$CUC_1M_1D_1WDM$ (Fig. 12.5) would be undesirable. In order to reduce the
amount of such distortion a closed die could be used so that pressure is
applied to the faces CDM and $C_1M_1D_1$. Whilst it is, of course, impossible by
this means to prevent the contraction which takes place in the region of
DWD_1, much of the overall distortion is reduced, and by preventing the
expansion of CUC_1 the amount of spring-back will be limited.

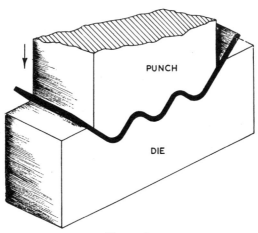

FIG. 12.8.

12.33

The operation of a simple forming die is illustrated in Fig. 12.9. A flat blank is fed into the recess either automatically or by hand. During the downwards stroke of the punch the blank is held in contact with the end of the punch by the spring-loaded pressure pad and the sides of the die turn the ends of the blank upwards. Fig. 12.9 shows the punch at the bottom of its stroke. As the punch is withdrawn the pressure pad acts as a stripper, pushing the

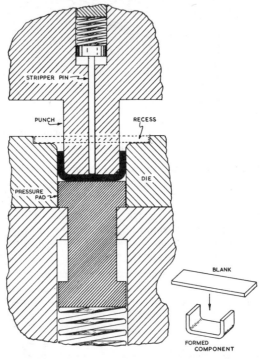

FIG. 12.9—Simple Forming Die for a Bending Operation.

work-piece to the top of the die and keeping it in contact with the receding punch. When the punch has moved clear of the die the part is ejected by means of the stripper pin. In addition to simple bending a degree of 'ironing' (stretching) takes place in an operation of this type if provisions have been made in the design of the die to keep edge distortion of the work-piece to a minimum.

In springs and similar products which are pressed from hard-rolled, or drawn strip the operations should be designed so that bending takes place at right angles to the direction in which the strip was rolled or drawn. Work-hardened materials will withstand more severe bending in this direction than they will 'with the grain', when cracking will very easily occur.

RUBBER PRESSING

12.40

In the previous chapter reference was made to the Marform process, which employs a rubber pad as a form of universal die in deep-drawing operations. The use of a rubber press for simpler forming processes, however, dates back much earlier—to 1939 in fact. In America rubber-pad forming is generally referred to as the Guerin process, and was used extensively during the Second World War for the manufacture of aircraft components in aluminium alloys. Rubber pressing is now employed for the production of pots and pans, tractor bonnets, stainless-steel trays, car-body panels, hub caps and other re-entrant shapes. The process is economical for short runs, particularly of prototypes in the car trade. Polished stock material is used for pressing many components. This is protected with a plastic coating which can be stripped off when the finished component is to be used.

12.41

Modern rubber presses usually have a stationary upper container which holds the rubber pad, whilst the lower platen, which carries the die and work-piece, is forced upwards into the rubber by means of hydraulic cylinders (Fig. 12.10).

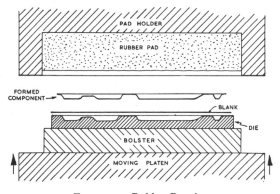

FIG. 12.10—Rubber Pressing.

The flexible rubber pad forces the work-piece down into the die cavity, and in this instance acts as a universal punch. Pressures in the region of 7·5–15 N/mm² are generally employed, and the complete cycle of placing the work-piece on top of the dies, pressing and unloading takes less than one minute. Frequently the moving platen carries a number of small dies, so that several pressings are made at a single stroke of the machine.

For rubber pressing aluminium alloys dies are made relatively cheaply from such substances as 'Delaron', a paper-base synthetic resin which can be shaped using orthodox wood-cutting machinery and in which an excellent surface finish can be obtained. Zinc-base alloys can also be used as die materials, and have the advantage that they can be remelted for further use. 'Improved' plywoods consisting of beech veneers bonded with synthetic resins are useful as die materials when the number of components required is small. Die costs are usually no more than one-tenth to one-quarter of those for more conventional steel dies used in other forming processes.

12.42

The amount of deformation which is possible at room temperature with many of the magnesium-base alloys is very limited. These alloys can, however, be subjected to extreme deformation at about 300° C without detriment, and the use of heat-resisting rubber pads has made the hot-pressing of magnesium-base alloys possible. Often 'slave mats' of heat-resisting rubber are used to cover the work-piece, thus protecting the main pad and prolonging its life. Die materials used for cold rubber-forming are generally unsuitable for use at high temperatures. Zinc alloys soften at the working temperature,

Courtesy of Messrs The English Electric Co. Ltd.

PLATE 12.1—A Rubber Press Used in the Production of Miscellaneous Aircraft Components.

whilst resin-bonded materials tend to suffer from de-lamination. Though mild-steel and cast-iron dies are suitable in many respects for continued use at 300° C they present difficulties arising from rates of expansion which are very different from those of magnesium-base alloys being pressed. Consequently, magnesium-base casting alloys, such as 'Elektron', are often used as die materials, since they expand at similar rates to the sheet being pressed. Magnesium-alloy die materials also machine easily, and the dies so produced are light in weight and easy to handle.

12.43

Recently the hot-pressing of titanium sheet by rubber-pad methods has been established using similar temperatures and techniques to those adopted for the hot forming of magnesium-base alloys.

SPINNING

12.50

Spinning is a process used to produce a hollow shape by the application of lateral pressure to a rapidly revolving blank, so causing it to assume the shape of a former which is rotating with it. This is one of the oldest methods of

Courtesy of Messrs The Northern Aluminium Co. Ltd.

PLATE 12.2—Spinning Aluminium Holloware at Messrs Swan Brand's Factory, Birmingham.

shaping sheet metal, and its efficiency depends very largely upon the skill of the operator in applying pressure to the rotating blank with the aid of simple hand-operated form tools. Deformation of the metal during spinning proceeds by a mixture of bending and stretching, so that it is a very suitable process for shaping ductile metals and alloys.

12.51

There are three features of spinning which govern its use as a forming process. First, since the equipment required in its operation is simple and hardwood formers are cheap to produce, it can be used to manufacture a small number of components where tool costs for a deep-drawing process would be prohibitively high. Second, many complex articles of re-entrant shape can be produced only by spinning. If the number of articles involved in such cases is large, then spinning may be used more economically in conjunction with pressing operations which have been employed to pre-form a blank. Finally, conical shapes are very easy to produce by spinning, whereas they are very difficult to produce by deep-drawing operations. Edge curling, seaming and heading processes may also form part of a spinning operation.

12.52
In simple spinning processes the equipment consists of a lathe in which the blank is held between a chuck and a tail plate, and simple forming tools which are generally bars with rounded ends. For external spinning (Fig. 12.11) a

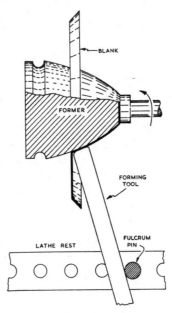

FIG. 12.11—Spinning.

former is usually attached to the chuck. This former corresponds to the internal shape of the finished component, and may be made from a hardwood such as maple or, in some cases, of metal. Formers may be solid, but if the component to be produced is of re-entrant shape, then the former must be segmented to facilitate withdrawal from the finished product. For internal spinning the blank is held at its circumference, and the former is often a shaped roller turning freely on an independent spindle. In this case deformation is effected by an internal tool which presses the metal outwards against the roller.

Adequate lubrication is necessary during the spinning process. For small-scale work beeswax, tallow or a mixture of lard oil and white lead are often used, whilst for larger work soap is the usual choice.

12.53

Tools used by the operator are of various shapes and of sufficient length to allow adequate leverage and control during use. To facilitate spinning the operator places a fulcrum pin in the appropriate hole in the lathe rest and steadies the tool against the pin with his left hand. He is then able to guide the nose of the forming tool, and so gradually work the blank on to the former. This operation calls for considerable manipulative skill and experience in being able to judge, for example, when the metal has received sufficient cold-work to necessitate annealing.

Care must also be taken that excess work is not put into the blank at any point, or undue thinning may take place and lead to fracture of the material. Usually the opposite state of affairs prevails at the rim of the component, since as the circumference of the original blank is reduced, there is a tendency for the metal at the rim to thicken. A similar situation exists in cupping and deep-drawing processes (11.12), and is controlled by the pressure of the blank-holder. During spinning, however, there is no similar control, and the required ironing of the component is dependent upon the manipulative skill of the operator as he gently coaxes the metal on the former by a stroking action of the tool.

Spinning speeds vary considerably with the type of material used and with the diameter and thickness of the blank employed. The thicker and harder the metal and the larger the diameter of the blank, the slower will be the spinning speed. In producing a small component about 25 mm in diameter from thin copper foil a speed of 2 500 rev/min. might be used, whilst in the spinning of a component from a brass blank 2 m in diameter and 5 mm thick a low speed of 250 rev/min. would be employed.

12.54

Typical products of the spinning trade are ornaments in copper and brass, musical instruments, cooking utensils, components used in chemical plant, stainless-steel dairy utensils and many others. Older readers may remember the spate of aluminium fruit bowls which reached the market soon after the end of the Second World War when much money was chasing very few goods. These bowls were very easy to produce by a simple spinning operation over an elementary former. They were then anodised and the anodic film subsequently dyed, but the organic dyes used frequently faded with a few days' ownership of the bowl by the disgruntled purchaser.

12.55

Of recent years progress has been made in mechanising the spinning process in order to reduce physical fatigue of the operator and at the same time increase production rates and the degree of control over the dimensional accuracy of the product. The new method originated in Sweden, and was used for the manufacture of 18–8 stainless-steel dairy utensils, but its application has now spread to other countries for the shaping of aluminium, copper,

Courtesy of Messrs The London Aluminium Co. Ltd, Witton, Birmingham, 6.

PLATE 12.3—A One-piece Aluminium Milk-churn Body Being Removed from a 'Flow-turning' Lathe.

Courtesy of Messrs The London Aluminium Co. Ltd, Witton, Birmingham, 6.

PLATE 12.4—General View of a Spinning Shop with a Power-driven Flow-turning Lathe in the Mid-distance Tooled for Producing the Deep Containers Shown in the Foreground.

brass, mild steel and titanium. It is practised in different countries under such titles as 'flowing-turning', 'flow-forming' and 'stretch-planishing'.

12.56

In the 'flow-turning' process thick-gauge material is made to flow plastically by pressure rolling it in the same direction as the roller is travelling, so that a component is produced in which the wall thickness is much less than that of the original blank. The principles of flow-turning are indicated in Fig. 12.12, though the actual machines at present in use vary very widely in individual

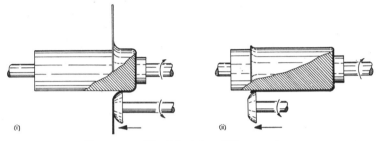

FIG. 12.12—The Principles of Flow-turning.

design. Aluminium cooking utensils for use on electric hot-plates are manufactured by this type of process. The side wall of a cast pot is made thinner by flow turning, whilst the base retains its initial thickness and also remains flat, so that it will provide maximum conductivity of heat.

STRETCH-FORMING

12.60

Stretch-forming is a process used for forming simple or complicated contours in sheet metal. It was the first introduced in the aircraft industry just before the Second World War, and soon became important in the production of metal-skinned aircraft. The process is also firmly established in the coach-building trade, as well as in the aircraft industry, where it is used as one of the principal methods of forming sheet metal, extrusions and rolled or drawn sections.

12.61

In any forming operation permanent deformation can only be produced in the work-piece if it is strained beyond its elastic limit. In stretch-forming this is accomplished by applying a tensile load to the work-piece so that the elastic limit is exceeded and plastic deformation takes place. The operation is carried out over a form tool or stretch block, so that the component assumes the required shape.

12.62

The earliest type of machine used for stretch-forming was of the rising-table type (Fig. 12.13). Here the work-piece is firmly gripped between jaws and the stretch block is mounted on a rising table which is actuated by means of a

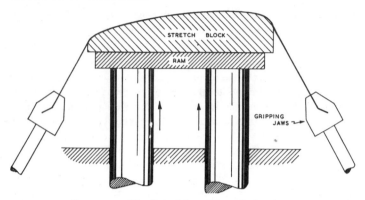

FIG. 12.13—The Principles of Stretch-forming.

hydraulic ram. Stretching loads of up to 4 MN are obtained with this type of machine, which can be used for a wide range of components.

Long panels with only limited longitudinal curvature are generally stretch formed in a moving-jaw or tangential stretching machine. In this type of machine the stretch block remains stationary whilst the jaws gripping the end of the sheet move tangentially to the ends of the stretch block under the action

Courtesy of Messrs The English Electric Co. Ltd.

PLATE 12.5—Vertical Stretch-forming Machine Used in the Production of Aircraft Fuselage Skin.

of hydraulic rams. Maximum stretching loads of up to 3 MN are developed
by this type of equipment, which is used for the stretch-forming of aircraft
fuselage panels up to 6 m in length and 2 m in width. When in operation each
jaw moves at about 2·5 mm/s.

12.63
In the machines already mentioned plastic deformation takes place as the
material is stretched over the form tool. A similar process, generally termed
stretch-wrap forming, is also used. In this process the work-piece is firmly
gripped and, whilst still straight, a load is applied which is sufficient to stress
it to its elastic limit. Then, whilst on the verge of the plastic state, the work-
piece is wrapped round the stretch block, the load then being increased
slightly to give the material a final stretch.

One type of machine used in stretch-wrap forming is shown in Fig. 12.14.
Here the work-piece is gripped between two sets of jaws, one set of which is
fixed to the rotatable table and the other set to a tension cylinder which is

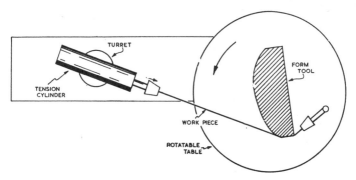

Fig. 12.14—Rotary Machine for Stretch-wrap Forming.

mounted on a movable turret. The initial stretching load is applied with the
work-piece straight. The table is then rotated to a pre-set stop so that
the work-piece is wrapped progressively round the form tool from one end to the
other. The load is kept constant during the operation by automatic adjustment
in the tension cylinder. After wrapping is complete the material is given a
final stretch.

12.64
Stretch blocks are generally made from wood or compressed resin-bonded
plywoods, but other materials, such as cast synthetic resins, zinc-base alloys
or reinforced concrete, are also used. When only low pressures are involved
during stretching a light lubricating oil is generally applied to the stretch
block by brush or spray, but for work entailing heavy pressures between the
stretch block and the component high-pressure grease is usually smeared on
to the tool.

Although stretch-forming is applied mainly to the heat-treatable alloys of
aluminium, any ductile metal can be shaped by this method. Stainless steel

and titanium are stretch-formed on a commercial scale, whilst magnesium alloys are stretch-formed whilst hot.

COINING

12.70

Coining is a cold-forging operation in which deformation takes place entirely by compression, and is confined mainly to the manufacture of coins, badges, medals, keys, identification discs and small metal plaques. The size of the work is limited because of the enormous pressures which are required to

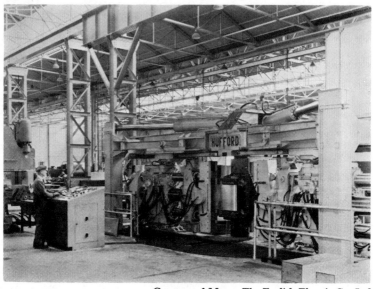

Courtesy of Messrs The English Electric Co. Ltd.

PLATE 12.6—A Stretch-wrap Forming Press Used in the Production of Narrow-wing Skin Section for Aircraft.

make metal flow whilst cold. Frequently pressures in excess of 1 500 N/mm^2 are required to produce sharp impressions, though presses capable of higher duty are generally employed in order to ensure a sufficient working margin.

12.71

The coining operation is carried out in a closed die (Fig. 12.15), and no provision is made for the extrusion of excess metal. Consequently, considerable attention must be paid to the gauge of the blanks in order to avoid any possible damage to the die by the development of excessive pressures due to the volume of the work-piece being too great.

The pressure required depends mainly on the extent to which the metal has to flow and upon its malleability, but it is also increased by a higher speed of working. Often the resultant thickness of the coin is greater than that of the original blank, and considerable flow of metal must then take place.

If a small indentation is made in a thin metal sheet supported on a hard foundation a bulge forms around the indentation. When this bulge is prevented from forming by the pressure of a die the whole work-piece must undergo lateral deformation. Thus, metal must flow sideways despite the restraining forces imposed by friction between the metal and the die surfaces. Consequently, with thin blanks the energy required to effect coining is enormous.

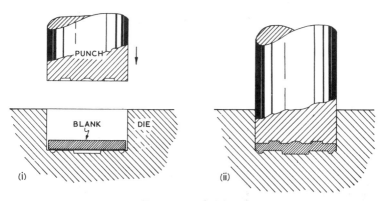

FIG. 12.15—Coining.

12.72
In the production of coins, blanks are first sheared from hard-rolled strip, and these blanks are then 'rimmed' by rolling the edges. After being annealed and pickled they are fed by automatic mechanisms to the minting press, where they receive the required impressions by upper and lower dies.

Coining is also used to obtain accurate dimensions in a part which has already been formed by another process. The operation is then generally referred to as 'sizing'.

EMBOSSING
12.80
Embossing differs from coining in that little or no change takes place in the thickness of the blank pressing. The energy required to emboss metal is therefore much less than in coining, since little lateral flow takes place in the blank.

The material used for embossing operations is generally thinner than that used for coining, and the process is effected by means of male and female dies (Fig. 12.16). The process therefore involves a combination of bending and stretching rather than flow under compressive forces which prevails in coining operations.

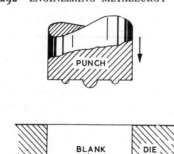
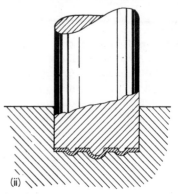
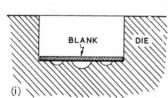

FIG. 12.16—Embossing.

HIGH ENERGY-RATE FORMING

12.90

The principles of high energy-rate forming—or HERF—were mentioned briefly in connection with its application to forging processes (8.22), and pneumo-mechanical methods of employing energy at a high rate were described. In this context it is the *rate* at which energy is dissipated by the work-piece rather than the total amount of energy used which is important. Thus, it is estimated that by detonating 0·1 kg of a suitable high explosive, energy is released so quickly that it is dissipated at a rate equivalent to approximately 6×10^6 kW. Consequently, since force can be transmitted more efficiently and quickly by fluids than by orthodox mechanical devices, many HERF processes rely on the use of chemical explosives or high-voltage electrical discharges under water to provide this high-rate release of energy. Currently, HERF processes are operating which use the following sources of energy:

(i) chemical explosives;

(ii) high-voltage electrical discharge;

(iii) electro-magnetic fields;

(iv) pneumo-mechanical methods involving the kinetic energy of fast-moving masses as in the 'Dynapak' machine (8.37).

The origins of HERF are by no means new. Fishlock and Hards in their 'New Ways of Working Metals' suggest that that important piece of furniture found in saloons of the American West, the spitoon, was the product of explosive forming. Whilst this may be no more than a colourful legend, it is known that towards the end of the 1880s—a period of great technological progress—embossing was carried out by this method.

12.91 Explosive Forming

A chemical explosive is a substance which takes part in a chemical reaction, releasing very rapidly a large volume of gas and, generally, considerable amounts of heat in the process. Most explosives are solids or liquids containing nitrogen combined with carbon, hydrogen and oxygen. On detonation nitrogen gas is suddenly released whilst the carbon and hydrogen also form gaseous products with the oxygen. In a HERF process this rapidly-expanding volume of gas is made to do work at a high rate.

High explosives are generally used in HERF processes since the reaction is completed in a very short time (of the order of microseconds). Consequently energy is dissipated at the required high rate. Low explosives on the other hand require a finite time for the reaction to be completed. 'Cordtex' and other detonating-fuse materials are useful in HERF processes. These are usually based upon the high explosive penta-erythritol tetranitrate (PETN), $C(CH_2.NO_3)_4$. On detonation this forms a large volume of gas very quickly:

$$C(CH_2.NO_3)_4 \rightarrow 4H_2O + 3CO_2 + 2CO + 2N_2 + Heat$$
(gas)

Another high explosive of use in metal forming processes is cyclo-trimethylene trinitromine (RDX). This became famous as the explosive used by Dr Barnes Wallis in bombs for the dam-buster epic of the Second World War.

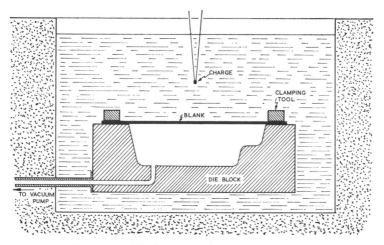

FIG. 12.17—The Principles of Explosion Forming.

Fig. 12.17 illustrates the principles of an explosive-forming process. Here the charge is suspended in water above the blank and is referred to as the 'stand-off' method. On detonation of the charge, shock waves are transmitted by the water (which is incompressible) to the metal blank forcing it to take the shape of the die. The die cavity is evacuated prior to detonation.

In practice quite small units can be used, in appearance not unlike small pressure vessels. Nevertheless the process is not suitable at this stage for 'shop-floor' production, or for mass production generally. Inevitably labour costs are high in dealing with dangerous explosives since skilled and careful operatives must be employed. Moreover, plenty of space must be available in order to locate such plant at a safe distance from other activities.

Many die materials are available. Clay and plaster are useful for one-off components, whilst concrete, hard wood, epoxy resins, aluminium, zinc-base alloys and mild steel all have their uses dependent upon the length of run required. Dies are relatively cheap to produce, not only as a result of the use of these materials, but because a 'half-die' only is necessary as compared with a conventional pressing operation.

Other advantages of explosive forming include:

(i) Large components up to 2·5 m in diameter can be formed. This is beyond the capacity of normal presswork;

(ii) 'Spring-back' is much less when high explosives are used. Hence closer dimensional tolerances are possible;

(iii) The capital cost of equipment is small compared with that for conventional forming processes;

(iv) Re-entrant and other difficult shapes can be formed more easily than by other methods.

The process is particularly suitable at present for prototype production or for very short production runs. The 6·7 m long segments for the American 'Saturn S II' moon rocket were shaped in this way.

12.92 Electro-hydraulic Forming

This is similar in application to explosive forming but the explosive charge of the latter process is replaced by a high-energy electric arc produced in water.

Electrical energy is 'trickled' into a capacitor bank (Fig. 12.18) which stores the necessary energy to produce the high-energy spark. As the spark

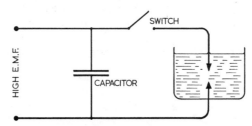

Fig. 12.18—The Principles of Electro-hydraulic Forming.

passes between the electrodes, heating of the water is such that ionisation takes place and produces a high-temperature gas bubble in about 4 microseconds. As the speed of expansion of the bubble is greater than the speed of sound, shock waves are generated in the water.

The process is best suited to small-scale production and has been successfully used in the forming of dental plates in stainless steel as well as other small parts.

12.93 Electro-magnetic Forming

In this process a considerable charge of electrical energy is built up in a similar manner to that used in the electro-hydraulic method mentioned above.

Instead of being discharged across a spark gap, however, the energy is released through a coil causing the rapid build-up of a magnetic field to an extremely high flux density. In turn this induces a high current in the work-piece which is placed within the coil (Fig. 12.19 (i)). Since the insulated

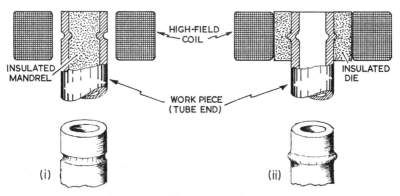

FIG. 12.19—Electro-magnetic Forming.

mandrel does not allow the field to pass *inside* the work piece, the induced 'magnetic pressure' acts only on the outside of the tube. Thus, as the two fields repel each other, the work-piece is thrown with great radial momentum against the mandrel/former. By interposing the insulated former between the coil and the work-piece (Fig. 12.19 (ii)) the latter can be forced in the opposite direction.

This particular HERF process is at present used mainly in the manner outlined above, namely the shrinking and expanding of tubes, or the shrinking of collars on to tubes. By using the 'Magnaform' process a collar can be shrunk on to a tube at a cost of approximately 0·75p as compared with using a 10p 'jubilee' clip.

BIBLIOGRAPHY

1 'The Final Forming and Shaping of Wrought Non-ferrous Metals', Symposium (Institute of Metals).
2 'Metal Spinning', Machinery's Yellow Back No. 7.
3 'Aluminium Forming', Reynold's Metal Co., Louisville, Kentucky.
4 'Presswork and Presses', J. A. Grainger (Machinery Publishing Co.).
5 'Fundamentals of the Working of Metals', G. Sachs (Pergamon Press).
6 'Pressworking of Metals', C. W. Hinman (McGraw-Hill).
7 'Aluminium, Vol. III—Fabrication and Finishing, Ed. K. R. van Horn (American Society for Metals).
8 'Principles of Magnesium Technology', E. F. Emley (Pergamon Press).
9 'Press Practice with Rubber Dies', Machinery's Yellow Back No. 18.
10 'Recent Progress in Metal Working' (Institute of Metals).
11 'New Ways of Working Metals', D. Fishlock and K. W. Hards (Newnes).

Chapter thirteen
THE HEAT-TREATMENT OF STEEL

13.10

Basic principles of the heat-treatment of steel were discussed in Part I, (chapters eleven, twelve and thirteen). The present chapter, therefore should be read as supplementary to these, and is meant to serve as an introduction to some of the industrial techniques and equipment used in the heat-treatment of steels.

A study of Part I (chapters eleven and twelve) will have indicated to the reader that any heat-treatment process applied to steel involves:

(*a*) heating the steel uniformly to some predetermined temperature;

(*b*) cooling it at a rate which will produce in it the desired type of structure.

Whilst from early times steel has been successfully heat-treated by craftsmen using knowledge based on long experience in the visual estimation of temperature, twentieth-century heat-treatment generally demands the control of such temperatures by the use of an efficient pyrometer system. Only in this way can uniform properties be obtained in large numbers of identical components.

13.11

In the hardening of a piece of hypo-eutectoid steel it is obvious that unless the steel is heated throughout beyond its upper critical temperature, then some ferrite may be retained in the structure both before and after quenching. At the same time the steel must not be heated too high above the upper critical temperature before quenching, or grain growth with all its attendant ills will take place. Consequently, the temperature range from which the piece of steel can be quenched is in practice quite small, and the adoption of pyrometric control is therefore almost essential. Further, many of the heat-treatment processes applied to steel are conducted at temperatures below red heat, and it is therefore not possible to estimate these temperatures by colour. The need for pyrometrically controlled furnaces then becomes obvious.

13.12

Structural faults associated with the use of unsuitable temperatures are not the only difficulties which can arise in the heat-treatment of steel. A furnace atmosphere which is chemically unsuitable may have adverse effects upon the chemical composition, and hence upon the physical properties of the surface layer of steel. Oxygen in the furnace atmosphere will cause decarburisation of the surface of the component being heat-treated. In the case of tool steels this will lead to loss of hardness, and in any steel to a loss of uniformity of properties over a cross-section. It may therefore be necessary to adopt some form of atmosphere control in the furnace. Although the structure obtained as a result of heat-treatment is not directly dependent upon the rate of initial heating, in practice the heating stage should be carried out as quickly as possible in order to minimise grain growth and decarburisation at the surface

Courtesy of Messrs Electric Resistance Furnace Co. Ltd, Weybridge.

PLATE 13.1—Electric Resistance Furnace for Heat-treatment Processes up to 1 000° C. A gas screen is provided to protect the charge during the heat-treatment cycle.

of the component being treated. The main requirements of a heat-treatment furnace therefore are that it shall be capable of maintaining an accurately controlled temperature and have a heat input sufficient to deal rapidly with the size of charge for which it is designed. Adequate atmosphere control must also be provided in order to reduce to a minimum changes in carbon content of the steel being heated.

FURNACES USED IN HEAT-TREATMENT

13.20

Gas and electricity are heating agents which permit the most accurate control in heat-treatment furnaces, and are consequently the most commonly used. Gas furnaces can be of the directly fired type in which the products of combustion of the burning fuel enter the heating chamber. Alternatively, they can be indirectly fired so that the furnace hearth is isolated from the products of combustion. Such a furnace will obviously have a lower fuel efficiency, but deleterious reactions between the surface of the charge and the products of

Courtesy of Messrs Birlec Ltd, Birmingham, 24.

PLATE 13.2—Batch-type Electric Resistance Furnaces for Annealing, Normalising, Hardening, Tempering and Carburising of Steel.

combustion will be avoided. A third type of gas-fired furnace is the radiant-tube variety, in which gas, burning inside metal tubes projecting through the heating chamber provides a source of radiant heat. As with the indirectly heated furnaces, the charge is similarly isolated from the products of combustion.

13.21

Electric furnaces are generally of the resistance type, in which heat is generated by a current passing through a high-resistance conductor of metal or silicon carbide. In some salt-bath furnaces the salt itself acts as the conductor and is heated by the electricity passing through it. Of recent years high-frequency induction furnaces have found increasing application in many heat-treatment processes.

Whatever the source of heat, annealing, normalising, hardening, tempering and other heat-treatment processes are carried out in a wide variety of furnaces, ovens, liquid baths and induction units. The choice of equipment depends upon several factors, among which are the degree and accuracy of temperature required, the limits on surface scaling and decarburisation, and the volume of production.

13.22

Furnaces may, in general, be classified as being of the batch or of the continuous type. Batch furnaces, which include the liquid-bath variety, are most suitable for short production runs and for dealing with the treatment of miscellaneous parts with varying heating cycles. The use of liquid-bath furnaces limits undesirable surface reactions and permits of rapid and uniform heating and accurate temperature control. A particular benefit arising from the use of a salt bath is that, on immersion in the liquid salt, a work-piece

Courtesy of Messrs Electric Resistance Furnace Co. Ltd,
Weybridge.

PLATE 13.3—Sectional Model of 'Cyclone' Air-circulating Type of Electric Resistance Furnace for Tempering Steel Parts.

becomes encased in a 'cocoon' of frozen salt which acts as an insulator and protects it from thermal shock due to too rapid a rate of heating. Continuous-type furnaces are characterised by higher thermal efficiency than the batch type, and are naturally more economical for relatively long production runs on identical components.

13.23
Batch-type furnaces which are installed to deal with a large output are generally of the horizontal type; that is they are charged horizontally through

a door at one end of the heating chamber. These furnaces, whether heated by gas or electricity, range in size from small units (Plate 13.1), used for hardening and tempering in the tool room, to large-capacity furnaces (Plate 13.2), used for various annealing, normalising, hardening and tempering processes on a full-scale production basis. Fig. 13.1 illustrates an interesting example of a modern horizontal gas-fired, batch-type furnace used for tempering and annealing processes at temperatures up to 675° C. In this furnace the atmosphere is circulated by a fan system in order that a uniform temperature shall

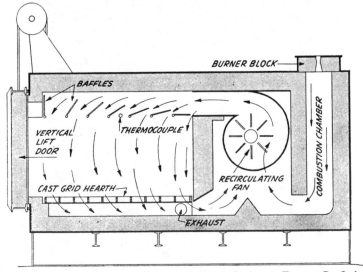

Courtesy of Electric Resistance Furnace Co. Ltd.

Fig. 13.1—Gas-fired Batch-type Furnace.

be attained throughout the charge. The equipment is supplied with heating-chamber capacities varying between 0·15 and 45·0 m³.

Some horizontal batch furnaces, designed for use with a protective atmosphere, are provided with a cooling chamber at the end farthest from the charging door. When the period of heat-treatment is complete the charge, which is contained in suitable trays, is pushed into the cooling chamber so that it may cool in a non-oxidising atmosphere.

One of the best-known vertical batch-type heat-treatment furnaces is that shown in Fig. 13.2. This is a small electrically heated, air-circulating furnace used extensively for tempering processes at temperatures up to 700° C. In this furnace the atmosphere circulation promotes uniformity and precise control of temperatures as well as the rapid transfer of heat from the nickel–chromium heater elements to the charge.

13.24

Larger vertical pit furnaces, generally electrically heated (Plate 13.4), are used for various heat-treatment processes up to 1 000°C. Vertical bell-type furnaces are sometimes used when strict control of the furnace atmosphere is necessary. In these furnaces the work is loaded on to a platform over which a heat-resisting steel hood is placed. A protective atmosphere is then circulated through the hood before the electric heater bell is lowered over the complete unit.

13.25
Salt-bath furnaces are essentially of the vertical batch type. Fig. 13.3 illustrates the principle of the electrode salt bath. In this type of furnace one or more pairs of electrodes are immersed in the salt, which, in the molten state, is a conductor of electricity. Each pair of electrodes is closely spaced,

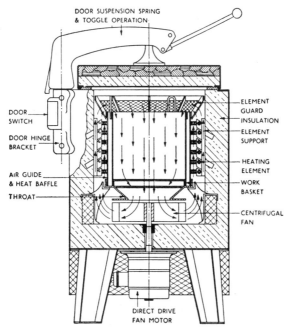

Courtesy of Wild-Barfield Electric Furnace Ltd.

FIG. 13.2—General Arrangement of a Vertical Forced-air Circulation Furnace.

and when an electric current flows through the molten salt in the gap between the electrodes the salt becomes heated by direct resistance. The electrodes are grouped so that a circulation of the salt is produced by electro-magnetic force generated around each pair of electrodes. When work is immersed in the bath it is effectively isolated from contact with the atmosphere so that decarburisation and oxidation are prevented. Moreover, when the work is withdrawn from the bath it remains coated with a thin protective film of salt until the moment it enters the quenching medium. If an appropriate salt mixture is employed a furnace of this type can be used for liquid carburising cyanide hardening; hardening in neutral bath; tempering; annealing; and the heat-treatment of high-speed steel.

Compositions and uses of some typical salt mixtures used for the salt-bath treatment of steels are given in Table 13.1. During use chemical changes are likely to take place in some of these mixtures. Chloride baths tend to become oxidised on long exposure to the atmosphere, and the oxychlorides which are formed have a decarburising effect on the surface of the work being treated. Similarly, any metallic oxides which are formed in the bath will have a

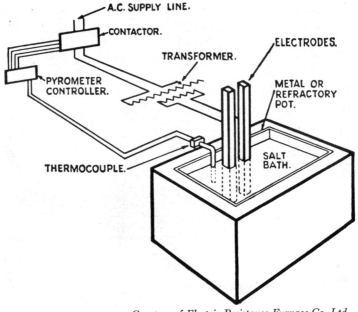

Courtesy of Electric Resistance Furnace Co. Ltd.

FIG. 13.3—Principle of the Electrode Salt-bath Furnace.

decarburising action on the work. Consequently, some form of 'rectification' must be applied to the fused bath when this becomes necessary. Borax or boric acid additions are used to convert oxychlorides to a sludge which can be removed from the bath; silica additions combine with metallic oxides to form silicates, which settle as a heavy sludge. This sludge should not be permitted to fall on to the electrodes, or overheating of the latter will take place and lead to a reduction of their working life. To avoid the formation of this heavy sludge, rectification may be obtained by the alternative method of suspending a graphite rod in the bath. Graphite chemically reduces any metallic oxides to free metal, which tends to adhere to the rod, with which it can be withdrawn.

13.26

Lead-bath furnaces also fall into this category, and are used for heating small parts in the temperature range 350–900° C. The lead pot is heated by gas, and the principal advantage of the furnace is the maintenance of a uniform bath temperature due to the high heat conductivity of the lead. The latter also effectively seals the work from the atmosphere.

13.27
Continuous furnaces are provided with some form of mechanism, usually a chain hearth, to carry the work through the heating zone. A protective atmosphere is nearly always used. Since the furnace is continuous in operation, the entrance and exit of the heating chamber must be sealed by some flexible

Courtesy of Messrs G. W. B. Furnaces Ltd, Dudley.

PLATE 13.4—Electric-resistance Heated Vertical Pit Furnace Used for Hardening Axle Shafts.
The quench tanks are adjacent to the furnace.

device, such as a chain curtain. Ingress of air is therefore prevented by arranging a small positive pressure of gas in the heating chamber and by equipping the furnace with an entrance tunnel through which gas flows gently, flushing away any air tending to enter the furnace. Similarly, a cooling tunnel is built on the exit side, so that the work will have cooled to a safe temperature before reaching the outside atmosphere. Such a furnace is similar in design to that shown in Fig. 14.7.

Continuous furnaces of the controlled-atmosphere type can be adapted for a process which involves heating followed by quenching. The quenching tank is placed adjacent to the end of the heating chamber so that the work-pieces fall from the moving hearth into the tank. The tank itself is covered by a hood which ensures that the protective furnace atmosphere extends above the quenching medium (Plate 13.5).

13.28

In addition to continuity of output and high thermal efficiency, continuous furnaces have the advantage that uniformity of treatment is assured when large numbers of components are to be treated. Both temperature and time of treatment are automatically controlled, whereas with batch furnaces the *time* of treatment often depends upon the human element.

Courtesy of Messrs Birlec Ltd, Birmingham, 24.

PLATE 13.5—Continuous Conveyor Furnace Used for the Bright Hardening of Steel Parts.

The heated components are discharged through a protective atmosphere into the quench tank shown on the right of the photograph.

THE CONTROL OF FURNACE ATMOSPHERE

13.30

The effects of oxygen in promoting scaling of metallic surfaces during heat-treatment are well known, and reference to the surface oxidation of non-ferrous metals and alloys will be made in the next chapter. During the heat-treatment of steels, however, an additional difficulty is encountered in the decarburisation, which inevitably accompanies scaling of the surface when the heated steel is exposed to an atmosphere which contains free oxygen or, in certain circumstances, other gases which contain combined oxygen.

13.31

Under some conditions of temperature and concentration these gases will give up their combined oxygen at the surface of the hot steel, so that scaling and decarburisation of the latter take place. Thus carbon dioxide and water vapour, though often classed as non-reactive gases, can react at high temperatures with the surface of steel—

$$\boxed{Fe} + CO_2 \rightleftharpoons FeO + CO$$

$$\boxed{C} + CO_2 \rightleftharpoons 2CO$$

$$Fe + H_2O \rightleftharpoons FeO + H_2.$$

Thus if present in the atmosphere of a heat-treatment furnace both carbon dioxide and water vapour may become oxidising agents. Sulphur dioxide can cause oxidation of the surface of steel in a similar manner.

13.32

The presence of reducing gases, such as hydrogen, carbon monoxide and methane, in the furnace atmosphere cannot, of course, lead to oxidation and scaling of the surface of the steel. They can, nevertheless, lead to alterations in the carbon content of the surface provided such reactions are favoured by suitable conditions of temperature and concentration. Hydrogen can give rise to *decarburisation* by combining with some of the carbon present at the surface of the steel—

$$C + 2H_2 \rightleftarrows CH_4.$$

Carbon monoxide and any unburned hydrocarbons of the methane type are, however, more likely to lead to *carburisation* of the surface if these gases are present in sufficient concentration—

$$\left. \begin{array}{l} 2CO \rightleftarrows CO_2 + C \\ CH_4 \rightleftarrows 2H_2 + C \end{array} \right\} \text{Dissolves in steel.}$$

The carbon which is liberated as a result of the above reactions is absorbed at the surface of the steel.

In all of the above reactions the relative concentrations of the gases involved will largely govern whether any particular gas shall have a carburising or a decarburising action on the steel. The furnace temperature, too, will affect the degree of dissociation of the furnace gases and, in general, the higher the temperature, the greater the extent of chemical reactions at the surface of the steel.

13.33

Greater thermal efficiency is generally obtained in a furnace in which the products of combustion of the fuel are allowed to circulate through or over the charge. In those furnaces which use solid or liquid fuel control of the resulting atmosphere is difficult, since oxygen must be admitted to the furnace chamber in order to effect combustion of the fuel. Moreover, such fuels often contain appreciable amounts of sulphur, and this will encourage scaling of the charge as mentioned above. These difficulties can be largely overcome by using a furnace of the muffle type, in which the heating chamber is completely isolated from the fuel and the products of its combustion (Fig. 13.4). Unfortunately such a furnace has a low thermal efficiency and, moreover, in order to exclude air from the furnace chamber some synthetic type of inert atmosphere must be passed into it. The production of these synthetic atmospheres is expensive.

When furnaces are fired by town gas, however, much closer control of the atmosphere is possible, since the gas and air are mixed before they enter the furnace chamber. Consequently, for many heat-treatment purposes the muffle can be dispensed with, since only the products of combustion reach the charge, the gas–air ratio being adjusted so as to avoid an excess of oxygen entering the furnace chamber.

Even so, at temperatures above 1 000° C products of combustion, such as carbon dioxide and water vapour, can react with the surface of the steel, giving rise to oxidation and decarburisation as already indicated. In such cases therefore it is safer to use a separate synthetic atmosphere which is circulated over the charge in a totally enclosed muffle chamber. Frequently

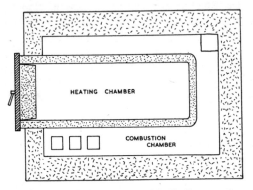

FIG. 13.4—Principle of the Muffle Furnace.

these atmospheres are based on burnt town gas from which water vapour and sulphur dioxide have been removed by condensation in a refrigerator system. The remaining gas is then mixed with some unburned town gas in such proportions as will give a balanced non-reactive atmosphere at the working temperature of the process.

13.34

'Pyrogenic decomposition' is also used to modify the composition of town gas in such a way as to render it suitable for use as a non-reactive atmosphere. In this method town gas is passed through a heated steel tube packed with mild-steel swarf and turnings. Those substances present in the gas which are likely to react with the surface of steel will do so with the mild-steel turnings. In this way reactive substances in the gas will be eliminated, so that a gas which is inert to the surface of the steel will pass into the furnace chamber. In particular, oxygen and sulphur are removed from the gas by this treatment, and an atmosphere consisting largely of hydrogen and methane is the result. Such an atmosphere, however, is useful only below 1 000° C, since above this temperature the dissociation of methane may lead to reactions at the surface of the steel, promoting carburisation.

'Endothermic generators' are widely used to provide either a protective or a carburising atmosphere from a hydrocarbon such as propane or methane by allowing the gas to react with a controlled amount of air. The resultant atmosphere consists mainly of carbon monoxide, nitrogen and hydrogen with small controllable quantities of carbon dioxide and water vapour.

13.35
Frequently electric furnaces operating at low temperatures, such as in the tempering of steel, do not use a protective atmosphere, and air is allowed to circulate in the heating chamber. The atmospheres used in high-temperature electric furnaces, however, are often based on town gas or 'cracked' ammonia. Since the latter is also widely used in the production of inert atmospheres for the heat-treatment of copper and many of its alloys, this aspect of atmosphere control will be dealt with in the next chapter (14.52).

13.36
Charcoal is used as a raw material for the production of a non-reactive atmosphere in the electric furnace treatment of some steel parts where decarburisation must be avoided. Since charcoal is almost free of sulphur, a clean atmosphere is produced which contains approximately one volume of carbon monoxide to two volume of nitrogen along with traces of carbon dioxide. Such an atmosphere is more expensive to produce than one from cracked ammonia, but it is superior in that its use completely eliminates decarburisation.

QUENCHING OPERATIONS

13.40
The choice of a quenching medium is governed by the type of steel being treated and the resultant properties which it is required to possess. Thus, whilst 10% brine or 5–10% caustic soda solutions are occasionally used to provide the very rapid cooling conditions necessary to produce maximum hardness in a plain-carbon tool steel or a case-hardening steel, oil quenching and air quenching are commonly used to harden alloy steels.

13.41
Water and oil are the two chief quenching media, however, and the bulk of all quenching is done in one or the other. Water provides a quenching rate roughly three times as fast as that of oil, and is used mainly with plain carbon steels. Since alloy steels now form a much more important group than the heat-treatable plain carbon steels, oil has probably become more widely used as a quenching medium than water.

13.42
Fused salts (Table 13.1) or molten lead are used as quenching media in such processes as austempering or the hardening of some high-speed steels. Hot-salt quenching provides rather slow cooling relative to molten lead, and is therefore unsuitable for austempering those steels in which the austenite–pearlite transformation begins after only a short time-lag (12.46—Part I).

13.43
Air-hardening is used for those steels with an alloy content high enough to reduce transformation rates to a point where martensite is formed when the steel is cooled in a current of air. In fact, thin sections in steels of this type will often cool quickly enough in still air to become fully hardened, whilst very heavy sections may need to be oil-quenched in order to obtain similar

TABLE 13.1—*Typical Salt-bath Compositions*

Composition %										Melting point (°C)	Working range (°C)	Uses
Sodium chloride	Potassium chloride	Barium chloride	Calcium chloride	Barium carbonate	Sodium carbonate	Sodium nitrate	Sodium nitrite	Potassium nitrate	Sodium cyanide			
—	—	—	—	—	—	—	40–50	50–60	—	140	160–650	Austempering, martempering. Tempering of carbon- and low-alloy steels
—	—	—	—	—	—	40–50	—	50–60	—	225	260–650	Tempering carbon- and low-alloy steels and high-speed steels
30–40	—	—	—	—	—	30–50	—	—	15–40	550	620–820	Quenching high-speed steels
15–25	—	25–35	45–55	—	—	—	—	—	—	480	510–760	Tempering high-speed steels
—	50	—	—	—	50	—	—	—	—	540	620–820	Annealing carbon- and low-alloy steels
45–55	45–55	—	—	—	—	—	—	—	—	675	730–900	Neutral hardening
15–25	20–30	50–60	—	—	—	—	—	—	—	595	675–930	Pre-heating high-speed steels
10–30	—	70–90	—	—	—	—	—	—	—	705	760–1100	Heating high-speed steel for hardening
—	—	98 min.	—	—	—	—	—	—	—	980	1040–1340	Heating high-speed steel for hardening
4–8	—	92–96	—	—	—	—	—	—	—	870	950–1260	Heating high-speed steel for hardening / Annealing stainless steels
15–25	—	—	—	20–30	—	—	—	—	45–50	620	820–950	Cyanide hardening

properties in them. The general practice, however, is to cool such steels in an air blast, since this treatment produces a martensitic structure in the thickness of section which is usually employed. Sometimes a blast of protective gas, such as cracked ammonia or burnt town gas, is used to give a 'bright-hardened' finish.

THE PRINCIPLES OF QUENCHING

13.50

When a piece of heated steel is plunged into a liquid quenching medium the outer surface will cool more rapidly than the core, as indicated by the two curves in Fig. 13.5. Though they differ in steepness, both curves consist

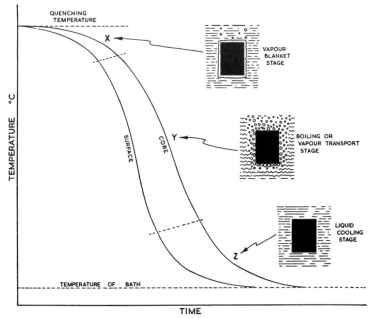

FIG. 13.5—Characteristic Quenching Curves.

essentially of three portions X, Y and Z, which are known respectively as the vapour-blanket stage, the vapour-transport or boiling stage and the liquid cooling stage. Any liquid gives a curve of this general form, provided that its boiling point is below the quenching temperature of the specimen.

13.51

As soon as the hot work-piece is plunged into the bath it becomes surrounded by a blanket of vapourised quenching medium, and cooling can only take place by conduction and radiation through this vapour blanket. Since vapours have low thermal conductivities compared with liquids, cooling during this stage of the quenching process is slow. This situation is undesirable, since slow cooling in the upper temperature range may permit some transformation of the steel to take place in this temperature range. That is, the cooling curve may cut into the nose of the modified T.T.T. curve (12.44—Part I), with the result that some pearlite is formed.

13.52
When the temperature of the specimen has fallen such that a continuous film of vapour can no longer be maintained at its surface, liquid comes into contact with the surface of the hot metal and vigorous boiling begins. Heat is thus abstracted rapidly from the work-piece in the form of latent heat of vaporisation of the quenching medium, and the cooling curve becomes correspondingly steep. Moreover, the evolution of bubbles of vapour gives rise to strong convection currents around the work-piece, and these constitute a more positive cooling action than can be obtained from simple conduction, which in this instance is of minor importance. Cooling during this vapour-transport stage must take place at a speed equal to or greater than the critical cooling rate of the steel if its partial transformation at high temperatures is to be avoided. Since the temperature of the work-piece during this vapour-transport stage is above the M_s line (12.43—Part I), extremely rapid cooling through this range will not harm the structure, since it is still completely austenitic.

13.53
When the work-piece has cooled to approximately the boiling point of the quenching medium boiling ceases and the vapour-transport stage ends. Cooling during the final or liquid cooling stage therefore proceeds by conduction and convection only, and is very much slower than in the vapour-transport stage. The relationship between the M_s temperature of the steel being quenched and the temperature range of the third or liquid-cooling stage for the quenching medium is important. If the work-piece is still cooling rapidly by vapour transport when the M_s line is reached, then distortion or cracking of the specimen will be likely to occur because the outer skin will change from austenite to martensite an appreciable interval before the inner core begins to change. If, however, the liquid cooling stage begins just above the M_s line, then the rate of cooling will have been considerably reduced by the time the temperature of the work-piece reaches that of the M_s line. Quench cracks or distortion will therefore be less likely to form.

13.54
This largely explains why oil is superior to water as a quenching medium when the avoidance of quenching cracks is important. As indicated in Fig. 13.6, the liquid cooling stage for oil begins at a higher temperature than that for water. In fact, it begins above the M_s line for the steel. Consequently, the temperature gradient within a work-piece which has been quenched in oil is considerably reduced by the time the M_s line has been reached.

13.55
In the vapour-transport stage the curve for water slopes more steeply than that for oil. This means that water is much more effective as a quenching

medium for those steels with high critical cooling rates (12.44—Part I). For this reason water is generally used for quenching plain carbon steels, whilst oils can be used for those alloy steels which have much lower critical cooling rates. This advantage in respect of water is, however, offset to some extent by the greater insulating effect of steam during the primary or vapour-blanket stage. Whilst the steam blanket does not necessarily persist longer than the

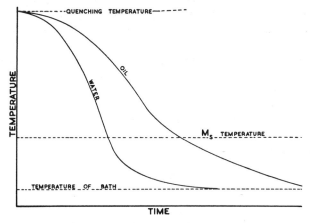

FIG. 13.6—Comparative Quenching Curves—Oil and Water.

oil vapour blanket, its conductivity is lower and its overall retarding effect slightly greater. This insulating effect increases as the bath temperature rises, because the boiling point of water is much lower than the lowest temperature at which oil begins to boil.

13.56
The quenching power of oils varies little up to bath temperature in the region of 80° C. This is due to the fact that viscosity falls as the temperature rises and this effect offsets to a great extent that of the rise in temperature, which naturally retards heat transfer from the work-piece to the oil. Moreover, since the oil is still well below its boiling point, the duration of the vapour-blanket stage is not materially altered. Consequently, whilst aqueous media must be maintained at a low temperature of, say, 25° C if their quenching power is to be maintained at a constant level, the temperature of oil baths can be allowed to vary between shop temperature and 80° C without significant change in the quenching power of the medium.

13.57
The cooling rate during quenching is dependent largely upon the degree of agitation which prevails. Not only does agitation continuously bring fresh cold liquid to the surface of the work-piece but it also helps to break down the initial vapour blanket, and thus accelerate cooling in the primary stages of quenching. The ideal condition therefore is to circulate the quenching medium and at the same time move the work-piece about in the bath. In this

way a very considerable increase in the cooling rate is achieved, and oil which is violently agitated can be made to provide as rapid a quench as static water.

QUENCHING OILS

13.60

Whilst it is on the whole advantageous that a quenching oil should be warm, it must not be used at a temperature where ignition is likely to take place. One essential property of a quenching oil therefore is that it must have a high flash point relative to the working temperature of the bath.

Some oils tend to oxidise and, in consequence, thicken rather quickly during use. This inevitably leads to an increase in viscosity of the oil and a corresponding reduction in its quenching power. Moreover, scum may form on the surface of the bath and heavy sludge deposit on the cooling coils of the tank.

13.61

The main requirements of a quenching oil therefore are that:

(*a*) it shall promote uniform rates of cooling;

(*b*) it should not emit vapour at low temperatures;

(*c*) it should not oxidise or thicken during use.

Quenching oils fall into two main groups—fatty oils and mineral oils. The former are of animal or vegetable origin and include:

(i) mammalian oils—tallow oil, lard oil, neat's-foot oil;

(ii) marine mammalian oils—whale oil, sperm oil, seal oil;

(iii) fish oils—cod oil, herring oil;

(iv) vegetable oils—rape oil, groundnut oil, olive oil, coconut oil, cottonseed oil, palm oil, castor oil.

All of these oils, like organic compounds in general, are composed fundamentally of the elements carbon, hydrogen and oxygen. They consist mainly of mixtures of compounds known as glyceryl esters (compounds related to glycerol) and fatty acids, such as stearic, oleic and palmitic.

13.62

Mineral oils are produced during the distillation of crude petroleum, and may be used as straight mineral quenching oils, or they may be blended with a small quantity of fatty oil. In general, mineral oils are regarded as being superior to fatty oils as quenching media. Fatty oils have a greater tendency to oxidise during use and exposure to the atmosphere. They therefore tend to deposit sludge and scum more quickly and to become generally thicker. Not only does their quenching power deteriorate in this way but loss due to 'drag out' is also increased. Moreover, fatty oils are unsatisfactory for use in conjunction with salt-bath heating furnaces, since reactions between residual salt clinging to the work-pieces and the oil leads to the formation of metallic soaps, which tend to insulate the work-pieces and also reduce the life of the bath. Finally, fatty oils often develop evil-smelling compounds under the action of hot steel, as any reader who has used whale oil as a quenching medium will appreciate. Mineral oils are relatively free from these disadvantages and this fact, coupled with the near-extinction of the whale due to over-hunting in recent years, has led to mineral oils becoming more popular as quenching media.

QUENCHING EQUIPMENT

13.70
Quenching tanks vary in size from vessels of a few litres capacity containing static quenching media to large installations involving thousands of litres of quenching medium which is circulated and cooled.

As stated earlier in this chapter, in order to harden a component satisfactorily, it is necessary to bring a sufficient quantity of cold quenching medium into contact with its surface. Relative motion between the quenching medium and the work-piece must therefore be achieved by moving either or both of them.

13.71
Slender components may need to be held still in order to avoid distortion by the mechanical pressure of the quenching medium; otherwise the work-piece is nearly always moved about in the quenching bath. This motion not only circulates the medium so that the work-piece does not remain enclosed in an overheated layer but is also helps to disperse the vapour blanket which is formed in the initial stages of quenching. The quenching of a limited number of small components is usually carried out by hand agitation; the parts being held in tongs or suspended on wires. Large components are often hung in the quenching medium on chains, by means of which they are swirled about in the bath until cool.

13.72
For mass production, however, some form of mechanical transfer of the work-piece to the tank, followed by automatic agitation, is required. Small and medium-sized parts can be hardened effectively by being fed into the quenching tank and allowed to fall through it into a basket. The height of fall through the quenching medium must be enough to ensure that when the components reach the basket they have already cooled past the nose of the relevant T.T.T. (12.44—Part I) curve, otherwise a slow cooling rate whilst they are lying in the basket may lead to softness.

The work basket may be replaced by a moving conveyor at the bottom of the tank if output is large enough to justify this, whilst large components may be introduced into the quenching tank down skid rails or on rollers. In some automatic systems the work-pieces are carried from the furnace on trays, which then pass into the quenching tank, where they remain until the components are cool. In those furnaces which employ a continually moving hearth and a protective atmosphere in the heating chamber, transfer from the furnace to the quenching medium may be made in a sealed compartment charged with protective atmosphere. This system reduces to a minimum the possibility of scaling and decarburisation.

13·73

When only limited quantities of small work-pieces are to be quenched shallow tanks holding 0·5–0·75 m³ of quenching medium are adequate, and circulation of the medium is achieved by hand agitation of the work-piece. If deep tanks are used, then a measure of gravity circulation of the medium occurs due to convection currents.

For continuous production on a large scale both circulation and cooling of the quenching medium by mechanical means are necessary. The usual method is to pump the quenching medium through an external cooling circuit consisting of a system of radiators or heat exchangers. Alternatively, internal cooling coils carrying cold water or refrigerated brine into the quenching tanks themselves. When an external cooling system is employed it is usual to incorporate in it a cleaning unit, particularly when the quenching medium used is oil. Gauze strainers to remove scale and other solid materials from the oil are used, whilst the inclusion in the circuit of a filter to remove sludge and water maintains the oil in a condition of maximum efficiency.

13·74

The volume of quenching medium necessary to cool a given mass of steel can be calculated easily, provided the hardening temperature of the steel and the permissible temperature rise of the quenching medium are known.

Let M = mass of the steel (kg);

C_s = average specific heat of the steel (J/kg °C);

T_h = hardening temperature of the steel (°C);

T_q = temperature of the steel when it is removed from the quenching tank (°C);

S = relative density of the quenching medium (kg/m³);

C_q = specific heat of the quenching medium (J/kg °C);

T_r = permissible temperature rise of the quenching medium (°C);

V = volume of quenching medium required (m³).

Then:

Heat given out by steel $= M \cdot C_s \cdot (T_h - T_q)$

Heat absorbed by the quenching medium $= V \cdot S \cdot C_q \cdot T_r$

$$\therefore V \cdot S \cdot C_q \cdot T_r = M \cdot C_s \cdot (T_h - T_q)$$

Hence:

$$V = \frac{M \cdot C_s \cdot (T_h - T_q)}{S \cdot C_q \cdot T_r}$$

This is the minimum volume of quenching medium which is capable of absorbing the heat liberated by the work when no cooling system is employed. When circulating and cooling systems are used the amount of quenching medium will be less than this.

13·75

A process known as press quenching is often used in hardening mass-produced components, such as gears, when uniform hardness and freedom from distortion are essential. The gears are transferred from the heating furnace to a quenching press, where they are firmly held between upper and lower dies. This corrects any slight distortion acquired during heating. Quenching oil is then admitted to the press, and the dies prevent any distortion from taking place during quenching. By this method quenching conditions are standardised and uniformity of properties in the product assured.

GAS-CARBURISING AND CASE-HARDENING

13.80

Case-hardening processes which depend upon the carbon enrichment of the surface of a low-carbon steel may employ either solid, liquid or gaseous media (19.20—Part I). Nowadays solid compounds and liquid baths are used only for small-scale operations, and large-scale production relies almost entirely upon gaseous reagents. In addition to the general surface cleanliness associated with gas carburising, foremost amongst other advantages of the process is the fact that large-scale production can be adopted on the continuous-flow principle.

13.81

The principal carburising gases are 'saturated' hydrocarbons of the paraffin series, namely, methane, CH_4; ethane, C_2H_6; propane, C_3H_8; and butane, C_4H_{10}. These are compounds of the general formula, C_nH_{2n+2}, and are far superior as carburising media to 'unsaturated' hydrocarbons such as the ethylene series (of general formula, C_nH_{2n}) which tend to deposit soot on the surface of the components during carburising due to a rapid release of 'excess' carbon when decomposition of the gas occurs.

Natural gas (mainly methane), 'LPG' (liquified petroleum gases) and 'manufactured' gas are sources of these carburising agents. Unfortunately, petroleum derivatives often contain large amounts of the soot-forming unsaturated hydrocarbons.

Liquids may also be used to produce carbon-rich gases. These include terpenes, benzene and 'oxygenated' hydrocarbons such as alcohol, ketones and glycols. Such liquids are fed in droplet form on to a heated target plate where thermal dissociation occurs to produce a carburising atmosphere containing carbon monoxide, carbon dioxide, water vapour and methane. Liquid feed-stock is very convenient to use with batch-type furnaces. Moreover, although the cost of these liquids is generally higher than that of gases, no external pipework is required to convey the gas to the furnace.

13.82

In a gas-carburising process it is usual to dilute the carburising agent with some form of 'carrier gas'. These carrier gases vary in composition from almost pure nitrogen to mixtures containing nitrogen, hydrogen, carbon monoxide and small quantities of methane and carbon dioxide and usually obtained by the partial combustion of town gas. 'Endothermic' mixtures containing little or no carbon dioxide are the most useful since carbon dioxide has a decarburising effect (13.31) and its presence must be counteracted by increasing the proportion of carburising gas mixed with the carrier.

Courtesy of Messrs Wild Barfield Ltd, Watford.

PLATE 13.6—A Pit-type Batch Furnace used for gas carburising extension steels of
rock drills.

Components such as these are suspended in a jig to prevent distortion during heat
treatment. The hydraulically-operated cover is seen swung to the left with the
atmosphere-circulating fan visible on the underside. The furnace retort remains in
position but can be cooled by external air flow to reduce the charge temperature to that
for quenching. Such furnaces may be heated by gas or electricity.

Courtesy of Messrs Wild Barfield Ltd, Watford.

PLATE 13.7—The Wild Barfield 'Ace' Sealed-quench Furnace, the operation of which
is indicated in Fig. 13.7.
In the above photograph a charge basket is seen on the loading table. These batch-type
furnaces may be heated by gas or electricity.

This in turn may lead to sooting of the surface. The amount of carburising
gas in the mixture may vary between 1% and 15% depending upon the
composition of the carrier gas and also upon other conditions prevailing. It
should be noted that in an 'endothermic' gas the carbon monoxide present
also has a carburising action (13.32).

13.83

Furnaces used for gas carburising may be either of the batch type or continuous
in operation. *Pit-type batch furnaces* similar to those shown in Plates 13.4 and
13.6 are very popular. These may be heated either by electric-resistance
units or gas-fired radiant tubes; a circulating fan being incorporated in the
sealing lid of the furnace chamber. The charge may be carried in the heating
chamber itself which, in this case, will need to be gas-tight; or it may be
carried in a separate gas-filled retort which is then lowered into the heating
chamber. Pit furnaces are often of considerable depth in order to accommodate long axle shafts and the like, suspended on a jig in a vertical position so

(1) Charge *A* is being heated in the carburising furnace, whilst *B* is in the purged air-free antechamber. *C* is on a loading table outside the furnace.

(2) *A* is transferred from the furnace to the gas-filled antechamber.

(3) The platform is lowered so that *A* is quenched and *B* is in a position to be loaded into the furnace.

(4) *B* is transferred from the antechamber to the furnace.

(5) *C* is moved into the antechamber.

(6) The platform is raised so that charge *A* is removed from the quench tank.

(7) *A* is recovered from the antechamber, and will be replaced by a new charge so that the above sequence can be repeated.

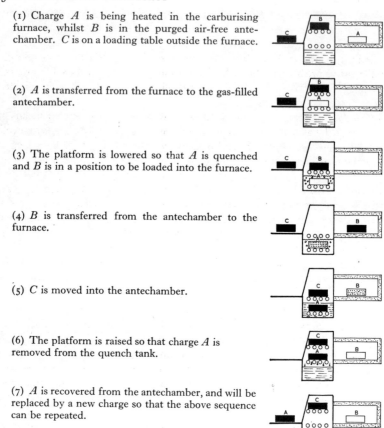

FIG. 13.7—The sequence of operations in the Wild Barfield 'Ace' sealed-quench furnace. *A*, *B* and *C* represent work baskets containing components being gas-carburised and subsequently hardened.

that a minimum of distortion will occur during treatment. The necessary quenching tank is generally sited alongside the furnace (Plate 13.4).

Horizontal Batch Furnaces are very convenient for the treatment of small- and medium-size components contained in rectangular baskets (Plate 13.7). Such furnaces are sometimes of the sealed-quench type, the operation of which is illustrated in Fig. 13.7. This system allows the complete treatment to be carried out without any contact between the charge and the external atmosphere. Again, these furnaces may be heated either by gas or electricity and have a built-in controlled system which adjusts the temperature of the charge from that of carburising to that of quenching.

Rotary-drum Batch Furnaces are used for gas-carburising and carbo-nitriding (19.46—Part I) and have the great advantage of eliminating the use of work baskets, the components being fed directly into the furnace retort. Constant slow rotation of the retort ensures uniformity of treatment.

Where large outputs are involved some form of continuous furnace is generally preferable. Such furnaces can be so constructed that, providing a small positive pressure in the carburising atmosphere is maintained, ingress of air is not possible (Plate 13.5) and either cooling or quenching can be effected in a controlled atmosphere.

In *Shaker-hearth Continuous Furnaces* the work is moved along by means of reciprocating shaker motion which can be regulated to control the time-cycle and hence, the case depth. Such furnaces are generally used for light-weight components which require shallow case depths of no more than 0·25 mm.

Pusher-type Continuous Furnaces are particularly versatile and will deal adequately with diversified charges. The work is pushed through the carburising zone on trays and, after treatment, may be quenched or cooled slowly. Pusher furnaces are generally constructed with purging vestibules at both charging and discharge ends in order to reduce contamination of the carburising atmosphere by air. Heating is more often than not by radiant tubes. Since these furnaces are relatively expensive their installation must be justified by a large output.

13.84 Variable Factors of the Process

The general object of carburising is to produce a carbon concentration at the surface of approximately eutectoid composition or just above. With high carbon concentrations in the carburising atmosphere, carburising may take place at such a rate that a considerable build-up of carbon occurs in the surface layers because diffusion of carbon inwards cannot keep pace with surface absorbtion. Conversely, the use of an atmosphere low in carbon may lead to a concentration of carbon in the skin of much less than eutectoid composition.

The diffusion of carbon into the surface of steel proceeds according to Fick's Laws (8.34—Part I). As might be expected, the rate of carbon absorption by austenite increases with temperature (19.20—Part I), though most gas-carburising is carried out between 900 and 950° C, depending mainly upon the depth of case required. A carburising temperature in the region of 920° C allows a reasonably high rate of carburisation without excessive deterioration of furnace equipment.

At any particular carburising temperature:

$$\text{Case depth} \propto \sqrt{\text{time of treatment } (t)}$$
$$\text{or Case depth} = K\sqrt{t}$$

At 900° C the value of K is approximately 0·533, hence

$$\text{Case depth} = 0 \cdot 533 \sqrt{t}$$

where the case depth is measured in mm and 't' in hours.

The value of 'K' increases with the temperature to 0·635 at 925° C so that the time necessary to produce a case of the required depth can be roughly estimated. Naturally, the time-cycle will need to be extended in order to allow for heating to the carburising temperature and also cooling to the quenching temperature, once carburising is complete.

13.85 Hardening

Despite theoretical considerations which favour a multi-stage heat-treatment after carburising (19.24—Part I), the bulk of gas-carburised components are hardened by quenching them direct from the carburising furnace. This is a much less costly policy since reheating becomes unnecessary. For this form of hardening a continuous furnace is preferable to the batch type since a cooling zone can be incorporated, in which the temperature of the work is allowed to fall from that of carburising to about 840° C prior to quenching. The work is fed into the quench tank which is integral with the rest of the equipment and under the same continuous protective atmosphere. A conveyor 'belt' (Plate 13.5) then discharges the hardened components from the system.

In some cases a separate heat-treatment process may be desirable as opposed to direct quenching. The following factors will generally influence the choice of process: (1) the size and shape of the component; (2) the need for selective carburising; (3) any subsequent manufacturing operations; (4) the type of steel being carburised.

13.86 Tempering

The bulk of gas-carburised components are put into service without being tempered after hardening. Some components, however, seem to benefit from tempering at a temperature between 150 and 200° C. Such low-temperature treatment has little effect on hardness but may possibly improve toughness. In fact there seems little reason metallurgically why very low temperature treatment should have any effect on the microstructure and properties since in this temperature range the mobility of carbon atoms is probably very low. Consequently, for the bulk of less critical applications tempering is generally omitted. Where important components, such as those associated with aircraft construction, are concerned tempering is generally carried out, the philosophy being that if such low-temperature tempering does no good, it will certainly do no harm.

BIBLIOGRAPHY

1 'Steel and its Heat-treatment', Vols. I, II, III, D. K. Bullens (John Wiley; Chapman and Hall).
2 'The Heat Treatment of Steel', E. Gregory and E. N. Simons (Pitman).
3 'Ferrous Metallurgy' (Vol. III—'Metallography and Heat-treatment', E. J. Teichert (McGraw-Hill).
4 'High-frequency Induction Heating', F. W. Curtis (McGraw-Hill).
5 'Controlled Atmospheres for the Heat-treatment of Metals', I. Jenkins (Chapman and Hall).
6 'Controlled Atmospheres in Heat-treatment', G. T. Dunkley (Pitman).

7 'Protective Atmospheres', A. G. Hotchkiss and H. M. Weber (Wiley; Chapman and Hall).

8 'Heat Treatment of Metals', Special Report No. 95, (Joint Committee of the Iron and Steel Institute and the Institute of Metals).

9 'Heat Treatment of Metals', Institute of Metals Refresher Course 1962 (Iliffe).

10 'Quenching and Martempering', ASM Committee (American Society of Metals).

11 'Induction Hardening and Tempering', ASM Committee (American Society of Metals).

12 'Furnace Atmospheres and Carbon Control', ASM Committee (American Society of Metals).

13 'Gas Carburising', ASM Committee (American Society of Metals).

14 BS 3446: 1962—Glossary of terms relating to the manufacture and use of refractory materials.

15 BS 4437: 1969—Method for the end quench hardenability test for steel (Jominy test).

Chapter fourteen

THE HEAT-TREATMENT OF NON-FERROUS METALS AND ALLOYS—I

14.10

Not only is heat-treatment applied to nearly all non-ferrous metals and alloys in the form of annealing processes, but in the case of many aluminium alloys (and a few copper alloys) heat-treatment is also a means of obtaining a variation in mechanical properties by promoting precipitation hardening. Annealing processes are carried out primarily to soften a material and generally to allow its capacity for cold-work to be regained. In passing, it should perhaps be mentioned that it is not possible to 'temper' hard-worked non-ferrous alloys (other than those of the precipitation hardening type) in order to obtain a degree of hardness intermediate between that produced by cold-work and the 'dead-soft' or fully annealed condition. Such attempts at tempering will generally lead to the material softening completely, and the only satisfactory method of producing a desired degree of hardness is by controlling the amount of cold-work in the final cold-working operation.

14.11

In most of these heat-treatment processes accurate technical control is necessary, for whilst an error of 100° C in the annealing temperature of pure copper would have little effect on either its grain size or mechanical properties, an error of as little as 10° C in the treatment temperature of a precipitation-hardening aluminium alloy may be disastrous. This is not to suggest that the annealing of pure copper is at all a haphazard procedure. If the annealing process is carried out in an electric furnace, then the need for fuel economy will dictate that the copper shall be annealed in conditions commensurate with the lowest possible combination of time and temperature. Moreover, the use of inert atmospheres during the annealing of copper and other metals allows a 'bright annealed' finish to be obtained, with consequent improvement in quality of surface and reduction in metal loss by pickling or other de-scaling processes.

THE EFFECTS OF ANNEALING ON COLD-WORKED METALS

14.20

When a metal is deformed by cold-work slip takes place along certain planes in the crystals so that the latter becomes strained and their internal structure distorted. The strain manifests itself as an increase in tensile strength and

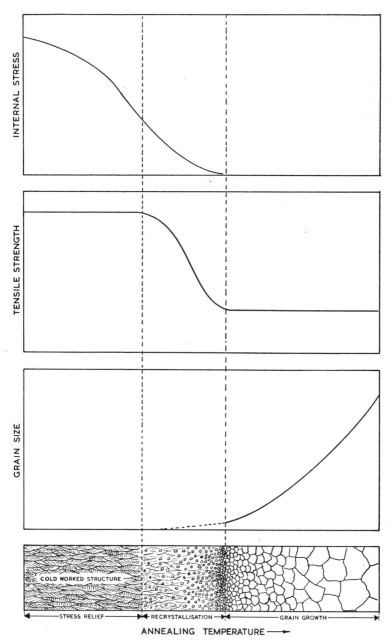

INTERNAL STRESS

TENSILE STRENGTH

GRAIN SIZE

COLD WORKED STRUCTURE

STRESS RELIEF — RECRYSTALLISATION — GRAIN GROWTH

ANNEALING TEMPERATURE ⟶

FIG. 14.1—Typical Changes in Structure and Mechanical Properties during an Annealing Process.

hardness and a reduction in ductility, and the degree of work hardening and resistance to further deformation depend upon the amount of cold-work applied.

If this work-hardened material is now heated to a sufficiently high temperature it softens and recrystallises, and the effects of cold-work are removed. The material is then in a condition suitable for further cold-working operations.

An annealing process takes place in three stages—stress relief, recrystallisation and grain growth (5.30—Part I). These changes do not take place instantaneously, so that, particularly at low temperatures sufficient time must be allowed to elapse in order that each stage shall reach completion. When the temperature to which a cold-worked metal is subjected is high enough the complete process takes place so quickly as to appear instantaneous, but at low temperatures the influence of time can easily be assessed. The degree of recovery and grain growth in a cold-worked metal during annealing then depend partly upon the time and temperature employed during the process.

14.21

The speed of growth of the new crystals during recrystallisation depends not only upon temperature and duration of the heating process but also upon the amount of deformation during the previous cold-working operations. Heavy cold-work tends to give a relatively fine-grained structure on annealing, whilst light cold-work usually results in much larger grains, and consequently, an annealed structure which is much less satisfactory from a mechanical point of view. The growth of large grains during recrystallisation following small amounts of deformation is caused by the formation of a relatively small number of nuclei during the time available for recrystallisation. With increasing degrees of deformation an increasing number of points of high stress are present, leading to recrystallisation from a larger number of nuclei, and hence to a greater number of grains, which are consequently smaller. Fig. 14.2 illustrates the type of relationship which exists between annealing temperature, the degree of previous cold-work (as indicated by % reduction in thickness), recrystallisation temperature and the resulting grain size.

If material is to be supplied as sheet in the annealed state (possibly for subsequent deep-drawing processes) it should therefore be heavily cold-worked in the last operation prior to the final annealing process if a satisfactory grain size is to be obtained.

14.30 ANNEALING ALUMINIUM AND ITS ALLOYS

14.31 (a) Work-hardened Alloys

The recrystallisation temperature of pure aluminium falls as the amount of previous cold-work increases. It is increased by the presence of impurities and by the alloying constituents present in the case of alloys. However, in order that recrystallisation shall proceed fairly quickly, it is necessary that the recrystallisation temperature be exceeded. Consequently, although the recrystallisation temperature of commercially pure aluminium is only in the

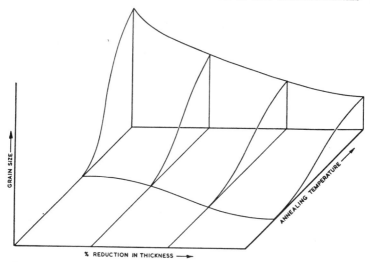

FIG. 14.2—The Relationship between Degree of Previous Cold Work, Annealing Temperature and Resultant Grain Size.

region of 150° C, in industrial practice temperatures of between 340 and 420° C are commonly used for annealing cold-worked aluminium and its alloys. Even higher temperatures are sometimes necessary in order to volatilise process oil from the surface.

To ensure the formation of the desired fine-grained structure in the material undergoing annealing, close control of those factors which promote the growth of large grains is necessary. Grain growth is aided by the use of high temperatures and long periods of treatment, therefore both temperature and time of treatment should be kept to the minimum commensurate with complete penetration of heat throughout the furnace charge.

The rate of heating through the recrystallisation temperature should be as rapid as possible, since this, too, is conducive to the production of fine grain. A slow rate of heating in this region tends to inhibit the formation of nuclei, and consequently give rise to large grains. Hence the furnace controls may be set at a temperature higher than that which the charge is to reach in order to produce rapid heating in the initial stages. Thus, the control may be set at 500° C so that the whole charge may reach, say, 400° C in less than an hour. The general practice is to employ a holding (or soaking) period of about 1 hour. Alloys which are not heat-treatable can then be cooled at any convenient rate.

Once softened a non-heat-treatable alloy cannot be hardened again except by cold-work. This will not be possible if the material has been finished to a specific size.

14.32 (b) Heat-treated Alloys

It is sometimes necessary to soften a heat-treated aluminium alloy so that further cold-forming operations can be carried out, but where possible it is better to buy material which is already in the soft condition. Heat-treatable material which has been softened for cold-work will need to be heat-treated again, but it should be appreciated that where the original properties obtained were a result of a combination of heat-treatment *and* cold-work, reheat-treatment after annealing will not result in the 'as-manufactured' properties being fully attained.

Annealing of a heat-treated alloy will not only remove the effects of any cold-work but it will also neutralise the results of the precipitation hardening treatment (17.50—Part I) by causing the sub-microscopical particles to coalesce until almost complete precipitation of the phase has taken place, thus

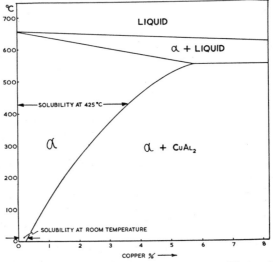

FIG. 14.3—Part of the Aluminium–Copper Thermal Equilibrium Diagram.

reducing strength and hardness. Some solubility of the phase still exists at the annealing temperature, and in order that full softening shall occur, the material should be cooled slowly enough from the annealing temperature to allow precipitation of the phase to take place.

A heat-treated aluminium alloy may be fully annealed by heating it to 400–425° C, maintaining it at that temperature for 1 hour and allowing it to cool slowly in the furnace at a rate not exceeding 20° C per hour to 260° C in order to facilitate precipitation of the dissolved phase. The material can then be withdrawn from the furnace and cooled in air.

It may be impossible to complete the cold-forming operation in one stage, so that an intermediate anneal will be necessary. Since the alloy is already in its fully precipitated condition, this intermediate anneal will only be such as is necessary to remove the effects of cold-work, and usually involves soaking the alloy for up to 2 hours at 350° C followed by cooling in air.

Air cooling from 350° C may cause the retention in solution of some of the phase which was precipitated by the initial full-annealing process. Consequently, precipitation hardening may subsequently occur. The effect is more apparent with material which has been annealed in a salt bath and washed immediately afterwards to remove the coating of salt. This washing has the effect of quenching the material and retaining the constituent in solution. Therefore any forming should be carried out within 24 hours of annealing, that is, before precipitation hardening has begun.

The annealing of heat-treated 'Alclad' sheet (22.61—Part I) is inadvisable since repeated heat-treatments (the initial heat-treatment, annealing and final heat-treatment) cause diffusion of the core constituents into the Alclad coating so that its resistance to corrosion is reduced. In a similar way the annealing of some of the heat-treatable alloys reduces their corrosion resistance because of subsequent electrolytic action between the precipitated phase and the base metal (22.25—Part I).

14.33 Furnaces Used for Annealing Aluminium Alloys

These are usually similar to those employed for the solution treatment of aluminium alloys (15.40). Both salt baths and air furnaces are used, but the latter are by far the more popular, since, although salt baths have certain advantages, particularly in rapidity of heat transfer, metal annealed in them must be washed and dried—processes not necessary when annealing is carried out in air furnaces. Moreover, since temperature control is less critical in an annealing process than in solution treatment, the slight advantage that salt baths have in respect of accuracy of temperature control does not warrant their use on this score.

The air furnaces used for annealing aluminium alloys are usually specially designed. Since temperatures employed in annealing are approximately 100° C less than those used in solution treatment, the products of combustion from gas-fired furnaces would be much less likely to cause blistering of the charge. It is therefore not necessary to protect the charge from the products of combustion by enclosing it in a muffle.

Some trouble may be experienced with staining when the load is charged cold to such a furnace. This is due to products of combustion condensing on the cold load, and it may be overcome by preheating the load to about 100° C in a dry atmosphere before transferring it to the zone where the products of combustion are circulating. The preheating chambers are usually of the enclosed muffle type and are heated by gas or electricity.

ANNEALING COPPER AND ITS ALLOYS

14.40

Generally the reason for annealing copper and its alloys is to bring about recovery and recrystallisation following cold-work, but sometimes the aim of the process is merely the relief of stress or, in some cases, the homogenisation of a cast structure.

14.41 (a) Homogenising Annealing

It is sometimes impossible to cold-work an alloy because of brittleness arising from a lack of homogeneity in the cast ingot. Tin bronzes, containing up to

10% tin, are so heavily cored in the cast state (16.42—Part I) that, though nominally α-phase alloys, they may contain considerable amounts of the brittle intermetallic compound $Cu_{31}Sn_8$ (the δ-phase) segregated between the primary α-phase dendrites. The presence of this brittle constituent causes the ingot to crack during cold-rolling.

A 'homogenising' anneal is therefore applied in order to eliminate or decrease segregation by promoting diffusion, which leads to uniformity of chemical composition throughout the casting. The time and temperature employed depend largely upon the rate of diffusion of the solute atoms in the crystal lattice of the solvent metal. Thus zinc diffuses readily in copper, whilst the diffusion of tin is very slow. Bronzes are therefore given a homogenising anneal at between 650 and 800° C for periods of up to 6 hours in order to promote diffusion and produce a more or less homogeneous solid-solution structure which can be cold-worked with safety. Homogenisation is also sometimes carried out in the case of silicon bronzes, nickel silvers and cupro-nickel.

The process is often referred to as 'solution annealing' since the object generally is to absorb some phase into solid solution. It should, not, however, be confused with 'solution treatment' as applied to the precipitation-hardening alloys, where heating is followed by a quenching operation, the object of which is to retain a phase in super-saturated solid solution at room temperature.

14.42 (b) Stress Relieving

Residual or 'locked-up' stresses in cold-worked alloys often manifest themselves during service in the form of 'season cracks'. Hard-drawn brass tube and rod and deep-drawn brass components which are subjected to mildly corrosive conditions over long periods are affected in this way. Brass covers of old electric-light switches will often be found to be badly season-cracked (16.33—Part I).

The basic cause of season-cracking (alternatively referred to as stress-corrosion cracking) is the combination of tensile stresses acting in the surface of the cold-worked material and corrosion at the crystal boundaries. Due to corrosion, points of stress concentration are set up, and this, coupled with the consequent weakening of the metal, leads to the formation of cracks.

Brasses with more than 20% zinc are the most susceptible of the copper alloys to season-cracking. The susceptibility increases with the zinc content. Copper, cupro-nickel and the bronzes, on the other hand, are almost free from season-cracking troubles.

The object of any heat-treatment to remove the susceptibility of a material to season cracking is to relieve the internal stresses *without* appreciably softening the material. Indeed, the alloy may be required in a hard-drawn condition, and it is therefore important to use a stress-relieving temperature which is *below* the recrystallisation temperature of the alloy. Both the time and temperature of treatment depend to a large extent on the previous mechanical and thermal treatment the material has received and upon the final properties required. As a general rule, stress-relieving heat-treatment takes place at a temperature about 50–100° C below the recrystallisation temperature for a period of 1–2 hours, but where optimum mechanical properties are required a lower temperature may be used for a period up to 24 hours. Under these latter conditions there is little or no decrease in strength of hardness, and with very severely cold-worked materials there may even be an increase in these properties (Fig. 14.4).

Hence the best practice in thermal stress-relieving is to use the lowest temperature at which stress relief will take place in conjunction with the

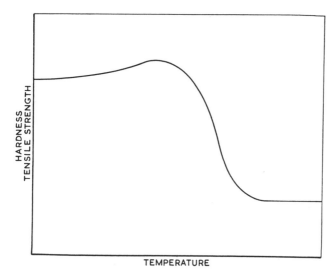

FIG. 14.4—The Relationship between Tensile Strength and Annealing Temperature for Some Heavily Cold-worked Materials.

longest time that is compatible with the needs of industrial production. Since the temperature needs to be accurately controlled and the danger of local overheating avoided, the best type of furnace to use is one employing a liquid bath of well-agitated salt or oil or, alternatively, an air furnace employing high-velocity forced convection.

70–30 brass is usually stress-relieved at 250–270° C for about 1 hour, but a temperature as low as 150° C employed over a longer period may produce the required stress relief whilst maintaining better overall mechanical properties.

14.43 (c) Recrystallisation Annealing

When a metal is cold-worked a point is ultimately reached beyond which it cannot withstand further deformation without permanent structural damage taking place. Before this stage is reached therefore, the metal must be annealed at a sufficiently high temperature to allow recrystallisation to proceed and so restore the initial capacity for cold-work.

The temperature and time of an annealing process for a copper alloy vary considerably and depend upon such factors as the initial degree of cold-work, the mechanical properties required and the composition of the alloy. Thus pure copper may be annealed at a temperature as low as 400° C in order to effect recrystallisation, whilst a temperature of 850° C might be used to anneal cupro-nickel, the presence of nickel rendering recrystallisation and grain-growth sluggish.

Accuracy of temperature control is more important in the case of some alloys than others. For example, the grain size of pure copper is only approximately doubled if the annealing temperature is raised from 400 to 900° C, whilst in the case of 70-30 brass a similar rise would cause the grain size to increase tenfold and lead to a deterioration in mechanical properties and an 'orange peel' effect on the surface.

In view of the variable effects of previous cold-work, it is difficult to specify a 'standard' annealing treatment for any given alloy, since an increased amount

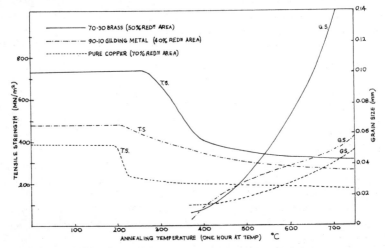

Fig. 14.5—Changes in Tensile Strength and Grain Size with Annealing Temperature for Some Copper Alloys.

of cold-work before annealing lowers the recrystallisation temperature. Similarly, the smaller the degree of cold-work prior to annealing, the larger the resultant grain size.

Time has less influence on grain growth than has temperature, but with any annealing temperature an increase in the time of treatment will lead to an increase in the grain size.

During the cold-working of copper alloys on an industrial scale the initial annealing operations are usually carried out at a higher temperature than the finishing ones. This helps in homogenising the structure and removes the effects of coring at an early stage. The conditions of the final annealing process, however, determine the grain size of the finished material, so that as the finishing stage is reached the tendency is to *increase* the percentage reduction in thickness at each 'pass' and *decrease* the annealing temperature. Both of these factors are conducive to the production of a small uniform grain size. In practice, the grain size is reduced to something approaching that desired in the finished product two or three anneals before the final. This ensures a more uniform grain size in the finished product.

The grain size required depends largely upon the use to which the material is put. In the case of the deep-drawn copper–zinc alloys a small grain size of 0·015 mm might be desirable when the surface finish is important and the degree of forming slight, whilst a large grain size of 0·100 mm would give high ductility but a rough surface exhibiting 'orange peel'. For the best combination of surface and drawing properties, therefore, a medium grain size of 0·04–0·05 mm would be chosen.

From the foregoing remarks it will be seen that it is difficult to specify any fixed annealing schedule for a particular copper alloy in view of the varying properties of the initial material and the different results required. Most copper alloys, however, are recrystallisation annealed for periods of up to 1 hour at some temperature within the range indicated in Table 14.1.

TABLE 14.1—*Recrystallisation Annealing Temperatures for Various Copper Alloys*

Alloy	Recrystallisation annealing temperature range (°C)
Pure copper	400–650
Cartridge brass . . .	425–725
65–35 brass . . .	425–700
Muntz metal . . .	425–600
High-tensile brass . .	425–600
95–5 tin bronze . . .	475–700
Cupro-nickel . . .	650–850
Nickel-silver . . .	600–825
95–5 Aluminium bronze .	425–750

BRIGHT ANNEALING

14.50

An annealing process is usually carried out at a temperature above that at which oxidation of the metal or alloy begins to take place. Whilst the thin film of oxide formed on the surface of most aluminium-base alloys is sufficient to protect them from further attack, this is not so in the case of the copper-base alloys, and during annealing in an atmosphere containing oxygen they become coated with a layer of scale, the thickness of which will depend upon the temperature and time of treatment.

If the metal surface has become scaled in this way it must be cleaned before the next forming operation by pickling in a suitable reagent, followed by thorough washing to remove all traces of the reagent. Pickling inevitably causes some roughening of the metal surface, so that, both in the interest of surface quality and the general economy of production, it usually pays to use some form of bright annealing process in cases where the output justifies laying down a plant.

Bright annealing involves heating the cold-worked material in an atmosphere which is, to all intents and purposes, oxygen-free. This means that the charge must be heated in a furnace chamber which is gas-tight or very nearly so. In the latter case a slight positive pressure of the inert atmosphere in the furnace chamber will cause a small flow of the atmosphere outwards, and thus prevent the ingress of air. Details of controlled-atmosphere furnaces will be given later (14.61).

14.51

In choosing a furnace atmosphere for bright annealing it should be remembered that some metals are adversely affected by the presence of hydrogen. Thus the hydrogen content of the atmosphere must be kept low in annealing tough-pitch copper, or it may become embrittled due to 'gassing' (16.22—Part I).

Copper was formerly bright-annealed on a commercial scale in an atmosphere of steam, though this method is now rarely used. The annealing container is fitted with one vent only and sealed by a non-return valve which allows the explusion of gases but prevents air from being drawn into the chamber until the valve is opened when the charge has cooled. A small quantity of water and charcoal are placed in the container along with the copper to be annealed and the container charged into the furnace. Evaporation of the water effectively purges the container of air, and during the heating process chemical reactions between the steam and charcoal produce some hydrogen and carbon monoxide, which help to clean the surface of the copper of any slight initial oxidation. Unfortunately the hydrogen concentration can build up to such an extent that embrittlement of copper containing oxygen will take place. Water-staining, too, is a defect often encountered in the bright annealing of copper in steam.

14.52

The best results are obtained by bright annealing copper in an atmosphere of 'burnt ammonia'. This type of atmosphere is expensive to produce, but if the furnaces operate on a closed circuit so that the air-contaminated gas can be regenerated its use becomes economically possible.

Ammonia gas enters the gas plant (Fig. 14.6) and passes over a heated catalyst (spongy iron impregnated with rare-earth oxides), which causes the ammonia to dissociate into hydrogen and nitrogen:

$$4NH_3 = 2N_2 + 6H_2.$$

This mixture is fed into a burner with a controlled amount of air so that nearly all the hydrogen is burned:

$$\underset{\substack{\text{Dissociated} \\ \text{ammonia}}}{2N_2 + 6H_2} + \underset{\text{Air}}{3O_2 + 12N_2} = 6H_2O + 14N_2.$$

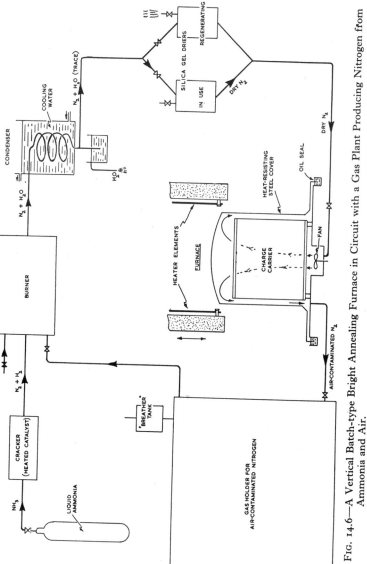

FIG. 14.6—A Vertical Batch-type Bright Annealing Furnace in Circuit with a Gas Plant Producing Nitrogen from Ammonia and Air.

The bulk of the water is removed by condensation and final traces by passing the gas through a silica-gel drier. The resultant gas contains about 1–2% hydrogen and the remainder nitrogen, which is obtained both from the ammonia and from the air used for combustion of the bulk of the hydrogen.

This gas is used to purge the furnace chambers, and the return gas, which, as mentioned earlier, is now contaminated with air, is passed to a large storage tank and then regenerated by passing it through the gas plant with the amount of dissociated ammonia necessary to combine with the oxygen present in this air. The only serious loss of gas which takes place therefore is when a furnace chamber is opened to remove the annealed charge.

14.53
Burnt town's gas and charcoal gas are also widely used for the bright annealing of copper. The former contains about 90% nitrogen, with up to 10% carbon dioxide and small amounts of hydrogen and carbon monoxide and is obtained by burning ordinary town's gas with a controlled amount of air. Suitable charcoal gas is obtained by the almost complete combustion of charcoal in a low-temperature burner which results in a gas containing roughly 80% nitrogen and 20% carbon dioxide. In each case desulphurisation of the gas may be necessary to avoid staining the charge. Sulphur gases can be removed by passing the burnt mixture through a lime tower.

14.54
Vacuum annealing offers alternative treatment in the case of copper, beryllium bronze and phosphor bronze. The type of furnace used (14.80) is similar to that employed for the treatment of refractory metals like titanium, tungsten and zirconium.

14.55
Whatever atmosphere is used, the furnace chamber containing the charge of copper is purged with it until the oxygen content is very small. The temperature can then be raised, a small flow of gas being maintained during the heating process in order to prevent any chance of air ingress and to help carry away volatilised rolling or drawing oil. The charge is allowed to cool to 150° C before it is exposed to the air.

With the exception of brass, most other copper alloys can be bright annealed under conditions similar to those which suit copper. Brass presents a special problem, since some zinc volatilises from the surface of the brass at the annealing temperature. This zinc condenses again during cooling and produces a 'bloom' on the surface of the brass. Moreover, zinc reduces carbon dioxide and water vapour at temperatures above 350° C, with the result that the bloom contains some zinc oxide. To prevent the initial volatilisation of zinc from the surface of the charge, an inert atmosphere which has already been saturated with zinc vapour before being passed into the furnace can be used. The vapour pressure exerted by this zinc present in the furnace atmosphere prevents volatilisation of any zinc from the surface of the charge. The formation of an oxide bloom can be prevented on alloys containing more than 5%

zinc by using an inert atmosphere consisting of desulphurised, dried burnt fuel gas which has been saturated with methyl alcohol.

FURNACES FOR ANNEALING COPPER AND ITS ALLOYS

14.60

Furnaces used for annealing copper and its alloys may be of the batch or continuous type, though the former are generally the more often used.

14.61 Batch Furnaces

Of batch furnaces the conventional rectangular muffle is the most widely used, and may be heated by electricity, gas, fuel oil or even coal. Such a furnace is usually very adaptable and can be used for annealing flat sheet, strip or tubes, as well as coiled materials.

Courtesy of G. W. B. Furnaces Ltd, Dudley.

PLATE 14.1—Circular Bell Furnace, for Annealing Copper Cable.
A retort covers the charge on the first base. The second base is open but loaded, whilst a cooling cover is in position on the third base. The fourth base is being heated by the furnace bell.

Horizontal cylindrical furnaces are sometimes used for the treatment of tubes or long rods, whilst vertical cylindrical furnaces are employed for annealing coils of wire and strip, as well as baskets of small components. The vertical bell-type furnace (Fig. 14.6) is generally used for bright-annealing processes. It is heated electrically and usually employs forced circulation of the atmosphere. A charge carrier is placed on the furnace platform and a heat-resisting steel hood lowered over it so that the lower rim of the hood rests in a channel containing oil, sand or water, which seals the interior of the chamber from the outer atmosphere. A protective atmosphere is then circulated through the chamber for long enough to purge the air from it. The furnace heater bell is then placed over the steel hood so that the latter, along with the charge it contains, is raised to the annealing temperature (Plate 14.1). After removing the heater bell the charge must be allowed to cool to about 150° C before the steel hood is raised, otherwise exposure of the hot charge to air would lead to oxidation of its surface.

14.62 Continuous Furnaces

One of the disadvantages of batch annealing is that variations in properties may occur in material annealed in different parts of the furnace due to temperature differences from point to point. In continuous annealing the product moves at a uniform speed through a heated zone held at a definite controlled temperature, so that in its passage through the furnace the whole of the charge undergoes the same heating and cooling cycle.

Courtesy of G. W. B. Furnaces Ltd, Dudley.

PLATE 14.2—Continuous Furnace with Disc Roller Hearth, for Annealing Titanium Sheet.
Illustration shows discharge end with cooling air ducts.

Continuous furnaces are of three main types; the roller conveyor, the mesh belt (Fig. 14·7) and the continuous-strand furnace. In the first of these light-metal trays are used to carry the charge through the heating zone and out into the atmosphere, though long rods and tubes are annealed in the roller-hearth without the use of tray conveyors (Plate 14.2).

Mesh-belt conveyor furnaces (Plate 14.3) are used extensively for annealing sheets and also small pressings. The latter are charged on to the mesh belt, which carries them into the heating zone and then into a cooling tunnel, after which they fall from the end of the belt into a pickling tank. The speed of the belt is so arranged that annealing is just complete as the components leave

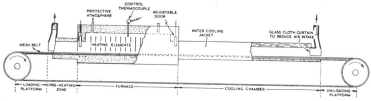

FIG. 14.7—Principle of the Mesh-belt Conveyor Furnace Used for the Bright Annealing of Non-ferrous Materials and Many Other Applications.

the heating zone. Plant of this type has been installed for annealing brass and copper sheet up to 1·4 m wide with outputs of over 1 tonne/hour.

Strand annealing of thin strip up to 1 mm thick is carried out in horizontal furnaces. The strip in uncoiled at one end of the furnace and re-coiled at the other, each subsequent coil being either welded or 'stitched' to its predecessor. After passing through the furnace the strip is usually drawn through a pickling bath, then through a washing bosh and finally through some form of drying equipment before being re-coiled.

Courtesy of Wild–Barfield Electric Furnaces Ltd, Watford.

PLATE 14.3—Continuous Mesh-belt Conveyor Furnace, from Discharge End. The cooling tunnel, in the foreground, is closed at its end by a flexible curtain.

In order to economise in floor space and also to avoid the use of supporting rollers, vertical furnaces have been more recently introduced for strand annealing.

Strand annealing has also been applied in the treatment of wire, and the process is essentially the same as that for strip. In this group the Snead furnace is interesting in that the electric current is passed through the wire which is being annealed, thus causing it to be heated to the required temperature.

FAULTS WHICH MAY OCCUR DURING ANNEALING PROCESSES

14.70

The main defects which can occur during an annealing process are associated either with the extensive oxidation of the surface of the material or with the production of coarse grain within the material. Excessive surface oxidation may take place as a result of heating the material at too high a temperature in an oxygen-rich atmosphere. A prolonged period of treatment will aggravate the condition. Apart from the control of both time and temperature of treatment to the minimum necessary for the production of satisfactory properties, the only alternative procedure is to use some form of protective atmosphere leading to the production of a bright or semi-bright surface finish.

14.71

As mentioned earlier in this chapter, coarse grain, and the attendant brittleness which accompanies it, may be due to conditions prevailing during annealing or to the degree of deformation carried out prior to annealing. The use of an excessively high temperature and, to a less extent, a prolonged period of treatment will both lead to the production of coarse grain. A low degree of cold-work prior to annealing will have a similar effect, due to the tendency for few nuclei to form as annealing proceeds.

Both surface oxidation and the formation of coarse grain are defects which are experienced to a varying degree with all the commercial non-ferrous metals and alloys.

14.72

A particular hazard affecting the annealing of copper containing oxygen was mentioned in Part I (16.22). If copper of this quality is annealed in an atmosphere rich in hydrogen, embrittlement will most probably occur. This embrittlement is caused by hydrogen forming a solid solution of the interstitial type (8.32—Part I) in the copper and reacting with the globules of cuprous oxide present. The product of the reaction is steam under pressure, which leads to the formation of tiny ruptures in the copper. As much as 1.0% hydrogen is permissible with annealing temperatures up to $500°$ C, but at higher temperatures the amount should be drastically reduced.

14.73

Residual lubricants may cause trouble, particularly during the annealing of copper and its alloys. Some oils volatilise completely, particularly if the charge is heated slowly, as in many of the bright-annealing processes. In some circumstances, however, the lubricant may undergo decomposition, leaving a deposit which is very difficult to remove. It is therefore advisable to eliminate as much of the lubricant as possible before the material is heated, regardless of the type of furnace or the material to be annealed. Excessive sulphur in either lubricant or fuel may cause discoloration of the metal in the form of red or reddish-brown stains.

14.74

'Fire-cracking' is likely to occur when heavily cold-worked alloys are heated too rapidly during annealing. The surface layer of the alloy becomes soft, whilst considerable internal stresses still exist in the interior of the material.

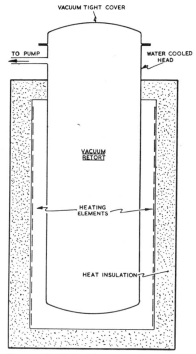

FIG. 14.8—Principle of the Hot-retort
Vacuum Chamber Furnace.

Relief of these internal stresses takes place automatically, leading to tearing of the soft, weak surface layer. Leaded copper alloys are particularly susceptible to this form of cracking. The remedy is to heat the material slowly and uniformly, so that internal stresses are gradually removed.

VACUUM ANNEALING

14.80

The chemical affinity of titanium for most other elements was referred to in a brief mention of the metal in Part I (18.72). Consequently, titanium can be most conveniently annealed in a vacuum furnace. Such treatment also ensures that hydrogen is extracted from the metal during annealing. In addition, tantalum, molybdenum, tungsten, zirconium and other metals are annealed in this way and the absence of an oxidising atmosphere ensures a bright-annealed product.

14.81

Vacuum furnaces are generally of the electric-resistance-heated type. In some models the vacuum chamber or retort is heated externally, whilst in others the heater elements are built inside the vacuum chamber. In the first or hot-retort type (Fig. 14.8) the vacuum chamber is made of stainless steel, Inconel or a Nimonic alloy (18.30—Part I), the maximum temperature required governing the material to be used. The hot-retort type of furnace is employed for work involving temperatures up to 1 000° C.

14.82

The introduction of the internal-element or cold-retort furnace (Plate 14.4) enabled temperatures in excess of 2 000° C to be attained in a vacuum chamber on a production basis. In this furnace the heater elements are located immediately outside the charge area but inside the vacuum chamber. Radiation shields, or heat reflectors, are arranged on the outside of the heating elements

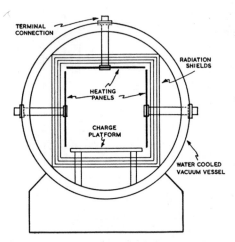

FIG. 14.9—Principle of the Internal-element Vacuum Chamber Furnace (End Elevation).

(Fig. 14.9), the complete assembly being contained in a water-cooled mild-steel or stainless-steel retort. Since the vacuum chamber operates near to room temperature, the vacuum seals are not subjected to high temperatures. Moreover, since there is no brick insulation, the thermal capacity of the furnace is low. This permits rapid heating and cooling of the charge. The fact that the heating elements are working in a vacuum enables graphite rods, cylinders or panels to be employed for this purpose. Graphite has many

HORIZONTAL TYPE GRAPHITE RESISTOR FURNACE

Courtesy of Wild–Barfield Electric Furnaces Ltd, Watford.

PLATE 14.4—Cold-retort Vacuum Furnace for High-
temperature Heat-treatment Processes.

attributes as a heating-element material, but it cannot be used in contact with
air because of the rapidity with which it oxidises.

14.83

The use of high-vacuum technology in metal heat-treatment has developed
rapidly in recent years, largely as a result of the demands of the aircraft and
nuclear-engineering industries. In addition to the heat-treatment of titanium
already mentioned, zirconium and uranium annealing processes are now well
established applications, whilst the sintering of beryllium and the brazing
of honeycomb sections are carried out under conditions of high vacuum.

Vacuum heat-treatment eliminates the possibility of any reaction taking
place between the charge and the atmosphere which would otherwise surround
it. In addition, heat-treating in vacuum gives the following advantages:

(1) A protective 'atmosphere' of high purity and uniformity is obtained.
(Since all spaces between the work-pieces are evacuated, the 'atmosphere'
is uniform throughout the work space.)

(2) In addition to hydrogen, other undesirable impurities are evaporated. High-vapour-pressure impurities, such as cadmium, magnesium and manganese, are removed in this way.

(3) Those chemical reactions which are influenced by conditions of temperature and pressure are accelerated by vacuum heat-treatment. Thus, vacuum treatment assists the dissociation of oxides and nitrides of iron, nickel, chromium and cobalt at relatively low temperatures.

Typical annealing temperatures and operating vacuum pressures are given in Table 14.2.

TABLE 14.2

Material	Annealing temperature (°C)	Operating vacuum pressure N/m²
Austenitic stainless steel	1 050–1 100	0·013–1·3
Zirconium	900– 950	0·013–0·13
Titanium	730– 750	0·013–0·13
Uranium	600– 700	0·013–0·13

The annealing of stainless steel, zirconium, titanium and uranium parts in vacuum results in high ductility and a very clean surface finish. Moreover, titanium is both annealed and de-gassed for the removal of hydrogen in a single operation. Some of the very large vacuum furnaces in the U.S.A. were built for this application, with capacities of up to 4·5 tonnes of titanium sheet.

BIBLIOGRAPHY

1 'Controlled Atmospheres for the Heat-treatment of Metals', I. Jenkins (Chapman and Hall).
2 'Chill-cast Tin Bronzes', D. Hanson and W. T. Pell-Walpole (Arnold).
3 'Controlled Atmospheres in Heat-treatment', G. T. Dunkley (Pitman).
4 'Protective Atmospheres', A. G. Hotchkiss and H. M. Weber (Wiley; Chapman and Hall).
5 'Equipment for the Thermal Treatment of Non-ferrous Metals and Alloys', Symposium (Institute of Metals).
6 'Heat Treatment of Metals', Institute of Metals Refresher Course 1962 (Iliffe).
7 'Aluminium, Vol. III—Fabrication and Finishing', Ed. K. R. van Horn (American Society of Metals).
8 BS 3446: 1962—Glossary of terms relating to the manufacture and use of refractory materials.

Chapter fifteen

THE HEAT-TREATMENT OF NON-FERROUS METALS AND ALLOYS—II

15.10

With the exception of those processes which are carried out to effect the absorption of some phase deposited as a result of coring in a cast structure, all of the annealing processes dealt with in the preceding chapter lead to some degree of stress-relief taking place in the material being treated. This relief of stress is usually accompanied by an increase in softness coupled with a corresponding loss in tensile strength. Where microstructural changes occur during these annealing processes they involve only recrystallisation.

15.11

In Part I (17.50) it was shown that the tensile strength and hardness of certain aluminium-base alloys could be increased considerably by suitable heat-treatment—loosely termed 'age hardening' or 'precipitation hardening'—and that this phenomenon was by no means confined to aluminium-base alloys, but could be applied to many alloys in which variation in the solid solubility of one metal in another took place. Whilst the heat-treatable alloys of aluminium no doubt constitute the most important group, the heat-treatable magnesium-base alloys, beryllium bronze and chromium-copper all have their particular uses.

It was further demonstrated that optimum properties were usually obtained when a suitable heat-treatment cycle, involving solution-treatment, quenching and precipitation treatment respectively, was applied. The metallurgical principles governing the process were dealt with adequately, and it will now be necessary to consider the practice of such heat-treatment.

SOLUTION TREATMENT

15.20

A study of the relevant part of the aluminium–copper thermal equilibrium diagram (Fig. 15.1) indicates that in order to obtain the necessary complete solution of copper in aluminium for a 4% copper alloy it is necessary to heat it at some temperature between A and C for long enough to absorb the intermetallic compound $CuAl_2$. In industrial practice it would be inadvisable to quote such a large permissible temperature range, since an error leading to the use of a temperature just above C would cause fusion of the alloy to begin, whilst the use of a temperature below A would mean that a considerable amount of $CuAl_2$ had not been absorbed into solution.

Moreover, most commercial alloys are more complex in composition than the simple binary alloy under consideration, and this may mean that the available temperature range between complete solution of the precipitated phase and the commencement of fusion is much smaller. Generally, the solution treatment of wrought aluminium alloys is carried out at some temperature between 450 and 540° C (Table 17.3—Part I), whilst for cast alloys a temperature between 490 and 550° C would be used, except in the case of

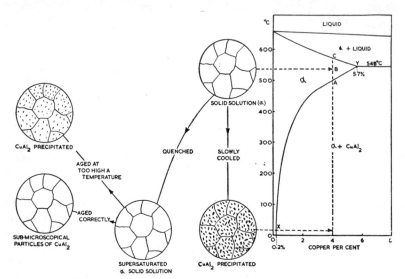

FIG. 15.1—Aluminium-rich End of the Aluminium-Copper Equilibrium Diagram Showing the Observed Microstructural Effect of Slow Cooling and Precipitation hardening.

the 10% magnesium alloy, which is heat-treated at 425° C (Table 17.4—Part I).

The permissible temperature range of solution treatment is usually of the order of 10–20° C, which makes accurate pyrometric control of the process essential. The temperature of the furnace must not be higher at any time during the period of treatment than the maximum temperature specified for that particular alloy, otherwise some fusion at the grain boundaries may take place. On the other hand, if the temperature falls below the minimum specified during treatment the optimum mechanical properties will not be developed, and in some cases corrosion may be accelerated due to the presence of undissolved constituents causing electrolytic action to take place.

15.21

The time specified for treatment should be measured from the moment when the coldest part of the charge reaches the minimum treatment temperature. When solution treatment is carried out in an air furnace the charge may take some time to attain the correct temperature, and an appropriate allowance must be made. The thickness and nature of the material and the size of charge also affect the rate at which its temperature will rise. Thus the solution treatment of some thin wrought sections may be complete in a matter of 10 minutes after the charge has attained the minimum solution-treatment temperature, but with heavier wrought sections it is generally satisfactory to allow 20 minutes for each 10 mm in thickness of section. It is generally necessary to solution-treat castings for a much longer period (Table 17.4—Part I), since their precipitated constituents are in a much coarser form, and consequently take far longer to dissolve.

15.22
As indicated in the previous chapter (14.32), the heat-treatment of clad sheet will always lead to diffusion of some of the core constituents into the surface layer. The shortest possible treatment time should therefore be employed with material of this type.

15.23
Since the control of temperature between fine limits is necessary, siting of the pyrometers is important, whether the furnace be of the air or salt-bath type. It is often essential therefore to carry out a temperature survey of the furnace by placing a large number of thermo-couples (inserted in thin-walled tubes) in different parts of a typical charge, as well as at various points throughout the furnace. If readings are then taken at intervals for all of the couples and the results plotted on one graph hot or cold spots in the furnace will be indicated. A temperature difference of more than 10° C between any two couples should be considered serious and steps taken to reduce it.

From the results of such a survey the location of the permanent thermo-couples can be determined. A *recording* couple should be placed in such a position as to give the most accurate temperature indication for the bulk of the charge, whilst a *controlling* couple should be located in the hottest part of the furnace, thus ensuring that the maximum permissible temperature for the charge is not exceeded.

FURNACES USED FOR SOLUTION TREATMENT

15.40
The design of a furnace to be used for the solution treatment of an aluminium alloy will depend largely upon the type of material to be treated. Two varieties of furnace are in common use: the air furnace in which heated air is circulated through the charge; and the salt bath containing a mixture of molten salts in which the charge is immersed. In either type the furnace may be heated by electricity, gas, oil or some solid fuel.

15.41 Air Furnaces
These are very adaptable, and since they can be used over a temperature range wider than that possible with salt baths, they can be employed for precipitation treatments or annealing as well as for solution treatment. Since they can be quickly started up or shut down, they are convenient for intermittent operations —a useful factor in small-scale manufacture.

A most necessary feature in the design of an air furnace is provision for rapid and uniform transfer of heat to the load. With gas- or oil-fired furnaces it is generally necessary to enclose the charge in a muffle chamber in order to protect it from direct contact with the products of combustion, which might cause high-temperature blistering.

In all types of air furnace artificial circulation of the heated air is necessary so that uniformity of temperature throughout the charge can be attained. The available heat imput must also be sufficient to bring the charge rapidly

Courtesy of G. W. B. Furnaces Ltd, Dudley.

PLATE 15.1—Tube-type Aluminium-alloy Solution Heat-treatment Furnace Installation.
Illustration shows the charge on a carrier in position above the quench tank on quench elevator platform.

up to the treatment temperature, whilst temperature control in the heating chamber should be maintained to within $\pm 5°$ C of the specified temperature if the material is to be uniformly treated.

Air furnaces for the solution treatment of sheet and extruded sections consist generally of a horizontal chamber of rectangular cross-section heated by electricity, gas or oil and employing fairly rapid air circulation. The furnace is equipped with withdrawal mechanism to transfer the charge rapidly to a quench tank placed in front of the furnace. Although forgings and castings are sometimes treated in a furnace such as has just been mentioned, a pit-type is more often employed. This consists essentially of a cylindrical chamber sunk in the ground, the castings or forgings being contained in a removable basket. A quench tank is placed alongside the furnace.

Tubes and long extrusions of small cross-section are often treated in a vertical furnace. This consists of a tall cylindrical heating chamber supported above a pit which is fitted with a runway, so that either a charge carrier or a quench tank can be moved beneath the furnace. The load is attached to a 'spider' and hoisted up from the charge carrier into the body of the furnace, where it hangs vertically. After solution treatment is complete the charge can be lowered directly into the quench tank, which has been moved in the meantime beneath the furnace. Not only is a rapid quench assured in this way but distortion of the work is also minimised, since vertical suspension of thin sections prevents their sagging whilst hot. The uniform quench across the cross-section of the material will also limit distortion.

15.42 Salt Baths

A salt bath generally consists of a rectangular tank in which salts are maintained in a molten condition by means of a pyrometrically controlled electric heater, for, whilst gas or oil firing are also in use, electric heating is the more popular. In electrically heated baths the elements are usually encased in nickel sheaths and are either suspended around the inside of the tank or laid along the bottom. Such heaters provide a rapid, efficient method of heating, and their maintenance costs are low.

Possibly the best material for the construction of the tank itself is 'Armco' iron (Plate 11.1A—Part I), since its resistance to corrosion is superior to that of other materials, viz., cast iron or welded mild steel, which are also used.

The working temperature must be maintained within similar limits to those obtained in an air furnace. It may therefore be necessary to agitate the charge in order to stir the molten salt and so ensure uniformity of temperature throughout the tank. It is also essential to stir the bath when fresh salt is added, and a sufficient volume of salt must be used to prevent excessive chilling when a load is charged to the tank.

A eutectic mixture of equal parts of sodium and potassium nitrates melts at the low temperature of $220°$ C and would therefore seem to be ideal for providing a molten bath, since its use would reduce to a minimum the internal stresses on the tank caused by thermal expansion when a solidified bath was being remelted. Since potassium nitrate is expensive, the pure sodium salt, melting at $310°$ C is more often used, whilst the addition of 10% sodium nitrite lowers the melting point of the latter by $20°$ C. Proprietary mixtures containing sodium and potassium nitrates and nitrites are also obtainable. Pure sodium nitrate is cheapest, but the use of one of the mixtures having a lower melting point involves a much smaller 'drag-out' loss.

This drag-out loss is one of the main disadvantages in the use of salt baths. When the charge is removed from the bath for quenching it may take with it up to 10% of its own weight in molten salt. This will be a total loss unless some process for reclaiming the salt from the quench water is employed. Moreover, when a shutdown is necessary the salt must either be siphoned from the tank or else allowed to freeze in the tank, and this latter practice always introduces the danger of explosion when starting up again due to salt melting at the bottom of the tank and exerting pressure on the still solid salt above. Explosions are also possible when loading due to moisture entrapped in the charge, whilst small explosions may take place as molten salt drips into the quench tank. Warping and twisting also tends to be greater and quench cracks more numerous than when air furnaces are used.

Other precautions in the use of nitrate salt baths might be mentioned here. Contact between the molten salt and any carbonaceous or organic matter (oil, coke, wood or clothing) must be avoided, or a fire may result, since nitrates are powerful oxidising reagents. Similarly, combustible gases must not be allowed to come into contact with the fused salt, and in the case of gas- or oil-fired baths an emergency shut-off valve should be situated at some distance from the tank. With such bottom-heated tanks, neither work nor 'sludge' should be allowed to collect on the bottom, since local overheating may cause the tank to be burned through. Fresh salts which are suspected of being damp must not be charged to a molten tank, but added when the bath is frozen. To control a nitrate fire dry sand should be used, and *on no account* should water or any other liquid extinguisher be employed.

The main advantage of salt baths over air furnaces are that they are cheaper to instal and that more accurate temperature control is possible. The rate of heat-transfer to the load is also greater, thus reducing heat-treatment time—a particular advantage in the case of clad materials, where diffusion of the core elements into the high-purity coating is a hazard.

In no circumstances should the heat-treatment of magnesium-base alloys (18.10—Part I) be attempted in a salt bath. Magnesium oxidises readily under some conditions, and immersion in a bath of strongly oxidising nitrates will lead to a reaction of explosive violence. The salt-bath treatment of aluminium alloys containing more than a few per cent of magnesium should also be regarded as dangerous. The precipitation-hardening alloys of copper—beryllium bronze and chromium–copper (16.71 and 16.72—Part I)—can be treated successfully in salt baths.

QUENCHING

15.50

When the solution-treatment process is complete the charge must be quenched as quickly as possible. Rapid transfer of the charge to the quenching tank is essential, since any delay will allow precipitation of phases to take place during the relatively slow cooling which obtains between the time the charge is removed from the furnace and actual quenching. Precipitation of phases due to delays in quenching will lead to poor mechanical properties and a lower resistance to corrosion.

The quench tank should therefore be adjacent to the furnace and on a slightly lower level and should contain clean water at a temperature *below* 30° C. (The temperature is best kept down by allowing a continuous flow of clean water to the tank.)

After being quenched the material should be washed in clean water in order to remove traces of salt, which may lead to corrosion.

REFRIGERATION

15.60

After solution treatment and quenching the alloy is in its most ductile and malleable condition, and any forming operation is therefore best carried out at this stage. It is obvious that the forming process must be finished as soon as possible after quenching, or hardening will begin to take place. This is particularly true of alloys which age-harden naturally at room temperature.

It is not generally practicable to plan production so that the output of the heat-treatment plant keeps in step with the capacity of the forming-process plant, and it is inevitable that from time to time material would need to be sent back for retreatment.

15.61

Precipitation hardening can, however, be considerably retarded by storing the quenched stock at low temperatures, and refrigeration equipment is employed for storing rivets, sections and sheet. For example, a grade of duralumin which at normal temperatures ($20°$ C) would need to be cold-formed within 2 hours of quenching, could be stored for up to a week at $-20°$ C without deterioration in ductility.

For large-sized stock, such as sheets, cold-storage rooms are used, but smaller material can be stored in thermally insulated boxes along with solid carbon dioxide. Mobile refrigerators can be used to transfer quenched stock from one part of the factory to another.

PRECIPITATION TREATMENT

15.70

Whilst some alloys can be allowed to age-harden naturally at normal temperatures, it is necessary to treat others at a higher temperature in order to obtain in them their optimum properties.

The relationship between the time and temperature of treatment and the mechanical properties obtained was discussed in Part I (17.53), and it was seen that in general the higher the temperature used, the shorter was the time necessary to produce optimum mechanical properties. Moreover, if this time were exceeded for any given temperature the properties began to deteriorate due to visible precipitation taking place.

Precipitation treatment must often be planned in order to accommodate material of varying sectional thickness. Thin sections tend to heat up more quickly than heavy sections, so that if a high-temperature–short-time treatment were employed variations in properties between thin and thick sections would be inevitable. Therefore it is general practice to carry out precipitation treatment at relatively low temperatures for correspondingly long times in order to minimise differences in properties due to the time-lag in reaching treatment temperature of heavy sections over thin.

15.71

Precipitation treatment is usually carried out in air-circulating furnaces of the types already mentioned in connection with solution treatment. After treatment the charge is generally air-cooled. Salt-baths can only be employed for this work if a salt mixture capable of fusion at a low temperature is used, and the charge must in any case be washed after treatment to remove the adhering salt.

Courtesy of G. W. B. Furnaces Ltd, Dudley.

PLATE 15.2—Large-capacity Batch-type Furnace for the Precipitation Treatment of Aluminium Alloys.
Note air circulation ducts on inside wall of chamber.

FAULTS WHICH MAY ARISE DURING HEAT-TREATMENT
15.80

The principal faults which can occur during either the solution or precipitation treatment of aluminium alloys are connected with the use of incorrect treatment temperatures.

15.81 Overheating During Solution Treatment

It was pointed out early in this chapter (15.20) that if an aluminium alloy was solution treated at too high a temperature, that is the solidus temperature of that particular alloy was exceeded, then fusion at the grain boundaries would begin. The results of such fusion are usually evident in a micro-section of the material, since the subsequent quenching operations results in the formation of a cast type of structure in that metal which had begun to melt and which was chilled on quenching.

Overheating may also lead to cracking of the material during quenching. These cracks may not be visible, and the use of such material will obviously constitute a source of danger.

The term 'burning' is often employed to refer to the very severe overheating of alloys during solution treatment, and whilst this may suggest to the reader that oxidation of the material has taken place, this is by no means the most serious fault associated with the term when used in this context. 'Burning' is indicated by a darkening of the surface of the alloy, and possibly by the formation of cracks and blisters during subsequent quenching.

15.82 Blistering During Solution Treatment

This fault is sometimes encountered with material which has been treated in an air furnace heated by gas or oil and in which the products of combustion have come into contact with the charge. Air furnaces fired by gas or oil should therefore be of the totally enclosed muffle type, so that the charge is completely separated from the products of combustion.

Water vapour in the furnace atmosphere may also lead to blistering. This may be derived from moisture on the charge or its carrier, or merely from humidity in the atmosphere of the shop itself. Such blistering may be inhibited by introducing some hydrocarbon, such as tallow or creosote, into the furnace along with the charge. The hydrocarbon burns when the temperature has risen sufficiently, and deposits a coating of carbon (lamp black) on the charge, which is still relatively cold. This coating protects the surface from attack by water vapour. The hydrocarbon may either be painted on to the charge or it may be placed in the heating chamber in a container.

15.83 Over-ageing and Reversion

During precipitation treatment heating should not be continued after the optimum properties have been reached, otherwise precipitation on a scale which is visible under the microscope will take place, and the material will begin to soften. The alloy is then said to be 'over-aged'.

The higher the precipitation-treatment temperature used, the sooner optimum properties are attained, and the sooner over-ageing takes place. Properties approaching those of freshly solution-treated material can be obtained in an alloy which has been fully aged at room temperature by reheating it to about 300° C. This treatment is stopped when minimum hardness is reached and the alloy aged again at room temperature. The complete cycle of softening and re-ageing is usually called 'reversion'.

BIBLIOGRAPHY

1 'Controlled Atmospheres for the Heat-treatment of Metals', I. Jenkins (Chapman and Hall).
2 'Controlled Atmospheres in Heat-treatment', G. T. Dunkley (Pitman).
3 'Protective Atmospheres', A. G. Hotchkiss and H. M. Weber (Wiley; Chapman and Hall).
4 'Equipment for the Thermal Treatment of Non-ferrous Metals and Alloys', Symposium (Institute of Metals).
5 'Magnesium Casting Technology', A. W. Brace and F. A. Allen (Chapman and Hall).

6 'Control of Quality in the Production of Wrought Non-ferrous Metals and Alloys. III. The Control of Quality in Heat-treatment and Final Operations', Symposium (Institute of Metals).

7 'Aluminium, Vol. III—Fabrication and Finishing', Ed. K. R. van Horn (American Society of Metals).

Chapter sixteen
PRESSURE-WELDING PROCESSES

16.10

Today the term 'pressure welding' usually implies methods of metal joining which involve the use of electricity or some other sophisticated energy source, but it should be remembered that the first welding operation ever used by man was a pressure-welding process. Pressure welding was undoubtedly part of the trade of Tubal Cain (21.10—Part I), and there is direct evidence of its extensive use by the Ancient Greeks more than 2000 years ago.

This simple form of pressure welding is still employed by blacksmiths all over the world. Most readers will have seen a blacksmith at work, and will know that he heats the two pieces of iron to be welded to a temperature in excess of 1000° C and then forges them together by a series of hammer blows. The metal faces are thus brought into intimate contact with each other by this procedure, so that recrystallisation takes place across the interface, knitting the two halves together. Moreover, the hammering process breaks scale from the surfaces and also causes recrystallisation of the metal adjacent to the joint, leading to a much more satisfactory structure.

Many modern pressure-welding processes are termed 'solid-phase' welding operations since no fusion of the work-piece occurs and joining is due to the application of pressure which causes crystal growth across the metal interface. Such processes often involve heating the parts to be joined, either by electricity or by an oxy-acetylene flame. In recent years, however, cold-welding processes have been developed which make use of high-explosives and ultrasonics as well as more orthodox methods of applying pressure.

Most of the processes are 'autogenous', that is, they do not employ weld metal obtained from an external 'filler rod' but form a weld from the metal of the work-pieces themselves.

OXY-ACETYLENE PRESSURE WELDING
16.20

In this process the parts to be joined are carefully shaped and cleaned so that they can be butted quite tightly together under pressure. Heat is then applied from a multiple arrangement of oxy-acetylene torches, causing recrystallisation and diffusion to take place across the metal interface at a temperature well below the solidus of either of the materials being joined. This type of close-faced pressure welding is the only process (other than that of cold welding) where joining takes place completely in the solid.

Whilst the method is generally applied to the butt welding of solid and tubular shapes which are provided with accurately machined abutting surfaces, lap welds may also be made by this process. The parts may be placed in a jig which aligns them and by means of which axial welding pressure may be applied. A single or double ring of oxy-acetylene burners encircles the periphery of the work-pieces, and as heating commences a pressure of 5–10 N/mm² is applied to the abutting surfaces (Fig. 16.1). The ring burner

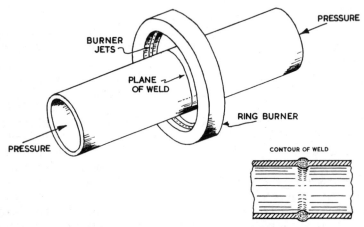

FIG. 16.1—Oxy-acetylene Pressure Welding.

is made to oscillate either in a plane parallel to the axis of the work-pieces, normal to the axis of the work-pieces or in a combination of the two movements. In this way uniform heating is obtained in the region of the work-pieces to be welded. When the welding temperature has been reached the pressure is increased to 20–30 N/mm² (for steels) in order to complete the weld. The heating flames are then shut off.

16.21

In an alternative method the faces to be joined are made reasonably square and then held a small distance apart whilst they are heated by an oxy-acetylene flame. When the faces have reached a state of incipient fusion the parts are brought together under pressure to effect a welded joint. An allowance must be made in both processes for a shortening of the parts being joined. This is due to upsetting of the material in the region of the joint.

Since the equipment required for oxy-acetylene pressure welding is relatively simple, the process lends itself to outdoor work, such as the joining of sections of cross-country pipe-lines and rail tracks. At the same time the operating conditions are such that they can be adapted to complete automation. Various sections in carbon steels, alloy steels and some non-ferrous alloys are welded in this manner.

16.22
Because of its method of manufacture, the joint resulting from an oxy-acetylene pressure-welding process has a strength almost equal to that in the base metal itself. The joint is homogeneous, and there is little evidence of the junction, except where there has been a difference in composition in the materials being joined.

INDUCTION PRESSURE WELDING
16.23
This process makes use of the heating effect produced when an electric current is induced in the work-piece. In other respects the process resembles oxy-acetylene pressure welding.

The induction coil, which surrounds the work in the region of the proposed weld, is connected to a power source, the frequency of which must not be so high as to cause skin-heating only. If a relatively low-frequency current is used fairly uniform heating across the joint is obtained. Since heating is very rapid and very localised a minimum of oxidation and distortion are produced. Moreover, a shielding atmosphere can be used if desired.

ELECTRICAL-RESISTANCE WELDING
16.30
In electrical-resistance-welding processes the parts to be welded are heated by an electric current which passes through them. With such a method of heating temperature can be strictly controlled, so that welds with consistent properties can be produced, making the process very suitable for mass-production methods. Resistance welding is particularly suitable for joining light-gauge materials which are generally less successfully joined by fusion-welding processes.

Electric-resistance welding is more widely used than any other pressure-welding process, and comprises spot, projection spot, seam, butt and flash welding operations.

16.31 Spot Welding. In the spot-welding process the parts to be joined are clamped firmly between a pair of heavy electrodes which are connected in the secondary circuit of a step-down transformer system. The maximum resistance in such a circuit exists at the surface of contact of the two parts being joined, and if we assume that no arcing takes place at this surface we can determine the heat developed in the region of the weld from the expression:

$$H = I^2 R\, t$$

where H = the heat developed (joules);
$\quad I$ = the current passing through the work (amperes);
$\quad R$ = the electrical resistance of the work (ohms);
$\quad t$ = the time the current flows (seconds).

Only a fraction of the actual heat generated at the joint will be used in raising the metal to welding temperature. Much heat will be lost by conduction to the adjacent metal and to the electrodes (which are usually water cooled), whilst some heat will also be lost by convection and radiation. Therefore the above expression can be amended to read:

$$H = k \cdot I^2 R t$$

where k is a factor which takes into account the heat losses mentioned above.

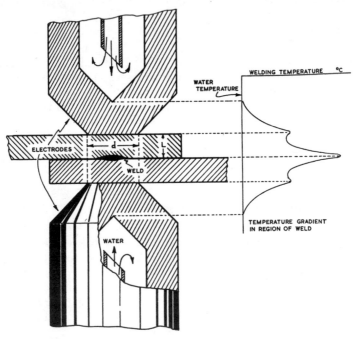

FIG. 16.2.

The total resistance between the electrodes in Fig. 16.2 is the sum of three separate resistances:

(a) the specific resistance of the parts being joined;
(b) the resistance of the metal interface between the parts being joined;
(c) the resistance at the points of contact between the electrodes and the metal parts.

Both (b) and (c) are variable and depend upon factors such as the pressure applied by the electrodes, the shape and size and surface condition of the electrodes and the surface condition of the parts being joined, particularly with regard to the extent of surface oxidation.

The quantity of heat, H, necessary to raise the cylinder of metal diameter, d, and height, $2L$, held between the ends of the electrodes (Fig. 16.2) to the welding temperature is given by the expression:

$$H = \frac{\pi d^2}{4} . 2L . S . C(T - T_0)$$

where L and d are in metres and

where S = relative density of the metal being welded (kg/m³);

$\qquad C$ = its specific heat (J/kg °C);

$\qquad T$ = welding temperature (°C)

$\qquad T_0$ = temperature of the surrounding atmosphere (°C)

Since T_0 is small compared with T it can be neglected.

Therefore $\qquad\qquad$ H $= \frac{\pi d^2}{2} . L . S . C . T$

By equating this expression to the one obtained for the heating effect of the current, the current requirements can be estimated.

$$\frac{\pi d^2}{2} . L . S . C . T . = k . I^2 Rt.$$

Hence $\qquad\qquad\qquad\qquad T = \frac{2k . I^2 Rt}{\pi d^2 LSC}.$

It follows from the above that for a given welding temperature T a metal with a low specific resistance will need a correspondingly high welding current. Pure copper and pure aluminium therefore need very high welding currents, whereas stainless steel, which has a high specific resistance, can be spot welded relatively easily.

16.311 It might be assumed from the above expression that any metal can be welded using a given current if the latter is allowed to pass through the work long enough. This is obviously not true since a stage would be reached where the rate of conduction of heat away from the region of the weld would balance the rate at which heat was being produced between the electrodes, so that the temperature could rise no further. In successful spot welding the actual joining operation usually takes place in less than 0·5 seconds, and in order that accurate timing can be established with those metals (e.g. aluminium and its alloys) which are difficult to weld, electronic timing devices have been developed which control welding time to ±0·001 second.

16.312 The pitch of spot welds (Fig. 16.3) must be large enough when welding those metals with high specific conductivities. For example, it is impossible to locate spot welds close together when joining copper sheets by this method, since the welding current tends to short-circuit through the weld previously made. Consequently, for pure copper the pitch must be at least five or six times the diameter of the weld.

16.313 Pressure is applied by the electrodes just before the current begins to flow, and is maintained for a brief interval after the automatic timer has broken the circuit. In this way oxide films are broken and the pieces brought together into intimate contact before the current begins to flow, so that the passage of the current is restricted to the area between the electrodes. More-

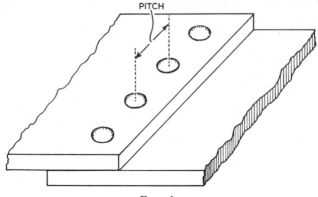

FIG. 16.3.

over, the application of pressure *after* the flow of current has ceased reduces the formation of cracks and porosity and promotes recrystallisation, which results in a fine-grained structure in the weld.

16.314 Spot welds may be produced by either 'direct' or 'indirect' processes. Fig. 16.4 (i) shows the usual direct method of producing a single spot weld,

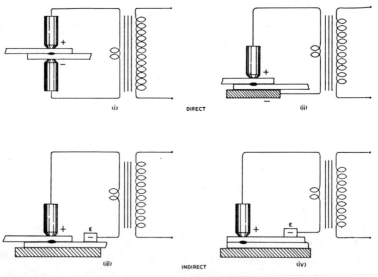

FIG. 16.4—Methods of Producing Spot Welds.

whilst Fig. 16.4 (ii) indicates a variation on the direct method. Figs. 16.4 (iii) and (iv) represent typical indirect methods of producing single spot welds. In each case the electrical circuits is completed through a contact block, E, which has a relatively large contact area, so that no weld is formed at this point.

Spot welds may also be made in multiples by using suitable machines.

Typical electrode and circuit arrangements for multiple welding are shown in Fig. 16.5.

Methods of producing a spot weld such as are indicated in Figs. 16.4 (ii), (iii) and (iv) and in Fig. 16.5 (iii) can be used when it is essential to avoid indenting the 'show' side of the work. With all of the other electrode arrangements indicated in Figs. 16.4 and 16.5, visible indentation of both surfaces adjacent to the weld will result.

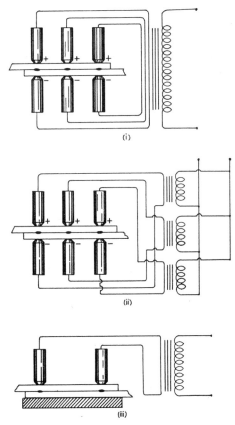

FIG. 16.5—Multiple Spot Welding.

16.315 SPOT-WELDING MACHINES may be either of the stationary (pedestal) type or of the portable (gun) type. Stationary machines may be further classified according to the path which the moving electrode follows. In one type the moving electrode follows a vertical straight path, and the electrode force is usually derived from a pneumatic or hydraulic cylinder or a motor drive. In the other type the moving electrode moves in an arc and is actuated by a lever or rocker arm (Fig. 16.6). Here the electrode pressure is derived either from a foot treadle, a motor-driven cam or a hydraulic or pneumatic

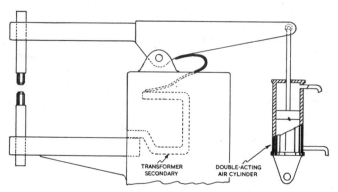

FIG. 16.6—Principle of the Rocker-arm Spot Welding Machine.

cylinder (as illustrated). Pneumatic cylinders are most frequently employed in modern machines. Multiple-spot welding machines are capable of making a number of spot welds in a single operation.

Portable machines are used in cases where it is easier to take the welding equipment to the work than it is to move the work to the welding machine.

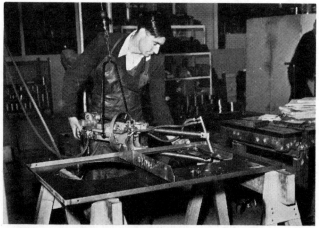

Courtesy of Messrs A. R. O. Machinery Co. Ltd, London, S.W.13.

PLATE 16.1—A Portable Spot-welding Gun of the Air-operated Type.

This illustration shows the gun in action welding a cabinet door panel.

They are also used for tacking when work has been accurately located in a fixed jig, and where assembly work is being carried out on the conveyor-belt system.

16.316 All of these spot-welding machines have three component sections in common:

(1) a mechanical system designed to apply the necessary force to the electrodes;

(2) the electrical transformer circuit, together with a current-controlling device;

(3) a timing system to control accurately the duration of the flow of current and the period during which pressure is applied.

The electrodes used in resistance welding carry currents up to 77·5 A/mm², whilst the pressure applied usually varies between 75 and 100 N/mm². The material used for electrodes must therefore be mechanically strong and at the same time have a sufficiently high electrical conductivity so that the electrodes themselves do not heat up to such an extent that they weld on to the work. Copper-base alloys, such as beryllium bronze and chromium–copper (16.71 and 16.72—Part I), in the heat-treated forms fulfil most requirements, though in cases where the metals being welded have a high specific resistance (e.g. stainless steels and nickel–chromium alloys) copper–tungsten alloy electrodes are employed. These are made by powder-metallurgy methods (6.11), but since their specific resistance is very high, they are not often used for spot or seam welding.

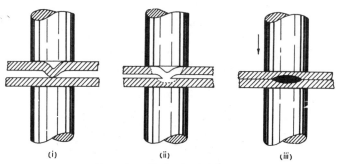

(i)	(ii)	(iii)

FIG. 16.7—Projection Welding.

16.317 The diameter of the tip of the electrode relative to the thickness of metal between the electrodes influences the quality of the weld. If the tip is too large very high currents will be required, which may result in localised overheating and oxidation of the metal in the neighbourhood of the weld; whilst if the tip is too small the weld may lack sufficient strength, since it does not cover a large-enough area. A rough guide to tip size is given by:

$$d = (2 \cdot 5 + T) \, \text{mm}$$

where d is the diameter of the tip and T the total thickness of the metal between the electrodes. In spot welding two pieces of metal of unlike thickness or unlike composition electrode tips of different sizes may be used to produce the correct heat balance in the weld. For example, in welding copper to steel the electrode with the smaller tip would be used in contact with the copper because of the much higher electrical conductivity of the latter.

16.32 Projection Welding. In this modification of the spot-welding process the current flow and the resultant heating are localised to a restricted area by embossing one of the parts to be joined (Fig. 16.7).

As compared with ordinary spot welding, an extra operation (embossing) is involved here, but as against this a number of advantages accrue. In cases where thick sections have to be joined projection welding can be used where spot welding would not be possible due to the heavy currents and pressures

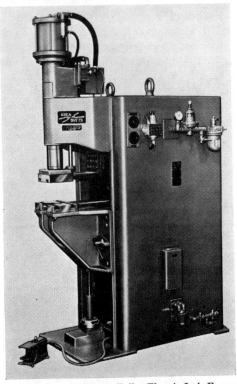

Courtesy of Messrs Fuller Electric Ltd, E. 17;
and AB Aseavetsmaskiner, Stockholm.

PLATE 16.2—A Projection Welding Machine.

required. Moreover, in projection welding a better heat balance can be obtained in difficult-to-weld combinations of compositions and thicknesses, and the finished appearance is often superior, since the electrode on the finish side will have a large contacting area which considerably reduces electrode indentation. Electrode life, too, is longer because of the large contact areas employed and the harder higher-resistance alloys used. Pressures and current densities are also lower than in spot welding, and these factors, too, will reduce wear and distortion of the electrodes.

In addition to the extra embossing process involved, the main disadvantage of projection welding is that it is limited to combinations of metal thickness and composition which can be embossed.

16.321 The design of the projection is important. It should form easily without causing any distortion in the part during forming, and it should be strong enough to support the initial electrode pressure before the current begins to flow. During welding the projection should collapse without undue spread of metal, and should thus leave the two parts in intimate contact.

16.322 The projection-welding cycle is similar to that used in spot welding. The stages in the formation of a projection weld are illustrated in Fig. 16.7. In (i) the projection in the upper piece is held in contact with the lower piece, whilst in (ii) the current is flowing and, being localised to the region around the projection, is heating the metal in that area. At (iii) the heated projection has collapsed under the pressure of the electrodes forming the weld.

16.33 Seam Welding. Seam welding is a resistance-welding process similar in principle to spot welding, but in which a continuous weld is produced

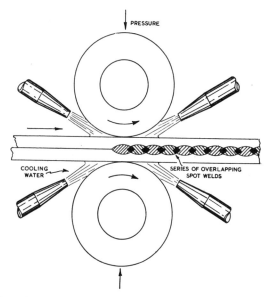

FIG. 16.8—Seam Welding with Intermittent Current.

by passing the work between rotating wheel-shaped electrodes (Fig. 16.8) which exert the welding pressure and conduct the welding current. As with spot welding, the welds may be formed by either direct or indirect methods, and may be either single or multiple, that is, a single seam or several parallel seams may be produced simultaneously.

16.331 A seam weld may be produced by either a continuous or an intermittent method of operation. In continuous-motion welding the electrodes rotate at a constant speed and the welding current either flows continuously or is interrupted. In the latter case a series of overlapping spot welds is produced, as indicated in Fig. 16.8. In intermittent-motion welding the electrodes travel the distance necessary for each successive weld and then stop. The current is then switched on and the weld made, the whole process being controlled automatically.

Courtesy of Messrs Fuller Electric Ltd, E.17;
and AB Aseavetsmaskiner, Stockholm.

PLATE 16.3—A Seam-welding Machine.

16.332 A serious difficulty encountered in seam welding is warping of the material being joined. Several methods are used to reduce such warpage. On long seams, for example, the parts are first joined by 'tacking' them together with a series of short seam welds. The work is then passed between the electrodes again and the missed portions welded together. A more common method of reducing warpage is to employ water-cooling jets immediately before and after the electrodes.

16.333 SEAM-WELDING MACHINES are similar in basic contruction to spot-welding machines, except that the electrodes are mechanically driven rotating discs. Several types of drive may be employed to actuate the electrode. In some machines one electrode is shaft driven whilst the other idles, but in others both wheels are driven. In the latter type of machine it is essential that the wheel diameters are maintained equal in order to avoid differences in the peripheral speed of the electrodes as they wear.

16.334 Changes in peripheral speed of the electrodes due to wear can be overcome by using a type of friction drive to the electrodes. One or both of the electrodes is driven by a friction wheel at the periphery of the electrode. The power-driven friction wheel is usually made of hardened steel knurled on the engaging surface. This knurling cuts into the face of the electrode wheel, or, alternatively, into the side of the wheel adjacent to the face. Whichever arrangement is used, the peripheral speed of the electrode will be the same throughout its life, and will be independent of changes in diameter due to wear.

In a third type of electrode arrangement the work is clamped to a bar electrode and pushed under an idler-wheel electrode, external power being used to push the work causing the idler to rotate.

16.335 The wheel electrodes may be set so that the seam weld is produced either transversely or longitudinally to the body of the machine. In the latter type the length of the weld is limited by the depth of the 'throat' of the machine, whilst in the former welds of any length can be produced, since the work moves across the front of the machine. Many machines, however, are 'universal'; that is the electrodes can be rotated about a vertical axis through 90° so that a weld can be made in either direction.

Various contours are used for seam-welding electrodes, the four basic types

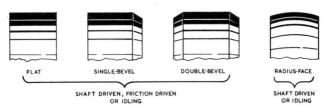

FIG. 16.9—Contours of Seam-welding Electrodes.

being indicated in Fig. 16.9. Radius-crowned electrodes are possibly the easiest to manipulate, and usually give the best appearance to the weld. Flat-faced or bevelled wheels are more difficult to set up, so that the two flat surfaces are parallel. If the faces are not parallel the work is indented unevenly.

The most common method of cooling the electrodes and the work is by direct sprays, as shown in Fig. 16.8, but when it is desirable to avoid wetting the work, internal cooling of both the shaft and the electrode wheel may be employed.

16.34 Flash Welding. Flash welding is a process which can be used for joining together the ends of sheets, rods, wire or tubes. The two work parts are placed in the clamping jaws of a machine, and as the parts are brought together into light contact a voltage sufficiently high to cause arcing between the ends is applied (Fig. 16.10). Arcing continues as the two parts advance, until the work attains a welding temperature, sufficient pressure being applied to produce a continuous weld. 'Flashing' and upsetting are accompanied by the expulsion of metal, slag and oxides from the joint.

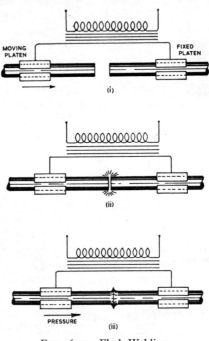

FIG. 16.10—Flash Welding.

16.341 In this process it is important that the moving platen is advanced at the correct speed in relation to the current used. If the speed is too high, then the work parts will come together too quickly, stopping the arcing action prematurely and resulting in an inadequate weld. If the speed is too low the arcing action may be intermittent, and again heating will be insufficient to form a good weld.

16.342 The applied pressure and the distance of travel of the moving platen must not be too great, or an excessive amount of plastic metal in the region of the weld will be forced out. On the other hand, if the pressure or distance of travel are insufficient a coarse crystal structure in the region of the weld may result from a lack of mechanical work following the heating action.

It is sometimes difficult to flash-weld heavy sections, because arcing will not take place readily between two large bodies of cold metal. This is sometimes overcome by preheating the two ends or by bevelling the surfaces to be welded. Alternatively, a higher open-circuit voltage can be used at the beginning of flashing than later in the cycle.

16.343 FLASH-WELDING MACHINES consist essentially of a main frame carrying the transformer and control equipment; a mechanical system to force the work-pieces together; a set of clamps to hold the work; and a circuit to supply the welding current.

Courtesy of Messrs Fuller Electric Ltd, E.17;
and AB Aseasvetsmaskiner, Stockholm.
PLATE 16.4—A Flash-welding Machine in Action.

These machines generally operate in the horizontal position. A stationary, non-adjustable platen is fixed to one end of the frame, whilst at the other end of the frame the moving platen is suitably mounted and connected to the upsetting mechanism. The platens are generally of cast iron or steel with copper terminals so that they may be connected to the secondary circuit of the transformer and clamps for holding the work-pieces and conducting the current to them.

The upsetting mechanism is either manually operated, motor driven, or operated by hydraulic or pneumatic pressure.

16.35 Butt Welding. Butt welding differs from flash welding in that no

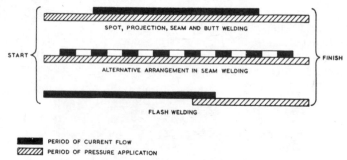

FIG. 16.11.

arcing takes place between the surfaces being joined, the heat being produced solely by the electrical resistance at the abutting surfaces to the passage of a current. Moreover, in butt welding pressure is applied before the current begins to flow and is maintained throughout the heating period, whereas in flash welding only a light contacting pressure is applied during the period of arcing (Fig. 16.11).

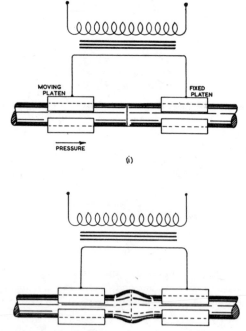

FIG. 16.12—Butt Welding.

16.351 In butt welding the parts are brought into solid contact and the current then passed through the contact area until a sufficiently high temperature has been reached to permit the forging of a weld (Fig. 16.12).

The best results are generally obtained in butt welding if the two pieces are equal in cross-sectional area and of equal specific resistance. If they are equal in specific resistance but not in cross-sectional area the part having the larger cross-sectional area should project from the clamping die farther than the other part, whilst if they are of unequal specific resistance the part with the lesser resistance should project farther from the die than the other.

16.352 In order to facilitate heating at the abutting surfaces the areas are sometimes restricted by bevelling the ends. The surfaces to be joined must be clean, parallel and reasonably smooth, otherwise local overheating may occur in the region of any projections. Such projections may even melt before the areas which are not in contact begin to heat up.

16.353 BUTT-WELDING MACHINES are basically similar to those used in flash welding (16.343 above), and differ mainly in the methods used to produce motion during welding.

THE PRODUCTION OF SEAM-WELDED TUBES
16.40

It is generally supposed that the earliest pipe to be used by man was in the form of a hollow tree-trunk. Probably the oldest *metal* pipe known was a copper one discovered in the temple at Abusir near the Pyramids. This pipe is thought to be some 5000 years old.

The manufacture of seam-soldered lead pipe by the Romans is, of course, well known. Used in conjunction with a system of aqueducts, several of which are still to be seen in various parts of southern Europe, lead pipe allowed the Romans to develop water supply, sanitation and drainage to an advanced stage. As the Roman Empire declined most of the sanitary measures which had been established perished with it. The filth and pestilence of the Dark Ages which followed culminated in the destruction of about a quarter of the population of Europe by the Black Death.

Even as late as the seventeenth century wooden water mains were in use in London, and it was not until the beginning of the nineteenth century that the work of two Englishmen, Osborne and Russell, led to the establishment of machine methods for manufacturing tubes by lap and butt seam welding. Prior to this, all tubes had been made by hand from plates which were first rolled into cylindrical form, then heated and the overlapping edges welded together over a suitable mandrel.

Metal tubes are of two main types, seam-welded and seamless, the production of the latter being described elsewhere (7.60; 9.50 and 10.40) in this book. Welded tubes and pipes are employed in vast quantities as conduit for electrical cables, and for carrying water and gas at low pressures. It must not be assumed, however, that seam-welded tubes are necessarily mechanically weak. Welded tubes are in fact generally only about 10% less strong than seamless tubes of similar composition. Large-diameter lap-welded pipes have in fact been used in hydro-electric installations.

Millions of feet of electric-resistance-welded tube are used every year in the motor-car, motor-cycle and cycle industries alone. Furniture frames, boiler tubes, condensers, heat exchangers and evaporators are further typical applications of electrical-resistance-welded tube, while for pipe-work used in chemical plant stainless-steel tube is produced by the same process.

16.41 The Butt-weld Process. The basis of the butt-welding process of tube-making was introduced in 1825 by Cornelius Whitehouse, who succeeded in producing a satisfactory tube by drawing a heated flat strip through a bell-shaped welding die. The manufacture of butt-welded pipe has followed the same general principle ever since Whitehouse's original invention, in that forming and welding operations are accomplished by drawing suitably heated strip through a welding bell. In the production of seam-welded tubes and pipes the initial strip or plate is known as 'skelp'. Skelp used in the manufacture of butt-welded pipe is not square at the leading end but is trimmed at an angle (Fig. 16.13), so that when it is pulled through the bell it will curve into the form of a cylinder.

16.411 The skelp is first charged to a heating furnace, and when the welding temperature of about 1 350° C has been reached the leading end of the skelp is gripped by an operator using a pair of tongs, over the handles of which he

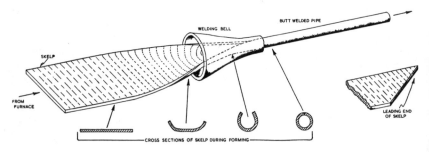

FIG. 16.13—The Butt Weld Process of Tube Making.

then slides a welding bell. The operator attaches the handles of the tongs to an endless moving chain which drags tongs, skelp and bell out of the furnace together. The bell is caught in a stand just outside the furnace, so that the skelp is pulled through the bell and is formed into a pipe, the edges of the original skelp being welded firmly together.

16.412 The seam-welded pipe passes first to the sizing rolls and then to a cooling bed. After the pipe has cooled, a further set of sizing rolls is used to bring it to its final size and shape and also to remove scale, both internally and externally. The pipe is then straightened and its ends trimmed. Finally, the pipes are transferred in bundles to a water bosh, where loose scale is removed.

The butt-weld process is used in the manufacture of pipes up to about 75 mm diameter.

16.42 The Lap-weld Process. In the butt-weld process described above the edges of the skelp meet or abut together before the welding operations, whilst in the lap-weld process they are actually overlapped before being welded. In order that the final weld shall be neat and smooth, the edges of the skelp are scarfed (Fig. 16.14 (i)). In the case of skelp used for the production of tubes up to 0·18 m diameter this operation is carried out on the cold strip by means of cutting tools, but for tubes above that size the plate is heated and its edges shaped by passing it between scarfing rolls.

The skelp is then heated to about 900° C and pulled through a turn-up die, the principle of which is similar to that of the welding bell used in the butt-weld process described above. In the lap-weld process, however, the die is fitted with a mandrel, and after passing through this stage the skelp has been converted to an *unwelded* cylinder with overlapping edges (Fig. 16.14 (ii)).

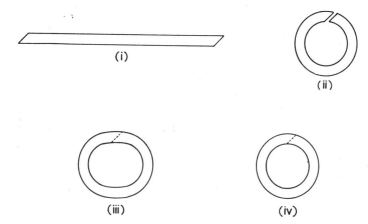

FIG. 16.14—Stages in the Lap Weld Process of Tube Making.

16.421 The skelp is then reheated to the welding temperature (1 350° C) and passed through a pair of welding rolls which are equipped with a mandrel and are similar in design to those shown in Fig. 8.12. The lap, which is kept uppermost, is squeezed between the top roll and the mandrel so that the overlapping edges are welded together. In order to avoid scoring the sides of the tube in the welding rolls, the horizontal axis of the groove is made greater than the vertical axis. Consequently, at this stage the tube is slightly oval in cross-section (Fig. 16.14 (iii)).

16.422 After the weld has been inspected the tube is reheated and passed through a pair of rolls cut with a groove of smaller diameter than that in the welding rolls. The walls of the tube are thus thinned, smoothed and elongated, whilst the weld is consolidated and the overall microstructural properties improved. The tube now passes between a pair of sizing rolls which bring it to a perfectly circular cross-section (Fig. 16.14 (iv)), after which it is straightened by reeling.

16.423 For tubes of greater diameter than 0·3 m the turn-up die is replaced by a roll-forming mill, through which the plates are passed whilst hot and bent up into cylindrical form. The welding process is similar to that used for small-diameter tubes, the lap being squeezed between the upper roll and a mandrel.

Lap-welded pipes are used for carrying water, oil, gas, steam; and for scaffolding and tubular roof structures.

16.424 A modified lap-weld process is used in the production of pipes with a diameter greater than 0·4 m. The plates are first roll formed to a cylindrical shape as described above, but because of the large dimensions of the work, the welding process is usually accomplished in sections. A 450 mm length of lap is heated from above and below by gas burners, and when the welding temperature has been reached the tube is moved between two rollers, one of which has a concave surface and is in contact with the outside surface of the tube, and the other a convex surface and which is in contact with the internal surface of the tube. The upper or concave roller is carried at the end of a hydraulic ram which exerts the required welding pressure. The short length of weld is inspected and, if satisfactory, a further section is similarly treated.

16.425 After it has been successfully welded throughout its length the tube is reheated and rolled round and round in the forming mill until it has cooled to black heat. The tube is then circular and quite straight.

Hydraulically welded pipes, which can be produced with diameters up to 1·8 m, are used for carrying water, oil, sewage and low-pressure steam, as well as being used for the manufacture of rollers employed in paper-making machinery.

16.43 The Continuous Butt-weld Process. This process, which is used mainly in the manufacture of small-diameter pipes in dead mild steel, is capable of very high production rates. The skelp is both shaped and welded by the use of rolls, so that production can be carried out continuously and at high speed.

16.431 Fig. 16.15 shows the general sequence of operations during the process. In order to maintain continuity the leading end of a new strip is flash welded (16.34) to the back end of the strip already under-going shaping and welding. The ends of the strips are first trimmed square, and are then flash welded together using a current of about 10^4 amperes at 7 volts. Pinch rolls are used to remove any roughness from the surface of the strip in the region of the weld. These rolls operate at a greater peripheral speed than those in the forming and seam-welding trains, and in this way a considerable accumulation of strip builds up in the looping bay. This enables the joining of strips to be carried out without stopping the process.

16.432 From the looping bay the strip passes into a tunnel furnace, where it is heated to a temperature of about 1350° C. As the strip leaves the furnace its edges are cleaned of scale by means of an air blast in order to facilitate the formation of a clean weld. The strip then passes into the forming rolls, in which it is bent into the form of a cylinder, but at this stage the edges are prevented from coming into contact by a small projection near the mouth of the rolls. A small jet of oxygen is allowed to play on the unwelded edges of the skelp so that they are raised quickly to the welding temperature. Immediately, the skelp passes into the welding rolls, where the weld is completed.

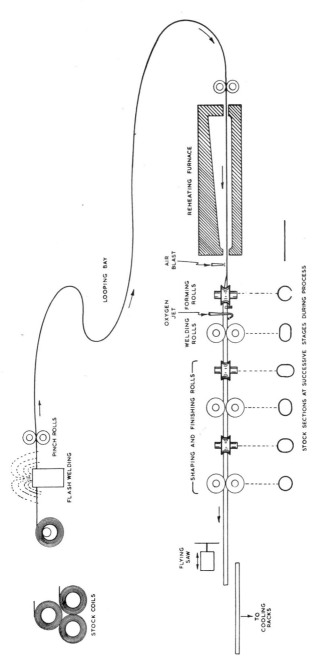

STOCK COILS

FLASH WELDING

PINCH ROLLS

LOOPING BAY

REHEATING FURNACE

AIR BLAST

OXYGEN JET

FORMING ROLLS

WELDING ROLLS

SHAPING AND FINISHING ROLLS

FLYING SAW

TO COOLING RACKS

STOCK SECTIONS AT SUCCESSIVE STAGES DURING PROCESS

FIG. 16.15—The Continuous Butt Weld Process of Tube Making.

The tube then passes through four sets of shaping rolls, which form its cross-section to oval shapes and finally to circular, as indicated in Fig. 16.15. At the same time further consolidation of the weld takes place as the tube passes through the shaping rolls.

16.433 The tube is cut into lengths by a flying circular saw which moves forward at the same speed as the tube which it is cutting. The cut tubes fall on to a moving cooling rack, which conveys them to sizing rolls, after which

Courtesy of Messrs Tube Products Ltd, Oldbury.

PLATE 16.5—Electric-resistance-welded Tube.
The strip passing through the forming rolls which produce the initial tube shape.

they are cooled by water sprays whilst being carried on another rack. Finally, the ends of the tubes are trimmed and the finished product is usually tested hydraulically to a pressure of $7 \cdot 5$ N/mm^2.

These tubes are used mainly for carrying liquids and gases. An idea of the rate of production can be gained from the information that tube leaves the shaping rolls at a speed of up to $1 \cdot 5$ m/s.

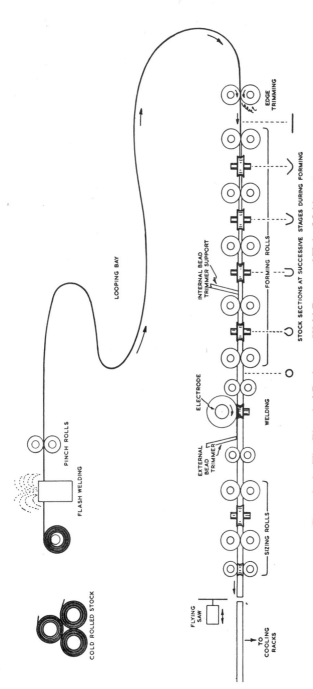

FIG. 16.16—The Electrical Resistance Weld Process of Tube Making.

16.44 The Electric-resistence-weld Process. In this process tube is produced from strip by a continuous butt-weld operation, but it differs from the continuous butt-weld process oulined above in that forming of the tube shape is carried out on the *cold* strip, only the edges subsequently being heated for the welding operation.

16.441 Fig. 16.16 illustrates a typical plant lay-out for this process. A train of about ten pairs of rolls is used to form the cold strip to a cylindrical shape and bring together the edges which are to be welded. The adjacent edges are then raised to welding temperature by the passage of an electric current across the joint. This is accomplished by means of two insulated disc electrodes which are fixed on either side of a wheel. This assembly presses down on to the seam so that one disc is held in contact with one edge and the other disc

Courtesy of Messrs Tube Products Ltd, Oldbury.

PLATE 16.6—Electric-resistance-welded Tube.
The tube passing under the rotating copper welding electrodes, where the butting edges are welded by the passage of a heavy current. The electrodes are liquid cooled.

is held in contact with the opposite edge. The heated edges are pressed firmly together by a pair of horizontal rolls, thus producing a sound weld. The pressure from these horizontal rolls causes fins to form on both the internal and external surfaces of the weld. These are trimmed off immediately, as indicated in Fig. 16.16. The tube is then passed through a train of sizing rolls and finally cut into sections by a flying saw.

In the electric-resistance-weld process only the edges of the skelp are heated. Consequently, little scale is formed. Moreover, only simple cooling tables are needed to receive the lengths of tube.

Resistance-welded tubes can be made in sizes up to 0·4 m diameter. Since higher welding temperatures can be applied than is possible in the continuous butt-weld process, tubes can be made from steel with higher carbon contents in the region of 0·3%.

FRICTION WELDING

16.50

This is a process in which one of the work-pieces is rotated, the other remaining stationary. Whilst rotation is taking place the work-pieces are brought together under pressure so that heat is generated at the metal interface (Fig. 16.17). The conversion of mechanical energy into heat by means of friction is a process the engineer usually opposes, but in this instance it can be regarded as an efficient way of converting mechanical energy into heat energy. This conversion occurs only in the weld area so that very little heat energy is wasted.

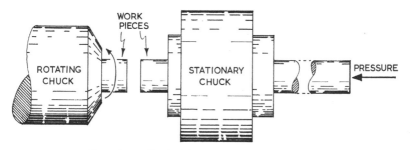

FIG. 16.17—Typical Set-up for Friction Welding.

16.51

As relative rotation between the work-pieces takes place under pressure, heat due to dry friction is generated and a stage is reached where pressure welding can occur. Such welding begins as seizures at local points, these seizures being followed by ruptures. This state of affairs is indicated by fluctuations in torque. In the following stage heat is generated by mechanical deformation of the metal rather than by dry friction, and the increase in heat energy produced is sufficient to reduce the metal to a plastic state. A 'flash' or collar of metal is then formed due to extrusion from the interface as a joint is produced. Since pressure is applied throughout the operation, welding occurs at the lowest possible temperature.

16.52

Friction welding can be used for materials up to several centimetres in diameter and the relatively low welding temperature involved results in high-quality joints. A further advantage of the process is that dissimilar materials can be successfully joined. Thus carbon steel can be satisfactorily welded to titanium, aluminium and zirconium as well as to high-speed steel. A type of brazing process in which a disc of the brazing alloy is interposed between the two metals to be joined, is also under development.

COLD-PRESSURE WELDING

16.60

If two pieces of metal are brought into intimate contact with each other under a high normal pressure and a shearing force is then applied which is sufficient

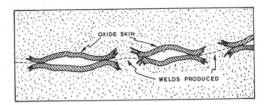

FIG. 16.18.

to cause one surface to slide over the other, then a weld will be produced between the two surfaces. Two pieces of freshly cleaned lead wire can be made to weld in this way by twisting them together, and the weld produced has a strength approximately that of the base metal.

16.61

The essential requirement of such a process is to obtain true metal-to-metal contact between the surfaces. This is extremely difficult, since a metal surface which has been newly pickled soon becomes covered again with an oxide film which, though extremely thin, is sufficient to prevent intimate contact between the metal surfaces. If the surfaces are sheared whilst in contact, however, fragmentation of the oxide film occurs, allowing some metal-to-metal contact to take place. Welding will occur at these points (Fig. 16.18).

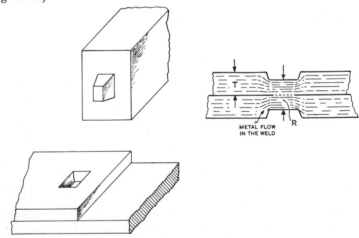

FIG. 16.19.

16.62

Any metal can be made to weld to some degree by shearing the two surfaces together at a sufficiently high normal pressure. In practice, however, the results are often erratic and (at the time of writing) only a few metals are being welded by this process. The most successful adaption of the process involves bringing the metal sheets into contact and then pressing a punch into them (Fig. 16.19). The interface between the sheets is thus *stretched* whilst it is under compressive stress. Stretching of the surface causes fragmentation of the oxide film and permits intimate metallic contact under pressure, which leads to welding.

16.63

The depth of penetration by the punch which will produce a satisfactory weld varies from metal to metal. For pure aluminium the best weld strength is obtained when the cross-section of the metal is reduced by the punch to about 33% of the original combined thickness of the sheets. The value 33% is sometimes referred to as the 'figure of merit' and is given by $\dfrac{R \times 100}{2T}$, where R is the thickness of the weld and T the thickness of one sheet. Table 16.1 gives typical values for the figure of merit for several combinations of metals.

TABLE 16.1

Material	Figure of merit
Pure aluminium . . .	33
Duralumin	20
Aluminium to copper . . .	16
Lead	16
Pure copper	14
Aluminium to iron . . .	12
Iron	8

16.64

In addition to lap-welding by the spot method as outlined above, cold seam-welding can also be employed. Thus, by the use of suitable tools, seam-welded tubes can be produced. Moreover, cans can be sealed by cold welding their lids into position, providing suitable tools are designed which will cause the necessary sliding together of the rims of both lid and can.

Cold butt-welding of wire and tubes has also been developed (Fig. 16.20). Here the parts to be welded are clamped in split dies so that the part projects beyond the die face in each case. When the dies are brought together, metal between the die faces is extruded laterally to provide the necessary flow in close contact so that welding occurs at the interface.

16.65

It is most important that the surfaces to be joined are completely cleaned before the cold-welding operation is attempted. Scratch-brushing and pickling are necessary to remove the thick oxide film and also to degrease the surface. A thin film of oxide forms immediately on the surface when the pickled sheet is exposed to the atmosphere, but if welding is carried out within an hour this thin oxide film will be fragmented sufficiently to permit metal-to-metal contact. Absolute cleanliness is essential for successful cold-welding, and handling of the metal surface with the bare hands after pickling will often result in a defective weld.

16.66

The main requirement of the material being cold welded is that it must be sufficiently ductile to withstand the heavy reduction necessitated by the process. The metal in the region of the weld must also be sufficiently ductile after joining to fulfil the engineering requirements of the material. The most successful cold-pressure welds have been produced in aluminium and copper and certain of their alloys. The cold welding of higher-strength metals and alloys necessitates greater punch pressures to effect the required deformation, and it becomes increasingly difficult to design tools which will withstand the pressures necessary to deform strong alloys.

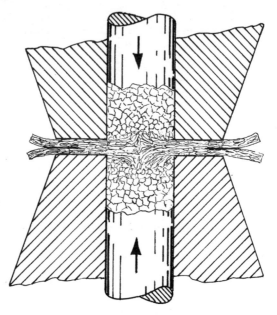

FIG. 16.20—Cold Butt-welding.

Heat-treatment of the joint after cold-welding may be useful in a few cases. Thus, recrystallisation and grain-growth across the interface may provide a tougher joint. On the other hand brittle films around the interface could be the result in the case of dissimilar metals which, when heated together, react to produce an intermetallic compound (8.40—Part I). A careful study of the relevant equilibrium diagram is therefore a prerequisite to any such treatment.

EXPLOSIVE WELDING

16.70

Explosive welding was discovered in 1957 when it was noted that during some explosive forming operations (12.91) the metal blank became bonded to the metal die. Since then explosive welding has been widely developed, particuarly as a means of cladding (22.61—Part I) one metal with another. More recently explosive-welding techniques have been introduced for the production of butt and lap welds and for the welding of tubes to tube plates.

16.71
In order to effect welding by this method, one of the work-pieces must be accelerated to a high velocity and make impact with the other work-piece at a suitable small angle of incidence (Fig. 16.21 (i)). As a result of this high-

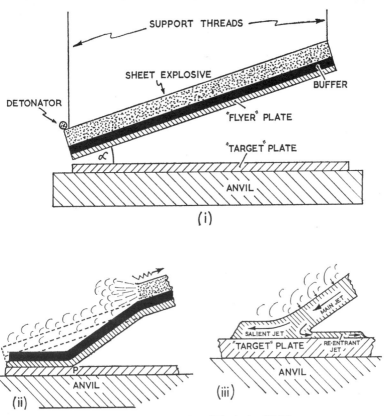

FIG. 16.21—The Principles of Explosive Welding.

velocity oblique impact, welding together of the two work-pieces occurs with the generation of very little heat in the weld region. Consequently there is no oxidation and no heat-affected zone.

16.72
A typical arrangement for the cladding of plate is shown in Fig. 16.21 (i). A moving, or 'flyer', plate is inclined at a small angle of incidence, α, to the stationary, or target, plate. The latter is supported by a steel anvil whilst the flyer plate is protected from erosion and surface damage during the explosion by a buffer coating of rubber or PVC. If a single explosive charge is used it is supported away from the flyer plate at a suitable stand-off distance. When sheet or plastic explosives are used for bonding large areas they are placed in

contact with the buffer (Fig. 16.21 (i)) and detonated at the end where the flyer plate and target. are closest together. The flyer plate may strike the target at a speed of 150–300 m/s and the pressure produced at the interface may be of the order of 700 to 7000 N/mm².

Under the impact of the explosion the flyer plate collapses, and at the point of impact, P (Fig. 16.21 (ii)) between the flyer and target a very high fluid pressure is generated in the materials. This fluid pressure is so high that the shear resistance of the materials of the flyer and target is negligible in comparison and as a result the material in the region of impact behaves for a very short time as a fluid of low viscosity. It can be shown, by application of the laws of fluid mechanics, that the flyer plate divides into two jets—a salient jet and a re-entrant jet (Fig. 16.21 (iii)). This re-entrant jet has a small mass but a high velocity so that it has an excellent scouring effect on the surface of the target.

Metallographic examination of bonded assemblies reveals a ripple configuration as indicated in Fig. 16.22, due to the generation of waves at the

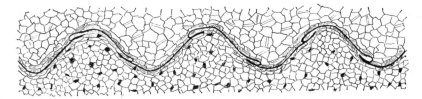

FIG. 16.22—The Microstructural Result of Waves Generated at the Interface, during the Cladding of Mild Steel with Stainless Steel by Explosive Forming.

interface. Superficial examination of the rippled joint might suggest that bonds are mechanical, depending upon the interlocking of the ripples on each work-piece, but closer examination shows that the surfaces are also metallurgically welded.

16.73
Many combinations of dissimilar metals can be welded by this process of which possibly the most significant are titanium to steel; copper to stainless steel; bearing metal to steel; and aluminium to steel.

ULTRASONIC WELDING
16.80
Those vibrations which can be received by the human ear to create the phenomenon we call 'sound' have a frequency range of approximately 20 to 16 000 Hz (cycles per second). Ultrasonic energy, however, is a vibratory energy with a frequency higher than this and in cold-working operations a value of some 20 000 Hz is generally used. In recent years 'ultrasonics' have found application in some machining processes; in measurement of thickness; and in non-destructive testing (21.81—Part I), as well as in cold-working processes.

16.81

Ultrasonic welding is a cold-joining process in which a bond is produced by ultrasonic vibratory energy in the weld region. The work-pieces are clamped between a vibrating probe and an anvil. The vibrating probe, called a *sonotrode*, induces lateral vibrations at the metal interface such that surface films are effectively broken. Bonding then occurs due to slip between the clean surfaces under pressure. Although there is a temperature increase in the weld area due to frictional heat generated before welding occurs, the heat produced is insufficient to cause distortion or a heat-affected zone. Once a weld has been produced slip between the work-pieces ceases and, instead, tends to take place between the sonotrode and the upper work-piece which, in consequence, would be marked. Hence, the operation is stopped as soon as welding is complete. For similar reasons the design of the sonotrode and the pressure between it and the work-piece must be chosen to minimise lateral movement between the two.

16.82

The equipment includes a 20 kHz ultrasonic generator, a transducer, a velocity transformer with a sonotrode tip and a suitable anvil (or reflecting sonotrode) (Fig. 16.23). The length and point of balance of the velocity

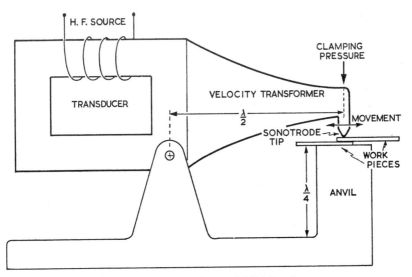

FIG. 16.23—The Principles of Ultra-sonic Welding Apparatus.

transformer are critical. Maximum efficiency is obtained by using a short velocity transformer such that its length is equivalent to $\lambda/8$ (where λ is the wavelength of the vibration used). Where such a member would be inconveniently short, a length of $\lambda/4$ or $\lambda/2$ may be used provided the tip coincides with an antinode. The sonotrode must be of strong material, titanium alloys, aluminium bronze or high-tensile steels generally being used for this purpose, whilst the tip may be of copper, stainless steel, titanium or Inconel. The anvil or reflector sonotrode should be massive and of length $\lambda/4$.

16.83

In addition to spot welding, both line and seam welding can be accomplished by this method. For line welding a sonotrode with a laterally-elongated tip is used, whilst for seam welding a disc is machined on the end of the velocity transformer. The complete vibrator is then revolved against a revolving anvil.

16.84

Possibly the main advantage of ultrasonic welding is the relative absence of generated heat. Consequently dissimilar metals can be joined without fear of the formation of intermetallic compounds and the brittleness they would introduce to the weld. Moreover, the work-pieces can be joined without risk of oxidation or distortion, whilst reactive metals can be welded without the need for controlled atmospheres. Although materials to be joined must be degreased, chemical deoxidation of the surfaces is unnecessary because of the vibrational action in breaking up oxide films immediately before welding occurs.

16.85

Ultrasonic welding is particularly useful in joining thin foils, though aluminium up to 2·5 mm thick can be welded. Steels, aluminium, copper, nickel, titanium, zirconium and their alloys have been successfully welded, whilst examples of dissimilar metal combinations which can be made with advantage include aluminium to stainless steel and aluminium to copper.

DIFFUSION BONDING

16.90

In cold-welding processes, high pressures are required to break up oxide films by lateral extension and also to extrude clean metal through the resultant cracks so that considerable plastic flow of the metal occurs. Such treatment is unsuitable for relatively brittle materials and it is in such cases where diffusion bonding is useful. Diffusion bonding is a technique for joining similar or dissimilar materials without requiring fusion at the interface.

16.91

The surfaces of the components to be joined must be prepared so that they are clean and fit closely against each other. They are then held together at a pressure well below that corresponding to the yield strength so that no deformation occurs, and heated to a suitable temperature usually in a vacuum or a controlled atmosphere. An example of an arrangement used for the 'pressure cladding' of steel with brass is shown in Fig. 16.24. Here the brass/steel 'sandwiches' were separated with sheets of brown paper and heated to 850° C in a reducing atmosphere to prevent surface oxidation.

Bonding occurs by atomic diffusion at the interface where, in the case of dissimilar metals, a solid solution will form. If such a solid solution is of the substitutional type, atoms will diffuse fairly slowly by means of 'vacancy

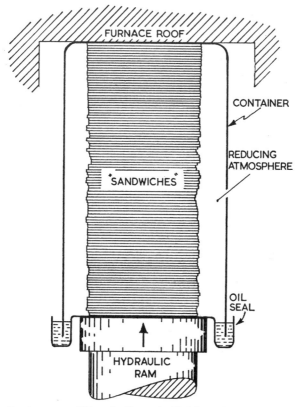

FIG. 16.24—Equipment to Effect the Pressure Cladding of Steel by Brass, using the Principles of Diffusion Bonding.

jumps' (8.34—Part I) whilst interstitial solid solutions will form more quickly as the small solute atoms penetrate rapidly through the interstices of the parent metal.

16.92

Alternatively, a third metal, in the form of foil, may be interposed between the two work-pieces in order to act as a bonding material by forming a different solid solution at the interface with each work-piece. This method is feasible in the case of two components which are themselves mutually insoluble in the solid state, but each of which form a solid solution with the third metal. In some cases the third metal actually melts during the process and alloys with both work-pieces. Such processes are in fact no more than brazing operations (17.50) and should not be regarded as true diffusion bonding which is a solid-phase process.

16.93

Useful work has been carried out with diffusion bonding in making metal-to-ceramic joints as well as metal-to-metal joints. In either case an intermediate material may or may not be used. Joints involving the use of noble metals are particularly successful because of the relative ease of obtaining freedom from surface films.

BIBLIOGRAPHY

1 'Resistance Welding (Theory and Use)', American Welding Society (Reinhold Pub. Corp.).
2 'Electrical Resistance Welding', H. E. J. Butler (Newnes).
3 'Resistance Welding in Mass Production', A. J. Hipperson and T. Watson (Iliffe).
4 'Metallurgy of Welding', W. H. Bruckner (Pitnam).
5 'Welding Practice', Vols. I, II and III, E. Fuchs and H. Bradley (Butterworths Scientific Publications).
6 'The Welding of Non-ferrous Metals', E. G. West (Chapman and Hall).
7 'Welding for Engineers', H. Udin; E. R. Funk and J. Wulff (Wiley; Chapman and Hall).
8 'Welding Engineering', B. E. Rossi (McGraw-Hill).
9 'The Solid Phase Welding of Metals', R. F. Tylecote (Arnold).
10 'The Science and Practice of Welding', W. J. Patton (Prentice-Hall, Inc.).
11 'Welding Design and Processes', B. R. Hilton (Chapman and Hall).
12 'Automatic Welding', R. Hammond (Alvin Redman).
13 'Friction Welding of Metals', V. I. Vill (Reinhold Pub. Corp.).
14 'Welding Technology', J. W. Giachino, W. Weeks and G. S. Johnson (The Technical Press).
15 'Metals and How to Weld Them', T. B. Jefferson, G. Woods (James F. Lincon Arc Welding Foundation, Cleveland, Ohio).
16 'Welding Metallurgy', G. E. Linnert (American Welding Society).
17 BS 807: 1955—Spot-welding electrodes.
18 BS 980: 1950—Steel for automobile purposes. Tubes.
19 BS 1138: 1943—Test pieces for production control of aluminium alloy spot welds.
20 BS 1140: 1957—General requirements for spot welding of light assemblies in mild steel.
21 BS 2630: 1955—Projection welding of low-carbon steel sheet and strip.
22 BS 2937: 1965—General requirements for seam welding in mild steel.
23 BS 2996: 1958—Projection welding of low-carbon wrought steel studs, bosses, bolts, nuts and annular rings.
24 BS 3065: 1965—The rating of resistance welding and resistance heating machines.
25 BS 3847: 1965—General requirements for mash seam welding in mild steel.
26 BS 4215: 1967—Spot-welding electrodes and electrode holders.
27 BS 4577: 1970—Materials for resistance welding electrodes and ancillary equipment.

Chapter seventeen
SOLDERING AND BRAZING

17.10

Soldering and brazing processes differ from fusion welding in that there is no direct melting of the metal parts being joined. The soldering or brazing alloy melts and flows freely over a temperature range below the solidus temperature(s) of the work-pieces, though some solution of the latter by the molten solder or brazing alloy may occur. Capillary action causes the brazing or soldering alloy to flow between the two closely adjacent surfaces of the work-pieces.

Both soldering and brazing processes are particularly useful for joining two dissimilar metals. Pairs of alloys which would be difficult to join by any other method can safely be joined by these processes, since a large variety of brazing and soldering alloys is available covering temperatures from below 100 to nearly 1100° C.

Joining by either soldering or brazing can be employed when it is important not to overheat the parts being joined. The choice of process and alloy used may also depend upon a number of other factors, such as the strength, corrosion resistance and colour of the joint. When a brazing alloy contains silver as an important constituent the joining process may be termed 'silver soldering' or 'hard soldering'.

SOLDERING

17.20

The use of tin–lead, tin–lead–antimony and tin–lead–cadmium alloys for joining metals is often referred to as 'soft soldering' in order to distinguish it from 'hard soldering' processes which employ silver solders. These latter are more akin to brazing alloys, and will be classified as such in this chapter. The use of the term 'soft soldering' is therefore restricted to those alloys which melt at temperatures below 350° C, whereas hard solders are fusible above 600° C.

Before a metallic surface can be soldered it must be capable of being 'wetted' by the solder. In order that this can occur there must be liquid solubility between the solder and one or more of the constituent metals of each work-piece. The atoms of at least one of the component metals of the solder may form a solid solution with the metal surface being soldered but combination of two metals from the liquid solution may result in the formation of an intermetallic compound (8.40—Part I).

In ordinary tin–lead solders it is the tin which alloys with the surfaces being soldered. Tin forms intermetallic compounds with both iron and copper, as indicated in the portions of their respective equilibrium diagrams, which represent the tin-rich alloys (Fig. 17.1). Lead, on the other hand, has no affinity for either iron or copper, the alloys of which metals form the bulk of materials which are soldered. The main functions of lead as an addition to solder are to produce an alloy with a melting point lower than tin itself and also to cheapen the solder.

Zinc, like tin, also alloys with iron and copper, and its good wetting properties are utilised in hot-dip galvanising processes (22.62—Part I). Its relatively high melting point and the readiness with which it oxidises, how-

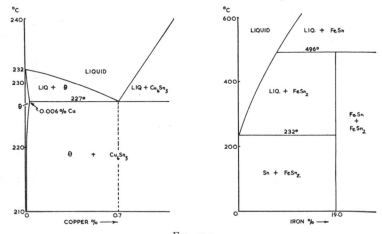

FIG. 17.1.

ever, preclude its use as a solder, though, alloyed with copper, it is extensively employed as a hard solder or brazing alloy.

Although wetting ability is often associated with the formation of intermetallic compounds, excessive formation of these compounds due to maintaining the joint at an unduly high temperature for a prolonged period ultimately lowers the strength of the joint. Maintaining the assembly under these conditions of temperature and time allows diffusion of the molten solder and the metal surface into each other to take place to a greater extent than when temperature and time of contact are limited. A concentration gradient is thus set up in the region of the joint so that other intermetallic compounds in the series may also be formed. The overall amount of intermetallic compound in the joint is thus increased, and since these compounds are invariably brittle, the brittleness of the joint is increased.

The ability of a solder to wet a surface is also affected by the cleanliness of the surface. Dirt which adheres mechanically to the surface may be removed by abrasion, pickling or de-greasing, depending upon the nature of the deposit. Even after such operations have been employed to clean the surface to be soldered, an extremely thin film of metallic oxide immediately forms on most

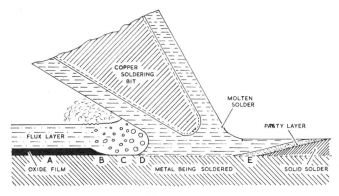

Fig. 17.2.

metallic surfaces and inhibits its wetting by solder. Some form of flux is therefore used to dissolve this oxide film and also to protect the metallic surface thus uncovered until it has been effectively wetted by the solder.

Fig. 17.2 illustrates the action of a suitable flux during a soldering operation. At *A* the oxidised metal surface is covered by a layer of flux solution, which begins to boil as the soldering bit moves towards it. The boiling flux rapidly becomes more concentrated and dissolves the oxide film (*B*), leaving a clean metal surface covered by a layer of protective flux (*C*). Immediately the molten solder wets this clean surface and begins to alloy with it (*D*). As the soldering bit moves away the film of solder cools and solidifies (*E*).

A soldering flux should therefore possess the following properties:

(*a*) it should be fluid at the soldering temperature and either have a solvent action on the oxide film or combine with it to form a slag;

(*b*) it must protect the metal surface from re-oxidation;

(*c*) it must be of such a nature that it can be displaced from the surface being soldered by the molten solder.

17.21 Soldering Fluxes
These can be divided into two main groups:

(1) solutions containing inorganic substances, the chief of which are zinc chloride, ammonium chloride and hydrochloric acid;

(2) fluxes based on resin.

The fluxes of the first group all leave a corrosive deposit on the surface of the work, and such residues must therefore be washed off completely as soon as possible after soldering. In electrical work, where washing is either difficult or impossible, a non-corrosive resinous flux must be used.

17.211 ZINC CHLORIDE ('killed spirits') is probably the most widely used of fluxes in the first group. It is made traditionally by adding zinc clippings to hydrochloric acid ('spirits of salts') until the following reaction ceases:

$$Zn + 2HCl = H_2 + ZnCl_2 \text{ (zinc chloride)}.$$

The presence of excess zinc indicates that the hydrochloric acid has been neutralised or 'killed'. Alternatively, 0·25–0·3 kg of fused zinc chloride stick dissolved in 1 litre of water gives a similar flux solution. The container in which zinc chloride sticks are stored must be tightly stoppered, since the substance is extremely deliquescent. In order to improve the wetting action of zinc chloride and other aqueous flux solutions a small amount of any soapless detergent may be added.

As soldering proceeds most of the water is evaporated from the flux solution and the layer of molten zinc chloride which remains dissolves the oxide film from the surface of the metal. Since the melting point of zinc chloride (260° C) is rather high for the soldering of many materials, 10% ammonium chloride is often added to the flux solution. This forms a eutectic mixture with the zinc chloride which melts at a lower temperature.

A paste-type of flux of similar composition contains:

> 65% petroleum jelly;
> 25% zinc chloride;
> 3·5% ammonium chloride;
> 6·5% water

Such a flux has the advantage that it will not run off a sloping surface which is to be soldered. Moreover, it can be mixed with powdered solder and the mixture conveniently brushed on to the surfaces which are to be soldered. Soldering is then effected in an oven or by induction heating.

17.212 HYDROCHLORIC ACID (50% solution) is useful as a flux when soldering zinc, whilst a mixture containing this actual solution and an equal amount of zinc chloride flux solution is a good flux for soldering stainless steels.

17.213 ORTHOPHOSPHORIC ACID (40% solution) is an effective flux for steel, copper and brass. Its residue is much less corrosive than that of either zinc chloride or hydrochloric acid, and in fact it appears to form a protective coating on steel. This is probably due to localised 'phosphating' (22.81—Part I) of the surface.

17.214 RESIN-TYPE FLUXES. Resin or 'rosin' is tapped from the trunks of pine trees by making a suitable incision in the bark. It does not corrode metallic surfaces, but, when molten, has a mild solvent action on some metallic-oxide films. Since it melts at a low temperature (about 120° C), it can be used in powdered form as a flux. A rather better coating, however, can be produced by brushing on a solution of resin in some suitable solvent.

Methylated spirit is the common solvent for resin, though industrial alcohol is used where a purer flux is required. The resin is crushed and warmed with about three parts by weight of alcohol until a uniform solution is obtained. The warming is best carried out with the aid of an electrically heated water-bath in order to avoid the risk of fire.

Propyl alcohol, butyl alcohol and carbon tetrachloride can also be used as solvents for resin where a solvent is required which does not evaporate so easily as ordinary (ethyl) alcohol.

The principal merit of resin fluxes is that their residues are non-corrosive.

They are therefore particularly suitable for soldering electrical components, pressure gauges, delicate instruments and all parts where the removal of the flux residue by washing is difficult.

17.215 ACTIVATED RESIN-TYPE FLUXES. Ordinary resin-based fluxes are quite suitable for soldering surfaces which have already been tinned, but on bare steel, copper and brass surfaces the solvent action of resin on the oxide films is very slow indeed. It is usual therefore to include in the flux a small amount of some chemical activator. The most suitable substances are the hydrochlorides of organic amines—hydrazine hydrochloride, aniline hydrochloride and glutamic acid hydrochloride are the ones generally used. Their function is to decompose, releasing hydrochloric acid, which behaves as a volatile activator and leaves behind a harmless residue.

BASIC OPERATIONS IN SOLDERING

17.30
The basic steps in the production of a soldered joint are as follows:

17.31 Shaping and Fitting the Metal Parts Together
Molten solder flows between two closely adjacent surfaces due to capillary action, and so long as there is sufficient space for the solder to penetrate, the closer the surfaces are together, the further will the solder penetrate, as indicated in Fig. 17.3. Therefore parts should be fitted closely in order that

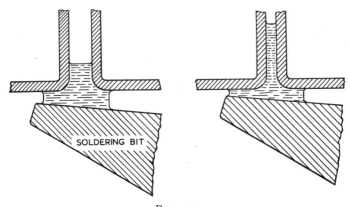

SOLDERING BIT

FIG. 17.3.

the space between them shall be filled completely with solder. With surfaces that have not previously been tinned a clearance of about 0·12 mm is satisfactory, but with tin-plate and other tinned surfaces a clearance of 0·02 mm is sufficient.

17.32 The Surfaces to Be Joined Are Cleaned
The method of cleaning employed depends upon the nature of the dirt or other material to be removed. Paint, rust, dirt and thick oxide scale are generally removed by abrasion in the form of filing, scraping, sand-blasting and the use of emery paper or steel wool.

Various forms of grease are best removed, on a commercial scale, by trichlorethylene vapour. The components to be de-greased are suspended near the top of a tank, in the bottom of which trichlorethylene is boiling. Cooling coils round the sides of the tank cause the trichlorethylene vapour to condense on the components and then drip back into the bottom of the tank, washing the dissolved grease with it. Since only pure trichlorethylene condenses on the components, these are quickly cleaned of all traces of grease. In small-scale treatment trichlorethylene can also be used in liquid form to

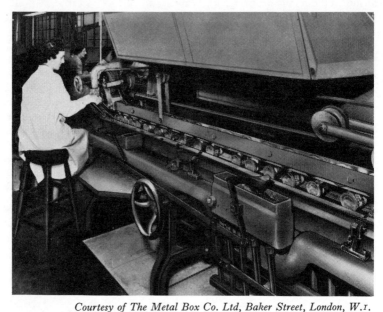

Courtesy of The Metal Box Co. Ltd, Baker Street, London, W.1.

PLATE 17.1—An Automatic Machine in which the Tagger Top is Soldered on to a Cutter Tin Lid.

wash or wipe grease from a metallic surface. It has the advantage that, unlike many organic solvents, it is not inflammable.

Failing trichlorethylene in either liquid or vapour form, grease can best be removed by immersing the articles in a hot alkaline detergent bath. Such detergent baths usually contain varying amounts of caustic soda, washing soda and sodium silicate or, alternatively, sodium silicate and trisodium phosphate with a small quantity of some wetting agent.

Acid pickling is occasionally used to remove rust from iron and steel surfaces before soldering. 50% hydrochloric acid solution is most frequently used, and immersion may vary between a few seconds and 10 minutes.

After pickling or alkaline de-greasing the components must be rinsed and then dried quickly.

17.33 The Surfaces to Be Soldered Are Coated with Flux

At this stage in the process the parts may also be assembled. On a small scale the parts are usually held together in a vice or with pliers, but in the production shop some form of specially designed jig is generally used.

17.34 The Surfaces to Be Soldered May Be 'Tinned'

The object of this operation is to ensure that the surfaces to be joined are completely wetted by a very thin film of solder, so that when the joint is soldered penetration by the solder is both rapid and complete.

In hand soldering solder is applied to the surface by a copper bit, and any surplus is drawn off by the same bit, but in large-scale soldering tinning may be accomplished by dipping the parts into molten solder.

17.35 Solder Is Applied to the Joint

The copper soldering bit is the traditional tool of the tinsmith. In addition to acting as the source of heat for melting the solder, it is used to convey the molten solder to the work and also to draw off any surplus solder when the joint has been made. There are many modifications in design of the simple soldering iron. Electric and gas-heated irons will no doubt be familiar to the reader, but it must be remembered that in many mass-production processes various forms of mechanically operated soldering bit are used. In tin-can manufacture, for example, the can ends are soldered on by rolling the assembled can along a roller which dips in molten solder (Fig. 17.4).

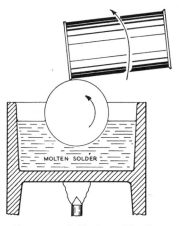

FIG. 17.4—Soldering a Tin Can.

Flame soldering with the aid of a mouth blow-pipe is useful when it is necessary to restrict the heating of the component as a whole, whilst large blow-torches are often used when filling in dents and weld marks on automobile bodies with solder.

When large numbers of small components have to be soldered it is often convenient to do this by painting the parts to be joined with a paste containing both flux and solder and then placing them either on a hot-plate or in an oven maintained at a suitable temperature. Alternatively, the assemblies can be placed on a conveyor belt which carries them through a small high-frequency heating coil.

Assemblies such as commutators and internal-combustion engine radiators are soldered by dipping them into molten solder, after first cleaning and coating them with a non-corrosive flux.

17.36 Surplus Solder Is Removed and the Joint Allowed to Cool

In mechanised processes the joints are usually so designed that removal of surplus solder is not necessary, though in tin-can manufacture a buff is occasionally used to wipe off any excess. In hand soldering, of course, the copper bit is used to draw off any surplus solder.

SELECTION OF A SOLDER

17.40

Although soft solders are basically tin–lead alloys, some of them contain varying quantities of antimony, cadmium, bismuth and silver. Antimony is sometimes present because the solder has been made from scrap white-bearing metal (18.42—Part I). Such solder is unsuitable for soldering either zinc or brass because of the brittleness of the antimony–zinc intermetallic compounds which are formed. Antimonial solders are also unsuitable for some types of can manufacture, and in general their wetting properties on untinned surfaces are inferior to those of plain tin–lead solders. Possibly the only advantage in the use of antimonial solder is in the higher creep strength obtainable as compared with an ordinary tin–lead solder, but it must be admitted that the main reason for producing solders containing antimony lies in the necessity of utilising secondary scrap.

Both bismuth and cadium may be added to tin–lead alloys in order to produce a very low-melting-point fusible alloy (18.60—Part I). Though not strictly speaking solders, these alloys are sometimes used as such when it is essential to produce a joint at the lowest possible temperature. They have wider application, however, as fusible plugs for automatic fire extinguishers, boiler plugs, safety plugs for domestic pressure cookers and time-lag fuses.

When copper is soldered using a plain tin–lead solder the intermetallic compound Cu_6Sn_5 is always produced at some point in the joint. The brittleness which the presence of this compound introduces may sometimes be serious, and in such cases copper may be soldered with an alloy consisting of 97·5% lead and 2·5% silver; for whilst lead and copper are insoluble in each other, silver alloys with each, and thus forms a metallic bond between the two. Such a solder is also useful in maintaining its strength at higher temperatures than is the case with ordinary tin–lead alloys.

The selection of a particular alloy will depend on such factors as the strength of the joint required, the method of application and the permissible temperature, as well as upon economic considerations. Some typical solders are shown in Table 17.1.

TABLE 17.1—*Soft Solders*

Sn (%)	Sb (%)	Other elements (%)	Melting range (°C)	Applications
95	0·5	—	183–223	Electrical instruments
65	1·0	—	183–186	High strength—'quick setting' due to small liquidus/solidus range
62	—	—	183	'Fine solder'—the eutectic alloy hence no 'pasty' stage (see Fig. 21.1 —Part I)
50	0·5	—	183–214	General purposes—hand or machine soldering
50	3·0	—	185–203	General purposes where an antimonial solder can be used
40	—	—	183–236	Tin-can soldering
40	—	Bi 25	96–160	Soldering glass to metal in syringes (Br. Pat. 360919)
32	1·9	—	185–245	Cable-wiping solder (P.O.)
16	—	Bi 52	96	The ternary eutectic—for low-melting point soldering
12·5	—	Bi 50 Cd 12·5	70	The quaternary eutectic—low-melting-point solder
—	—	Ag 2·5	304	The eutectic alloy—used where a high-strength joint is required in soldering copper, also for strength at high temperatures

NB. The balance is lead in each case.

BRAZING AND SILVER SOLDERING

17.50

The term 'brazing' was employed originally to describe the use of a copper–zinc alloy as a filler material for joining two metal parts. Pure copper and copper alloys containing tin, nickel, phosphorus and silver, as well as zinc, are now used in a similar manner in joining processes of this type.

Brazing is used where a ductile joint is required which will have not only good strength but also resistance to fatigue and corrosion. Such joints are also able to withstand higher service temperatures than soft-soldered joints.

Steel, cast iron, copper, bronze and brass are the alloys commonly joined by brazing, whilst metallurgically good joints can be obtained by brazing together dissimilar metals. Even copper and aluminium can be joined in this way if an aluminium–silicon alloy is used as the brazing solder. When two dissimilar metals are to be joined by either soldering or brazing it is important to employ a filler material which does not form brittle intermetallic compounds with either of the materials being joined.

As with soft soldering, joints can be made singly or in mass production by using a suitable method of heating the work. Often two or more parts are assembled by pressing, pinning, clamping or spot welding before a permanent brazed joint is made between them.

17.51 Some Metallurgical Aspects of Brazing

The brazing solder must melt and flow freely at a temperature below the solidus of either of the alloys being joined, and it is therefore necessary to choose a brazing solder which will provide a reasonable temperature margin. Where temperatures can be controlled accurately, as in various automatic mass-production methods of brazing, the temperature differential may be as low as $30°$ C, but when brazing by hand with the torch or blow-pipe it is safer to employ a temperature differential in the region of $100°$ C unless the operators are exceptionally skilled in the use of these tools.

17.52

The brazing solder must, of course, 'wet' the metals being joined. It must not oxidise too freely, and such oxides as are formed must be easily dissolved by the flux used. The presence of phosphorus in some brazing solders helps to maintain their free-flowing properties, since it volatilises and bubbles through the molten flux layer, reducing any copper oxide which is present.

17.53

The bond formed between the brazing solder and the metal being joined depends either upon some diffusion of the solder into the base metal taking place or, alternatively, upon alloying between one or other of the elements of the solder and the base metal at their interface (Fig. 17.5). The brazing solder must not diffuse too freely into the base metal, however, and similarly it must not dissolve too much of the base metal at the working temperature. The greater the mutual solubility of the solder and base metal, the wider must they be separated during brazing, otherwise there is a tendency for them to alloy with each other rather than for the solder to penetrate into the base metal. On the other hand, spacing must not be too great, or capillary action will not be strong enough to cause penetration into the base metal.

17.54

The brazing solder should not appreciably dissolve gases such as hydrogen at the working temperature, or a porous joint may result when these gases are liberated during the solidification of the solder. Most of the copper-base brazing alloys and the silver solders are satisfactory in this respect.

The surfaces to be joined must be chemically clean before brazing is attempted. Their oxides must be capable of being dissolved by the flux used at the working temperature. The dense oxides of chronium, aluminium and beryllium present a particular difficulty in this respect.

17.55

The brazing of annealed or normalised base metals will cause no appreciable change in their physical properties other than a slight increase in crystal size,

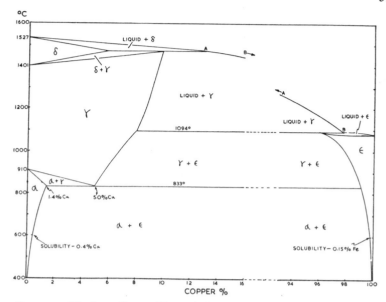

FIG. 17.5—The Iron–Copper Thermal Equilibrium Diagram Indicating the Mutual Solubility of the Two Metals.

but when the base metals are in a work-hardened condition some degree of softening is inevitable. If a low-temperature brazing alloy is used, however, and if the working time is kept as brief as possible softening may not be serious, and sufficient strength may still be retained in the metal adjacent to the joint.

17.56
In the case of heat-treated materials, such as steel or precipitation-hardened aluminium alloys and beryllium bronze, the relationship between the heat-treatment temperature and the brazing temperature must be carefully considered. In some cases it may be necessary to heat-treat first and then braze.

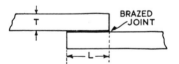

FIG. 17.6—Brazed Joint in Sheet
or Flat Bar.
($L = 2$ or $3 \times T$.)

This would certainly be the case with beryllium bronze, since the low-temperature alloys used to braze it would probably melt at the solution-treatment temperature of this alloy. Conversely, steel which has been brazed with pure copper (at say 1 150° C) can still be heated safely to above its upper critical temperature for quenching without serious deterioration of the brazed joint. Naturally silver solder would be unsuitable as a brazing alloy for steel parts which had then to be heat-treated.

17.60 Design of the Joint

The depth of lap in a joint can be calculated by equating the strength of the joint to that of the weaker of the two base metals being joined. The strength of the joint in shear will be equal to the area of the lap multiplied by the shear strength of the brazing solder.

If the maximum strength of the base metal is to be utilised by means of a brazed joint in shear, or partly in shear and partly in tension, the usual practice is to make the area of the brazed surface between two and three times the area of the cross-section of the base metal.

In a scarfed joint (Fig. 17.7):

$$\text{Brazed area} = \frac{\text{Cross-sectional area of base metal}}{\text{Sin } \theta}$$

θ	Brazed area
$30°$	$\dfrac{\text{Cross-sectional area}}{0\cdot5000} = 2 \times \text{Cross-sectional area}$
$25°$	$\dfrac{\text{Cross-sectional area}}{0\cdot4226} \simeq 2\cdot5 \times \text{Cross-sectional area}$
$20°$	$\dfrac{\text{Cross-sectional area}}{0\cdot3420} \simeq 3 \times \text{Cross-sectional area}$

Therefore the angle of the scarfed joint θ measured from the axis of the base metal should be between 20 and $30°$ in order that the area of the brazed joint should be between two and three times the cross-sectional area of the base metal.

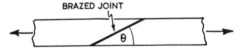

BRAZED JOINT

FIG. 17.7—Scarfed Joint in Wire or Sheet.

17.70 Brazing Fluxes

The temperature attained in a brazing process is much higher than that prevailing during soft soldering. As in the latter process, the presence of even a thin film of oxide prevents proper bonding between the brazing solder and the work-pieces. The need for a suitable flux which will not only protect the metal from oxidation but will also dissolve any existing oxide films on the surface of the work therefore becomes apparent.

17.71

Ordinary borax, which melts at about $750°$ C, producing a mobile liquid, is probably the most widely used brazing flux. It will dissolve the oxides of most of the common metals, with the exception of aluminium, chromium and beryllium. The ordinary hydrated salt contains about 47% water of crystallisation, which is expelled when the salt is heated, causing it to froth vigorously. For brazing and other metallurgical processes, therefore, the dehydrated or 'fused' variety of borax is to be preferred. Fused borax must be kept out of contact with moisture, or it will absorb water of crystallisation again.

17.72
Borax is the sodium salt of boric acid ('boracic powder'), and combinations of of the two substances are also used as brazing fluxes, the chief merit of boric acid being that it flows freely at a somewhat lower temperature than borax.

17.73
For brazing at lower temperatures, fluorides of the alkali metals are commonly used, sometimes in conjunction with borax and boric acid. These fluorides will also act as a flux for the refractory oxides of aluminium, chromium, silicon and beryllium.

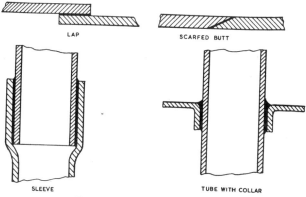

LAP SCARFED BUTT

SLEEVE TUBE WITH COLLAR

FIG. 17.8—Types of Brazed Joint.

No flux is required when brazing copper with an alloy rich in phosphorus. As mentioned earlier, the phosphorus which is vaporised as the brazing solder melts reduces the copper scale on the surface of the work.

METHODS OF HEATING
17.80
A number of different methods is available for supplying the heat necessary to effect brazing.

17.81 Torch Brazing
Torch brazing is no doubt the most widely used method, particularly where the work is of a jobbing nature or the assembly too large for other forms of heating to be used. For low-temperature work town's gas and air can be used in the torch, but higher temperatures demand the use of oxy-acetylene. The latter combination also provides a quicker rate of heating,

which is advantageous in speeding up the brazing operation and also in localising the effects of heat on the work-pieces.

A neutral or slightly reducing flame should, in general, be used in torch brazing, though for tough-pitch copper a slightly oxidising flame is necessary in order to prevent hydrogen-embrittlement of the metal adjacent to the joint (16.22—Part I).

17.82 Furnace Brazing

Furnace brazing methods are applicable where medium- or small-sized components are being brazed in large numbers. The brazing solder is sometimes placed in the joint in the form of a granular powder, but when two flat surfaces are to be joined a stamped washer or strip of the brazing alloy is generally placed in position before the assembly is charged to the furnace (Fig. 17·9).

A protective atmosphere of either burnt town gas or cracked ammonia (14.52) is used in the furnace chamber in order to dispense with the need for coating the joint with flux. The furnaces used may be either of the batch type or the continuous-conveyor type. In the former the work is stacked in racks, which are then covered by a gas-tight 'bell' of the type used in bright-annealing furnaces (Fig. 14.6). The air is purged from the bell by circulating the protective atmosphere through it before the heating process begins.

Courtesy of Messrs Birlec Ltd, Birmingham, 24.

PLATE 17.2—A Mesh-belt Conveyor Furnace Used for the
Furnace Brazing of Components.
This furnace is rated at 60 kW.

The continuous-conveyor furnace (Plate 17.2) is more often used than the batch type just mentioned. The assemblies are placed on a conveyor belt of heat-resisting alloy and are passed through the furnace, metal chain or refractory curtains being used at the entrance and exit to reduce the contamination of the inert atmosphere by the ingress of air (Fig. 14.7).

Close temperature control of the process is necessary, so these furnaces are heated by gas or electricity.

17.83 Induction Brazing

If a coil carrying a high-frequency alternating current is placed around or near to a piece of metal eddy currents are induced in the surface of the metal adjacent to the coil. These eddy currents are transformed into heat energy due to the electrical resistance of the metal and to the hysteresis loss in the case of magnetic materials. Thus induction heating is particularly useful in the case of iron and steel, which have strong magnetic properties as well as fairly high specific resistances.

The high-frequency current may be produced either by a motor generator, a spark generator or a valve generator, and the coil itself is usually in the form of a copper tube through which cooling water flows. One advantage of such

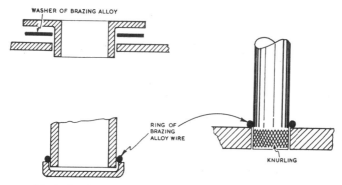

FIG. 17.9—Methods of Pre-placing the Brazing Alloy for Furnace or Induction Brazing.

a system is its adaptability. Whilst small components can be placed in the coil for treatment, large assemblies can remain stationary whilst the coil is moved. With hollow work-pieces the coil may even be placed inside the assemblies to ensure heating on the internal surface should this be necessary.

Since it is generally necessary to design an inductor coil for each job, this method of heating is usually more adaptable to mass production than to the brazing of individual components. Moreover, due to the extreme rapidity with which the heat can be localised, it is rarely necessary to use protective atmospheres, since oxidation is slight.

17.84 Resistance Brazing

Resistance brazing is similar in some respects to resistance welding, in that modified spot- and seam-welding machines (employing copper or copper-alloy electrodes) and butt-welding machines are used. A piece of the brazing alloy is located at the interface of the work parts. Flux may be used or, alternatively, a stream of hydrogen may be flushed over the joint whilst the current is flowing.

Sometimes the electrodes in resistance brazing consists of carbon rods which generate the necessary heat by virtue of the high resistance which they offer to the passage of an electric current. Hence this process differs from the

one just mentioned in that heat is developed externally to the metal interface.
The brazing solder, which is generally in the form of rings or washers, is dipped
in flux before being placed in position.

17.85 Dip Brazing

In this process the whole assembly is dipped into a bath of the molten brazing
alloy, the surface of which is covered by a layer of molten flux. The brazing
solder is drawn into the joint by capillary attraction, and remains there when
the assembly is withdrawn from the bath. At the same time most of the
solder drips off the outer surface, and the remainder is removed either by
mechanical means or by electrolysis.

17.86 Salt Bath Brazing

Salt-bath brazing methods are unique in that the heating medium also
acts as the flux. The parts to be brazed are assembled with a thin piece of
brazing alloy in the joint and then dipped into the salt bath, which is maintained at the required brazing temperature. Alternatively, a ring of the
brazing wire is placed round the edges of the joint, and on immersion of the
assembly in the salt bath this melts and is drawn by capillary action into
the joint.

BRAZING SOLDERS

17.90

Strictly speaking, the term 'brazing' refers to the use of brass as a material to
produce a joint between the two work parts. Indeed, brasses are very widely
used to produce ductile joints in steels and, to a lesser extent, for brazing those
copper alloys which have solidus temperatures above 1 050° C. Brasses used
as brazing solders usually contain less than 60% copper. Consequently, their
micro-structures contain considerable amounts of the hard β-phase (16.30—
Part I). During the brazing process some of the zinc is lost by volatilisation
and oxidation, so that the resultant joint is composed of the tough ductile
α-phase.

Brasses to which small amounts of other elements have been added are
also used as brazing alloys. Among elements commonly added are silicon, to
act as a deoxidant, silver, to increase fluidity, and nickel and manganese, to
increase the toughness and strength of the joint.

17.91

Copper in the unalloyed form is widely used to braze steel. It is applied to
the joint in the form of wire, powder, foil or a paste of powder in cellulose
lacquer. Alternatively, the copper may be deposited on the surface to be joined
by spraying or electrodeposition. Molten copper flows readily into a prepared
joint, and will penetrate much farther than brass or silver solder. Since the
melting point of steel is at least 300° C above that of copper, the latter is an
ideal brazing material for many ferrous materials.

17.92

The copper–phosphorus brazing solders are used mainly for joining copper
and those copper alloys which contain no nickel, since with nickel-bearing

TABLE 17.2—*Brazing Brasses*

Copper (%)	Zinc (%)	Other elements (%)	Melting range (°C)
50	Balance	Total impurities 0·85	860–870
54	,,	,, ,,	870–880
60	,,	Total impurities 0·90	885–890
54	,,	Total imp. 0·85; Sn 1·0	860–870
60	,,	,, ,,	880–890
61	,,	Si 0·5 max.	880–890
59	,,	Si 0·2; Ag 1·0	880–890
50	,,	Ni 10·0; Fe 1·0; Si 0·5; Mn 0·5	860–900

TABLE 17.3—*Phosphorus-bearing Brazing Alloys*

Copper (%)	Silver (%)	Phosphorus (%)	Melting range (°C)
Balance	14	5	625–780
,,	—	7	705–800
,,	—	6	705–930

TABLE 17.4—*Silver Solders*

Ag (%)	Cu (%)	Zn (%)	Cd (%)	Melting range (°C)	Characteristics and uses
80	16	4	—	740–795	High electrical conductivity—copper, brass and steel
65	20	15	—	695–720	Copper, brass, bronze and steel
61	29	10	—	690–735	Good conductivity—copper, brass, bronze and steel
50	15	16	19	620–640	Low melting point—copper alloy steels, nickel alloys
43	37	20	—	700–775	General engineering purposes—copper, brass, bronze, steel, nickel
33·3	33·3	33·3	—	700–740	Joining ornamental brass
17	50	33	—	790–830	Copper, brass, bronze and steel
10	52	37	1	840–855	Copper, brass and steel

alloys and also ferrous alloys the formation of hard, brittle phosphides is possible. Phosphorus vaporised during the brazing process acts as a deoxidant and reduces copper oxide which is formed at the joint. Moreover, due to the loss of some of the phosphorus, the melting range of the solder is raised so that a brazed joint can be made near to an existing one of a similar type without the latter being affected by the brazing temperature, provided that the latter is efficiently controlled.

17.93
For joining metals in the lower-temperature range of 600–800° C silver solders are used, whilst pure silver may occasionally be used as a filler metal for joining copper and some copper alloys. Typical brazing alloys and silver solders are given in Tables 17.2, 17.3, and 17.4.

BIBLIOGRAPHY

1 'Tin Solders', S. J. Nightingale (British Non-ferrous Metals Research Association).
2 'Properties of Soft Solders and Soldered Joints', J. McKeown (British Non-ferrous Metals Research Association).
3 'Industrial Brazing', H. F. Brooker and E. V. Beatson (Iliffe).
4 'Brazing Manual', American Welding Society (Reinhold Pub. Corp.).
5 'Welding Engineering', B. E. Rossi (McGraw-Hill).
6 'High-frequency Induction Heating', F. W. Curtis (McGraw-Hill).
7 'The Joining of Metals', Symposium (Institute of Metals).
8 'Filler Metals for Joining', O. T. Barnett (Reinhol Publishing Corp.).
9 'Soldering Manual', AWS Committee (American Welding Society).
10 'Solders and Soldering', H. H. Manko (McGraw-Hill).
11 'Welding Technology', J. W. Giachino, W. Weeks and G. S. Johnson (The Technical Press Ltd).
12 BS 219: 1959—Soft solders. Amendments, March & November, 1963.
13 BS 441: 1954—Rosin-cored solder wire, 'activated' and 'non-activated' (non-corrosive).
14 BS 499: 1965—Welding terms and symbols. Part I—Welding, brazing and thermal cutting glossary.
15 BS 1723: 1963—Brazing.
16 BS 1845: 1966—Filler rods for brazing (silver solders and brazing solders).
17 BSAU 90: 1965—Soft solders for automobile use.
18 BS 4416: 1969—Methods for penetrant testing of welded or brazed joints in metals.

Chapter eighteen
ARC-WELDING PROCESSES

18.10

In electric-arc welding processes the arc is used as the source of heat, which is transferred to the weld metal partly by direct radiation and partly by the gas or ions in the arc stream. Such methods of welding may be autogenous, that is, the weld metal is derived from the two work-pieces being joined, but in most cases weld metal supplied from an external source produces the joint. In the latter case a non-consumable tungsten electrode may be used, the weld metal being obtained from a separate filler rod. Other processes make use of a consumable electrode which is used to strike an arc on to the work-pieces, and which itself melts to provide the weld metal.

In order to dispense with use of flux, some processes utilise an inert-gas shield to protect the weld metal, and that metal adjacent to the weld, from oxidation. However, the provision of a shield or blanket was not the sole purpose of the gas used in the now obsolete atomic-hydrogen arc process, for in this instance ionisation of the hydrogen used provided a method of heat transfer from the electrodes to the weld metal.

CARBON-ARC WELDING
18.20

The use of carbon electrodes formed the basis of one of the earliest arc-welding operations. The process, which is now virtually obsolete, was available in two forms—an indirect method employing an arc between two carbon electrodes (Fig. 18.1 (i)), and a direct method in which the arc was struck between a single carbon electrode and the work (Fig. 18.1 (ii)). In the direct-arc process it was necessary to increase the heat intensity produced by concentrating the arc stream electro-magnetically by means of a coil carrying the welding current as shown in Fig. 18.2.

The carbon arc process was used for welding steel sheet, copper and, sometimes, aluminium, but is of little interest now except in 'arc-gouging'. Here the carbon arc is used to melt small areas of the metal to be gouged. The molten metal is then removed by a blast of compressed air issuing from a jet in the electrode holder.

METALLIC-ARC WELDING
18.30

Metallic-arc welding using manually operated equipment is by far the most widely used fusion-welding process. In this process the metal electrode which

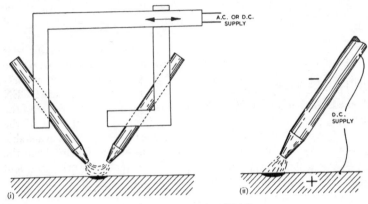

A.C. OR D.C.
SUPPLY

D.C.
SUPPLY

FIG. 18.1—Carbon Arc Welding.

is used serves both to carry the arc and to act as a filler rod which deposits molten metal into the joint. The use of a bare electrode permits considerable oxidation of the weld metal and this is not satisfactory when a weld of high strength is required. Consequently coated electrodes are invariably used

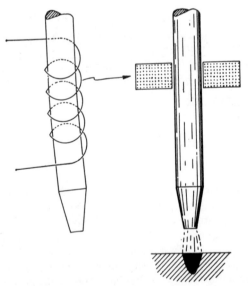

FIG. 18.2.

resulting in the formation of a layer of slag at the surface of the weld, whilst combustible materials in the coating generate gases which form a protective blanket over the metal in the region of the weld.

Either alternating or direct currents may be used for metallic-arc welding. When a.c. is used the arc must re-ignite at each half-cycle as the polarity is reversed. This causes some instability of the arc, which, however, can be overcome by the use of arc-stabilising agents in the flux coating of coated electrodes.

When d.c. is used there is obviously a choice of polarity, and this choice is affected by the fact that the positive pole of the arc becomes hottest. If the *electrode* is connected to the *negative* side of the generator whilst the work-piece is connected to the positive side of the generator this is termed DCEN (or in America, 'straight polarity'). When an arc is struck both the end of the electrode and the metal of the work-piece directly under the tip of the electrode melt and become mixed under conditions which induce considerable turbulence. The pressure produced by the stream of ions flowing from the electrode causes a 'crater' to form in the molten metal of the work-piece, and into this crater falls the molten metal from the electrode (Fig. 18.3). As the arc travels onwards along the joint, metal flows back into the crater, and intimate admixture of the electrode metal and the base metal takes place.

The depth to which melting of the base metals occurs is called the penetration of the arc, and with an uncoated electrode this penetration is less if DCEP (or in America, 'reverse polarity') is used, that is, if the *electrode* is connected to the *positive* side of the generator. Metallic-arc welding with uncoated electrodes was therefore generally carried out using DCEN in order to obtain maximum penetration.

In modern metallic-arc welding processes coated electrodes are used, arc conditions being controlled largely by the nature of the coating chosen. For example, non-ferrous electrodes are used on DCEP polarity for several reasons. When using this polarity the arc itself has a cleaning effect on the pool of weld metal, breaking up and dispersing refractory oxide films which are prevalent with many non-ferrous metals. Moreover, greater heat is generated in the electrode and this may be useful in melting flux coatings on those metals of high thermal conductivity. More important still, however, the transfer of metal particles from the electrode to the weld is smoother with DCEP.

18.31

If an uncoated electrode is used the weld is surrounded with an atmosphere containing oxygen and nitrogen, and both oxides and nitrides may therefore form in the weld metal. As a result, ductility and impact toughness of the weld are impaired. These difficulties are largely overcome by the use of coated electrodes. Electrode coatings contain both slag-forming ingredients, which produce a fluid coating over the weld as it cools, and gas-forming materials, which generate an atmosphere of carbon monoxide, carbon dioxide and hydrogen around the arc. It must be noted, however, that the reason for using coated electrodes in the first instance was stabilisation of the arc. This was achieved by including materials which would produce ionisation and consequently a steady current through the arc. It must be appreciated that when using a.c. the arc is extinguished fifty times per second and, in the absence of ionised material, a steady arc could not be maintained.

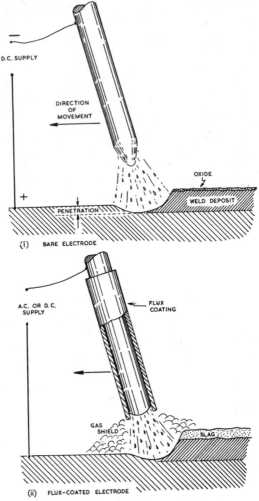

FIG. 18.3—Metallic-arc Welding.

The principal materials used in electrode coatings include:

(i) *Carbonaceous matter* which consists mainly of cellulose-type materials of the formula $(C_6H_{10}O_5)_n$. The function of this is to produce a gas shield on combustion:

$$C_6H_{10}O_5 + 3O_2 \rightarrow 6CO + 5H_2O$$

Thus an atmosphere of reducing gas surrounds the molten metal as it is carried from the electrode to the joint. Since the atmosphere is strongly reducing it is possible to include alloying elements in the electrode coating either as ferro-alloys or as oxides.

(ii) *Silica*, SiO_2, which combines with metallic oxides present to form a fusible slag (1.52—Part I).

(iii) *Titanium oxide*, TiO_2, which is added to stabilise the arc. The high affinity of titanium for nitrogen possibly reduces the tendency for nitrides to form in the weld.

(iv) *Calcium Carbonate*, $CaCO_3$, as limestone. This decomposes to form lime, CaO, and hence, a basic slag. It also controls the melting rate of the electrode.

(v) *Calcium Fluoride*, CaF_2, as fluorspar. This increases slag fluidity.

(vi) *Sodium Oxide*, Na_2O, which is combined with some of the silicon as a silicate. This acts as a binder for the coating and also promotes fluidity in the resulting slag.

(vii) *Ferro-silicon* to act as a deoxidant.

(viii) *Iron powder* which will increase the rate of deposition and improve arc behaviour.

In Britain, electrode coatings are classified into a number of groups according to type and application. This classification is covered by BSI specifications (see Bibliography).

The function of the slag produced by the electrode coating is not only to protect the weld metal from oxidation but also to act as a flux which dissolves oxides and other impurities already present in the molten pool of weld metal. Moreover, the slag, by virtue of surface tension, promotes intimate admixture between the metal from the work-pieces and that from the electrode, and also helps to produce a smoother contour in the weld itself. The slag must have high fluidity to enable it to rise quickly to the surface of the weld metal, and so prevent the trapping of slag particles below the surface of the weld.

The slag coating also provides thermal insulation, which reduces both the rate of solidification of the weld metal and its subsequent rate of cooling in the solid state. Dissolved gases and other impurities thus have a much greater opportunity of escape. The slower rate of cooling of the solidified weld helps to reduce hardness in that metal adjacent to the weld with those steels which tend to precipitate martensite (21.92—Part I).

18.32

Most engineering metals and alloys may be welded by the metallic-arc process. In welding carbon and low-alloy steels the coated electrodes are usually of low-carbon steel. For welding those alloy steels in which martensite is likely to form on cooling, low-alloy electrodes are generally employed. Such steels are also sensitive to hydrogen embrittlement, so that the electrode coating must be free from hydrogen-forming cellulose. Instead, titanium oxide and limestone are generally included, the limestone providing the carbon dioxide to form the protective blanket around the weld. Electrodes of austenitic composition (up to 25% chromium and 20% nickel) are also useful when formation of martensite is to be avoided. Cast iron is usually welded with nickel-rich or monel electrodes, whilst most non-ferrous metals and alloys are welded with electrodes of a composition similar to the metal being welded.

Courtesy of Metropolitan-Vickers Electrical Co. Ltd.

PLATE 18.1—Metallic-arc Welding in the Construction of a Penstock for a Scottish Hydro-electrical Scheme.

18.33 Hard-facing Electrodes

Special electrodes are sometimes used to deposit a hard facing on a component with the object of producing a wear-resistant surface. Metal-working dies, rock-crushing rolls, well-drilling tools and excavating equipment may be treated in this way. In some cases the deposited coating hardens as the weld cools whilst in others further treatment is required.

Hard-facing electrodes fall into the following main groups:

(i) Electrodes depositing weld metal which can subsequently be heat-treated;
(ii) Austenitic steel electrodes producing a coating which work-hardens in service. These include high-manganese steel (13.83—Part I) and stainless steels (13.44—Part I).
(iii) Electrodes, commonly of high-chromium steel (13.35—Part I), producing a weld which hardens due to martensite formation during the cooling process.

(iv) Electrodes which deposit a soft weld metal with hard particles dispersed through it. These materials include 'Colmonoy', which consists of hard chromium carbide and boride particles in a nickel matrix; and 'Stellite' (14.22—Part I). Often these electrodes are in the form of tubes which carry the hard constituent as a powder.

AUTOMATIC FLUX-SHIELDED WELDING
18.40

In a metallic-arc welding process where *coated* electrodes are used, the current must be conducted through the length of the core wire. Since comparatively high currents must be carried, there is a limit to the length of electrode which can be used because of the resistance-heating effect along the wire. Consequently manual metallic-arc welding is essentially an intermittent process and its adaption to a continuous operation, whilst still retaining the flux shield, involves some modification in order to make it possible to transmit current to the electrode. A number of successful methods of continuous flux-shielded welding have been developed.

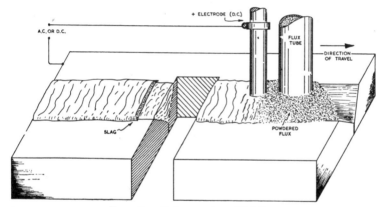

FIG. 18.4—Submerged-arc Welding.

18.41 Submerged-arc Welding

The submerged-arc process (Fig. 18·4) is essentially an automatic form of the metallic-arc welding process which can be used in the straight-line joining of metals. A tube which delivers powdered flux into the prepared joint in advance of the electrode is built into the electrode holder. This powered flux envelops the melting end of the electrode and completely covers the arc. Much of the flux melts and rises to the top of the molten weld metal, where it forms a coating of protective slag. Any unmelted flux is removed by a suction system and can be used again. The slag coating is easily detached from the metal surface when cool.

The electrode is in the form of bare coiled wire and is generally copper-plated to ensure low-resistance electrical contact between the wire and the contact shoes.

The process results in a very smooth weld surface being produced. The surrounding work surface is free from spatter, a fault which is often in evidence with welds produced by the ordinary metallic-arc process. The weld metal is completely protected from the atmosphere so that oxidation is at a minimum. Moreover, the arc is very quiet and there is no discomfort from glare or fumes.

Some claim that the submerged-arc process is not a true arc-welding process and that the current is carried electrolytically by the molten flux. It is fairly certain, however, that an arc is formed even though some of the heat generated may be due to resistance heating by current transmitted by the molten flux.

The process is widely used for welding low- and medium-carbon steels and low-alloy steels; though copper, aluminium and titanium can be welded if suitable fluxes are employed. Submerged-arc welding has found application in the fabrication of pressure vessels, boilers and pipes and in shipbuilding and structural engineering generally.

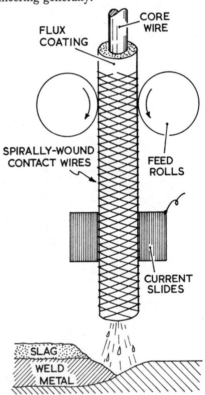

Fig. 18.5—Welding with a Continuous Covered Electrode.

18.42 Continuous Covered Electrodes

Long coated electrodes in coil form can be made conductive by helically wrapping the flux coating with both right- and left-hand spirals of wire. Since the wire spiral protrudes above the coating it makes adequate contact with the current slides in the welding head (Fig. 18.5). When a carbon dioxide shield is also employed this increases the protection offered to the weld and at the same time allows greater latitude in choosing the flux. Moreover, the current can be increased to give improved efficiency in what are sometimes called 'open-arc' methods. These allow the welder to observe conditions in the weld pool and in this respect have an advantage over submerged-arc welding.

This process is very suitable for welding longitudinal seams and finds use in structural engineering and shipbuilding.

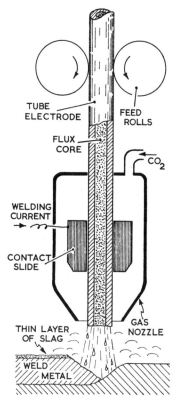

TUBE ELECTRODE

FEED ROLLS

FLUX CORE

CO_2

WELDING CURRENT

CONTACT SLIDE

THIN LAYER OF SLAG

GAS NOZZLE

WELD METAL

Fig. 18.6—Using a Cored Electrode.

18.43 Cored Electrodes

These are used in another flux/gas arc process indicated in Fig. 18.6. Here the flux is carried *inside* the electrode which consists either of a tube as indicated in the diagram, or of a strip of metal folded around the flux.

The auxiliary gas is generally carbon dioxide. If such a gas shield is not used then the flux should contain materials which will decompose to liberate non-oxidising gases in the region of the weld.

One disadvantage in the use of cored electrodes is that the amount of flux which can be carried is limited by the bore of the wire. If the wire diameter is increased in order to increase the quantity of flux which can be contained, this spreads the arc concentration and consequently decreases its penetration. A Japanese process known as 'Mitsubishi Dual Shield Welding' (Fig. 18.7) seeks to overcome this state of affairs. Here a wire of small diameter is used and to make up for the flux deficiency an inner shield of argon is employed to help protect the weld pool. Thus the hottest zone is blanketed by slag and by the

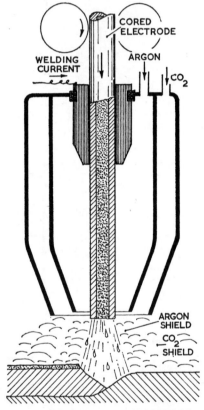

FIG. 18.7—Mitsubishi Dual Shield Welding.

inert gas, argon, whilst the cooler metal surrounding the weld is adequately protected by carbon dioxide which, at low temperatures, is not very reactive (18.54).

18.44 Magnetic Flux/Gas Arc Welding

Cored electrodes tend to be rather bulky. This can be overcome to some extent by using bare electrode wire in conjunction with a separate magnetisable flux. This flux is carried by a stream of carbon dioxide through a nozzle which surrounds the electrode wire. Since an electro-magnetic field will form around

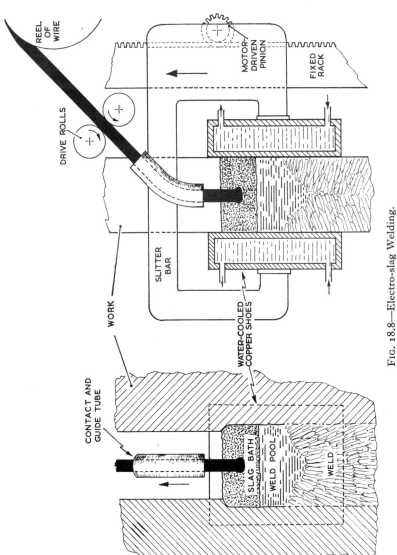

FIG. 18.8—Electro-slag Welding.

the electrode as long as it is carrying a current, the finely-divided magnetisable flux will stick to the wire forming a thick coating. In addition to serving as a vehicle for carrying the flux powder, the carbon dioxide provides a gas shield for the metal adjacent to the weld pool. This method also allows better inspection of the progress of welding as compared with the submerged-arc process.

18.45 Electro-slag Welding

Thick work-pieces can generally only be welded by orthodox methods if multi-run techniques are employed to build up the weld. The main feature of electro-slag welding is that heavy sections can be joined in a single run by placing the plates to be welded in a vertical position so that molten metal is delivered progressively to the vertical gap rather as in an ingot-casting operation. The plates themselves form two sides of the 'mould' whilst travelling water-cooled copper shoes dam the flow of weld metal from the edges of the weld until solidification is complete (Fig. 18.8).

In some respects the process resembles submerged-arc welding in that molten metal is produced beneath a blanket of slag. Here, however, the arc is used only to initiate melting and thereafter heat is generated by the electrical resistance offered by the slag which is sufficiently conductive to allow the current to pass through it from the electrode to the weld pool beneath. The slag consists of a mixture of silicates derived from lime, magnesia, alumina, maganese dioxide and silica, together with up to 20% calcium fluoride which improves both its fluidity and its electrical conductivity.

As the electrode wire melts the level of the weld pool rises and the automatic water-cooled weld shoes (Fig. 18.8) are raised at a suitable rate to keep pace with solidfication and delivery of molten metal. The molten slag bath above the weld pool acts both as heat source and shield to protect the weld from oxidation. During welding slag temperatures up to 2000° C are produced. This leads to considerable melting at the edges of the work-pieces so that intimate mixture of the materials of electrode and work-pieces takes place. This 'dilution' of the weld metal must therefore be taken into account in assessing the properties of the weld. On the other hand, since the edges of the work-piece are melted in this way, little edge preparation is required as compared with other processes.

At high temperatures iron can reduce oxide materials such as manganous oxide and silica in the slag, and the concentration of FeO in the weld pool tends to increase. The presence of FeO may lead to porosity in the weld due to the reaction:

$$FeO + C \rightarrow Fe + CO \ (4.21—Part \ I).$$

Consequently electrode wire may contain up to 2% manganese to act as a deoxidant.

Since the electro-slag process was developed in the U.S.S.R. in 1953 a number of variations of the process have been introduced. In addition to the wire-electrode method outlined above, a plate-electrode modification can be used in which plate or bar electrodes are suspended in the weld gap and lowered slowly as they melt in the slag bath. Consumable guides can also be used to provide filler metal.

The principal metallurgical advantages of electro-slag welding are:

(i) There is a reduced risk of cold cracking in the work-pieces because of the relatively slow rate of heating and cooling;
(ii) There is little danger of gas porosity because gases have time to escape. Entrapped slag is also unlikely for the same reason;
(iii) Once stable welding conditions have been established there is little trouble with hot cracking.

Possibly the main disadvantage of the process arises from the high temperature reached coupled with the slow rate of cooling. Both factors lead to the formation of coarse crystals which are of the columnar type as a result of the direction in which heat is extracted by the water-cooled shoes.

The process was developed for joining large castings and forgings in order to produce very large composite structures. Its use has since been extended to cover many branches of the heavy engineering industries. Although developed mainly for welding mild- and low-alloy steels, it can be used for some high-alloy steels and also for titanium.

18.46 Electro-gas Welding

This process employs a basically similar technique to that used in the electro-slag process in that vertical welding between water-cooled copper shoes takes place. In the electro-gas process, however, heat is generated by an electric arc struck between a flux-coated electrode and the weld pool. Since only a thin coating of protective slag is formed, additional shielding is provided by carbon dioxide or argon fed into the weld area from jets built in the top of each copper shoe. Although slag is being fed continuously to the weld it does not accumulate above the weld pool but tends to solidify at the weld surface adjacent to the water-cooled shoes.

Electro-gas welding can be used at greater speeds than those possible in the electro-slag process and it can also be halted and restarted with much less difficulty. It is used, therefore, in the site fabrication of storage tanks and in shipbuilding.

GAS-SHIELD ARC WELDING

18.50

So far in this chapter we have been dealing principally with arc-welding processes in which some type of coating flux is used to protect the weld area from attack by atmospheric gases, though the use of a gas shield to offer auxiliary protection had been mentioned in connection with some of the automatic metallic-arc processes. In true gas-shielded arc welding no flux is used, complete protection being effected by a blanket of suitable gas around the weld area.

Some of the so-called 'inert' gases are by no means chemically inert to all metals. Thus nitrogen can be used safely as a protective shield when welding copper but it will certainly form brittle nitrides with magnesium and some other metals. Similarly, carbon dioxide is reasonably non-reactive under many circumstances but it can have an oxidising action on iron at high temperatures. Thus, the only truly *inert* gases are those which are monatomic and have a completed outer electron shell (1.77—Part I). Even these gases can be made to form some compounds, albeit rather unstable ones, under special conditions and the present tendency amongst chemists is to refer to them as 'noble' gases since like the noble metals gold and silver they are most reluctant to combine with other elements. These noble or inert gases include helium, neon, argon, krypton and xenon, all of which occur in small quantities in the atmosphere:

Gas	% by volume in the atmosphere
Argon	0·94
Neon	0·001 5
Helium	0·000 5
Krypton	0·000 11
Xenon	0·000 009

Since of these gases argon is by far the most plentiful, it is the one which is generally used in true inert-gas arc-welding processes. In America, however, considerable quantities of helium are forthcoming from natural gas deposits. These contain 80% methane and up to 1·5% helium, so that in the U.S.A. and Canada helium is also used for gas-shielded welding.

Both argon and helium are expensive and in recent years a better appreciation of its limitations has led to the use of carbon dioxide, CO_2, as a shielding gas when circumstances permit.

In gas-shielded arc welding the arc can be struck between the work-pieces and a tungsten electrode, in which case a separate filler rod is required to provide the weld metal. This is referred to as the 'tungsten inert gas' (or TIG) process. Alternatively the filler rod can also serve as electrode as it does in other metallic-arc processes. In this case it is called the 'metallic inert gas' (or MIG) process.

18.51 The TIG Process

This process was developed in the U.S.A. during the early years of the Second World War for welding magnesium alloys, other processes having proved unsatisfactory because of the corrosive action of fluxes on chemically-reactive magnesium. The success of the process soon led to its adoption for welding aluminium alloys for similar reasons. Since it can be mechanised easily and gives high-quality welds, TIG welding has become very popular for precision work in the aircraft, atomic energy and instrument industries (Plate 18.3).

In the TIG process a tungsten electrode is used in order that it will withstand the high temperatures generated without suffering undue erosion. The electrode is surrounded by a nozzle (Fig. 18.9) which conducts the shielding gas to the weld area. This nozzle may be ceramic material (Plate 18.2) to render it temperature-resistant, though torches designed to carry currents in excess of 100 A are usually water-cooled.

The type of current supply used depends upon the particular application and the material being welded. In some cases alternating current is quite suitable, particularly when it is of high enough frequency to stabilise the arc. The use of d.c., however, allows greater flexibility in operation. When DCEN (or 'straight') polarity is used the electrode, being cathodic, tends to run at a lower temperature than it would under conditions of DCEP (or 'reverse') polarity. Consequently when using DCEN polarity more heat is generated

Courtesy of The British Oxygen Co. Ltd.

PLATE 18.2—A TIG Welding Torch with Ceramic shield.

at the surface of the work-piece and there is a deeper penetration of the base metal, whilst the electrode remains cooler, erodes less quickly and retains a finer point (Fig. 18.10). When DCEN polarity is used electrons flow from the tip of the electrode to the work whilst positive ions travel in the opposite direction. Meanwhile the inert gas shields the metal sufficiently to allow coalescence to take place in the case of steels, copper and some copper alloys. If DCEP polarity is used, however, electrons bombard the surface of the

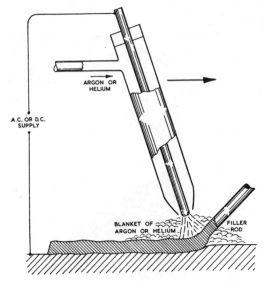

FIG. 18.9—The Principle of the TIG Welding
Torch.

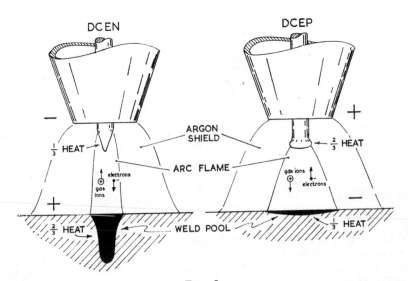

FIG. 18.10.

work. Oxides on the surface of the molten weld metal interfere with the flow of electrons and prevent ready coalescence of the liquid metal. The bombardment of the oxide film by the gas ions, however, has a marked cleaning effect on the surface of the weld metal by breaking up tenacious oxide films. Consequently, light alloys, which oxidise easily, are effectively welded using DCEP polarity, though the use of a.c. provides a useful compromise between rapid metal melting and surface cleaning in such cases.

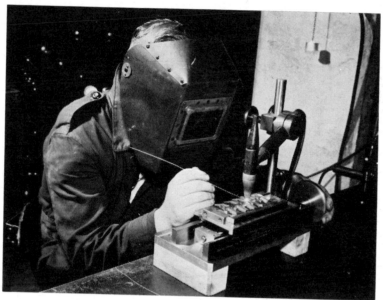

Courtesy of The British Oxygen Co. Ltd.

PLATE 18.3—TIG Welding of Aircraft Components.

The TIG process is one of the most versatile methods of welding, employing currents from as little as 0·5 A to as much as 750 A. Small currents, used with delicate air-cooled torches, are used for welding materials of the order of 0·05 mm thick. At the other end of the scale water-cooled torches carrying up to 750 A are used for welding thick copper and similar materials of high thermal conductivity and which, therefore, require a high-rate heat input.

18.52 The MIG Process

This process uses a consumable electrode which is generally in the form of coiled, uncoated wire fed by a motor drive to the argon-shielded arc. Apart from the use of the inert-gas blanket, the process does not have much in common with TIG welding. Whilst in the latter process it is usual to employ DCEN polarity in order to avoid over-heating and undue erosion of the tungsten electrode, in MIG welding d.c. is invariably used with DCEP polarity. In this way the surface cleaning effect of DECP referred to above is utilised, and since melting of the electrode is in this case intentional there is no great problem of overheating. Very high current densities are used in this process, electrode wires varying in diameter between 0·75 and 2·25 mm only.

For the MIG welding of non-ferrous metals and alloys argon, or sometimes, mixtures of argon and helium, are used. It is found that for welding ferrous materials the addition of about 1% oxygen to the argon is beneficial. This may seem a surprising statement in view of the fact that an inert atmosphere of argon is used principally to exclude oxygen from the weld area. However,

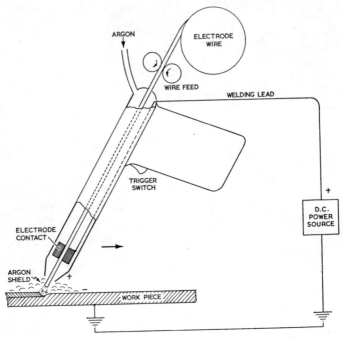

FIG. 18.11—The Principles of a MIG Welding 'Gun'.

its presence in small quantities seems to produce a much smoother transfer of metal from electrode to weld pool. More important still, the fluidity of the weld pool, and the readiness with which the weld metal 'wets' the work-piece, is improved by the presence of small amounts of FeO arising from the oxygen present.

Most MIG welding equipment is designed for semi-automatic operation, in which the operator guides the torch or gun but has little else to do once the initial control settings have been made. The electrode wire may be fed from a small spool mounted in the gun itself (Fig. 18.11) or it may be delivered from a large coil mounted externally to the gun. Pre-set automatic controls govern the flow of gas and cooling water (necessary when large welding currents are involved); speed of electrode delivery and current conditions.

In addition to the advantage arising from the possibility of semi-automatic operation, the MIG process is associated with the following features:

(i) ease of positional welding;
(ii) suitability for welding non-ferrous metals;
(iii) absence of flux;
(iv) general cleanliness.

Consequently the MIG process is one of the most diversely used welding methods in terms of the number of different applications with which it can successfully cope. Those industries where it finds application include automobile manufacture; shipbuilding; aircraft engineering; heavy electrical engineering and the manufacture of tanks, pressure vessels and pipes.

18.53 The PIGMA Process

The 'PIGMA'— or 'pressurised inert gas metal arc'—process was developed in the U.S.A. essentially for the welding of aluminium alloys. A modified MIG process is conducted in a vessel filled with inert gas under pressure, and it is claimed that a reduction in porosity is obtained as compared with that often encountered in aluminium alloys welded by the orthodox MIG process.

18.54 The CO_2 Welding Process

As mentioned earlier in this section (18.50) only monatomic gases can be described as completely 'inert' under normal chemical conditions. Carbon dioxide, CO_2, though relatively non-reactive at normal temperatures, can have an oxidising influence at high temperatures at which some dissociation takes place, particularly in the presence of iron:

$$2CO_2 \rightleftharpoons 2CO + O_2.$$

Oxygen thus released will combine readily with iron in the weld pool, producing the *soluble* oxide FeO. During subsequent solidification of the weld metal this oxide reacts with carbon present in the weld pool:

$$FeO + C \rightleftharpoons Fe + CO.$$

Since solidification is partly complete at this stage, bubbles of carbon monoxide, CO, generated are trapped, giving rise to gas porosity (4.20—Part I). Consequently carbon dioxide is only really effective as a shielding gas if the electrode wire contains manganese, silicon and, sometimes, aluminium in sufficient quantities for adequate deoxidation of the weld pool before solidification commences. Deoxidation products remain as fine inclusions in the weld metal or as traces of slag on the surface. Typical electrode wire contains approximately 1.8% manganese and 0.5% silicon and at least half of these amounts are used up in the deoxidation process. However, even when the extra cost of this electrode material is taken into account the 'CO_2 process' is still very attractive from an economic point of view for welding mild steels and low-alloy steels, since carbon dioxide is considerably cheaper than argon.

The normal CO_2 process then is a modified MIG process in which argon has been replaced by carbon dioxide, and in which electrode wire rich in deoxidants must be employed. Some modification in the power supply may also be necessary, since different shielding gases can cause a difference in arc voltage and this, in turn, affects the efficiency of metal transfer from electrode to weld pool.

ATOMIC HYDROGEN-ARC WELDING

18.60

In this process an arc is struck between two tungsten electrodes which are contained in the body of the torch. Each electrode is surrounded by a stream of hydrogen (Fig. 18.12) which is supplied to the torch from a cylinder. In common with other arc-welding methods, the size of the tungsten electrodes is dependent upon the rate of heat input required for the material being welded.

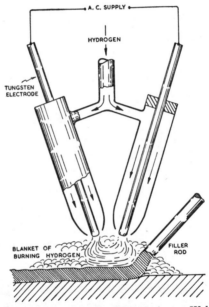

FIG. 18.12—The Principle of Atomic Hydrogen Welding.

On passing into the region of the arc, ionisation of some of the hydrogen molecules takes place, each hydrogen molecule dissociating into two positively-charged hydrogen ions and two negatively-charged electrons. Heat energy is absorbed from the arc by the dissociation process, which can be expressed by the following equation:

$$H_2 + Heat \rightleftharpoons 2H^+ + 2 \text{ electrons.}$$

Since the reaction is reversible, heat energy is given out again as the ionised hydrogen cools and reassociates to the molecular form. When the torch is directed at the metal being welded this release of heat energy takes place at the metal surface, and thus the hydrogen transfers heat from the arc to the weld. Moreover, the newly formed molecular hydrogen burns, and the heat of combustion also serves to raise the temperature of the weld metal still further.

In addition to producing heat in the ways mentioned above, the ionisation process serves to cool the tungsten electrodes and thus prolong their working life. The molecular hydrogen which is formed by reassociation at the surface

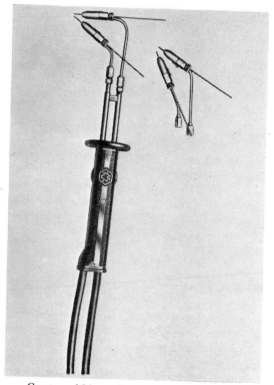

Courtesy of Metropolitan-Vickers Electrical Co. Ltd.
PLATE 18.4—An Atomic Hydrogen Welding Torch.

of the weld metal forms a blanket which protects the work from oxidation, both during welding and whilst the work is cooling from the welding temperature.

The operating voltage in the atomic hydrogen-arc method is higher than that for any other arc-welding process because of the high potential necessary to produce ionisation of the hydrogen. The process can be adapted to either manual or automatic operation, and as in gas or carbon-arc welding, the weld metal may be obtained either by melting the parent metal or by the addition of metal from a filler rod. The presence of the protective blanket of hydrogen permits the welding of ferrous materials without flux, thus allowing the operator an unrestricted view of the weld during manufacture. Those aluminium alloys, however, which can be welded by this process require the use of some flux.

18.61

This atomic hydrogen-arc process is unsuitable for welding many aluminium- and copper-base alloys because of the strong tendency of hydrogen to dissolve in these metals, particlarly whilst they are molten. Most of the dissolved gas is precipitated as the metal solidifies, giving rise to porosity in the weld metal. Those grades of copper which contain some oxygen must not be welded by this process, since reaction between the atomic hydrogen and the cuprous oxide globules present causes considerable intercrystalline porosity in the metal adjacent to the weld (16.22—Part I). When welding medium- and high-carbon steels some carbon is lost due to a reaction between some of the carbon and hydrogen resulting in the formation of the gas methane, CH_4:

$$C + 2H_2 \longrightarrow CH_4 + \text{heat.}$$

It is usual, therefore, to employ a filler rod of high carbon content in order to make up this loss.

In view of the metallurgical difficulties encountered in using the atomic hydrogen-arc process it is perhaps not surprising that it has been replaced almost entirely by modern inert gas processes. It is now used only for a few specialised applications. These generally involve the welding of delicate parts since it is possible to regulate the working current and electrode size between wide limits.

PLASMA-ARC WELDING

18.70

In the present context 'plasma' is the term applied to a mass of extremely hot gas which has become ionised, that is, its atoms or molecules have been broken up to form a mixture of electrons and positive ions. This state is achieved by passing a suitable gas such as argon—or a mixture of argon with hydrogen or nitrogen—through a constricted electric arc. Under these conditions ionisation of the gas takes place and a jet of plasma issues from the nozzle of the torch or gun.

The sun's surface consists essentially of high-temperature plasma, though even higher temperatures of up to 15 000° C can be produced artificially in these 'electric flames'. The use of plasma as a high-temperature heat source is finding application in the cutting, drilling and spraying of very refractory materials like tungsten, molybdenum and ceramics, as well as in welding.

18.71

In the 'transferred arc plasma' process an arc is struck between a tungsten electrode and the work-piece (Fig. 18.13a). The extent to which the arc is constricted as it passes through the nozzle to some degree governs the temperature which is produced and since, in this process, heat tends to be liberated mainly at the surface of the work-piece, this technique is suitable for

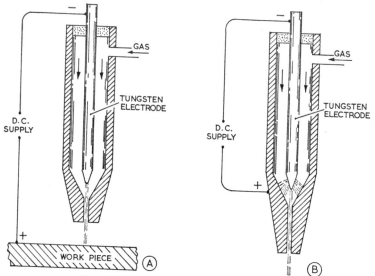

FIG. 18.13—Plasma-arc Welding Torches—
(a) The 'Transferred-arc' Plasma Process;
(b) The 'Plasma-jet Projector'.

cutting very refractory materials. It is also useful in welding in what is in effect a high-speed version of the TIG process. If an auxiliary gas shield proves necessary this can be supplied as an annular flow concentric with the flow through the plasma chamber.

This process is particularly useful in the manufacture of seam-welded stainless-steel tubes and in the welding of reactive metal compacts.

18.72

A separately-insulated water-cooled nozzle forms the positive electrode in the 'plasma-jet projector' (Fig. 18.13b) which works on the principle of the 'non-transferred' arc. A plasma flame up to 0·75 m long can be produced from the nozzle. Unlike the 'transferred' arc dealt with above and where most of the heat is generated in the work-piece, here most of the heat is concentrated in the flame whilst the work-piece remains comparatively cool. Hence this 'plasma gun' is particularly useful in spray-welding very refractory materials including tungsten carbide/nickel; alumina/chromium and titanium carbide/chromium cermets (14.21—Part I). The materials involved may be fed into the flame as powders from two separate ports so that the composition of the cermet deposits may be graded. Alternatively, the powders may be pre-mixed and supplied from a single port. Metal wire may also be fed into the plasma flame if necessary, though powder tends to produce a finer, denser deposit with a superior surface finish.

18.73

A shielded plasma jet spraying unit (Fig. 18.14) has been developed for the surfacing of mild steel plate with a nickel–chromium–boron–silicon alloy and

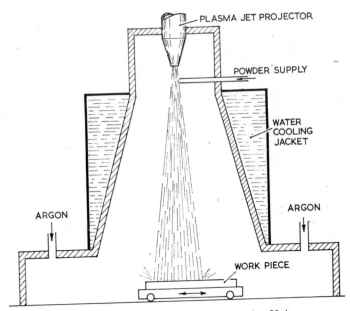

FIG. 18.14—A Shielded Plasma-jet Spraying Unit.

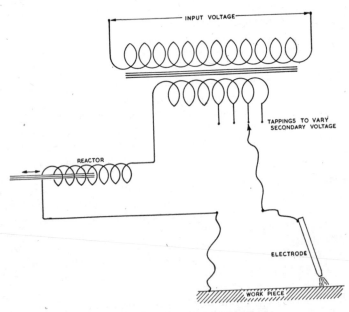

FIG. 18.15—Typical Circuit for A.C. Supply.

with other hard materials. Here an auxiliary argon shield is used to protect
the work from oxidation.

POWER SUPPLIES FOR ARC WELDING
18.80

In arc-welding processes large currents at low voltages are generally employed.
As indicated earlier in this chapter, both alternating- and direct-current
sources are used, though direct current certainly finds the wider application.

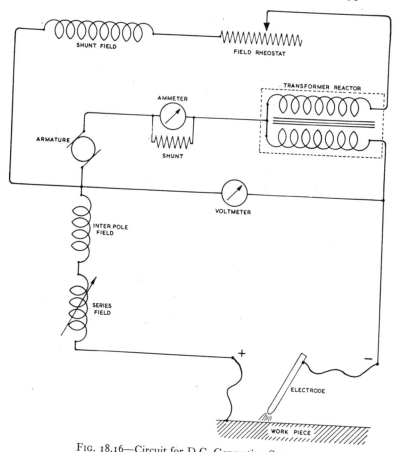

Fig. 18.16—Circuit for D.C. Generating System.

18.81 Alternating-current Supplies

Alternating-current supplies are readily obtained using a transformer circuit
of the type indicated in Fig. 18.15. Here a step-down transformer is used, and
the output voltage can be varied by means of tappings on the secondary
winding. In order to provide the momentary high voltage necessary for
striking the arc, a suitable reactor is included in the output circuit.

18.82 Direct-current Supplies

Direct-current supplies can be obtained from a transformer circuit similar to the one already mentioned but in which rectification has been introduced in the secondary circuit. Alternatively, a direct-current, compound-wound, variable-voltage generator can be used. This can be coupled to a mains-driven motor or to a prime mover such as a petrol or oil engine.

The main disadvantage of a generator set is that it is rather noisy. On the other hand, it is robust and easily transportable and should require only limited maintenance. Such a generator is also capable of furnishing the momentary high voltage necessary for striking the arc. The type of control circuit for such a set is shown in Fig. 18.16.

With transformer equipment the noise is much less than with a generator, but when rectification is employed the rectifier is more liable to damage by mechanical shock. This type of set is therefore more suitable for a fixed installation.

BIBLIOGRAPHY

1 'Metallurgy of Welding', W. H. Bruckner (Pitman).
2 'Welding Practice. Vols. I, II and III', E. Fuchs and H. Bradley (Butterworths Scientific Publications).
3 'The Welding of Non-ferrous Metals', E. G. West (Chapman and Hall).
4 'Welding for Engineers', H. Udin; E. R. Funk and J. Wulff (Wiley; Chapman and Hall).
5 'Welding Engineering', B. E. Rossi (McGraw-Hill).
6 'Procedure Handbook of Arc Welding Design and Practice', The Lincoln Electric Company.
7 'Electric Arc Welding Manual. Vols. I and II', Murex Welding Processes.
8 'The Joining of Metals', Symposium (Institute of Metals).
9 'Filler Metals for Joining', O. T. Barnett (Reinhold Publishing Corp.).
10 'Welding Transformers and Rectifiers', H. P. Zade (Macmillan, U.K.; St. Martin's Press, U.S.A.).
11 'The Science and Practice of Welding', W. J. Patton (Prentice-Hall Inc.).
12 'Welding Design and Processes', B. R. Hilton (Chapman and Hall).
13 'Electroslag Welding', Ed. B. E. Paton (Reinhold).
14 'Automatic Welding', R. Hammond (Alvin Redman).
15 'Manual, Semi-automatic and Automatic Arc Welding', E. Flintham (British Oxygen Co., Ltd).
16 'Inert Gas Arc Welding', Institute of Welding.
17 'Electric Arc and Oxy-acetylene Welding', W. A. Atkins and A. G. Walker (Pitman).
18 'Welding Technology', J. W. Giachino, W. Weeks and G. S. Johnson (The Technical Press Ltd).
19 'Metals and How to Weld Them', T. B. Jefferson and G. Woods (James F. Lincon Arc Welding Foundation, Cleveland, Ohio).

20 'Welding Metallurgy', G. E. Linnert (American Welding Society).

21 BS 638: 1966—Arc-welding plant and equipment. Amendment 1969.

22 BS 639: 1969—Covered electrodes for the manual metal-arc welding of mild steel and medium tensile steel.

23 BS 938: 1962—General requirements for the metal-arc welding of structural steel tubes to BS 1775.

24 BS 1077: 1963—Fusion welded joints in copper.

25 BS 1719: Part 1: 1969—Classification and coding of covered electrodes for metal-arc welding.

26 BS 1856: 1964—General requirements for the metal-arc welding of mild steel.

27 BS 2633: 1956—Class I metal-arc welding of steel pipe-lines and pipe assemblies for carrying fluids.

28 BS 2642: 1965—General requirements for the arc welding of steel to BS 968 and similar steels. Amendment 1968.

29 BS 2901—Filler rods and wires for gas-shielded arc welding.

30 BS 2493: 1971—Molybdenum and chromium-molybdenum low-alloy steel electrodes for manual metal-arc welding.

31 BS 2926: 1970—Chromium/nickel austenitic steel electrodes for manual metal-arc welding.

32 BS 3019—General recommendations for manual inert-gas tungsten-arc welding.

Part 1: 1958—Wrought aluminium, aluminium alloys and magnesium alloys.

Part 2: 1960—Austenitic stainless and heat-resisting steels.

33 BS 3571—General recommendations for manual inert-gas metal-arc welding.

Part 1: 1962—Aluminium and aluminium alloys

34 BS 4365: 1968—Industrial argon.

(*See also 'Bibliography', Chapter nineteen, for BSI specifications covering general topics.*)

Chapter nineteen
OTHER FUSION-WELDING PROCESSES

19.10
Although oxy-acetylene welding is by far the best-known welding process which makes use of the heat supplied by an exothermic chemical reaction, other welding operations, such as the thermit process, are used, in which the heat is also derived chemically. In the first case the fuel is, of course, the gas acetylene, C_2H_2, which is burned with a controlled supply of oxygen, whilst in the thermit process the fuel is aluminium powder which derives its oxygen supply from the iron oxide with which it is mixed.

GAS-WELDING PROCESSES

19.20
The oxy-acetylene welding process was introduced at the beginning of the present century when the first successful equipment was developed in Paris by Fouché and Picard. Several other gases had been tried in the search for a suitable heating flame. In 1888 Fletcher in this country produced some welding equipment which used coal-gas, but the advent of the oxy-acetylene flame displaced most other gas-welding methods, and despite the use of such gases as hydrogen and, in more recent years, propane, butane and hydrogen–fluorine mixtures, oxy-acetylene welding remains the most important of the gas-welding processes.

19.21
In gas-welding processes the heat necessary to produce fusion of the metal being welded is obtained by burning some gas issuing from the nozzle of a blow-pipe or torch. The gas issuing from the nozzle is already mixed with the amount of oxygen required to produce a flame, which may be chemically either oxidising, neutral or reducing. The chemical nature of the flame can thus be altered to suit the type of metal or alloy being welded.

Formerly gas welding ranked equal in importance to the metallic-arc method but since the introduction of shielding gases to the latter process, the use of gas welding has declined for metals where a flux is necessary. It remains an important process for welding steel sheet since equipment is relatively cheap.

The oxy-acetylene process is quite widely used in maintenance and repair work, since the torch can also be used as an auxiliary tool for heating metals and for brazing jobs. As with arc welding, the process may be autogenous or a filler rod may be used. Automatic oxy-acetylene welding is useful for joining sheet metal components in which edge joints are involved, the use of a filler rod then being unnecessary.

Since the gas flame is less compact and less efficient than the arc, the heat-affected zone tends to be more extensive with gas welding. This considerable heat spread also causes greater distortion than is experienced with arc welding. At the same time, this heat spread can be advantageous in welding those materials, particularly some alloy steels, in which air-hardening is likely to occur (13.15—Part I), since the rate of cooling which follows gas welding is generally much less rapid than with arc welding.

19.22 The Oxy-acetylene Flame

Both oxygen and acetylene can be stored conveniently in cylinders and their flow to the welding torch controlled easily by means of simple valves. Although lower than that of either propane or butane, the calorific value of

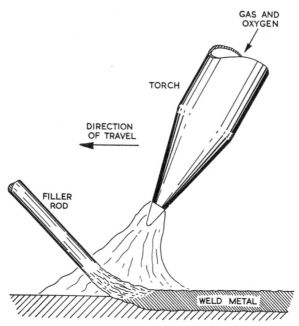

FIG. 19.1—The Principle of Gas Welding.

acetylene is nevertheless very high and, when the acetylene is mixed with the appropriate amount of oxygen, flame temperatures in the region of 3 500° C can be reached. If air is fed to the torch instead of oxygen the flame temperature is naturally lower because of the cooling effect of the large amount of nitrogen which passes through the flame and which takes no part in the chemical reaction. In these circumstances temperatures of 2 200–2 400° C are attained.

The proportion of oxygen to acetylene can be varied in order to produce a flame which is either neutral, oxidising or reducing. The complete combustion of acetylene is represented by the following equation:

$$2C_2H_2 + 5O_2 \longrightarrow 4CO_2 + 2H_2O + 53\cdot38 \text{ MJ/m}^3 \text{ of acetylene}$$
$$\text{1 vol.} \quad 2\tfrac{1}{2} \text{ vols.}$$

Thus, in order that complete combustion shall take place at the tip of the torch, 1 volume of acetylene requires to be mixed with $2\tfrac{1}{2}$ volumes of oxygen. In practice, however, the amount of oxygen used is much less than this. If a

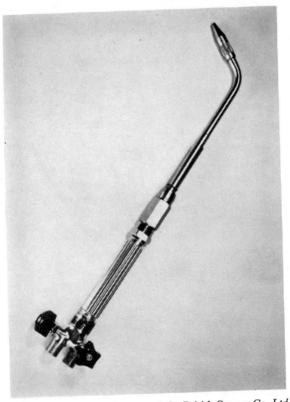

Courtesy of the British Oxygen Co. Ltd.

PLATE 19.1—A 'Saffire' Type 2 Oxy-acetylene Torch.

ratio of 1 volume of oxygen to 1 volume of acetylene is used, then incomplete combustion of acetylene takes place at the tip of the torch according to the equation:

$$C_2H_2 + O_2 \longrightarrow 2CO + H_2 + 18\cdot3 \text{ MJ/m}^3 \text{ of acetylene}$$
$$\text{1 vol.} \quad \text{1 vol.}$$

The carbon monoxide and hydrogen produced by this incomplete combustion then burn on contact with atmospheric oxygen in the outer envelope of the flame:

$$2CO + O_2 \longrightarrow 2CO_2 + 12\cdot7 \text{ MJ/m}^3 \text{ of carbon monoxide}$$
$$H_2 + \tfrac{1}{2}O_2 \longrightarrow H_2O + 10\cdot2 \text{ MJ/m}^3 \text{ of hydrogen.}$$

In practice, a ratio of $1\cdot04$–$1\cdot14$ volumes of oxygen to 1 volume of acetylene is used to give a chemically neutral flame. Such a flame is characterised by an almost white but sharply defined central cone with a reddish-purple envelope

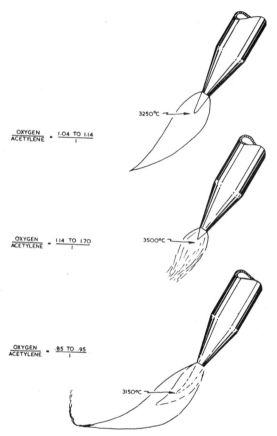

$$\frac{\text{OXYGEN}}{\text{ACETYLENE}} = \frac{1\cdot04 \text{ TO } 1\cdot14}{1}$$

3250°C

$$\frac{\text{OXYGEN}}{\text{ACETYLENE}} = \frac{1\cdot14 \text{ TO } 1\cdot70}{1}$$

3500°C

$$\frac{\text{OXYGEN}}{\text{ACETYLENE}} = \frac{\cdot85 \text{ TO } \cdot95}{1}$$

3150°C

FIG. 19.2—Types of Oxy-acetylene Flame.

(Fig. 19.2). A neutral flame is used for welding carbon steels and most ferrous and non-ferrous alloys, since it protects the metal from oxidation and no chemical action is introduced in the molten weld metal.

If the ratio of oxygen to acetylene is now increased to $1\cdot14$–$1\cdot7$ parts of oxygen to 1 part of acetylene an oxidising flame is produced. The flame itself becomes shorter and the cone much shorter and more pointed than in the neutral flame, whilst considerably higher temperatures are attained. A flame of this type would oxidise many metals and alloys. A weld produced in steel would be brittle and suffer from gas porosity because of reactions introduced in the molten weld metal by the presence of excess oxygen. Nevertheless, a slightly oxidising flame is used for welding copper, various bronzes and nickel silvers, since the oxidising conditions in the flame prevent the solution by the molten weld metal of hydrogen, which would lead to porosity in the solid weld. A more strongly oxidising flame may be used for welding brass.

Courtesy of The British Oxygen Co. Ltd.

PLATE 19.2—Using a Light-weight Oxy-acetylene Torch
in Automobile Work.

The pasty mass of zinc oxide which forms on the surface of the weld metal helps to reduce the loss of zinc by vaporisation.

When the ratio of oxygen to acetylene is adjusted to between 0·85 and 0·95 to 1, a reducing flame is produced. This flame is characterised by a white, luminous cone, surrounded by a white, feather-shaped zone, which in turn is contained in a reddish-purple envelope. The temperature of this flame is lower than that of a neutral flame, since the rate of combustion of the acetylene in the inner zone is much lower. A flame of this nature is used for gas welding of aluminium alloys, where the tendency of the metal to oxidise must be limited as far as possible. A reducing flame is also used for the gas welding of many alloy steels. An exception is the low-carbon, high chromium stainless steel (13.35—Part I). In this case the use of a reducing flame would lead to

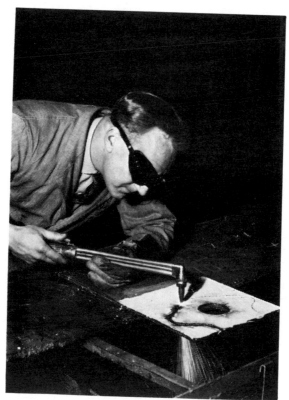

Courtesy of The British Oxygen Co. Ltd.

PLATE 19.3—Hand Profile Flame Cutting Using the Oxy-acetylene Torch.

the absorption of carbon by the metal adjacent to the weld, with the consequent development of brittleness due to martensite formation as the weld cooled (21.92—Part I).

19.23

The readily available heat source provided by the oxy-acetylene flame is often useful when gas welding hardenable steels. The flame can be used to preheat the metal around the weld and so reduce the rate of cooling to such an extent that martensite formation does not occur. Moreover, since the flame temperature is much lower than that of the electric arc, a less-steep temperature gradient is formed in the region of the weld, and this, in turn, leads to slower cooling.

19.24

The use of oxy-acetylene mixtures for what is loosely called 'flame-cutting' of steel up to 1 m thick might be mentioned here, though in addition to severing operations, planing, milling, turning and boring of ferrous metals can be accomplished in this way. A modified type of gas torch is used in which several small holes are placed circumferentially around a large hole situated in the tip of the torch. Through the small holes passes a mixture of oxygen and acetylene, whilst the large central hole carries a powerful stream of oxygen. The function of the oxy-acetylene mixture is to preheat the surface of the steel to such a temperature (about $900°$ C) that it will ignite under the action of the oxygen jet:

$$3Fe + 2O_2 \longrightarrow Fe_3O_4 + 4·88 \text{ MJ/kg}$$

The heat of combustion raises the temperature so that some of the surrounding iron melts and is blown away, along with the molten oxide which is formed, by the force of the oxygen jet.

Metals with lower affinities for oxygen, such as copper or nickel-base alloys, can be flame cut only if some easily ignited metal such as iron is fed into the flame (in powder or rod form) in order to provide the necessary high temperature. The base metal then melts and is blown away by the oxygen jet along with the oxidised iron.

19.25 Bronze Welding

The term 'bronze welding' refers to the joining of metals with high melting points, such as mild steel, cast irons, nickel and copper by the use of copper-alloy filler metal. Bronze filler rods containing about $4·5\%$ tin and $0·5\%$ phosphorus were originally used for this process, but since their liquidus temperature is only $30°$ C below the melting point of copper, 60–40 brass filler rods have become more popular, particularly for joining copper. These brass filler rods usually contain some silicon, which acts as a deoxidant and also improves fluidity, and additions of other metals, such as tin, nickel, iron and manganese, to improve the mechanical properties of the resultant weld.

Bronze welding differs from true welding processes in that little or no fusion of the work-piece takes place. The temperature employed need only be sufficient to cause 'tinning' or amalgamation to take place between the molten weld metal and the work-pieces. At the same time, bronze welding differs from ordinary brazing in the method of application of the filler metal. In brazing processes the solder is usually preplaced whilst solid and heat is then supplied from a gas torch; whilst the procedure in bronze welding follows closely that used in standard fusion welding by either the oxy-acetylene torch or electric-arc processes. Moreover, in brazing the molten filler metal is drawn by capillary attraction into the gap between the closely adjacent surfaces of the parts being joined, whereas in bronze welding the molten filler metal is directed into a relatively wide gap until the latter is filled.

As in other fusion-welding processes, so in bronze welding a groove or angle between the work-pieces is necessary. The faces of the groove are coated with a flux of the borax type, this being suitable for working temperatures up to 900° C. When bronze welding with the oxy-acetylene torch the flame should be adjusted until it is slightly oxidising, as indicated by an inner cone which is more pointed than that in a neutral flame. This oxidising flame is suitable for the bronze welding of most metals and alloys, a notable exception being aluminium bronze, which requires a reducing flame because of the rapidity with which aluminium oxidises.

The edges of the groove at the start of the 'run' are first heated to the melting point of the filler rod. The end of the rod is then placed immediately in front of the torch, which is held so that the end of the flame is about 3 mm away from the groove. Globules of metal melt off the end of the rod and are deposited in the groove, wetting the joint surfaces and forming a positive bond due to inter-diffusion of base metal and filler metal.

19.26
Although in this country the oxy-acetylene torch is generally used for bronze welding, electric-arc welding with an electrode or filler rod, the melting point of which is well below the solidus of the work-pieces, is sometimes carried out. Alternatively, an arc can be struck between a carbon electrode and the filler rod, so that less fusion of the base metals will take place.

Bronze welding, in common with other joining processes, has been used for many years in the building up of worn parts, but bronze welded joints are now also employed extensively in the manufacture of vessels, roofing and pipe systems, structures and machines.

19.27 The Oxy-hydrogen Flame
Hydrogen burns in oxygen according to the reaction:

$$H_2 + \tfrac{1}{2}O_2 \longrightarrow H_2O + 10\cdot2 \text{ MJ/m}^3 \text{ of hydrogen.}$$
$$\text{steam}$$

Unfortunately steam, which is the product of the above reaction, is likely to oxidise the surface of steel at a high temperature according to the equation:

$$Fe + H_2O \mathrel{\substack{\longrightarrow \\ \longleftarrow}} FeO + H_2.$$

It will be noted that this is a reversible reaction so that if the concentration of hydrogen in the welding atmosphere is increased the reaction will tend to proceed to the left. An excess of hydrogen is therefore necessary in order to make the flame reducing, and so usable as a welding source. Consequently the ratio of hydrogen to oxygen is usually above 2·5 to 1. The temperature of the oxy-hydrogen flame is lower than that of the oxy-acetylene flame making it more suitable for welding materials with melting points below that of steel, for example, aluminium, magnesium and their alloys.

19.28
Micro-welding techniques which have been introduced recently make use of miniature oxy-hydrogen torches. An oxy-hydrogen mixture in which the gases are in the proportions to give a nominally neutral flame is obtained by the electrolysis of water. The flame power can therefore be controlled by

varying the electrolysing current, so that the small welding unit requires only mains electricity and water in order to operate it. This led to the somewhat misleading title of 'water welding' being applied to the process.

Although nominally neutral, the flame is in fact oxidising and a neutral or reducing flame can be obtained by passing the gases over alcohol in order to increase the content of combustible material. Micro-welding is useful in joining miniature components in the electronics industry as well as being a useful tool in the jewellery trades.

THERMIT WELDING

19.30

The thermit fusion process originated in Germany in about 1900 when Dr. Hans Goldschmidt found that if a mixture of iron oxide and aluminium powder was ignited locally, then the two materials would react exothermically, so that the reaction spread rapidly throughout the mass, converting it into molten iron and a slag composed mainly of aluminium oxide:

$$8 \text{ Al} + 3 \text{ Fe}_3\text{O}_4 \longrightarrow 9 \text{ Fe} + 4 \text{ Al}_2\text{O}_3 + 15 \cdot 4 \text{ MJ/kg of aluminium.}$$

19.31

Aluminium powder and ground mill scale (Fe_3O_4) are mixed in the molecular proportions indicated by the above equation. (This tells us that 1 kg of aluminium powder will react with about 3·2 kg of iron oxide (Fe_3O_4) to produce approximately 2·3 kg of metallic iron, and release roughly 15·4 megajoules of heat energy in the process.) In order to start the reaction a local ignition temperature of about 1 150° C is necessary, whereupon the reaction spreads quickly throughout the mixture. The thermit mixture is generally contained in a refractory-lined crucible (Fig. 19.3) and an igniter, such as barium peroxide, is used. A small amount of this is mixed with aluminium or magnesium powder and placed in a mound on top of the thermit mixture. A piece of magnesium ribbon stuck into the top of the mound is generally used as a fuse.

Whilst the theoretical reaction temperature of about 3 500° C is not reached in practice, due to the heat absorbed by the walls of the crucible, temperatures in excess of 2 500° C may nevertheless be attained. In order to limit the temperature some fine steel scrap may be added to the basic thermit mixture, together with steel scrap containing any necessary alloy additions, such as nickel or manganese. Ferro-silicon and carbon may also be added to give a product similar in composition to cast iron. About 2% lime may also be included in the mixture in order to improve the fluidity of the aluminium oxide slag, and thus accelerate its rise to the surface of the melt. The composition of the charge in respect of steel scrap is adjusted to give a final pouring temperature of about 2 400° C.

The stopper pin at the bottom of the crucible is used to tap the molten steel into the welding mould (Fig. 19.3). When the metal has run from the crucible the operator diverts the flow of the molten slag which follows. Usually the sides of the space into which the weld metal is to run are made parallel by cutting them with a gas torch. Around the parts to be joined a wax pattern is built up with reinforcement contours similar to those required in the finished weld. A sheet metal box is then placed around the wax pattern and when the latter has hardened, moulding sand is rammed into the box around the wax

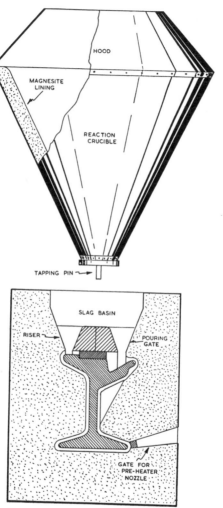

FIG. 19.3—Thermit Welding a Rail.

pattern, the necessary provisions for pouring gate, risers and heating gate having first been made. The wax pattern is then melted out by means of a flame directed into the heating gate so that it leaves a cavity which will later be occupied by the weld metal. Heating is continued in order to dry out the sand mould and also to preheat to redness the parts to be joined. When multiple sections are to be joined a two-part mould, together with a wooden pattern, are used instead of the box, sand and wax.

19.32
Thermit welding is particularly adaptable to the joining of heavy sections ranging from rail ends (Fig. 19.3), requiring a few pounds of metal, up to large marine frames which require several tons of weld metal. In all applications the normal foundry methods must be employed in order to control the incidence of gas porosity, shrinkage, slag inclusions and cracks.

Fractured iron and steel housings, frames and shafts of heavy section can also be repaired by thermit welding, whilst increasing use is being made of the process in the fabrication of large units from a number of relatively simple castings or forgings, thus avoiding the necessity of large, intricate castings.

19.33
The thermit reaction has also been used as a means of heating in the production of pressure butt welds in rails. In this application the molten charge produced by the thermit reaction is poured from the *top* of the crucible, so that the slag comes into contact with the rail ends and thus protects them from fusion welding. A skin of slag forms on the rail ends and prevents the molten iron from wetting them. At the same time the parts are heated to a high temperature, so that a subsequent application of pressure squeezes out the molten thermit metal and slag and produces a butt weld. When the weld is cool the surrounding thermit metal and slag are trimmed away.

19.34
The thermit reaction is also used in some instances to maintain the temperature of melts in large foundry ladles and to produce small quantities of steel for castings. It is also reported that a modification of the thermit process in which copper oxide replaces iron oxide has been employed in the U.S.A. for producing autogenous joints in copper cables.

19.35
The quality of the weld produced by the thermit process is usually regarded as being quite high, and in some instances its mechanical properties are superior to those of a steel casting of similar carbon content. This is probably due to the relative purity of the thermit metal, which is produced by the reduction of an oxide, whereas a steel casting commonly contains appreciable amounts of the impurities which were present in the pig iron from which it was produced. These impurities tend to segregate at the crystal boundaries of a cast steel, and it is significant that such a steel will fracture along its grain boundaries, whilst fracture in a thermit weld usually follows a transcrystalline path.

ELECTRON-BEAM WELDING

19.40
In electron-beam welding the kinetic energy of fast-moving electrons, striking the surface of the work-piece, is converted into heat energy. Such a beam can be controlled with precision to heat a small selected zone and so obtain a very

high temperature there. The operation is best carried out in a vacuum in order to avoid dissipating the kinetic energy of the stream by collisions between the electrons and the relatively massive molecules of atmospheric gases. Thus a suitable cathode (electron emitter) and anode are enclosed in a chamber in which a high vacuum can be produced and maintained. If a high electrical potential difference is established between the heated cathode and the anode, a stream of rapidly-moving electrons will leave the cathode and be accelerated towards the anode which in some cases can be the work-piece itself. The kinetic energy imparted to the electrons is transferred to the work-piece in the form of heat energy as the electrons bombard its surface. An increase in the accelerating potential difference results in a greater heat input at the surface of the anode. When using an accelerating voltage of the order of 15 kV, electrons may reach a speed of 224 000 km per second. The heat generated can be calculated from:

$$Q = 0.292\,E\,I$$

where Q is measured in joules per second; E in volts and I in amperes.

19.41

A very important feature of electron-beam welding is that an extremely deep and narrow penetration can be achieved as shown in Fig. 19.4. Since the rate of energy input is very high, the target metal is melted and immediately

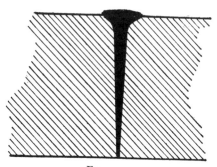

FIG. 19.4.

vaporised at the point where the beam impinges. A hole is thus produced and then deepened by the continual electron bombardment. The diameter of the hole is small and it is filled with metal vapour, which, it is claimed, helps to stabilise the beam. Movement of the beam relative to the work-piece causes the hole to advance through the metal whilst molten metal solidifies in its wake. The effect is rather like that when a hot needle is passed through wax. Since a very narrow weld is produced the process is particularly suitable for autogenous welding though the use of filler metal is not ruled out.

19.42

Several different types of electron-beam gun are available. In some of these the work-piece itself can be made the anode as mentioned above. The system is then said to be 'work accelerated' and, though simple, it imposes a number of

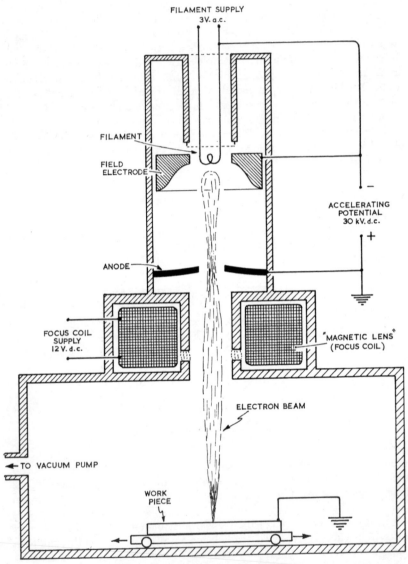

FILAMENT SUPPLY
3 V. a.c.

FILAMENT

FIELD
ELECTRODE

ACCELERATING
POTENTIAL
30 kV. d.c.

−

+

ANODE

FOCUS COIL
SUPPLY
12 V. d.c.

"MAGNETIC LENS"
(FOCUS COIL)

ELECTRON BEAM

TO VACUUM PUMP

WORK
PIECE

FIG. 19.5—Electron-beam Welding.

limitations as far as successful welding is concerned. Accurate focusing of the beam is difficult, the work must be electrically conductive and the gun must be used close to the work-piece. Consequently this type of gun has generally been used when a large number of similar components of simple shape are to be welded, for example, reactor fuel elements.

In the 'self-accelerated' type of gun the anode is in the form of a perforated plate through which the electron beam may pass and impinge on the work-piece beyond. In order to focus the beam accurately an electro-magnetic 'lens' system is required, the beam being focused by altering the field current which in turn alters the 'focal length' of the 'lens'. The principle of one type of self-accelerated electron-beam gun is shown in Fig. 19.5. The function of the shaped field electrode, which is at the same potential as the cathode, is to produce a field which will converge the electron beam. In other respects the electrical features of the apparatus resemble those of a thermionic valve of the diode type.

When a beam of electrons impinges on a metal surface X-rays are emitted and this is in fact the principle of the X-ray tube. In the latter the tungsten target needs to be water-cooled but in electron-beam welding we are interested basically in the heat produced and must regard the production of X-rays as an incidental and troublesome side effect. When using an accelerating voltage of up to 30 kV, the X-rays produced are relatively 'soft' (3.82—Part I) but when higher voltages are used harmful 'hard' X-rays are generated and some form of shielding is necessary.

19.43

Although the use of a high vacuum is desirable if deep penetration is to be achieved, progress has been made in the development of non-vacuum techniques. Since an oxygen molecule is some 60 000 times more massive than an electron it is to be expected that much kinetic energy would be wasted by collisions between electrons and molecules of atmospheric oxygen. Thus the type of gas present in the path of the electron beam influences the scattering of the beam and, as one might expect, helium with its relatively small monatomic molecules, has the least effect and permits the greatest depth of penetration. Invariably the depth-to-width ratio of non-vacuum welds is less than that with high-vacuum conditions.

19.44

Since electron-beam welding apparatus is relatively costly its application is somewhat specialised. The following features characterise the process:

(i) the ability accurately to control penetration;
(ii) its absolute chemical cleanliness;
(iii) the low heat input relative to the depth of penetration;
(iv) the accuracy possible in locating the weld.

These and other features make electron-beam welding an ideal process for welding refractory metals such as tungsten, molybdenum, niobium and tantalum and also the chemically-reactive metals beryllium, titanium, zirconium and uranium all of which benefit from being welded in a vacuum.

LASER WELDING

19.50
The fashion which developed during the Second World War for acronyms, that is, names coined from the initial letter of each important word of a descriptive title, left us with examples like FIDO, PLUTO and NATO. As time-saving appellations these may have been admirable, but to posterity they mean nothing unless accompanied by the necessary descriptive text. One would have hoped, therefore, that science had been spared such jargon in favour of etymologically-derived titles. For better or for worse, 'LASER' is the acronym representing 'Light Amplification by Stimulated Emission of Radiation'.

19.51
The device consists of a suitable generator of light pulses—or 'optical pump' —and an active element, and it produces a very high intensity beam of monochromatic light. The optical pump usually consists of a high-power flash tube filled with xenon or krypton and powered by capacitor discharge. It is similar in many respects to the 'electronic flash' equipment used by photographers. The active element in 'solid state' lasers is usually a single crystal of synthetic ruby (or crystalline form of aluminium oxide containing about 0·05% chromium) or alternatively a special glass containing 2–6% of the 'rare earth' metal, neodymium, and is generally in the shape of a rod with flat ends which are made highly reflective but one end being about 5% less reflective than the other.

Operation of the flash tube causes excitation of the chromium atoms in the ruby into a higher-energy state. These excited atoms return to their normal energy level and in so doing emit an intense but amplified light beam which is unidirectional and composed of radiations all of the same wavelength and on the same phase. Oscillation occurs within the ruby, with the reflective ends causing optical resonance so that an intense beam of monochromatic radiation emerges from the end with the least reflectivity. The beam is roughly parallel, of a diameter similar to that of the crystal and can be focused by lenses to provide sufficient heat to vaporise metals in its path. Equipment is available with which temperatures up to 40 000° C have been attained. An advantage of the coherent parallel beam of light is that it will travel great distances and lasers have in fact been used to 'bounce' radiation from the surface of the moon back to earth.

The principle of one form of ruby laser is shown in Fig. 19.6. Here the flash tube and ruby crystal are placed at opposite focii of an elliptical reflector in order that the maximum amount of light shall reach the crystal. Even so, such a laser is not more than about 1% efficient.

19.52
As might be expected, the popular press saw in the laser the long-awaited and almost legendary 'death ray' of science fiction. Introduced in 1961, the laser is still in its infancy and has enormous potentialities in many fields. It is being used in cancer research and has been employed successfully in 'spot

welding' detached retinas in the eyes. In the field of metal manufacture it will obviously find application in cutting, drilling, shaping and welding—particularly in *micro*-welding.

Since pulsed lasers are the only group of coherent light devices able to produce high-enough energy intensities to melt and vaporise many metals, their principal use is in *spot* welding. Continuous seam welds can, however,

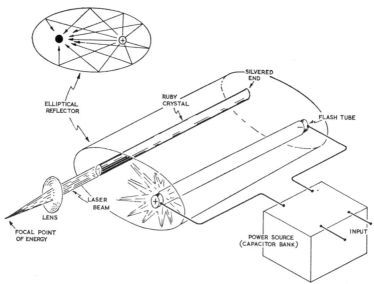

FIG. 19.6—One Method of Producing a LASER Beam.

be produced as a series of overlapping spots. Particular advantages of the laser beam when used as a welding tool include:

(i) There is no physical contact with the metal being welded and since the beam does not diverge, the distance between the laser head and the work is not important.

(ii) Very little temperature rise in the metal surrounding the weld;

(iii) Welding can be carried out in air or in a controlled atmosphere, whereas the electron-beam method requires a vacuum to give the best results;

(iv) The high-energy densities produced make it possible to weld very dissimilar materials;

(v) Very small wires and other small components can be welded successfully.

BIBLIOGRAPHY

1 'Practical Handbook on Oxy-acetylene Welding', Suffolk Iron Foundry.
2 'Metallurgy of Welding', W. H. Bruckner (Pitman).
3 'Welding Practice, Vols. I, II and III', E. Fuchs and H. Bradley (Butterworths Scientific Publications).

4 'The Welding of Non-ferrous Metals', E. G. West (Chapman and Hall).

5 'Welding for Engineers', H. Udin, E. R. Funk and J. Wulff (Wiley; Chapman and Hall).

6 'Welding Engineering', B. E. Rossi (McGraw-Hill).

7 'The Joining of Metals', Symposium (Institute of Metals).

8 'Gas Welding and Cutting', C. C. Bainbridge (Iliffe).

9 'Welding Handbook (Vols. II and III)', American Welding Society.

10 'The Science and Practice of Welding', W. J. Patton (Prentice-Hall. Inc.).

11 'Welding Design and Processes', B. R. Hilton (Chapman and Hall).

12 'Handbook of Electron Beam Welding', R. Bakish and S. S. White (Wiley).

13 'Electron Beam Welding', Machinery Yellow Back No. 51.

14 'Electric Arc and Oxy-acetylene Welding', W. A. Atkins and A. G. Walker (Pitman).

15 'Welding Technology', J. W. Giachino. W. Weeks and G. S. Johnson (The Technical Press Ltd).

16 'Metals and How to Weld Them', T. B. Jefferson and G. Woods (James F. Lincon Arc Welding Foundation, Cleveland, Ohio).

17 'Welding Metallurgy', G. E. Linnert (American Welding Society).

18 'Aluminium, Vol. III—Fabrication and Finishing', Ed. K. R. van Horn (American Society for Metals).

19 'Principles of Magnesium Technology'. E. F. Emley (Pergamon Press).

20 BS 499: 1965—Welding terms and symbols.
Part 1: Welding, brazing and thermal cutting glossary.
Part 2: Symbols for welding.
Part 3: Terminology of and abbreviations for fusion weld imperfections as revealed by radiogrophy.

21 BS 693: 1960—General requirements for oxy-acetylene welding of mild steel. Amendment 1966.

22 BS 709: 1971—Methods of testing fusion-welded joints and weld metal in steel.

23 BS 1126: 1957—General recommendations for the gas welding of wrought aluminium and aluminium alloys.

24 BS 1453: 1957—Filler rods and wire for gas welding.

25 BS 1542: 1960—Equipment for eye, face and neck protection against radiation arising during welding and similar operations.

26 BS 1724: 1959—Bronze welding by gas.

27 BS 2597: 1955—Glossary of terms used in radiology.

28 BS 2600: 1962—General recommendations for the radiographic examination of fusion welded butt joints in steel.

29 BS 2653: 1955—Protective clothing for welders.

30 BS 2704: 1966—Calibration blocks and recommendations for their use in ultrasonic flaw detection.

31 BS 3451: 1962—Testing fusion welds in aluminium and aluminium alloys.
32 BS 3683. Glossary of terms used in non-destructive testing.
Part 1: 1963—Penetrant flaw detection.
Part 2: 1963—Magnetic particle flaw detection.
Part 3: 1964—Radiological flaw detection.
Part 4: 1965—Ultrasonic flaw detection.
Part 5: 1965—Eddy current flaw detection.
33 BS 3923. Methods for ultrasonic examination of welds.
Part 1: 1965—Manual examination of circumferential butt welds in pipes.
Part 2: 1965—Automatic examination of welded seams.
Part 3: 1965—Manual examination of nozzle welds.
34 BS 4206: 1967—Methods of testing fusion welds in copper and copper alloys.
35 BS 4360: 1968—Weldable structural steels.
36 BS 4397: 1969—Methods for magnetic particle testing of welds.
37 BS 4570—Fusion welding of steel castings—Part I: 1970—Production, rectification and repair.

Chapter twenty
'NEW' METALS

20.10

At the beginning of the present century only a few of the sixty-odd metallic elements known to science had any engineering application. About a quarter of a century ago, however, the stimulus provided by the demands of the aircraft industry led to the development of a comprehensive range of high-strength alloys based on the light metals aluminium and magnesium.

The evolution of the gas turbine engendered a need for alloys capable of withstanding combinations of very high temperature and stress. This challenge was met by the development of the Nimonic series of alloys by a team of Birmingham metallurgists. More recently the search for a light material of high strength, coupled with a high melting point and good corrosion resistance, has resulted in the production and fabrication of titanium on an industrial scale.

In the rather specialised field of nuclear energy metallurgical research plays an increasingly important part, and metallic elements which were hitherto mere names in the more advanced textbooks of chemistry are now being produced at the instigation of the nuclear engineer.

BERYLLIUM

20.20

Although beryllium is classified as a 'new' metal, it was in fact discovered as long ago as 1797 by Vauquelin. The famous chemist Wöhler first isolated the metal in any quantity in 1828, but the commerical development of beryllium did not begin until 1916, when an American company became interested in it.

Beryllium bronze (16.71—Part I), a copper alloy containing 2% beryllium, first made its appearance as a commercial alloy in the early 1930s, but it is only in very recent years that attention has been focused on the possibilities of using beryllium in the pure form or as an alloy base. Beryllium is less dense than aluminium and, as one might expect, the aircraft industry is believed to be extremely interested in the possibility of using high-strength, beryllium-base alloys. At present, however, much of the beryllium being produced is absorbed by nuclear-energy projects.

20.21

Amongst metallic properties in which nuclear engineers are particularly interested is the behaviour of a metal to the passage of neutrous through it.

TABLE 20.1—*'New' Metals*

Metal	Symbol	Melting point (°C)	Relative Density	Crystal structure	Thermal neutron absorption cross-section (barns/atom)	Tensile Strength (at 20° C)		% elong. (at 20°C)	Hardness (D.P.H.) (at 20°C)	Remarks
						N/mm^2	tonf/in^2			
Beryllium	Be	1283	1·85	Hexagonal close-packed	0·009	327	21·2	2·74	109	Metal of a greyish colour, but large crystals are lustrous
Zirconium	Zr	1852	6·55	HCP below 862°C BCC above 862°C	0·18	437	28·3	30	180	A soft, ductile metal
Niobium	Nb	2468	8·6	Body-centred cubic	1·1	270	17·7	49	Approx. 40	—
Vanadium	V	1900	6·11	Body-centred cubic	4·8	437	28·3	35	165	Ductile or brittle fracture according to previous mechanical and thermal treatment
Hafnium	Hf	2130 ± 15	13·36	HCP blow 1950°C BCC above 1950°C	115·0	340	22·0	35	180	Brilliant lustre
Tantalum	Ta	2996	16·6	Body-centred cubic	21·3	309–463	20–30	40	65	A soft, ductile metal
Germanium	Ge	958·5	5·32	Octahedral	2·8	—	—	—	—	A silver-coloured brittle metalloid

Some metals, of which beryllium is one, are said to have a low neutron absorption, that is they do not react to any marked degree with neutrons which pass through them. Consequently, metals of this type are suitable for the manufacture of thin-walled containers used in reactor construction. Those metals, however, which tend to absorb neutrons (and in doing so take part in nuclear reactions) are also of interest to the nuclear engineer, since they are suitable for the manufacture of the control rods which are used to regulate the speed of nuclear reactions by absorbing neutrons.

The current trend towards operating reactors at higher temperatures also means that metals of both types must have a high melting point. They must also be able to withstand intense neutron bombardment without giving rise to the formation of dangerous isotopes. Moreover, the metal must be capable of fabrication to a variety of shapes, including very thin-walled tubing.

20.22
The neutron absorption of beryllium is very low indeed, and for a light metal it has a high melting point, making it suitable for use over quite a wide temperature range. The fact that it is light and at the same time has good strength and reasonable corrosion resistence has led to its being considered as a reactor material suitable for use in nuclear powered submarines.

20.23
In France beryllium is still known by the name 'glucinium'; a reference to the fact that many of its compounds have a sweet taste. The metal is, however, extremely toxic, and this constitutes one of the major difficulties in the fabrication of beryllium. Further, the metal lacks ductility, a fact which restricts the methods which can be used to shape it: Beryllium crystallises in the hexagonal close-packed form and, as mentioned previously (5.13—Part I), metals with this type of structure are generally more brittle than those which crystallise in one of the cubic forms. Nevertheless, beryllium has been successfully extruded to produce bar, tube and simple shapes. Hot-working the metal in a sheath is a common method of shaping beryllium, though working the base metal at moderate temperatures has proved successful.

ZIRCONIUM

20.30
In 1789 Klaproth discovered a new metal in the mineral zircon, but it was Berzelius, who, in 1824, succeeded in isolating zirconium. It was not until 1914 that Lely and Hambruger produced the metal in sufficient quantity to demonstrate that it was ductile. Then, during the First World War, rumours circulated that Germany had developed zirconium steels. Intensive research by the Allies, however, failed to produce an alloy of this type which had useful properties.

Eventually zirconium became known chiefly as an alloying addition to magnesium-base alloys (18.12—Part I), whilst its oxide zircona was developed as a high-temperature refractory. In 1944, however, research was instituted with the object of producing high-purity zirconium, and today it is regarded as being the most generally useful nuclear-engineering material for applications where low neutron absorptions are necessary.

20.31

In other respects too the use of zirconium in the field of nuclear engineering is quite an attractive proposition. As compared with beryllium, it is relatively plentiful, and is also superior to beryllium in respect of resistance to corrosion. Moreover, zirconium and its alloys can be fabricated with comparative ease, provided that the metal is not heated in contact with either oxygen, nitrogen or hydrogen. Each of these gases will form an interstitial solid solution (8.31 —Part I) in zirconium and lead to its embrittlement.

20.32

Unalloyed zirconium tends to be mechanically weak at high temperatures. In addition, under such conditions it is rapidly corroded by water vapour and carbon dioxide. These difficulties have been largely overcome by alloying, and most of the zirconium now used in nuclear engineering is supplied as an alloy, called 'Zircaloy II', which contains 1.5% tin, 0.12% iron, 0.05% nickel and 0.1% chromium.

Zirconium powder compacted with lead is useful in the form of lighter 'flints'. In the form of ferro–zirconium or ferro–silico-zirconium it may be used as a 'scavenger' in steel making, since it not only removes oxygen but also sulphur. Any residue refines the grain of steel, whilst the strength of some alloy steels can be increased in this way.

NIOBIUM

20.40

This metal was first discovered near Connecticut in 1801 by a British chemist named Hatchett. In recognition of its source he called it 'columbium'. At about the same time Ekeburg in Sweden discovered a 'new' metal in association with tantalum, and when later, in 1844, it was isolated by Rose he gave it the name 'niobium'. Soon afterwards 'columbium' and 'niobium' were identified as being the same metal, but the two names continued to be used on their respective sides of the Atlantic until recently, by international agreement, the name 'niobium' was officially adopted.

20.41

Niobium was first produced in any quantity by Balke in 1929, but has, of course, been used for a considerable time as a 1.0% addition to 18–8 stainless steels, in which it induces resistance to 'weld decay' (13.44—Part I).

20.42

Whilst zirconium is at the moment the most generally useful nuclear-engineering material for applications demanding low neutron absorption, the use of proposed higher reactor temperatures will necessitate the use of an alternative metal. In respect of low neutron absorption, niobium is next in order of usefulness. Moreover, it has a very high melting point ($2\,468°$ C). Unfortunately niobium also reacts with the pile gases, as well as with other substances with which it is likely to come into contact in the reactor, at temperatures in excess of $500°$ C.

20.43

The fact that niobium has satisfactory strength at high temperatures, how-ever, makes it a metal on which research is worth while, and it is possible that alloying may appreciably reduce its high-temperature reactivity. Some of the alloys of niobium have oxidation resistances several hundred times better than that of pure niobium. Unfortunately such alloys are generally rather brittle.

Although niobium is inferior to zirconium in respect of oxidation resistance, it has a very good resistance to liquid sodium and sodium–potassium mixtures such as might be used as coolants in reactors. Further, when of high purity, niobium is one of the most ductile metals known; though alloying additions of the kind necessary to reduce the reactivity of the metal at high temperatures also impair the mechanical properties and make the resultant alloys very difficult to work.

VANADIUM

20.50

The discovery of vanadium was mentioned in Part I (13.60). Following its isolation as a pure metal in 1867, it found its first commercial application in armour plates produced in 1896 at the Firminy Steel Works in France. It has, of course, been used as an alloy addition to certain steels for many years, and properties it imparts to such steels are well known (13.61—Part I). Vanadium pentoxide has long been used as a catalyst in the manufacture of sulphuric acid.

20.51

Since vanadium has a fairly low neutron absorption (Table 20.1), research has naturally been carried out to assess its suitability in other directions for nuclear-engineering purposes. So far it has been found to have the same limitations as niobium with respect to oxidation at high temperatures, and it seems unlikely that it can compete favourably with the latter metal.

The fact that pure vanadium is a soft ductile metal with a high capacity for cold-work has led many metallurgists to think that it may develop along similar lines to titanium, that is, as a high-strength material in the low-temperature fields of application.

HAFNIUM

20.60

One of the main disadvantages in the use of zirconium as a reactor material is the presence of small amounts of hafnium which materially increase the neutron absorption. Unfortunately hafnium is always closely associated with zirconium in the mineral deposits of the latter, and the reduction of the hafnium content to the few parts per million, which is all that can be tolerated in reactor-quality zirconium, becomes an expensive operation.

Both zirconium and hafnium belong to the same 'family' of chemical elements. Usually elements in any particular chemical family show a strong relationship to each other in so far as physical and chemical properties are concerned. Indeed, zirconium and hafnium do have many properties in which the family resemblance is apparent, and for this reason the separation of the two metals is difficult, and hence expensive. In repect of neutron absorption, however, they are at opposite ends of the scale, for whilst zirconium has a very low neutron absorption, that of hafnium is extremely high.

20.61

Amongst the 'new' metals hafnium has by far the greatest power of absorbing neutrons. It is in fact one of the strongest neutron absorbers available. In addition, it possesses good resistance to corrosion and is sufficiently ductile to enable it to be fabricated easily. Moreover, it is singularly free from radiation damage, and when the hafnium atom absorbs a neutron the 'daughter' element is a hafnium isotope. This reaction can be repeated several times, but each time a neutron is absorbed only hafnium isotopes are produced. Consequently, dimensional changes in the hafnium component under neutron bombardment are negligible. The absorption of neutrons by some elements gives rise to their transmutation to other elements. Such transmutation is often accompanied by a volume change which ultimately renders the component unfit for use.

Because of its marked ability to absorb neutrons, hafnium is a very useful element for the manufacture of rods for the control of nuclear reactors. Its use in nuclear engineering therefore depends upon a property which is diametrically opposite to that which makes its sister element, zirconium, useful.

20.62

The existence of hafnium was possibly first detected about ninety years ago, when a new metal christened 'ytterbium' was separated from a mineral of the rare-earth metal erbium. Subsequently, the new 'metal' was found to be an alloy of no less than four metals which later became known as ytterbium, thulium, lutecium—and hafnium. It was not until 1923 that hafnium was established as an element beyond doubt. Hafnium is found mainly in zirconium ores, which occur in many parts of the earth, and though scarce, hafnium occurs more plentifully in the earth's crust than does the metal mercury.

Prior to its use in nuclear engineering, metallic hafnium had been used on a small scale for the manufacture of cathodes in X-ray tubes. It had also found limited application in rectifiers and for the production of some electric-lamp filaments.

TANTALUM

20.70

Whilst the aircraft and nuclear-energy industries are particularly responsible for the development of many of these new metals, in other fields, too, new metallic substances are making their appearance. Amongst these new metals tantalum is particularly noteworthy, since it possesses a unique combination of high corrosion resistance and high ductility. Though generally regarded as a new metal, it was in fact first detected in 1820 by the chemist Berzelius. However, nearly a century elapsed before pure tantalum was produced in 1905.

20.71

In the pure state tantalum is corrosion resistant to most acids and alkalis. Since, when pure, it is also very ductile, it is used in the manufacture of acid-proof equipment in chemical plant. Being impervious to acid attack, sections as thin as 0·33 mm can be used in heat-transfer equipment.

Not only is pure tantalum unreactive towards animal fluids but it also provides a surface upon which flesh will grow. Consequently, it is used in bone surgery and for other 'implants' in the human body. Tantalum sheet and plate are used in cranial repairs, and woven gauze as a reinforcement to the abdominal wall in some hernia operations.

20.72

Tantalum can be anodically treated (22.71—Part I), and the film so formed is very stable and self-sealing. Moreover, this oxide film has excellent dielectric properties and, being impervious to the electrolytes used, has made tantalum a very useful metal for the manufacture of small electrolytic condensers. Foil of the order of 0·013 mm thick can be produced resulting in the manufacture of electrolytic condensers of about one-tenth the volume of ordinary aluminium-foil condensers of equivalent capacity. These small tantalum-foil condensers find wide application in modern electronic circuits.

GERMANIUM

20.80

Brief reference has been made in this chapter to 'families' of chemical elements. One such family contains, at its head, the non-metallic elements carbon and silicon, and in one of its branches, the metals tin and lead. During the last century when these family characteristics were being noticed by chemists and attempts were being made to classify the elements into appropriate groups, the Russian chemist Dimitri Mendeleef, predicted, in 1871, the existence of a hitherto undiscovered element, which he claimed would have properties intermediate between non-metallic silicon and metallic tin. He called this element 'eka-silicon' and forecast its properties. In 1886 the element 'germanium' was discovered by C. Winkler, and its properties were found to be almost identical with those of Mendeleef's predicted 'eka-silicon'.

20.81

Germanium is a 'metalloid'. That is, some of its properties are metallic in nature whilst others are non-metallic. Thus, whilst it has a silvery metallic lustre, its ductility is very low and it cannot be cold-worked to any useful extent.

As many readers will know, germanium is used in transistors and small rectifiers. For such purposes crystals of the element are grown from small 'seeds'. Alternatively, films of germanium can be electro-deposited.

20.90

The foregoing notes can do little more than indicate the enormous amount of research which is taking place into the metallurgy of these 'new' metals. It is, of course, difficult to predict the extent of their future development though it is safe to assume that their relatively high production costs will limit their use to the more sophisticated technological applications.

BIBLIOGRAPHY

1 'Rare Metals Handbook', C. A. Hampel (Ed.) (Reinhold Pub. Corp.).
2 'Reactor Handbook (Materials)' (McGraw-Hill).
3 'Guide to Uncommon Metals', E. N. Simons (Muller).
4 'Zirconium', G. L. Miller (Butterworth).
5 'Beryllium', G. E. Darwin and J. H. Buddery (Butterworth).
6 'Tantalum and Niobium', G. L. Miller (Butterworth).
7 'The Metallurgy of Vanadium', W. Rostoker (Wiley).
8 'Refractory Hard Metals', P. Schwarzkopf and R. Kieffer (Macmillan).
9 'Behaviour and Properties of Refractory Metals', T. E. Tietz and J. W. Wilson (Arnold).

INDEX